THROUGHOUT IT ALL, II

To Barbara,
God Bless You!

by
Doris Marie Davis

Doris Marie Davis
11/17/2006

PUBLISH AMERICA

PublishAmerica
Baltimore

ISBN: 1-4137-5636-0
PUBLISHED BY PUBLISHAMERICA, LLLP
www.publishamerica.com
Baltimore

Printed in the United States of America

I dedicate this book to GOD.
Because of Him — I survived!

Foreword

Throughout It All, book one of a three-book series, reveals gripping descriptions of Dawn's birth, early childhood, teenage years, onslaught of depression, teaching career traumas and three husbands. A portrayal of her forth husband and their marriage starts in the last three chapters. The book ends with Dawn's excitement about moving into her eighty-year old Victorian home.

This book *Throughout It All, II* continues with chapter 28, a college flashback, agonizing trials of her fourth, fifth and sixth husbands and her son's serious battle with drugs. Dawn's roller coaster years of surviving horrendous obstacles continues.

28...AN AWAKENING, AN AWARENESS

> ...We smile, but, O great Christ, our cries
> To thee from tortured souls arise.
> We sing, but, oh the clay is vile
> Beneath our feet, and long the mile;
> But let the world dream otherwise—
>   We wear the mask!
> **Paul Laurence Dunbar:** "We Wear the Mask"

I'll never forget the day I answered an ad in my local newspaper for part time help at the Enoch Pratt Library in Baltimore. It was my last year of undergraduate work.

"Hello, my name is Dawn Jennings. I'm inquiring about the ad in the paper for college students to work in the evenings. Do you have any vacancies?"

"Yes we do." She wanted to know my available days for work. After answering a list of questions, she finally asked what college I attended.

"I'm attending Morgan State University."

After a long pause, she answered, "A—h, um, I thi-nk that position is filled. L—et me check. Yeees, it's been filled."

Surprised by her answer, I said, "But the first thing I asked you was, 'Do you still have any vacancies?' and you said, 'Yes.' Do you remember that?"

"Yes, I remember, but I made a mistake. They're *all* filled."

I thought *more prejudice, even in the library.* My heart dropped but my mouth opened and asked more questions.

"Would you please explain how they were filled in less than a minute?"

Another long pause—she offered her evasive answer, "I'm sorry, but all of the positions have been filled," she said goodbye and hung up.

Had I applied in person, they *might* have hired me since I looked like them.

Or maybe they didn't want a student from *that* college—a Negro college. The library's refusal to hire me was its loss. A dedicated, hard working young married college student; I'd have been an asset to any library.

Theon and I made preparations to buy that eighty year old Victorian home even though I was not returning to work; plus our marriage had split at the seams. I continued my drapery business and Theon his mental abuse.

After Theon joined the Arthur Murray Dance School, we attended classes together pending his work schedule. His constant attention to the female instructors caught my eye. Whenever I'd mention his flirtatious actions, he became angry. One evening as we returned home, I mentioned his disrespectful conduct.

"What's wrong with you, Dawn? I'm only dancing with the ladies. I can't help it if they find me charrr—ming."

"I find it the reverse. *You* seem to be the charmer!"

"There you go again, always reading into my actions."

"I don't have to read into anything, not when you so obviously flaunt your attention at every dance. Like the other day when we were in the department store and you were gazing at that lady's legs. You actually turned your head all the way around and stared. Your intense gawking made the lady wonder why you were staring so long."

"Ah, you don't know what you're talkin' 'bout."

"You think so uh? I know more than you think I know. Yes, the lady had big pretty legs, but a quick glance from you would have been sufficient. But no, you turned *all* the way around, leaned your head down, as though you'd never seen a pair of big legs before."

"Ahhh, that was just your imagination, you didn't see all of that."

"I'm not blind. I know *exactly* what I saw!"

Bryan mentioned whenever he was out with Theon, he made passes at the clerks. What nerve he had in front of my children! But then I thought *if he'd disrespected me in public why would he respect my children's presence?*

I recall the time we both stood in front of the washing machine and dryer in the basement. I leaned over to get something off the shelf. Suddenly I was *knocked* on the floor! Shocked, I jumped up!

"What did you do that for?"

"You were in my way."

"I wasn't in your way and *don't* do it again."

"Ahhh, I only shoved you aside a little, I didn't know you'd fall."

"Well, after I fell, why didn't you help me get up?"

"You got up didn't you. You didn't need my help."

Less than a year—our marriage had split. Splinters flew everywhere...

One day when I arrived home from work I noticed that Theon's car wasn't parked out front.

"Mama has Theon gone to work?"

"I don't know Dawn. I never know when he leaves for work. He never tells me. He sure is a strrrange man. He's quiet and stays to himself when he's here. I hardly know when he's around."

The next day I asked him, "Theon why don't you talk to my mother sometimes or at least let her know when you leave for work."

"I don't go out of my way for *nobody!*"

"But Theon, that's my mother. The least you can do is let her know when you're going to work. You know she's not able to get up and down the steps that well. What kind of man are you anyway?"

"Well my mother ain't sick. I don't like being around sick people. Besides if she needs anything she can just call me."

"You're a cold heartless man! Why didn't you show that side of your darling personality while we dated?"

"I know how to get what I want. I hid that side until *after* we were married."

"You're a sneaky mean person. It's all coming out. Now I understand what your mother meant when I told her you were a gentleman and she said, 'You don't know Theon, he's *definitely* not a gentleman!' She knows your personality better than anyone else."

"She knows a little, but not *that* much."

"You're not the same caring man I dated, the man that had to be around me everyday, the man that went out of his way to do any little thing to make me happy."

"Well, I was *crazy* then! I'm *sane* now. Back to my real self, the *Man.*"

Theon's temperament worsened. A few days of harmony soon changed to meanness. Once after a terrible argument, we didn't speak for two days.

The third day when I asked him a question he said, "Why are you talking to me so soon? You're supposed to wait at least a week."

"A week. Why should I wait a week? I don't stay angry with anyone that long, especially if we live in the same house. I say what I have to say, and that's that. I treat people the way I want to be treated. I like being kind to people."

As we walked down the steps, he jerked around as soon as he reached the bottom landing.

"Y-e-a-h, so I've noticed. Sometimes you're so kind, you're *sickening!*"

"*Sickening*, how can you say such a thing? You don't appreciate people treating you kind, especially your wife?"

"*No!* Sometimes it's all right but not *all* the time. I like some confusion and this house is, *too* quiet. You need more *action* around here."

"You mean more fussing and arguing."

"Yeah, yeah we need more action around here, like wrestling and tussling. You don't like those kinds of games."

"No I don't because you always get rough. You think I'm one of those men you wrestled in your college classes and when you were a Marine. But I'm not. I'm a lady and your wife."

"Well, you just have to get tougher!"

"Ahhhh—I understaaand nooow. When I taught dancing you saw the rough side of me; the side that pushed my dancers harder and harder! I reminded you of your tough loud drill sergeant. But off the rehearsal floor I'm different. You need a sparring partner not a wife."

"No. I need a wife that's not afraid of a little action every now and then."

"Is that right? You need a ruffian, a street woman. You should have married that woman that held you hostage in her home. *Yes*, that's your type of wife, someone who'll argue and battle on command."

Theon rolled his shifty eyes then strolled toward the kitchen door. His mask had vanished. The real man emerged. He'd fooled my mother, my sons and me. Why me? Because I was in looove! I loved his boyish ways, polite mannerisms. Yes, this was *not* the same man I married. I didn't *know* this man. His respect, his kindness disappeared like an early morning fog. Who *was* this stranger sleeping in my bed? Who was this alien, this outsider sharing our home?

Two months after Marty joined the Air Force a dramatic change occurred in Bryan. The change, a slow process, escalated one night when I questioned him about not washing the dishes. Bryan had inherited Marty's striking attic bedroom. I used his small bedroom as my art studio to hold my drafting board, bookcase, desk, and art supplies.

One night I called upstairs to Bryan to come down and wash the dishes. Theon was working the night shift. Had he been home, there wouldn't have been a problem.

"Why do I have to wash dishes? I don't see Theon washing any dishes!"

"Bryan, Theon does other things to help in the house. He does chores while you're at school. Come on down and get these dishes washed!"

"I don't think it's fair. I'm not washing *nothing*!"

With that statement as I proceeded up the attic steps toward his bedroom he rushed to the head of the steps and kicked in the face of the small fan that cooled his room. Enraged by Bryan's behavior, for the first time—I feared my son! His twisted face; fuming, fiery eyes stared me down! He ached to hurt me. Startled, I stopped and stood still. For a few moments he examined his damaged fan, turned and walked back toward his bed.

"I'll get the dishes in a few minutes." He grumbled.

I retreated and headed to Mama's opened bedroom door—frightened, not for myself but for my son. What had happened to him? I stared out Mama's window into the backyard at the small vegetable garden that needed weeding. My rapid heartbeat cried for help! Each beat questioned Bryan's fate. Mama lay still in her bed as she did twenty hours a day, waiting for me to break the silence.

From the corner of my eye I noticed a roach crawling over her nightstand. As I bent over to kill it, I saw another one running up her light blue draperies. I thought *how strange to see roaches in Mama's room. I hadn't seen any before*. Curious, I pulled back the ceiling to floor draperies behind her bed; looked behind them, then *screamed!*

"Ohhh, roaches, roaches Mama! They've covered the back of your draperies!"

Mama left her bed and sat in her chair. I retrieved the vacuum cleaner from the hall closet; attached the smaller hose used for cleaning crevices; rushed to her bedroom and watched the hose suck up nearly a hundred roaches! Bryan hurried downstairs to see what was wrong. He moved Mama's bed from the window and took down the draperies while I completed the roach slaughter! By this time the pests were racing on the floor, headed for the hall and my bedroom. I hosed the few still running for their lives!

My body cringed at the sight of one. Killing almost a *hundred* was an experience I'll *never* forget! I thought I was dreaming. I'd never seen that many roaches in one area not even in New York City, the roach haven.

Two days later an exterminator came and sprayed the entire house. It amazed him that only Mama's room was infested. I explained Mama ate in her room daily. If she hadn't finished, her plate remained for her to eat the rest later. We *never* left another plate, only cookies etc. in tight containers. The exterminator revealed that roaches loved wood. They hid in dresser drawers and cabinets etc. and could *survive* on wood.

That February, snow had covered everything. One morning around one o'clock, after I returned from the bathroom, I pulled back the window curtain in our bedroom to check the depth of the snow and noticed my car was gone! I rushed over to the bed and shook Theon.

"Theon, my car is gone! Somebody has stolen my car!"

He jumped from the bed and looked out the window! I called the police and reported my car had been stolen. While we waited for the policemen, Theon checked upstairs in Bryan's room. Bryan was gone! We went downstairs to check the club basement. Tossed on the sofa were his pajamas, house shoes and robe. Theon opened the basement back door. Bryan's footprints were on each step that led up to the yard and out the backyard gate. No doubt, Bryan had stolen my car. Only fifteen; he didn't have a driver's license. Did he know how to drive! I didn't know. How could he do such a *stupid* thing? *Fury held me captive!*

As we waited for the officer, I told Theon about an incident that had occurred two weeks earlier in school as I stood on hall duty. A student of mine stopped to chat.

"Hi Mrs. Albens, I saw your son last night at the *Gardenia Club*."

"You saw Bryan where Samatha? I think you're wrong. Bryan was home last night, in bed. What time last night?"

"About twelve-thirty, I was juusst leavvving." Her answer was slow and hesitant.

Before I asked additional questions she turned to leave and said, "See ya Mrs. Albens I gotta hurry so I won't be late for class."

The officer arrived. We explained the problem. He suggested we wait until Bryan returned and call again. As we waited, I remembered incidents connected to the car. For the past few months I'd bought more gas than usual. I'd expressed my concerns to Bryan as we drove to school several mornings. He didn't reply but just stared out the window. Those actions weren't unusual for Bryan. He did not like school and was never eager to go. He could have been, an A student, with his quick bright mind. But he chose to wriggle through with C's, D's and a few B's. We'd discuss the value of an education but he rebelled, determined to do things *his* way. He'd been that way since birth.

At six months old. Bryan threw his milk bottle from the crib and refused to drink any more milk, not even from a cup! He received his supply of calcium through enriched foods even though he never ate much of anything.

Bryan had cried every time we tried to put him on the white potty-chair placed in the bathroom next to the toilet. He preferred to climb up onto the commode and straddle the toilet seat. Each time I saw him, raised on both hands, straddling the seat larger than he, I feared he'd fall in. He never fell and *never* used that potty-chair. Since Aunt Betty's toilet was lower to the floor, Bryan had potty trained himself during his summer vacation. He also refused to use his car seat.

He squawked every time we tried putting him in that seat. He insisted he'd sit the same way we sat. He did and never fell over. I always said Bryan was a man trapped in a baby's body.

Theon reminded me of something I did every night without any hesitation for worry.

"Dawn, remember you leave your keys and pocketbook downstairs every night. It was easy for him to take the keys."

By this time we were in Mama's room discussing our problem. She was as angry with Bryan as we were and gave us more insight to the dilemma.

"So that's why Bryan couldn't get up to go to school. He'd been out blue goosing half the night and was beat! I used to hear movement in the hall, but I figured it was you or Theon going to the bathroom. Taking your car Dawn was a *terrible* thing for that boy to do to you."

"I'm hurt Mama. But I'm more angry than hurt! When he returns I'm calling the police and let them handle it. He thought Theon had to work tonight but he starts day shift this morning."

I returned to our bedroom and noticed Theon standing by the window holding an envelope.

"Here, read this. It's a copy of a letter Bryan wrote Marty some time ago and asked me to mail it for him."

I pulled out the letter, and read it slowly. Bryan had told Marty, he was still taking my keys and driving my car at least twice a week. He described the fun he and his friends were having in *my* car emphasizing his *late* hours.

"Theon you mean you've known this all along and didn't tell me? Why! How could you know Bryan was stealing my car, driving without a license and keep it a secret? Tell me why you did such a thing?"

"I copied the letter, and kept it for a time just like this."

"You mean you've had this letter all this time! He might have wrecked my car, and killed himself! Explain to me why you did nothing. You don't care about my car or Bryan, do you?"

My heart pounded! I was so, *so mad!* Theon climbed into bed. I kneeled and prayed for my immature son. Catnaps stole my rest until I heard Bryan downstairs at five a.m. I called the officer then went downstairs to greet *Mr. Bryan.* God protected him; but *I was fuming!*

"Well Mr., do you know what time it is! Where have you been with my car half the night! Don't answer because I don't want to hear any lies come from your mouth!" One heated question after another poured out!

During my interrogating speech, the patty wagon arrived. The policeman knocked on the door. I answered. When he stepped inside, Bryan looked dumfounded. The officer questioned him about my car being stolen and explained his reason for being there. Bryan was shocked when the officer handcuffed him and ushered him out to the patty wagon. Since Theon had gone to work, I followed them to the police station at six o'clock that early cold Saturday morning, *fuming and disgusted!*

Bryan was questioned by an arresting officer in one room. I waited in another one, alone. Placed in a holding cell for over two hours, it provided him time to think about being locked up for stealing his mother's car plus driving without a license. Two hours later, the officer returned.

"Mrs. Albens, your son was shocked that you had him locked up. He said he never thought you'd do anything like that to him."

"Well I never thought he'd steal my car!"

"There isn't much we can do since he doesn't have a previous record. I decided to let him sit alone in a holding cell for a while. That'll give him time to think over his wrong actions. We talked at length about him driving without a license and allowing his friends to drive your car."

"His friends! You mean he let *his friends drive my car!"*

"Yes ma'am. If he'd had an accident with no license he'd never gotten a Maryland Driver's License."

"Good! He *still* doesn't need one! I am *so angry* with that boy! He could have killed himself plus the other boys with him. What's wrong with these children? Cars are not toys! They can hurt and kill!"

After Bryan's release, we walked across the parking lot in silence. No words existed to express my irritation with him! As we sauntered toward the car, he finally spoke.

"Mommy I'm sorry for what I did. I guess I didn't think about what could have happened. We just wanted to go to the club."

"Bryan you're only fifteen years old. You *stole* my car! *How* could you do such a thing!"

"I didn't think you'd find out."

"Is that right? Yes, I know, you just didn't *think, period!* Young people never think about the consequences of the crime. You never thought about anything except what Bryan wanted!"

"Mommy I never thought you'd have me locked up."

"I didn't either, but isn't jail for thieves?"

"I guess so."

"No guessing Bryan. When you stole my car, you became a thief."

"But I'm your son and I just borrowed it."

"Borrowed nothing! Borrow is when someone allows you to use his property with permission. You never asked me for anything! You stole it and could have had a wreck!"

"But I didn't."

"Thank God you didn't. Yes, you're my son and I love you very much. That's exactly why I called the police now, so I won't have to later! You have many years to drive cars and go to nightclubs. Besides, what club lets you in, you're under age?" Our conversation mellowed as I drove home, trying to gather my shattered nerves.

Two months into Marty's basic training, and one month after Bryan's vehicular episode, I received his unexpected letter. In essence Marty apologized for not alerting me earlier that Bryan had been stealing my car on school nights. My return letter explained our recent problem and expressed my ultimate disappointment in him for allowing his brother to continue such conduct. I believe Bryan had written him about the incident, although neither one admitted to such a letter about his unhappy experience in jail. Consumed with guilt, I'm sure Marty wrote me to clear his conscience.

When I confronted him later, he confessed, "I thought Bryan would eventually stop."

The car episode only increased Theon's ill feelings about Bryan, which initiated additional problems in our marriage; as though we needed *anymore*.

Negotiations for the Victorian house commenced. Mr. Seymour agreed to hold the mortgage while we assumed responsibility for the remaining two-thirds of repairs. We secured a real estate lawyer. Now August, still three months remained. That was enough time to finish painting the interior, cleaning, sanding floors, washing windows, stripping linoleum off three floors, etc. and to sell my house. Profits from the house would provide funds to ready *our* new home and moving expenses. We waited eagerly for a buyer. Buying the large old forgotten home depended on the sale of our present home.

On Theon's days off, he visited the house to make repairs and paint while Mr. Seymour's crew finished their jobs. Excessive walking and talking interrupted Theon's work therefore he didn't accomplish much. As weeks passed, Theon went, less and less. After my house sold to a fine young couple, I hired two men to complete Theon's neglected job of painting. What a waste of money since Theon had had *three* months to paint those rooms!

The house's low electrical capacity required me to clean before dark since it was during October and November and darkness fell early. Aged linoleum *stuck* to the hardwood floors necessitated scraping before any sanding commenced. When I bent over to pick up one corner of the worn torn linoleum in Mama's future room on the first floor, I discovered it *wasn't* stuck! Instead, newspaper dated *1929* had protected the floor for over fifty years! I removed the old linoleum and saved every sheet of the dingy faded paper. What a treasure I'd uncovered!

I was not as fortunate in the adjacent dining room. It took *days and days,* kneeling on a pillow, to scrape up that stubborn linoleum plus *another* room upstairs. Removing areas of plaster in the bathtub, the sinks, and shower was equally exhausting.

Numerous small pieces of linoleum were impossible to remove! The workmen said not to worry; their sanding machines would get the rest. They sanded seven rooms, a foyer and the staircase to the second floor. Three coats of polyurethane were applied in layers for several days before we moved, finalizing their fantastic job!

Everyday that I cleaned and scraped, I spoke to the old house as a friend.

"Soon you'll look grand again. Maybe it won't be as lovely as when you were first built, but close. I promise to renew your initial beauty and care for you the best I can as long as I'm here."

I'd stroll through the rooms and the halls and pray. I thanked God for the gracious old home, a home I'd *always* wanted, a Victorian home with a wrap around porch. I also thanked Him for the attic, my future haven and art studio/ sewing room. And of course I thanked Him for the dirty stone wall, cracked concrete basement floor, where after having been remodeled we'd entertain in future years.

Two weeks before we moved, I was completing a drapery order in the basement with Ceal, a young lady Theon had recommended. This was her second day sewing drapery hems in by hand. I needed help desperately. As we worked, we talked. As we talked, I learned. As I learned, I asked questions and received shocking answers!

"Ceal, how long have you known Theon?"

"I met Theon about three years ago but we didn't date. We started dating several months later—and then he met you."

"You mean the two of you were intimate?"

"Yes, *quite* intimate."

Her response was forlorn. A distant air touched her voice; a sense of disappointment echoed each word.

"When did you first know I made draperies, Ceal?"

"Theon's been calling me on the phone for a few months. He wanted to renew our relationship." With those words I stopped what I was doing.

"What did you say, Ceal?"

"Theon wanted to renew our relationship."

"You knew he was married. What did you say?"

"I told him no. He'd dumped me for you. Why should I want to see him again?"

With my back to Ceal, I excused myself and walked upstairs to Mama's room as tears flowed down my face. I held in the cry, until I reached her room, closed the door then cried in a soft blue pillow on her chair next to the bed. After a few minutes I revealed my problem between sobs.

Mama said, "Dawn she's trying to hurt you."

"She *did* hurt me!" I started crying again in the soft blue pillow to muffle the crying sounds that might escape through the vent to the basement.

"Theon married you and not her. She wants to get back at Theon through you. Don't let her know you're hurt."

"But Mama, the mere fact that he had the nerve to even *bring* one of his former girlfriends in my house is an *insult*! And right now he's still asking her to be intimate with him. What's *wrong*, with these men!"

I stayed a few more minutes and prayed, washed my face in the bathroom then returned to the basement. Ceal was still hemming when I returned. Attempting to converse was difficult, so I stopped. Thirty minutes later, Theon sauntered down the basement steps.

"Hello, young ladies, I see you're both still at work." I spoke but said nothing else. Theon continued bragging about something. As he walked and talked I grew angrier.

"Theon, I understand that you used to date Ceal."

"Y—es, I guess you could c—all it that."

"Yes, I do call it that, especially when you have sex with that person." I said.

"Sex, what are you talking about?"

"What about calling her recently and asking her to renew your relationship?"

"I did no such thing," he said.

Ceal was still sewing with her head bowed but after that remark it jerked up.

"Theon, you know very well, you asked me to start dating you again and I said no because you were now a married man." Ceal answered.

"I don't know what either one of you are talking about." He started walking toward the steps to leave.

"And where do you think you're going? Stay right here and answer these questions." By this time my voice was loud and Ceal was folding the completed drapery in preparation to leave. She'd completed *her mission*; satisfaction was hers.

"I don't have to answer anything, from you or anybody else, I don't care who it is." He proceeded up the steps to the kitchen.

"Ceal, I'll pay you for these two days. I'll handle the rest myself. Are you ready to leave?" I said.

"Yeah, I'm ready."

Ceal didn't own a car so I'd picked her up and carried her home both days. She told me how sorry she was because I was such a nice lady and *too* good for Theon. After I pulled away from her apartment building the anger I held in, rushed out in gasping cries and tears! They ran full force! They strove to cleanse my drowning pain, from yet another man, another husband, another *Bum!* I drove though streets with cars parked on both sides that blocked me in. My head ached. I cried frantically! The car moved as I remained robotic. We traveled across the city. We intermingled in traffic. We wove in and out side streets, up and down lanes across main arteries unknown to me. We moved by instinct. I prayed, *"God, please, please help meee!"*

Daylight ended; darkness emerged. Families ate dinner while others scurried home. Two hours had passed, I knew Mama was worried, so I pulled into a gas station and called home.

"Mama, I'm alright. I thought it best to drive a while to ease this hurt before coming home. Have you eaten?"

"Yes, Bryan gave me my dinner long ago. When are you coming home Dawn, it's getting dark outside."

"Tell Bryan I'm alright and I'll be home soon. I need to be alone with God a little longer. He always takes care of me. Mama—how do I always manage to marry the same wrong men?"

"You're too good to your boyfriends and husbands, Dawn. They don't appreciate you and the things you do. You're too good hearted, just like me. You'll *always* get hurt. It's just your nature to be kind to people and believe what you hear."

Mama was right. She was usually on target. She'd traveled that rocky road in life long before I was born. I kept thinking *God made all these men; there has to be one out there for me. A kind, considerate understanding male has to exist somewhere.* Will I ever find him; I wondered.

Unaware then, I searched for the love, through husbands, not received as a child. Mama found it *her* way. She too was love-starved, the same as I. I needed a man to fill that hollow space of loneliness. At least *that's* what I believed.

As a child I was too busy playing or studying to realize, Mama or Aunt Betty had ever said, *I love you.* I assumed sufficient food, clothes and a home meant love. No one tucked me in bed at night or gave me that loving hug. Only Marcus, my fourth grade sweetheart's love notes said those words and when we dated years later. Even family TV shows didn't alert me to what I wasn't getting: hugs, kisses, affectionate touches. I'd missed the vital essentials for developing into a mentally healthy adult. Daddy provided some of that love.

I returned home late after Theon had gone to work. The next day I called his mother and explained our problem. She replied, "Oh, Dawn, you know how men are."

In her nonchalant manner of speaking she inferred I should *accept* her son's faithless adulterous behavior.

"No, I *don't!* Why don't you tell—*me!*"

"Ah, you know what I mean; they have to sow their wild oats from time to time."

"Wild oats! So that's what you call it. I call it *adultery*! Do you have another name for it! If so, tell me!"

By then I was crying, trying to make her understand my point of view. But she saw *no* wrong. She said I shouldn't let that bother me and just go on with my life as though nothing had happened! *She must—have—been—crazy!!*

The next evening after dinner, I expressed my feelings toward Theon about the situation. Of course he denied everything! Flashbacks helped me recall the many mornings and evenings he'd come home late. It's extraordinary how the mind plows deep into your memory without consent. Ye-s, ye-s, ye-s, I remembered those mornings well. It was during that time his disrespect surfaced that he started his wandering. I noticed his amorous attention, starting to fade. It faded like a stained cloth soaked in Clorox. My *fourth* marriage, I was tired, so tired of marrying and divorcing. Why couldn't I just leave men alone? I was only ruining my life and self esteem while they simply moved on as though nothing ever happened.

We'd already signed papers to buy the house and invested a lot of money in necessary move in renovations. My house was sold. I was trapped. I sat at the kitchen table, face buried in my hands, "God what am I going to do? *Please* help me. I don't know what to do anymore!"

Theon's envy of my sons was obvious. He'd question items I bought them.

"What do they need that for? I never had that when I was their age. You just spoil those boys!"

He walked around the house angry most of the time, frowning and rolling his sinister eyes. When I said, "I do" at the altar, I do for what? I do for pain. I do for insults. I do for disrespect. I do for adultery. For him, our love had lasted as long as a butterfly lights on a pink Penta petal.

I was trapped, caught in my own web, strangled by threads of deceit, cynicism and meanness. While I waited on my disability decision from the school system, mental confusion anchored my body into physical fatigue. My doctor sent me to a psychiatrist after treating me for three months because I refused to take medication. How could I get well when one disaster after another kept tripping over each other!

29...TIME CHANGES SITUATIONS

Is't possible that so short a time
can alter the condition of a man?
Shakespeare: Coriolanus. Act V, Sc. 4

My Turkish psychiatrist Dr. Youtow's accent was difficult to understand. Later on my ears became attuned providing I watched his lips and listened intently. I shall never forget our first meeting.

"Dr. Youtow, I don't know why I'm here, Mr. Tillon should be here, not I. *He's* the one that's crazy!"

For two years I visited him twice a month. He helped me understand my emotional condition. Slowly the multiple causes for my problems unraveled. A selfish husband, a bed-ridden mother and my teenage son headed the list. Not knowing my real father, childhood and adolescent difficulties had affected my adult personality. In time I viewed myself in a different light and practiced the suggestions he offered. Indeed, a difficult task lay ahead for me. I wondered if I'd ever cross that safe peaceful road in life.

The day before Thanksgiving—we moved. The old Victorian house with boarded up windows, peeled dingy white clapboard, an overgrown weeded yard with some parts mowed and my private front forest was now home!

Moving was a strenuous job. The movers tackled heavy boxes, large furniture to be carried in the basement, on the second floor then upstairs to the attic. Tight passageways were awkward to maneuver. I wondered how those stout men squeezed through those narrow openings. As usual I labeled every box for each room. I'd moved so often I'd thought about writing a book titled, "How to Move with No One's Help" since I packed and negotiated everything myself.

Mama would said, "Dawn, sit down; rest yourself. You're too young to wear yourself out like you do. One day you're gonna' regret it and end up like me."

"Ah, Mama, I'll be fine. If I don't do it, no one else will?" I ignored her wisdom.

I drove ahead and guided the movers with their stuffed trucks to our newly renovated home located in a peaceful wooded area. They backed up the huge truck into the gravel driveway and started to unpack. While they unpacked the furniture and placed it on the lawn in the order to be carried into the house, I grabbed newspaper from my car, hurried to cover our shiny hardwood floors. I opened the door and *froze*! No glossy shine greeted me. I trembled and yelled!

"What is *this*! *Look* at these *floors*!" I dropped the stack of newspapers on the floor, rushed to the kitchen and called Mr. Phillips. He explained the problem and promised to return the day after Thanksgiving.

The men had applied three coats of polyurethane on all the floors. Wet, the floors had a brilliant sheen. Due to years of awesome neglect, the wood absorbed the liquid like a sponge! Mr. Phillips returned as promised and reapplied more Polyurethane to every floor. For *three weeks* we lived in a house of piled up furniture, moving it from room to room until every floor had been rolled twice. They finished a few days before Christmas. Gorgeous hardwood floors, white window shades with scalloped bottoms, peach painted walls and stained woodwork must have smiled. The weather beaten peeled white clapboard and boarded up windows remained intact until spring. I'm sure the house's original owners, who watched overhead, were grateful.

Theon's mother knew our moving date. She knew I didn't have time to cook, not to mention Thanksgiving Dinner. She *never* mentioned dinner or offered any help whatsoever. My dear friend Tanya invited us for Thanksgiving Dinner. With Theon working, Marty in the Air Force and Bryan living in Fayetteville, I went alone while Mama watched television. As usual Tanya had cooked an *outstanding* meal, a table set for "Queen Dawn." She sent my mother a dinner and gave me enough food that lasted us for days. Yes indeed she *was a blessing*! Theon's mother visited weeks later.

Days later Mr. Seymour our landlord came to discuss the settlement date set for November. Amazed when he entered, he yelled:

"Dawn what *have you done* to this house! I can't believe these are the same rooms I worked on this summer?"

I thought *after paying $1000 and three future weeks of agony they better glitter like gold!*

He stared speechless. The peach walls, shiny hardwood floors and new white window shades were stunning. He, Theon and I sat squeezed together on the sofa wedged in between piled up furniture.

"Mr. and Mrs. Albens why don't you just rent this house from me and buy it later?"

I gawked at that man! I thought *he must be raving mad!* All the labor, time and money I've spent making this house livable. He can't be serious. But he was.

"You could stay here and I'll be responsible for the maintenance."

I read his mind. I'd done such a good job with the house, now he wanted to renege on his deal. *No way* would we change *our* minds! During our tight, close meeting on the sofa, Mr. Seymour asked us to wait until February to settle the property. He wanted to avoid the sale of two houses in the same year on his taxes. In addition the rent we paid until February would be included in our down payment. We agreed to his terms and signed the papers. He left still in shock at the interior's renovation.

We endured three pinned-in weeks. We stepped up, around and crawled over furniture, as though traveling in a maze, to avoid a wet floor. What a terrible inconvenience we experienced just days prior to Christmas.

Mama's room, on the first floor, didn't have a door. However a door was underneath the porch. It needed cleaning and painting, but Theon refused to prepare the door and hang it. His eccentric, cold Dr. Jekyll/ Mr. Hyde personality switched from sweet and suave to villainous! This was another Nat, only Theon was sneaky, cruel, callous plus uncaring! I begged him.

"Theon, would you *please* get Mama's door from under the porch, and hang it. She doesn't have any privacy. I'll scrape and paint it myself, later on."

"It doesn't need a door." He shook his head and strutted out the house. I followed him outside to the porch.

"What do you mean, it doesn't need a door. That's my mother's bedroom and she needs a door. Don't you have a door to your bedroom? Well, she needs one to hers!"

"I *saaiid* it *doesn't* need one, so it *doesn't get* one! She stays in the bed all the time anyway so why does she even need a door!"

I watched him ease down the side porch steps, walk down the severely cracked sidewalk to his reddish-orange Datzun 280Z, back out the gravel driveway onto the dirt road then drive straight ahead out to Flannery Lane, leaving his cruel remarks behind.

Marty arrived home on his military leave a week before Christmas. How handsome he looked in his Air Force uniform. As we drove home from the airport, I explained about the house not having been painted on the outside because that money was set aside for the settlement in February. In addition we decided to keep the boards on the windows the entire winter—to help retain the heat. This was Marty's first time in *this* home. We'd moved so much he expected another home every few years. Aunt Betty called me her *wandering gypsy*! So did my friends.

As soon as Marty stepped inside the house he said, "Mom, where's the Christmas tree?"

"I haven't gotten one. I'm not putting up a tree 'til these filthy radiators are painted and Mama has a door to her bedroom." After he greeted Mama, he noticed her doorway.

"Why doesn't Grandmommy have a door?"

"Theon said she didn't need one."

"Do you have a door to fit her room?" He said.

"Yes, it's one under the front porch. It's dirty but I'll clean it if you'll put it up."

"Mom, I'll put up the door *and* paint the radiators. Then I'll get a tree. I've never had Christmas without a tree. It's not like you—not to have a tree."

"Thanks, Marty. I thought you'd finish those things for me. I'm tired, weary and disgusted. Aunt Betty and Bryan will be here in a few days. I really wanted everything finished before they got here."

Marty was gifted with his hands. He could repair anything. In the Air Force he was an Air Traffic Control Specialist.

Bryan drove his used car, a gift from Aunt Betty, from Fayetteville to Baltimore. The six hour trip was fine—until he reached home. Aunt Betty laughed and cried as she explained their dilemma.

"Bryan cou—ldn't reme—mber how to get h—ome. We kept ri—ding around 'til I realized he was lost and asked him."

"No I'm not lost, Aunt Betty; I just don't remember how to get uptown."

Bryan drove around aimlessly until he recognized a street that led him to a main artery.

"Mommy, I'd never driven to Baltimore. When I entered downtown, I was all turned around. I didn't know where I was, so I kept driving around until I saw a street I remembered. Riding the bus or riding in someone else's car was all I was used to."

We had our joke on Mr. Bryan! Born and reared in Baltimore, he couldn't find his way home! Theon avoided my family during their holiday visit. He'd come home from work, say a few words then go right upstairs to bed. Since our settlement date for the house had been pushed up to February, I dug deep into its money. Bryan needed school clothes. Christmas gifts and crucial house items were also bought. As usual I spent too much money making everyone happy while my bank account cried *Hellllllp!*

As February crawled closer, my heart beat faster. My retroactive school disability check was due, but I didn't know when. Mr. Seymour was reluctant to extend the settlement date to April.

"Mrs. Albens I'm losing money as it is. You knew the settlement date was in February, so what has happened?"

"I'm waiting on my school disability check. I worked with you, Mr. Seymour, for three months so you wouldn't have to report taxes on the sale of two homes, so why can't you wait for me?"

"That's different, you're not losing money; I am."

We talked until I persuaded him to wait. During that two-month interval I continued to unpack and endured Theon's disassociation with the house. A week before the closing, we received a letter from Seymour's real estate lawyer asking us to meet with him. We did. Seymour had his lawyer write up a document stating we would rent the property, with the rent going toward the future purchase until 40% of the purchase price had been paid. Then we could buy the property. I jumped up from my chair!

"Ooooh no! We are buying that property *now*! I've worked too hard, too long for him to keep my home. Tell me Mr. Stark why is he doing this to us, one week before our settlement date?" The lawyer tried to weasel out from answering my question, but I persisted. He finally told us the truth.

"Mr. Seymour still owes a balance on the property."

"You mean he doesn't own that property and is trying to sell it to us on his own terms? What's the balance?" I said.

"I can't reveal that information Mrs. Albens."

"I think I have a right to know. He's trying to pull a crooked deal. I don't like it at all. Tell him if he doesn't sell us that house as planned we'll bring a suit against him."

With that remark, Theon and I left his lawyer's office. I couldn't fathom the man's reasoning! His deceitful smiles and underhandedness in trying to keep his house after all the money and labor I'd spent, infuriated me!

"Theon, people never ceased to amaze me. He knew we were recently married and struggling to get that house. How *could* he do such a thing? The answer is simple, *greed*! He owns property in Hawaii, Arizona and Maryland. He doesn't care about us, only himself and *money*, money, money! I'm glad I don't treat people like that."

"Well Dawn, I study people. I knew immediately the type of man he was. He wants to make as much money on this property as possible. Wouldn't you?"

"Yes, but not his way."

The next day his lawyer called us and said Seymour was making arrangement to pay off the balance of $13,000 to the bank but it would take several days for his funds to be transferred. He had paid $20,000 for the property and sold it to us for $55,000, including the adjacent wooded lot. The settlement date was moved up a few days. We secured our own attorney to sit at the table with us. Immediately he detected a clause in the contract where Seymour wanted us to pay a certain fee that was to be shared by both parties. That fee alone saved us $700. A few other fees had to be shared. I never mentioned it to Seymour or his attorney.

Settlement day arrived and so did we, ready to see his reactions to the mistakes he'd made in his contract. Mr. and Mrs. Seymour sat across the table from the three of us while Mr. Stark Seymour's attorney sat at the end of the table to our right. When our attorney read the parts of the contract that revealed sharing closing expenses, Seymour was appalled. He'd not discussed his contract with his attorney. Instead he'd written everything himself.

"You mean that's all I'm going to get! Why that's $1,400 less than you were to pay!"

Both lawyers explained what had happened; the items he had misinterpreted. After several minutes of repeated explanations he understood but remained very angry. God was in control. He answered my prayer.

"God please help us through this ordeal in buying this house. There have been so many unexpected financial burdens. My nerves are shot!"

He always answered my prayers, in His own time, but always *on* time. God's methods in handling my problems never ceased to amaze me. I'd say, "Father God I don't know how you'll handle this problem, but I know you'll solve it in your own way."

After it was resolved, I'd say, "Thank you God. I knew you'd do it but I just didn't know how. Thank you!"

Jesus never said His children wouldn't have problems but He'd be with them through the turmoil and guide them over and around the hurdles to safety.

"But seek ye first the kingdom of God, and His righteousness and all these things shall be added unto you." Matt. 6:33 This is one of my favorite Bible verses.

We left Mr. Stark's office *financially* satisfied! Mr. Seymour's strategy to purloin our money—failed!

Theon had no interest in the house. Why? It wasn't what he wanted. Too much work was involved; he wanted a newer house. We didn't have money required for a down payment or the large monthly payments. Since he couldn't help with finances for renovating, repairing, moving or closing cost; as usual everything rested on me. Before we moved, his mother carried her friends over to see, *Theon's home* that *he* was buying to *fix* up. I had to *beg* and *plead* with that lethargic laid-back man to do *anything*!

The small kitchen, once a narrow back porch, had an old casement window over the sink. Everything in the kitchen was new but inexpensive except the double casement window and the old door. Inside hinges enabled the window to swing outward in the center, by using a hand crank on either side of each window. It was the same old window Mr. Smith had installed when he first closed in the back porch for his kitchen after his mother died.

Mr. Seymour had not insulated the kitchen as he said. His helper informed us *later* after we moved, of many things he said he'd done but had *not*! As I stood at the kitchen sink in front of the casement window that looked out into the back yard viewing the grape arbor, large pear tree, shed and other trees that winter, my feet and chest ached from the cold breezes that blew in between the cracks in the window and under the base cabinets.

I loved my old house, even though it remained boarded up waiting to be painted. I'd complained to Theon about my cold feet.

He'd say in a demeaning tone, "Put on some more socks and wear heavier pants. You know what to do. You've been in this world longer than I have, so you *should know* what to do!"

"Yes I do know what to do and so do you. And don't keep reminding me of my age. You knew I was older than you when we dated and married."

He suggested I stuff something along the bottom of the cabinets on the floor to keep out the drafts. When he refused to do it, I did it myself.

"Theon, would you please put some plastic on the outside of that casement window. Plastic would keep out the draft until we can replace the window in the spring."

"What's wrong with you? You're the artist. You'll do a better job anyway."

"But it's awkward leaning over the sink."

"Then stand in a chair or use the ladder."

"What's wrong with you Theon? Your name is on the deed just like mine. I think you could take a little interest in your home."

"This *ain't* my home! This is *your* home! I never wanted this old house in the first place. It was all your idea, not mine. I *hate* this house!"

"If you hate it so much, why did you sign your name on the contract?"

"I may be lazy, but I'm not a fool. Why should *I* pass up an opportunity to make some money on it in the future?"

"Is that why you married me, to help you make money?"

"We—ll, if you hadn't had anything; I wouldn't have married you. I don't fool around with women that don't *own* anything."

Those words *stabbed* my pride! How could he say that to me? He had some nerve telling me, he only married me because I had things worth money to him. Devastated again by his heartless words, I turned dragging my drained body from our bedroom. That egotistical, narcissistic, sneaky maniacal little boy was an *evil, evil man!*

Some men adore their wives and treat them like queens. It was good to know, they out there—somewhere—although I'd *never* had one.

Part of that cold winter I made draperies in the attic, wearing gloves, a heavy coat and hat. I recalled how I used to practice the piano in the cold hall in Fayetteville also wearing, a coat, hat and gloves during the weekdays when Aunt Betty's house wasn't heated. Theon had set up two saw horses in the unfinished attic with my sewing board placed on top. I'd covered the board with a blanket and sheets and played classical music as I worked. Extra outlets were installed in the attic for my Singer Industrial sewing machine and electric heater. A twenty-five foot telephone cord ran from a bedroom on the second floor then up the steps to the attic.

Prior to sewing in the attic, I'd rented the upstairs apartment over an upholstery shop on the corner from us when we first moved. Several nights when I came home after 11:00, I suspected a man was following me. When Theon was available he'd walk me home. Soon I started coming home at dusk. Later I left Mr. Fineman's second floor apartment and moved my sewing paraphernalia to our cold unfinished dingy attic.

Mama was satisfied knowing I was upstairs working on the draperies rather than having to walk home late at night, up that dark road, with trees lined on both sides, glaring animal eyes peering through the woods or anything else out there. I never worried though. Why, I knew God protected me. However, God did expect me to use *common sense* in all situations.

Theon worked a swing shift. Periods of time passed when our paths barely crossed, not due to his work schedule but to his lateness in coming home from work. Stubborn and set in his ways he'd say:

"You're not home so why should I come home."

"Because this is your home. Besides, people who work nights, usually come home in the morning, and go straight to bed."

"If I come home when you want me to, I can't make any extra money."

"What extra money?" I asked.

As usual he *never* answered my questions. I always had to ask him two or three times. Often I'd turned away in disgust.

"Sometimes I help the guys move furniture or repair things in their houses."

"Ahhhh, that's interesting, you don't have time to do anything in *your* house but you take time to repair things in somebody else's house."

"That's different; I don't get paid working here."

"Ma—nn you're *out* of your mind! Something is *really* wrong with you!"

Exactly one year after we moved into the house, the day after Thanksgiving, a terrible storm flooded the basement. Boxes of papers to file, school materials, furniture etc. were almost ruined. Everything not elevated was soaked. Theon refused to help me clean up the debris.

"I'm not putting *my hands* in that dirty water."

"But Theon put on your boots and some rubber gloves."

The water level had reached nearly two feet! I put on boots and slopped through the water sorting out ruined clothing, papers and other items. Theon helped for a short while then he returned upstairs to the den and watched television. The sump pump was broken. Water seeped up through the multiple cracks in the old broken concrete floor. Disgusted with my so called husband, I persevered several days of throwing out wet, wasted refuse. A few boxes were never opened and stained furniture remained, but elevated.

Bryan returned home late summer. His first winter in Fayetteville was unforgettable! The cold bathroom on the back porch, cold water, no heat in the house except in Aunt Betty's bedroom and warmed over food left on the small oil burner until he came home from school or work was not for him. He wrote me letters explaining how unhappy he was living under those conditions. I told him if I survived for nine years, he could endure it for one. During one of his collect calls, begging to come home, he emphasized everything he didn't like.

"But Mommy, that's you, we're two different people. Aunt Betty mixes all my food up together, on my plate. You know how picky I'm about my food. Everything has to be separate and not mingled in together."

"Well, Mr. Bryan, you had fine living conditions in Baltimore but you simply refused to obey. That's why you're keeping Aunt Betty's company for a while."

"I know why I'm down here. All in all it's not too bad. We get along fine but it's just the house. The house is nice, but she's too stingy to heat it during the week and still turns off the hot water heater at night. I get tired of getting up every morning in a cold house. Then go out to that *cold* bathroom and bathe in *cold* water."

"I guess it's time to come home. You're failing in school anyway. Aunt Betty had no business buying you that car in the first place."

"How was I supposed to get to school? It's too far to walk up to Haymount Hill to get the bus, besides Aunt Betty needed me to carry her places."

"Too far, to walk to Haymount Hill, that distance is nothing compared to the miles I walked to school for nine years. You want too much Bryan. You've been spoiled. You've had too many conveniences. Be thankful for what you have. I heard you're working more and going to school less. Is that job helping you get an education?"

"No, but it's putting money in my pocket."

"Yes, temporarily."

"When can I come home, Mommy?"

"Finish out this school year and bring up your grades. Then I'll send for you."

"Good, then I can drive my car to Baltimore!"

"Oooh no! You sell it. You've already spent too much money in repairs. It's an old car; it's not worth it. Besides, you need to concentrate on school if you want to graduate next year."

"I guess you're right, Mommy. I'll sell it just before I leave and use the money for my bus ticket." I couldn't believe he agreed with me.

"Now your thinking makes sense." He returned home shortly after school closed.

Early August I enrolled Bryan in the senior high school close to us. September he started a new school year with round-trip transportation a half block from our house. The county school bus stopped on the corner by our mailbox. It was the first time he'd had almost door to door bus service. As usual he was never satisfied! He still hated school and his relationship with Theon didn't improve. In fact it got worse.

My frazzled marriage dangled by a thread waiting to break and crash to the floor! Mama's rheumatoid arthritis hadn't improved either. And I, well I was caught in the middle of my family web that pulled and jerked me in every direction. My nerves split! Like the fibers of a spider web, strong, yet fragile, something always invaded its home. Only prayer, kept me rational enough to cope; to stay afloat.

Now a Christian Scientist, I shunned medicine, drank no alcoholic beverages or smoked. The devil had his field day though. He tried to torment my life. But, God carried me, He knew my limitations, like the Biblical character, *Job* who suffered with boils, was ridiculed by his friends, and lost all his possessions; but regained multiple wealth in the end through his faith in God.

One sunny autumn October afternoon, I stood in the kitchen preparing dinner. As I admired the grapes on the arbor, outside the window over the sink and realized my vegetable garden needed to be watered, Bryan dragged his weary body downstairs in a sorrowful mood. He flopped down in a kitchen chair and stared into space.

"What's the matter, Bryan?"

"Ummm, I don't know."

"What do you mean, you don't know?"

"Well there ain't nothing to do. I don't have any money. I don't have a car. So I don't know what to do."

"My dear, dear son, if that's your problem, you came to the right person."

"I'm not talking about *work*, Mommy, if that's the way you plan to solve my problem. All you think about is work, work and more work."

"My suggestions are not work but a pleasant way to fill your empty moments. Okay, you could water the vegetable garden. While the hose is doing its job, you could then cut the grass or finish painting the shed in the backyard. Or you could saw those hanging limbs…"

"*Ahhh no,* I knew your solution consisted of work. Why can't Theon do some of those things? I never see him do anything around here except cut the grass."

"He works swing shifts Bryan and you know our marriage isn't like it was in the beginning."

"Yes, so I've noticed. He sure has changed from the Theon you first dated. He's the king around here. I have to do all the dirty work while he does nothing."

Our once calm mother/son conversation ended in a heated argument about him, Theon and me. Hurt and devastated, I rushed from the kitchen through the dining room pocket doors and onto the front porch. Fatigued mentally and physically, I curled up into a tight ball on the cold floral cushion, double seated glider that faced the wooded area in front of the house. An *hour* of repeating the Twenty-third Psalm between sobs of hurt, my prayer was answered, soul soothed and tears subsided. I sat up, gazed straight ahead into the beautiful lush woods and the thousands of multicolored leaves that lay on the ground and inhaled fresh air. The trees now revealed their true silhouettes since their veils had disappeared. Body relaxed from hurt and anger, I returned to the kitchen and finished dinner.

Days, weeks of household tranquility were futile. My intimidating thoughts were frightening. Mama complained because I didn't spend enough time with her. Theon became so mean I didn't want to be near him. Bryan's transition from adolescence to manhood was unbearable. The house screamed, *help!* I struggled to hold my emotional seams in place, only God kept me sewn together.

One day during a moment of exasperation with Theon, I started screaming! My aching body followed the screams outside to my car. As the car backed out the driveway, Theon sprinted across the yard yelling!

"Stop the car Dawn, stop the car! Where are you going!"

"I don't kn—ow and I do—n't *care*! Just le—ave me al—one. All of you are dri-ving m-e *cra—zy*. I'm home on—-dis-abil-ity. My prob-lems are getting *worse* not better! I'm ti-red. I'm tired of li—-vi—ng. I'm tired of all these problems. I'm tired of family taking me for granted. I'm tired of contemptible men who only care about themselves. I'm tired of *everything*!"

I couldn't stop crying. Theon tried to console me. At that moment I wanted to die!! In his calm, charming, con artist voice he said, "Dawn, get out the car and come back into the house. You're overworked. You need to rest."

"Rest! Rest! You're telling me I need to rest! Do you know the meaning of word *need*, Theon? You have really *changed* since we married. I can't handle your meanness and sarcasm anymore. Dr. Youtow told you everybody in this family was contributing to my illness. Can't you see what you're doing to me? If it weren't for God I'd *been* dead! The only reason I'm alive is because God doesn't forgive suicide."

Theon continued his persuasion while I reminded him repeatedly of his mental cruelty and abuse toward me.

"You enjoy seeing me upset. You hurt me. You're a sadistic man."

He said nothing in his defense. He knew I was right. He knew himself well. Soft-spoken words flowed from his mouth that enhanced his charming deceitful smile. He couldn't fool me anymore. He tried to defend his character but he knew, I knew him, all too well.

I shared my problems with Mama after returning inside. She hated to see me crying and so distressed. She knew how hard I worked, trying to make that old house into a lovely home. She'd plead with me to slow down. If I didn't do the necessary chores, who would? Theon pouted every time I asked him to do something, while Bryan complained. I hated to ask them so I did the work myself. It was work for them. But for me, it was joy. Joy in mowing the lawn. Joy in landscaping the raw and neglected property. Joy in transplanting plants in the rain, while pushing my wheelbarrow and dressed in rainwear. Transferring plants during a mild rain assured their rooting and no yellow leaves.

Bryan and Theon's relationship deteriorated. After the stolen car incident the previous year, a police station counselor set up an appointment for the three of us to visit a psychologist and discuss ways to help Bryan.

In silence Theon, Bryan and I rode downtown in Theon's car. We entered the psychologist's office and sat semi-circular in front of his desk. During the session, the social worker failed to impress upon Theon the advantage he possessed in being closer to Bryan's age than I. Theon, cold and hard, refused to reason.

"I don't intend correcting anybody's behavior but once. He's no baby. He needs to learn how to talk to his mother then I won't have to correct him."

Theon continued his small talk. Bryan waited in the hall until the psychologist had finished with us. When Bryan returned, he and Theon promised to do better. Their relationship improved for a while. But eventually I asked Aunt Betty if Bryan could stay with her the remainder of that school year.

Now back home Bryan retained his same stubborn habits. Both Theon and Bryan were determined to have their own way, at any cost. The cost of course, only caused my depression to worsen.

My daily prayers were, "God please help me! I can't take anymore of this mental torture. Please, please *helllp meeee!"*

Bryan, a gregarious person, often invited his school friends to visit. They sat in the den upstairs next to our bedroom and listened to the Panasonic stereo Theon purchased when we dated. It was during our dating that my husband to be did everything to make me happy. My veil of love obscured Theon's true persona, his real character traits hidden behind a mask of deceit. The sweet humane façade was counterfeit.

One day I heard him bragging on how much his stepfather had paid for the unit.

"Ah man, Theon paid over $2000 for that set etc. and my mother paid $35 for that and $50 for that etc."

I'd told him *time after time* to stop bragging about how much we'd paid for things in the house. He didn't listen. Theon also reminded him he didn't like teenagers coming in and out the house. Bryan didn't listen.

Before Christmas, Bryan visited the Army recruiting office. He passed *every* test with excellent scores! A few days later I received a call from his recruiting officer; Bryan had changed his mind. He wanted to discuss Bryan's change of heart and came to our house the following day.

"Mrs. Albens I've a stack of tests here where young men have failed these tests and would give their right arm to get the scores your son got on his tests."

The recruiting officer and I discussed other issues while we waited for Bryan to come home from school. Bryan was failing. He knew if he didn't go into the service, he'd have to repeat the 12th grade. His pride refuted that option. After he came home we three discussed his future. His desire to finish the 12th grade in the service was paramount. I was told he would *definitely* be given the opportunity to complete his last year of high school in the service. Later he could enroll in college if he desired. On this condition, Bryan relented. I signed for him to enlist since he was only seventeen.

On a cold morning of February 1, 1981, the day before my birthday, I drove my younger son to the shopping mall where the recruiting officer was waiting with an army bus. I parked the car. We got out and stood near the car. Holding back tears as I held my second born I loved, so close.

I prayed silently, "Dear God please take care of Bryan. He's your son. I only gave him birth. My life has been terrible. I didn't provide him the stability he needed. Please take care of him."

Bryan promised he'd obey and stay out of trouble. We both knew what he needed, the masculine guidance and training I'd been unable to provide even after four husbands. Each time I married I wanted a father figure for my sons, but it backfired every time. What a bright and determined young mind he possessed: a mind that needed special attention, a mind that searched and wandered in wrong directions.

I placed my business card in his hand with Bible scriptures on the back. My dear, dear mixed up son tried to smile, but I saw his hurt face. I hated to see him leave but he knew he had to go. Either he or Theon would soon get hurt. I felt guilty. My confused life had spilled over into his. I assumed I was performing at my best, not realizing what my unsettled mind was undergoing. I led the life of a gypsy; always seeking new places and adventures. My search was on a roll, unraveling, getting tangled, untangled then rolling on to the next unknown resting point.

Later that spring I convinced Mama to attend a senior citizens center. Before I left for work, I helped her get dressed. Sunny mornings were easier in encouraging her to go. She received special door to door service for persons with physical problems. Each time she went I felt so relieved. My spirit was lifted—but not hers.

One day she said, "Dawn, I'm not going to that place anymore. I have to sit all day and there's no place to lie down and take a nap. I get tired. Besides, I don't know any of those women."

"But Mama, it takes time to know people. The more often you go, the more people you'll meet. What kinds of activities were you offered today?"

"Some ladies sewed on a quilt and some more painted on those stands that you use sometimes."

"Ah, you mean an easel?"

"Yes. Only they sat down at a table while they painted."

"And what did you do, Mama?"

"Nothing! I did some exercises sitting in the chair and I helped a lady work on a puzzle."

"That was great Mama! How many minutes did you exercise?"

"I don't know, I guess about five or ten. I don't know."

"What was the lady's name?"

"The lady's name, I think it was Agnes. Yes, it was Agnes! She said that she was

there four days a week, while her daughter was working."

"See, that's one lady you met. Now each time you go you'll meet more ladies and make new friends. Mama, I hate to see you stay in this house day after day, watching television all day long."

"But I like television."

"I know you do, but there's more to life than watching television, Mama," I said.

"I don't feel like getting dressed and it's starting to get too cold anyway. I'm *not* going anymore." She didn't.

30...MAMA'S NEW HOME

...Be strong!
It matters not how deep in trenched the wrong,
How hard the battle goes, the day how long;
Faint not—fight on! Tomorrow comes the song.
Maltbie Davenport Babcock: Be Strong!

Mama's rheumatoid arthritis worsened. We visited several doctors, but nothing helped. Soon she used a wheelchair. For every doctor's appointment I closed up that *heavy* wheelchair, dragged it down eight steps then rolled it to the car. I lifted that ton of metal into the car's back seat; then out again after we arrived at the doctor's office.

Mama took a few steps and held onto my shoulder as we descended each step slowly then crept down the sidewalk to the car. I didn't mind the doctor visits but handling that *heavy chair* by myself, was awkward especially up the steps. Mama ascended each step in pain! The neighbor behind my house would run across the backyard and help when he saw us struggling.

The onset of diabetes required that her medications and meals be on time. Her doctor mentioned a year earlier that eventually she'd have to be placed in a nursing home. But I *refuted* his statement. He consoled my hurt.

He explained, "Every week I help adult children face the same sad facts concerning their parents. I know it's not an easy decision but unless you can afford home care it's inevitable."

For months I avoided the predictable fact. Accepting the reality of placing Mama in a nursing home was heartbreaking. She'd lived with me for *twenty* years. She had accompanied me to the hospital the night my first son was born, while my husband was *out!* For many years she managed our home, cared for my children, washed our clothes, and cooked our meals while I worked two or more jobs. My heart ignored the doctor's decision but reality soon stood its ground. I prayed and struggled for acceptance.

Months of conflict forced me to face the fact; I had no other alternative. My mother needed twenty-four hour care, care I could not provide. I remembered Mama's pain as she struggled to get up and down the porch steps; the agony she experienced getting in and out the car. I prayed, "God please help me. I'm so tired! I don't want to put my mother in a nursing home. What am I supposed to do?"

After I contacted social services, Mama received health care for two to three days a week for three months before it stopped. During those months she was happier; she wasn't alone when I worked. She and one of the ladies became close friends and continued that relationship after the services stopped. The ladies bathed her, helped her get dressed and served her meals in her room. She always said, "I don't see why I have to get dressed. I'm not going anywhere!" The ladies were a blessing to Mama and to me!

Sometimes when Mama returned from the bathroom at night, adjacent to her bedroom, she'd slide on the floor when she tried to get in bed. She'd lie on the floor for two or more hours banging on the radiator pipe with her cane. Since our bedroom was upstairs, on the other side of the house, we never heard the banging unless Theon or I went to the bathroom. Mama became more dependent.

Mama had been hospitalized six times that year! I'd toured the city's hospitals. I recall one hospital when I'd arrived late. The time to leave was announced but I remained. A nurse spied me in the room and asked me to leave. I explained I was the patient's daughter and had only been there ten minutes and asked to visit a little longer.

"No. You have to leave now."

"This is the first hospital that my mother has been in where there was no thought given to a working family member."

The nurse left the room. I stayed. A couple of minutes later the hospital policeman came to the door and asked me to leave. He was harsh and treated me as though I were a criminal.

"Did the nurse ask you to leave!"

"Yes, but I just got here a few minutes ago. I asked her if I could stay just a few more minutes with my mother."

"Visiting hours, are *over*! You have to leave *now*!" His mean eyes pierced mine. As I walked down the hall he walked close to me as though I'd committed a terrible offense. After we got to the door, I said my farewell.

"Good day, sir. Thank you for escorting me to the door. It was indeed an honor. I also thank you for being so understanding about me wanting to spend ten more minutes with my mother."

He hurled a mean stare my way, turned around without a word then strolled down the hall.

Mama's last hospital visit was the one I feared. Her doctor insisted I start searching for a nursing home. My older friend, Simone, a volunteer at several nursing homes, suggested a good one, considering the reputation of some nursing homes.

I visited Mr. Barnett the director of a nursing home unannounced. As we walked down the halls I passed residents seated in wheelchairs, heads dropped, staring in space or asleep. I thought, *is this the way my mother has to spend the rest of her life?* Mr. Barnett was upbeat with his tour as I heaved a sigh of anguish and sorrow knowing this place would soon be Mama's new home. Even though it was clean and organized I resented having her there. We saw the cafeteria, the arts and crafts room etc. then returned to his office. With the arrangements completed and papers signed, we shook hands. I left with tears in my eyes; head dropped to my chest. My steps hastened down the long corridor, past the seated elderly citizens who helped build this fine country of ours, then out the front door as my tears gushed out like a shower in full force!

A few days later Mama was transferred to the nursing home from the hospital. I'd contacted the florist where I used to work and ordered a huge $40 bouquet of live flowers to greet her when she arrived. The flower arrangement was spectacular! But they had no effect on Mama. I walked into her room, lit by sunrays from two large windows, shared by five other residents. She sat in a wheelchair next to her bed. Turned sideways, her head rested on both folded arms on her bed. Instantly, I felt I'd betrayed my mother. I'll *never ever* forget that moment! My heart cried, "How could you do this to your mother, Dawn? You know how much she'd dreaded coming to one of these places."

Concealing my hurt, I walked over to Mama's bed bent down, kissed and hugged her. She refused to lift her head at first, but after a little babying and affection she finally relented and raised her head from the clean soft blue blanket folded neatly at the foot of her bed.

"Hi, Mama, how do you like the flowers I sent? I think it's one of the most beautiful arrangements I've ever seen. And the aroma is so sweet."

Mama said nothing. Her wet face signaled, she'd been crying. We talked for a long time. Before I left, I hung up the clothes I'd brought in her small closet near the door. I'd informed the director I'd take care of her clothes; nothing would go to their laundry in fear it would get lost.

"Mama, I have to go now but I'll be back tomorrow. I can't come every day but I'll come four to five times a week. I'll be here as often as I can and I will take care of your clothes, not the laundry here."

My daily attempts to cheer her up were hopeless. She refused to leave her bed; her health soon declined. The home's aides tried to raise her spirits—to no avail.

After several weeks of watching Mama deteriorate I called her former physician to *please* help my mother! He *did*! He contacted the nursing home, spoke to the doctor and changed her medication. She improved almost overnight! I thought she'd die. She would have, had I not intervened. She played bingo, attended arts and crafts classes and enjoyed *Church Services* every Sunday. Each time I visited she shared her day's events.

I thought *Mama had to go to a nursing home to attend church services.* I praised the Lord for that change!

One quiet autumn afternoon when I drove up my rugged driveway, I saw Kelly, my beautiful Calico cat roaming outside. I wondered how she'd gotten out. Then I noticed the side porch door was open, the door we always used. As I crossed the lawn, toward the side porch steps, Kelly ran toward me. The door had been forced open. I sat down on the concrete steps with my head buried in my hands, too frightened to know what to do next. Kelly rubbed against me wanting attention while I sat in shock! Not thinking, both of us entered the house. It appeared undisturbed, except for the door. A sharp instrument had pried open the lock! The old worn wooden panel exterior door had seen better days. After confirming nothing downstairs had been disturbed, I started upstairs, with Kelly running ahead. At the top of the staircase, in the hallway lay a pink sheet with items ready to be grabbed and taken from the house.

I reached the top of the steps and saw the den disheveled. My heart pounded! The shelves that held Theon's beautiful Pioneer stereo set: the tuner, cassette deck, and turntable that cost over $2000, was empty! The speakers remained only because they were too large to carry. The other rooms were untouched. At that moment I realized I had not called the police.

When they arrived, an officer said, "Ma-am you should *not* have entered this house. You could have been hurt if they had still been in here."

"I didn't think about that. I wanted to see what they'd stolen."

"Well if this happens again *don't*—come into this house. Go to a neighbor's and call us immediately."

I promised him I would. They took all the necessary information and left as Theon arrived home. Theon showed little emotion at first, but said in his slow, calm unassuming manner:

"I bet it was one of those guys Bryan brought into this house. I *told* him about bringing strangers home."

"How do you know it was one of them?"

"I'm willing to bet you money it was."

"Had Mama been here, it wouldn't have happened. She often mentioned people calling but said nothing. Now no one is home to answer the phone. They broke in about one-thirty. I'd been gone only an hour or so."

Distraught over the burglary and my broken beautiful Victorian paneled beveled glass front door I retired early. They'd tried that door, but the *old secure bolt lock* denied their entry. I noticed the broken glass was not covered and cold air was gushing through the large hole when I got up the next morning. I rushed back upstairs to ask Theon about the door.

"Theon, why didn't you cover the broken glass before you went to bed? All that cold air is rushing in through that large hole. Besides, it was dangerous uncovered!"

"Why didn't you cover it? You're the artist. What's wrong with *your* hands!"

"You're the man in this house. I thought you'd take responsibility and cover it."

Time and energy were wasted; he ignored every word. After two hours, I covered it myself. His stubborn streak didn't allow him to succumb, especially to me.

I realized too late my major mistake; I *married* him! Having sex outside of marriage was tough for me. I asked God to remove those sexual desires which ended in miserable male relationships. I wanted a husband. I wanted a *man*. But I'd married a boy, an immature, selfish self-centered boy. Even with his meanness I still loved this man, but why? Something was wrong with me. How could I love a man so demeaning and cruel? He never apologized. He never said *I'm sorry* but reveled in his heartless demeanor toward me. I stood my ground and argued, but always forgave him.

Theon came home from work later and later everyday. No matter what shift he worked he was always four or more hours late. One afternoon I questioned his lateness.

"Theon what are you doing so important you can't come straight home from work like you used to? After those long hours you pull, I'd think you'd want to come home and go to bed."

His wild bloodshot eyes gazed through me. "I can't make any money in the bed. Today a guy on my shift needed help in moving to his new apartment, so I helped."

"Well, what about the other days?"

He didn't answer, typical of him. Instead he dragged himself up the stairs his head dropped to his chest and went to bed.

Later that week, he stayed out all night and handed me another sad lie. The second time he stayed out all night that week I put all of his clothes in green plastic bags and stacked them on the porch. I was furious! Late that afternoon he showed up. I heard the key in the lock. The door opened and he started dragging the bags back into the house. Each bag he brought in, I threw back out on the porch! As he dragged one in, I'd throw it out. Finally he started to walk up the stairs. I rushed over and yelled.

"Where do you think you're going? You can't sleep in this house after staying out all night."

I grabbed the plastic bag of clothes he held, threw it toward the door, reached up and yanked his arm! He turned. His right arm flew around landing on my chest, knocking me down the three bottom steps onto the floor. I jumped up off the floor and grabbed his shirttail. It ripped! His arm flung around again, this time hitting me in the face.

"You better leave me alone unless you want to get hurt."

He was too tired to bother with me. I was *too* small to tackle him. I'd forgotten his size and strength. Getting hurt never occurred to me. The nerve of this man was awesome! He'd stayed out all night and had the gall to come home and attempt to go to bed. *WOW*!

This mean, sneaky, sly man *had* to go!! But how? I'd been through this with my first husband. I would not tolerate staying out all night anymore by a husband.

I slept downstairs that night. Before I retired, I threw his shoes *outside*. His clothes remained on the porch in bags. He was off the next day.

When he finally came downstairs, he said, "Dawn, have you seen my shoes?"

I walked into the living room, "Yes, I threw them outside where *you* belong."

"You did what?"

When he opened the door to go outside to find his shoes, I pushed him in his back as hard as I could.

He yelled, "My car is gone, my car is gone!"

That instant Theon lifted me off the floor by my long hair and threw me across the living room floor! My body crashed into the coffee table knocking the heavy candy dish with an alabaster base, on the floor. My right leg landed on the broken candy dish which cut a long gash in my leg. Blood flew everywhere! His car was gone! I lay bleeding on the floor.

"Look at what you've done to my leg! How could you do such a thing!"

As I phoned the police, all Theon said was, "They took my car, they took my car!" He never acknowledged my leg. Two policemen arrived and wrote the information in their report. When Theon told them that I had tried to push him out the door, one of the officers replied:

"That means you assaulted him. Did you push him?"

"Yes I did. He stayed out all night. That was his second time this week. I figured he needed to go back where he'd been all night. Obviously he didn't want to sleep here anymore."

I had called the police in my defense and they treated me as though I was the culprit, not Theon. I couldn't believe their argument. Stunned, I told them to leave.

"I called you to help me and you stand there defending his wrong. Get *out* of my house! Get out *now*! You see my bleeding leg, my hair and my torn clothes and you have the nerve to side with this man. All of you men are just alike! You defend each other. Get *out*! *Leave!*"

As they left, sneaky, smiling Theon followed them outside on the porch and said, "Thank you for coming officers." They shook hands laughing and joking as though all of this had been some type of joke or fun time. I stepped outside onto the porch.

"What's going on here? My husband could have killed me and you're befriending him. I don't believe this! What kind of a police department am I paying for anyway!"

I'd forgotten Theon was a correctional officer. I suppose the policemen regarded him as a fellow officer. My practitioner prayed for me by phone. I wrapped my leg. Later, I went to the police department to file a report but was told I had to see the Commissioner in the County Courthouse. The next day I went but he wasn't in so I returned the following day. We discussed the problem but no action was taken. I don't remember why.

I knew I was wrong in pushing Theon. But I was fed up; disgusted with men taking advantage of my kindness, my loyalty, forgiveness and good heartedness. I prayed for God to send me a Christian husband, but I always intervened and accepted what the devil squeezed in between the cracks. The devil knew my weaknesses. He thrived on them at my lowest points!

The weeds grew tall as it rained for days in early May. The grass and shrubs welcomed the sun as I waited and waited for Theon to help me in the yard. Days passed. His promises weren't honored. *Tomorrow* he'd say, *tomorrow*. Tomorrow never came. Finally, my good side fell asleep. The bad side woke up. God never smiled on this side but the devil reveled and beamed!

Theon came home from work, late as usual. It was Thursday. Before he left that morning he *promised* again he'd come straight home, from work and help me in the yard.

He passed me heading for the staircase smelling of alcohol and cigarette smoke. He strolled upstairs to the bedroom. It was almost dark, I was furious! I watched him undress, getting ready for bed.

"Everyday you come home too late to do anything in the yard. You *promised* me last night you'd help me today. What happened?"

"I got tied up."

"Tied up. Tied up alright, with alcohol and women!"

"That's your problem, you always thinking somebody's with some woman."

"Since you weren't here to help me as you promised, I did most of the yard work myself. The digging was hard because that shovel is so weighty and carrying that dirt made it even heavier."

"Good! This *is* your house. *Remember* I never wanted this old thing anyway. You're not doing that much work, so you do the yard work yourself!"

"Not working! I work every single day and you know that. Perhaps you don't call making and hanging draperies work, but I do. You know it's a lot of work because you've helped me. You're mean and selfish!"

I turned and walked to the bathroom at the end of the hall next to the kitchen. He followed me. When I turned to leave, he stood in the doorway. Without a word he *spit in my face!* Horrified at his revolting behavior, I stood shocked! Spit covered my glasses and dripped on my blouse. He turned and headed for the bedroom. I followed.

"What kind of man are you, to spit in your wife's face?"

"You just need to leave me alone, you b——!"

He pushed the bedroom door as hard as he could. Before it closed I put my foot up to keep it from slamming shut and cracking, since it was over eighty years old. When the door bounced back and Theon saw my foot up in the air, he thought I was trying to kick him. He rushed forward, lifted his right foot to kick me in my stomach. I ducked just in time before that heavy army boot touched my stomach and jammed me into the balustrade.

I ran in the kitchen yelling, "I'm gonna' call the police and tell them what you're doing to me."

He ran after me. "Well then, let me give you something to *really tell them!*"

That instant, Theon lifted my body over his head and *slammed* me on the floor! I knew I was dead. Instead, my eyes opened seeing blurry red. No way had I survived that slam! I lifted my head, felt my eyeglasses against my face; they'd broken. Spattered blood streaked the white wall and white tiled linoleum floor. Theon came over, bent down and attempted to help me up. His sneaky calm voice said, "Come on nooow, let's get up and wash your face."

I jerked away, got up and walked in the bathroom. In the mirror I saw a face covered with blood; its source unknown. I looked at Theon and said calmly,

"Why did you do this to me, why?" He raised his head and said coolly, "The devil made me do it. You need to leave me alone. You just need to leave me alone."

He was right; his *devil/father* had made him do it. Without cleaning my face, I returned to the kitchen, picked up the receiver from the wall telephone and attempted to call the police. Theon walked over, placed his hand gently over mine to keep me from dialing.

"Please don't call the police, Dawn, please." He got down on his knees and pleaded repeatedly, something I never thought I'd see this man do. I watched him down on his knees begging and pleading, over and over again, for me not to call the police.

"I'll do anything you want, but please don't call them."

When I saw he wouldn't let me call, I replaced the receiver, went downstairs, picked up my pocketbook and headed for the door. I still had not washed my face.

"Where are you going, Dawn? Don't go to the station, please don't go!"

Such begging and pleading, down on his knees was unbelievable. He

45

knew *that* report would cause him serious problems as a correctional officer. I relented. I had another plan.

"I won't call but I want your house key in the morning before you go to work."

"Okay, okay, anything you say; just don't call the police."

I slept or rather rested downstairs in the den. Every hour or so, I walked upstairs to check the gash over my eye. Even with the ice compact it had swollen the size of a peach. I thanked God my nose wasn't broken and my eye had not been injured. Each time I went upstairs to bathe my eye; I saw Theon's head was at the foot of the bed. He watched me, in case I decided he shouldn't live anymore. His eyes were *wide* open each time I ascended and descended those steps.

Because I called my Christian Science practitioner, his prayers eliminated all pain. Only the swelling was evidenced and bulged out beyond my broken eyeglasses. I explained my serious problem to him—admitting my blame. He said, "Dawn you should never hit a man because he will strike back."

"But I never hit him. My foot was on the door to keep it from slamming shut, not on him."

When Theon came downstairs, ready for work the next morning, I greeted him at the door with my hand extended to receive the door key.

"May I have the door key, Theon?"

"I'm *not* giving you *nothing*!"

"You pleaded with me last night and said you'd do anything."

"Yea, that was last night. I'm not giving you *nothing*!"

"Well, I'm going to report this to the police."

"I don't care what you do. I'm *not* giving you my key!"

After he left, I went to the police station. As soon as I walked through the front double doors, I heard exclamations from people seated in the waiting area.

"Man, somebody sure did her in. *Look* at that eye!"

With Barry's prayers, I was unaware that anything was wrong with my eye unless I looked in the mirror since I had no pain.

I approached the desk and stated I wanted to press charges against my husband. Again they told me I'd have to see the County Commissioner. So again I drove miles to the County Courthouse. When I arrived, the Commissioner was speaking to someone else so I waited in the hall. As soon as I walked in his office and took a seat in front of his desk, he stared at me curiously.

"Haven't I seen you in here before?"

"Yes sir, just a few months ago."

"Same thing, huh?"

"Yes sir, the same thing, only worse this time."

"Yes, I can see that. When did all this happen?" The Commissioner a kind man voiced deep concern. His face expressed sympathy.

"Last night. I tried to call the police, but he begged and pleaded so hard I decided to wait until he went to work to file the complaint."

He wrote the necessary information and said Theon would be served his papers that night.

Theon came home from work *on time* and went straight upstairs. Neither one of us spoke. I was sleeping in the den when the door bell rang at two a.m. I opened the door.

"I have a warrant for Theon Albens," the policeman said.

"Come in please." I went to the staircase in the foyer and yelled upstairs.

"Theon, there are two policeman down here who want to see you."

"See me. What do they want to see me for?"

"You know very well why they want to see you." Theon took so long in coming down, that one of the officers yelled upstairs himself.

"Mr. Albens, we're *waiting* for you to come downstairs. What's the problem?"

"I'm getting dressed."

"Well, *hurry up!*"

Theon waited several seconds before he dragged his sneaky, lying body downstairs. He stared in space as the policeman explained the problem and that he had to vacate the property.

"You may go upstairs and get enough clothes for the weekend. Your court hearing is on Monday." Theon returned upstairs in his slow moving pace. He stayed too long once again.

"Mr. Albens, you have to come down now! You've been up there long enough. *Do you need any help!*"

Theon didn't answer, typical of Theon.

"Did you hear me, Mr. Albens!"

Theon uttered a slowly, "I'm coming down now."

They left. I returned to our bedroom upstairs and attempted to sleep.

As soon as I drove into the parking lot Monday morning, I spied his car. Of course I parked as far away as possible. Inside the courthouse I located the courtroom for the hearing. To my surprise, I wasn't nervous. Theon saw me seated on the long bench and strolled my way. We spoke. He asked me to drop the charges. I refused. I discussed divorce. He listened. We discussed other financial matters like two intelligent human beings should have for a change.

When we entered the courtroom, I walked toward the front and sat on the right hand side. I thought Theon would have sat elsewhere but he sat next to me. I could have moved but I didn't. When our names were called we walked forward and stood in front of the Judge. He discussed our problem and asked many questions.

"Where did you spend the weekend, Mr. Albens?"

"I was scheduled for Military Reserve duty this past weekend."

That was the *first time I ever heard* Theon answer anyone's question without delay! After several more questions from the judge, about fifty years old and two-hundred thirty pounds he leaned forward and looked Theon sternly in the eye.

He said in a *firm* voice, "Mr. Albens I advise you to *keep your hands off your wife!*"

The judge issued an order that Theon was *not* to come on the property for one year, unless I gave him permission. The judge had honored my request. I didn't want him jailed only not to come on the property.

Several days passed before I visited Mama. I waited until most of the swelling had gone down. However, she noticed it as soon as I entered her room.

"What happened to your eye, Dawn? Theon, huh?"

"Yes." I avoided the gruesome details. She didn't need to know. Neither should I have experienced it. Some people might say I brought it on myself. But I say I shall never be a doormat for any man to trample on. I'd already taken *too* much from him. Bryan's first visit home from basic training was the following week. Mama knew Bryan would be *extremely* upset after he'd seen my eye.

"Dawn, when Bryan sees your eye, there's going to be trouble."

"No trouble, Mama. I will not discuss what happened with Bryan."

"You think so, huh? You know how Bryan hates Theon and how much he loves you. Just keep your eyes open and watch Bryan's actions."

"Don't worry, Mama. It won't be any trouble."

The following week I picked up Bryan from the airport.

Before hugging me he said, "Theon did that to you *didn't he?* I *better not* see him at the house or anywhere in Baltimore. He *will* pay for that!"

As we left the building in silence he kept staring at my right eye while we walked toward the car. As soon as we got inside and left the parking lot he repeated, "He *will* pay; he *will* pay for what he did to you."

"No, Bryan, no more trouble. You're in the service and don't do anything to ruin your career. He's not worth it."

"You're my mother and no man has the right to be beating on you!"

I changed the subject from Theon to his activities in the service. He wanted to see Mama before we went home. As we approached the nursing home he informed me he hated that his grandmother was in there. He loved her. She'd spoiled him rotten! She'd give him her *last* dime!

As we walked into the building, I saw his solemn, sad expression and understood completely because I felt the same way. He walked into the room and over to the head of her bed, then dropped on his knees to embrace her tightly. Both were *so* glad to see each other. Before he left, still on his knees, he took both her rheumatoid arthritic hands, lowered his head in them and said tenderly, "I love you, Grandmommy."

As we walked down the hall toward the front door, he said in a low-spirited voice, "Mommy, I hate to see my grandmother in this place."

"So do I Bryan, so do I. It's not so bad. I'm here every other day and I wash all her clothes. She's made several friends and enjoys playing bingo, and wins too! She keeps more money than I do. She's made the adjustment and understands she gets better care here since I'm working most of the time."

I gave Bryan birth, but Mama reared him. I started work at the raincoat factory when he was six weeks old. When he was nine months old, a teaching position became available so I left the factory. In addition I stopped working on his light green and yellow sweater I knitted on the bus everyday that I rode to work everyday. The unfinished sweater was placed in a plastic bag with the knitting needles holding the last stitch, left on a closet shelf, never completed.

Bryan never saw Theon throughout his short stay. During his visit, Theon called and wanted to see me. We met in a shopping center and talked in my parked car.

Sally, a former college roommate, urged me to visit her after she learned about my recent mishap with Theon. She insisted a change was what I needed to lift my spirits. Her exact words were:

"Come on down here and let me spoil you for a week and take your mind off your troubles."

I accepted. I needed to be spoiled by someone who cared. Low on funds, I called Maurice and asked him to lend me $100 to visit Sally. He knew Sally well. How could he forget those fun-filled college days we'd spent together: exciting parties, cold and rugged football games and her help with our small wedding reception. He agreed to the loan. I didn't mention my physical problem. He'd find out soon enough.

Strolling up the sidewalk to the row house, my first home, mixed memories surfaced. Some were good, others bad, some happy, others sad. Memories like the day of settlement on our house when we left the office with only one nickel between us. Memories of the day Bryan was brought home from the hospital. Memories of Marty running to the ice cream truck with his nickel while I was pregnant with Bryan. Memories of the driver giving Marty ice cream when he didn't have a nickel. Memories of Mama hiding money in my bathrobe pocket during Maurice's job layoff. Memories of snow piled so high that cars had to park on the treed street island in front of the house.

Maurice opened the door; I walked into my former row home toward the kitchen to avoid his face. When he saw my eye, he took several steps backwards in shock as his eyes widened in anger.

"I *never* did anything like that to you!"

I turned my face and took a few steps toward the kitchen door and stared out the window.

"Oh *yes* you did! Remember when I was pregnant with Bryan and the black eye you gave me after I confronted you about that woman calling you at my home? How soon people forget *their own* wrongs."

"What are you talking about?" He said.

"You know very well what I'm talking about. The time you slapped me so hard across my face when I was home sick and four to five months pregnant with Bryan. My doctor said you could have been put under the jail for hitting your pregnant wife! It was good I wasn't teaching because I couldn't have worked with a black eye."

He didn't respond to my statement but said, "Well I want to know what happened to your eye, *that* eye you don't want me to see. Theon did it, didn't he?"

I remained silent looking out the window into the backyard; the small yard, where Mama and I once had a productive aromatic flower and vegetable garden; the same backyard where Marty and Bryan played and entertained their friends.

"I see you've started your garden. It's May so what have you planted?"

"*Don't* change the subject, Dawn. *Why* did Theon do that to you!"

"Maurice, I'd rather not discuss it. Please, just give me the money and I'll leave."

He didn't pursue the subject but reached into his pocket, pulled out the money and handed it to me—slowly. His face revealed remorse, regret and rage! How sad he hadn't become infuriated with himself when his *hard slap* across my face left me with a black eye, while I carried his second unwanted child eighteen years prior!

31...TRUTH UNVEILED

My heart is opened wide to-night
For stranger, kith of kin.
I would not bar a single door
Where love might enter in.
Kate Douglas Wiggin:
The Romance of a Christmas Card

Fresh smelling country air, variegated green leafed trees, and the wide-open spaces of Chapel Hill, NC was the change I deserved. It took twenty minutes to drive through eight miles of flooded streets before I reached dry concrete. Drenching rain had preceded my entrance to the renowned city of the south.

Sally treated me royally! She and her husband, Handel owned a successful building contracting company. A few years earlier they'd built a fantastic home nestled in a scenic wooded section next to a small brook with water flowing over a mirage of stones and debris. Outstanding! My Christian friend was *rich*, monetarily and spiritually. During that week Sally and I watched various television ministries. Unfamiliar with most of them, they opened my eyes to a more in-depth study of the Bible.

One evening as we studied, Sally asked me, "Dawn, Christian Scientists don't believe that Jesus is the Son of God do they?"

"I don't know Sally, but I do."

We discussed the issue in depth. After I returned to Baltimore I continued watching the TV ministries. I kept a Bible in the car. One day while I was driving I heard a minister point out that Jesus was the Son of God. During the radio commercial I asked God for understanding.

"God, if you are Jesus and Jesus is you, please show me. I'm so confused."

Immediately the radio minister returned on the air and said, "Everybody

52

knows God is Jesus and Jesus is God, just read John 1." Stunned at the instant answer, I pulled the car over to the side of the street, opened my Bible to John 1:1 and read, "In the beginning was the Word and the Word (*Jesus*) was with God, and the Word was God...

Verse 14: *And the Word was made flesh, and dwelt among us...* "

I pondered, prayed and studied those fourteen verses plus more for *three years* before I left. The church believes that Jesus is *a son* of God. I believe what the Bible says, "Jesus is *the* Son of God" as stated in verse one. For twelve years I learned to turn to God for everything while I attended that church but that *one word* disturbed me.

In Fayetteville, I'd attended a Presbyterian Church. Impressed with the occasional Catholic services I attended with my best friend, Suzette in elementary school I decided to become a Catholic when I reached eighteen. As soon as I started college I joined and remained so for nineteen years.

After I met Audrey Mellon, a Christian Scientist where I taught, I changed my thinking once again. During that time my second marriage was in jeopardy. Audrey taught me how to study and pray to ease my heavy burdens. On many occasions just talking to her in school or on the telephone, I was healed instantly of physical problems. I learned from her that God hears our prayers and we *only* need to turn to *Him*. In Catholicism we didn't study the Bible. I yearned to know more. In addition, the priest's answer to my questions weren't complete.

Theon was an Episcopalian. During our marriage he attended his church only once, for his sister's wedding. He also attended mine once. He'd laugh at me when I tried to explain God's goodness and how adhering to His Word could help him become a better person.

"Dawn I like *me* the way that I am. People can't survive in this world thinking the way *you* do. Besides, it's no *fun* being good. Who wants to be good *anyway*?"

"I'm not perfect, but at least I'm not mean and irritable like you. You weren't like this when we dated. Why did you change?"

"I didn't change; I only covered up the side I didn't want you to see."

"What are you saying?" I said.

"I hid the real Theon until we were married. I know how to get what I want and I wanted you. You wouldn't have married me if you'd seen my true side."

"You're right about that. You've changed too much for me. We used to enjoy kissing; now you tell me kissing is dirty; it passes too many germs. You won't even let me hug you anymore. Is something wrong with me?"

"No, its not you, it's *me*."

"Well what's wrong with you?" He didn't answer.

"I remember when you cursed me after we were married one week. I couldn't believe you'd called me that name."

"Ahh, I didn't curse you. Everybody uses that word. You need to loosen up and stop trying to be Miss Goodie, Goodie Two Shoes."

Understanding Theon was impossible; he was set in his ways. Changing was *not* on his mind.

I continued to make draperies and Theon continued to call from his parent's home where he'd moved. He said he wanted to take care of me, be my husband, but remain at his mother's home.

"What are you *saying, Mr.?*" I listened.

"I'm saying that you're too tight on me, I don't have any freedom."

"You're a married man. How much freedom do you expect?"

"I shouldn't have to tell you everywhere I'm going. You won't let me talk on the phone to my friends."

"Are you talking about those women friends of yours?"

"Yeah. What's wrong with my friends calling me and me calling them?"

"Sounds to me like you need to stay where you are and lead a single man's life, because you won't do that in *this* house!"

"Ahh, come on, why don't you bend a little?"

"Bend. My back is broken from bending. Why don't you grow up? You need to make a decision whether you want to be married or be single and if you're a boy or a man?"

"I *am* a man."

"Well act like one!"

Baltimore's hot humid temperatures soon trickled to cool and calm. Autumn rushed in faster than usual. September meant school; school meant children. Two years had passed since I'd taught. After Theon had moved, I healed gradually. But was I ready to teach again? My Psychiatrist didn't think so.

"Dawn you will not be happy teaching. There is too much stress in the classroom for you. Besides, you have very high standards and society's criterion for education isn't on your level. *Don't* return."

"What am I going to do then, it's difficult to find employment. I'm either over qualified, haven't had enough experience in specific areas or the salary is too low. I'm stuck."

"Keep looking Dawn, you'll find something."

I did find something. I was hired as a graphic artist for Telecommunications in Baltimore City. Cable was opening up in the city. After my interview, the director, Ms. Marsh was so impressed with my portfolio, she instructed the photographer to include me in their staff pictures they were taking that day. I was shown around the offices and introduced as their staff's graphic artist. Already a city employee she inquired if the city would switch my teaching salary inasmuch as I'd still be a city employee. The position was pending on the personnel's decision. Their funding wasn't sufficient to pay my present salary.

I kept thinking *finally I'd work in my field as an artist!* Art teachers were considered as someone who made banners, decorated for assembly programs and kept the hall bulletin boards attractive. I loved teaching. But I refused to tolerate profanity, sarcasm and disrespect from any more children!

Two days later I received a call from Ms. Marsh. Personnel disapproved the switch. Regret was obvious as she revealed the sad news. At first I was hurt. But later I realized God had something else planned. I stopped searching for another job after many trips to Washington, D.C. for interviews, several T.V. stations, and commercial art companies. I'd even spent $1500 to Haldane Associates who taught me how to write a perfect resume in how to sell my skills. Interviewed by several interior design businesses, I was told to return after I'd completed my classes. Job hunting was a worthwhile experience, I learned a lot, but didn't get hired.

I canceled my disability funds and decided to return to work before I checked if a position was available in my area in September. Nothing was! Now, my only source of income was making draperies. The unemployment agency's clerk revealed I didn't qualify because I'd been out too long. She suggested I apply for Welfare. Later I learned had I spoken to the director I would have received unemployment.

To survive, I sewed draperies sixteen to eighteen hours on some days. Mama was concerned because I didn't look well; she always worried about me. But my God blessed me with drapery customers. I remember sitting on the den sofa one morning, head in my hands as I prayed for a customer. The oil tank was nearly empty, plus many bills were due.

"Dear God I need ..." Before I finished my sentence the telephone rang.

"Ms. Albens this is Ms. Snowden, I'm ready for you to make my draperies."

As we discussed business I thanked my dear God for answering my prayer. I never did underestimate the power of prayer. As I worked fatigued hour after hour everyday making gorgeous draperies of which I had none, I'd say *when I return to the classroom, I'll never leave again unless I have another job first!*

Theon helped pay some of the expenses but he wanted to play husband and reside at his parents' home.

"If you want to sleep with me then you move back and help pay these bills!" So in November he returned. I remember the day I asked him for *one* dollar.

He replied, "I just gave you a dollar yesterday, now you want another one!" His statement cut *deep*! .

"Yes, I want *another one, and another one, and another one!* You're my husband. I shouldn't have to ask you for anything, not after the way you've treated me!"

Before he gave anyone money he'd turn from the person, lean over and fish for his sacred bills. I prayed everyday that somehow this insulting man would leave my life. I never understand how anyone could be so wicked! Those despondent days reminded me of the film *Gone with the Wind* when Scarlett yelled in the desolate garden of her deserted slave's cabin holding up a dried carrot she'd almost choked on.

"As God is my witness, as *God* is my witness, I'll *never be hungry again!"*

My version was "God *is* my witness God *is* my witness, when I start work again I'll never ask another man for a penny!"

I lost weight during those five agonizing months, sewing, pressing and hanging draperies. So tired often I'd sit in a chair and cry 'til tears ceased to flow. Only my faith sustained my sanity. God heard my plea.

In January I attended a sorority dance. As I discussed my plight to a friend seated next to me, an assistant principal, she mentioned an art position available in February. Early Monday morning, I drove downtown to the board of education. When I entered Mr. Bollen's office, he motioned for me to have a seat as he spoke on the phone.

Before I uttered a word he smiled and said, "I had planned to call you Ms. Albens. An art position will be available in February."

His small but adequate office was instantly filled with joy! Light poured through his oversized window as I thanked God for my new position, not knowing where it was located or what grade levels I'd teach. It really didn't matter as long as I had *a job!*

The middle school principal, Mr. Todder escorted me to the art room. I met the teacher, who was leaving in two days. The room was *chaotic!* The adjacent storage room was worse! I stood on the threshold of the storage room and gasped! *Another* dirty art teacher! Only this time I was able to address the problems *before* she left. She agreed to get rid of unnecessary materials and projects. I handled the storage room myself. However bad the environment appeared to be, I'd *never* had my *own storage* room adjacent to my classroom! It was an ideal situation! By that time I'd spent many *years* cleaning up after filthy art teachers.

The building was only a few years old. Once again I was the only art teacher of which I relished. The female music teacher, across the hall from me was a sweetheart. Nothing ever seemed to bother her. I wondered how she remained so calm. Later I found out that she had a marvelous husband who adored her. His love supplied her with the calm she possessed.

As usual the custodial staff alerted the principal of my clean art room. They'd made the same remarks I'd heard at other schools. They soon found out it was my policy to maintain cleanliness, order and discipline. You couldn't have one without the other.

I'd taught with Ms. Spendoll the assistant principal, my first year teaching, so we weren't strangers. Our principal, Mr. Chase and had trained us *quite* well.

Meanwhile back at the homestead, Theon was himself, mean and arrogant.

"Theon, what time do you have?" I said.

"What are you asking me for; *didn't* I give you a watch!"

"Yes, but it's upstairs in the drawer."

"Well go upstairs and *put* it on!" He yelled.

I prayed, "Dear God, please *help* me! I can not live with this evil man anymore.,"

During the five months we were separated Theon phoned often.

"Dawn I do love you. I just don't know how to treat you. I guess I don't respect someone being kind to me. I consider that a weakness. When I'm not with you I miss you and when I am with you I don't know how to treat you. I just don't understand it."

"I do. You need help. You should talk to your minister and seek professional counseling as I did. Both of those sources have eased the pains you've caused me. Remember my doctor telling us that everyone in this house was responsible for my onset of a nervous breakdown? You refused to talk to him anymore. That was *your* loss."

His sister also revealed numerous problems experienced in his first marriage; the times he'd beat his wife, knock her into walls leaving holes and blackened her eyes etc. She'd return to her parents. He denied his wife the chance to return home even being pregnant with their second child. It was years before the family allowed him to see his daughter. I soon realized Theon hated women. He only loved Theon.

One Saturday afternoon as we drove downtown to a very large church for a drapery order, a psychologist on the radio discussed *why some men beat women*. He mentioned one thing that perked my interest.

"If a mother has been cruel to her son and he couldn't fight back, then he'd take all that stored up hate and inflict it on his wife."

I turned to Theon, "Did you hear what that doctor just said about you?"

"Interesting," he said.

He'd heard the doctor and understood every word. Mistreatments by his mother: nights spent on the porch when he came home too late; frying pans thrown at him in anger; dinners missed because of lateness etc. Those hidden inflicted pains were later taken out on his wives, his adversaries.

Theon's mother and biological father separated when he and his sister were very young. She worked long hours, plus raised two children alone; a strenuous feat. Whenever he angered her, he said she'd throw anything she had in her hand at him. Sometimes he ducked in time.

During high school he'd often come home late. At 6:00 p.m. all doors were locked. Therefore, he slept on the porch all night without dinner. This remorseful baggage remained in his subconscious mind. Unable to confront his mother whom he loved dearly, he fought male and female. We knew that emotionally abused children reacted in this manner. Even killing, was *mild* in his eyes. He was sadistic. He delighted in cruelty. He reached gratification from inflicting physical or mental pain on others, mainly women. His charm and kindness toward me lasted only short periods. I'd forgive him, thinking he'd changed but days later his demeaning ways returned. He *never* modified his behavior.

One day he *met* his Waterloo just like Napoleon.

At night we sat upstairs in the den, watching television or playing games. One evening, the phone rang. Since Theon sat closer, he answered. I knew by his facial expressions and the tone in his voice it was a woman. When he finished his conversation I asked him who it was.

"Ah, that was just a friend."

"Yes it was quite obvious to me that it was a *friend*. Was it a female or a male?" He didn't answer.

"Was it a female or a male friend?" I said again.

"What does it matter to you *who* it was? They wanted to talk to me, *not* to you."

"It matters a great deal to me. I don't want women calling you in this house unless it's pertaining to your job…"

"Since I help to pay the bills here I can have *anyone* call me that I want to."

"Not in *this house* you can't!"

Theon let the first name of the lady slip out during our heated conversation. The following day I checked his little black book in the top dresser drawer and not only did I find the woman's name and address but receipts from a motel and restaurant. I called several women before I got the right one. Each one gave me new insights on the *bum*!

Evelyn, the lady who'd called, was unaware he was married. The tone of her voice was convincing and we talked at length. He'd dated her during our separation. Nothing serious developed. She kept apologizing for having called my home and understood how I felt. When Mr. Theon came home from work, I showed him the receipts and told him about my conversations with those women!

"You're just messing up my friendships. I don't see why I can't have females call me. They're people I knew before I met you."

I looked at my husband and thought, *is he for real?*

"Theon you have your leg surgery next week. When you come home from the hospital your belongings will be packed."

Theon was in the hospital one week. I visited him everyday. Each time I visited I'd remind him that all of his belongings would be ready for his move. When he left the hospital in April, he came home. I helped him put his clothes in the car. He drove away looking sad and dejected, but I'd seen that look before, and forgave him. Not this time though, he was *gone—gone for good!*

He called at least twice a week. The man loved to talk, especially about himself. Several weeks passed before he confessed he'd slept in his car the first three nights after he left. Too embarrassed to ask his parents if he could return, he sulked in his car. His father said, "This is the *last* time. You need to grow up and act like a man." Theon needed counseling. He denied the necessity and refused any help.

I lived in that big house for eighteen months, alone. I was never afraid, not even when I cut the grass late at night. I had peace from him but not from men. After Theon left I slept upstairs just a few times. For some reason I didn't want to sleep in that bed anymore. I slept downstairs in Mama's room, now the den.

My friends and co-workers couldn't understand how I stayed in that large house, partially hidden in a densely wooded area and not be afraid. The neighbor behind me suggested I get a gun.

"A gun, what do I need a gun for?"

"Protection."

"Protection? God is my protection."

"But they don't know about God."

"But I do!"

Nothing happened to me those eighteen months of peace and tranquility. I dated a few men but they proved to be liars, and possessed no moral values. My church, Mama, the house, yard and job consumed my time. Satan had a way of disturbing my inner peace. He knew my weaknesses and thrived on them, but only if I voiced them out loud. He couldn't read my mind. Sometimes I learned to ignore his evil words and adhered only to good thoughts.

My younger son, Bryan encountered serious military problems. As usual he defied authority. His stubbornness caused him much grief. I knew unless he altered his thinking he'd never succeed in this world.

First, he was angry because he wasn't allowed to complete his high school education in the service. *Second*, he didn't like people yelling at him. *Third*, the Army was slow in issuing his two months back pay.

Bryan had dated Valarie Sue, a pretty white girl, also in the Army. They loved each other and wanted to marry. When she told her grandmother her plans to marry a light-skinned black guy, the grandmother became furious!

"I don't care what color he is, if you marry that *n*——- I'll *denounce* you from this family! I don't want no *n*——-*s* in my house or in *my family!*"

"But Grandma Bryan is a fine person. His mother is a teacher, his brother's in the Air Force and they have a real nice house in Baltimore."

"No never mind what they'd got. I don't want him or his family in my house, *ever*! Do you *hear* that Valarie Sue!"

Nothing changed her grandmother's mind. In spite of their love the engagement ended. Valarie Sue loved her grandmother but couldn't understand why she disliked people of other races; whom she had never met. Bryan bought the wedding rings I'd received from Theon. When she hadn't returned the rings, he and his Sgt. went to Georgia to retrieve them. Unexpected financial glitches delayed their return to the base. Bryan called his top Sgt. and explained the situation. He turned a deaf ear.

The fuel gage read *empty*! So did their wallets. A service station owner held the wedding rings as security for a tank of gas. Reported as AWOL when they returned, Bryan's problems only intensified.

After that incident, Bryan's paychecks showed severe discrepancies. His blatant refusal to obey his superiors caused him serious reprimands. On one occasion he strolled away from his Sgt. during a conversation. The Sgt. called him twice. Bryan ignored him and continued walking to the barracks. I'd called the Sgt. previously about his immature behavior. This time he called me!

"Mrs. Albens this is Sgt. Mallory, Bryan's Sgt. He's on his way out of the Army with an unsatisfactory rating because he will *not obey!*"

"What! What has he done now!"

"He still insists on having things *his* way."

He explained Bryan's numerous problems. He could not understand his persistence in disobeying the Army's rules. When I spoke to Bryan about his actions he replied.

"Mommy they're just prejudiced. They won't let me go to school, like the recruiting officer said they would. Besides they *yell* too much."

I knew the yelling was the main reason. Bryan objected to anyone *telling him what to do!*

"Bryan you're in the Army. They make men out of boys. Yes they yell and they're strict. That's their job. When Marty joined the Air Force he hated the yelling too, but he made the adjustment. Get yourself together young man and do *your* job! You listen and obey those men or you'll find yourself in *big, big* trouble!"

Bryan grew older but not wiser. He created his own turmoil. Just living day to day was a task. But he insisted more misery was required!

I'd forgotten Bryan's physical struggle at birth a near death experience, three days in an oxygen tent and his right arm's limitation in playing sports. Had the oxygen affected a portion of his brain? My darling young and foolish son, if only he knew he was ruining his future in not obeying rules. He didn't understand the Army was not an *end* in itself, but a *means* to an end.

Later I received an urgent phone call from Bryan.

32...TROUBLE, TROUBLE, TROUBLE

We estimate vices and weigh sins
not according to their nature,
but according to our advantage
and self-interest.
Montaigne: Essays II. v.

"Mommy, I need your help, I'm in trouble." How little did I realize that tormented plea was the *first* in his reckless future of pleas!

"What's wrong now, Bryan!"

"I neeeed a lawwyer. I've been in jail."

"In jail, for what!"

Between long breaths and sighs, he explained his mishap. Disappointed but not surprised, I listened to my young immature son.

"Benny and I got caught breaking into a trailer."

"Breaking in a trailer! Bryan did I raise you to steal or to *work* for your money!"

"I know what you're going to say, Mommy, but you just don't understand. They kept messing up my paychecks. I got tired of being broke all the time. They ruined my checks for two months and all that time I had very little money."

"So instead of being the *squeaking wheel* that gets the oil, you became the *stealing wheel*?"

"No, not really. It's just that—it's just that—I can't stay at Aunt Betty's house—and not have any money."

"That's exactly why I didn't want you to live off base in the first place. You'd have too much freedom; freedom to mingle with the wrong kind of people. Bryan, why do you *always* befriend those types of people?"

"I don't know Mommy—it just happens."

"I know why. It's because you enjoy that side of life."

There was a long pause, "I gu-ess you're ri-ght Mommy, I gu-ess you're right."

"I know I'm right. You *are* aware, that I don't have money—to give you—for a lawyer. You'll have to get a public defender."

"Benny's wife and mother sent him money to hire a lawyer. But I understand why you don't have the money. I'll talk—to a public defender tomorrow. It's better if I have a lawyer but if you don't have the money then I hope I don't go to jail."

"You should have thought of that before you and that no count Sgt. started breaking into trailers and stealing other people's property. What a *sorry, sorry* role model he is for young men away from home! How did you get out of jail?"

"I called Aunt Betty first, but she said *no*! She said she didn't have that kind of money to waste. So the Army got me out."

"Well young man, your sins will find you out. If you continue the way you're headed, one-day, you won't need a lawyer. You'll get killed or sent to prison."

I made three trips to Fayetteville because of Bryan's *stupidity*. But of course he relished doing wrong, why—I'll never know. My first trip was wasted. The court date had been changed but the paper work didn't reach his public defender in time to notify me. The second trip's failure was due to Bryan's determination to have his way. When I arrived after nine p.m. he wasn't home. He arrived minutes later as I sat in Aunt Betty's bedroom.

"Hi Mommy, can I use your car?"

"No, you can not use my car."

"But why?"

"Because, I just got here. After driving six hours that car needs to rest. Besides, I didn't drive four hundred miles for your enjoyment. I came to help you stay out of jail."

"I *know* why you came!"

He'd been drinking or smoking something. His voice escalated!

"Well just *keep* your g—d—- *car*. I'm going out and don't know what time I'll be back! You and that car…!" He used more profanity! Aunt Betty was *shocked*!

"Dawn I've never heard Bryan use that kind of language around me before."

"That's because you give in to him. I don't! If I don't submit to his whims, he gets furious. When Bryan's drinking he's a different person. I've only seen that side of him a few times."

My son's remarks hurt but I shed *not* one tear. I decided to return home that night however Aunt Betty persuaded me to wait until morning. I listened.

Bryan's court case was scheduled for 10 a.m. Up by eight and dressed; I put my belongings in the car, ready to leave. Bryan appeared in the doorway. He didn't speak nor did I. I kissed Aunt Betty goodbye and left. Another wasted trip, wasted money and wasted time for an *ungrateful* sick son! On July 12th he turned eighteen. I guess that two-digit number made him *think* he was a man. Rougher roads lay ahead before he'd *ever* reach that *status*!

I arrived home late afternoon and called Aunt Betty. Bryan's public defender had notified them his case had been postponed *again*! So that second trip was another waste of *my money!* Weeks later, after Bryan's apologetic call, I traveled Highway Interstate 95, a *third* time.

Bryan's greeting was warm, embracing and—sorrowful. He'd *begged* me to return. I relented, the typical reaction from a mother. Poor mothers; they do so much for their loved ones. Wives and mothers shoulder the world's woe. Men inflict pain while women absorb its grief and gloom.

The Public Defender Mr. Sardinous was outstanding! He'd checked three courtrooms prior to our arrival before selecting *the judge* to hear Bryan's case. He said one judge would have given Bryan ten years, even though it was his first offense. I sat in the courtroom and observed case after case of young men and women standing alone, without a parent. Why? After appearing so many times, they'd given up. Mr. Sardinous chose the third judge. He wasn't as harsh.

Mr. Sardinous sat up front. We sat toward the middle of the courtroom. At one point Bryan leaned over and whispered softly in my ear.

"Mommy, if I had two or three thousand dollars, I know where I can get a brand new Corvette."

Appalled, I whispered in his ear, "Are you *crazy*! We sit in a courtroom, where you face a possible ten-year prison sentence and you mention $3000 for a stolen car! *Have you lost your mind boy!*"

When Bryan's case was called Mr. Sardinous rose, stood tall and conducted his case well. He informed the judge I'd driven down from Baltimore three times in support of my son. Yes, my dear son who minutes earlier expressed his desire in the *courtroom* to buy a stolen car!! I prayed for God's help to keep Bryan out of prison. The sadness and sorrow in this situation had clouded our lives.

Bryan was sentenced to three years probation and $500 in restitution to the family that owned the trailer. I thanked Mr. Sardinous then floated out the courthouse on a transparent carefree cloud *thanking* God! The car sensed my exuberance, departed from the curb, headed toward Highway 95 with soaring invisible wings. Bryan also drove away, leaving the morning's distressful situation, for a high school football game. There he met a gorgeous young lady from Thailand.

She *loved* Bryan and was delighted with his company. What a sight they were together. Both had interesting styles of humor. Aunt Betty said or did anything to Bryan; he never got angry. He said at times, she ran him around the house with a broom in jest.

"Come here boy; let me spank your butt. It ain't been spanked in a long time. Come on, get on your knees and lean over my lap."

At times they acted like two little kids. Aunt Betty found laughter in anything. Although she held an iron hand on me she was more lenient with Bryan. He confessed why he gave in to my aunt so easily.

"Aunt Betty doesn't mean what she says, but *you* do. Besides she's much older than you."

Bryan also had a house key. I lived there nine years and *never* had one. She said I didn't need one.

"What did you need a key for gal? I'm here all the time. Bryan works late most nights. Having a key keeps him from disturbing my sleep."

I understood the reasoning; however I still should have had a key to the house.

During my stay, I met Bryan's girlfriend, Nardia. Her stepfather had married her mother while stationed in Thailand. They sent for Nardia and her brother Lamar, several years after returning to the states.

Nardia resembled a Thai doll in her multicolored short, *short* dress, rosy cheeks and long bouffant black hair. She sat on the bed next to Aunt Betty. This pretty girl, he'd met at the football game, had captivated my son's heart! She came to America at twelve years old not speaking English. Now an assertive sixteen, she spoke English rather well.

Aunt Betty marveled at Nardia's long hair. She'd pat it, rub it and twist it around her fingers. They adored each other.

"Gal, don't you think that dress is a little too short?"

Nardia reached over with her right arm and hugged Aunt Betty around the neck.

"Ah no Aunt Betty all the girls are wearing them like this. That's the style today."

I thought, yes they wear them short but *not that short!* When Bryan introduced me to his sweetheart, I knew instantly *she* was the one.

Late one night Bryan called collect. As we spoke, I heard heavy rain pounding on the telephone booth!

"Mommy I just had to talk to you."

"What's wrong Bryan?"

"I'm so mixed up. I didn't tell my girlfriend I was getting discharged from the service. She was impressed with me being in the Army because her father's in the service. Now I'll be out in a few days and I don't know how to tell her the truth."

"Does she know about the court problems?"

"No. I haven't told her anything."

"Well— I guess it's time to tell her the truth. Don't you think so?"

"Mommy, I'm standing in this phone booth, soaking wet, broke and disgusted for what I've done with my life. I was walking back to Fort Bragg in all this rain when I decided to call you. *Please* pray for me, Mommy. I just don't know what to do."

"Of course I will Bryan!"

I prayed for Bryan, as I had so many times in his eighteen years. Whenever in trouble, he called me. He knew I'd pray whether he asked or not. He knew God answered prayers! He left the phone booth and started his six mile walk back to the Base. Within minutes a car pulled over ahead of him and offered him a lift. As he ran toward the rear of the car, another car sped by on his left side so *fast* it missed him by inches. God protected him!

Yes, Nardia's pretty face, long black hair, and appealing figure, said the words *I do.* I've heard boys usually married girls similar to their mothers. Homesick and lonely, young military men also married early. So it was with Bryan, as it was with Marty. My sons married young, too young; just as I had.

Stationed at Tinker Air Force Base in Oklahoma, Marty married at twenty. He too met Renanta, a pretty girl on base from Elkart, Indiana. I'd never met her but had spoken to her several times on the phone. They married on June 1, 1982. A year later, Rolanda Jennings was born. Another year passed before I held my first grandchild and met my first daughter-in-law.

At the nursing home, I remained with Rolanda in the lobby while Marty and Renata went to Mama's room. Children weren't permitted. The next visit, Marty rolled Mama's wheelchair into the lobby. Then she saw Rolanda, her first happy and beautiful great-granddaughter who'd inherited her mother's captivating smile. God blessed us with the *first girl* in our small family.

Maurice stopped by my home to see his son and family. He played and laughed with Rolanda but I knew he really didn't like children. That gorgeous sunny day, we took pictures recording precious moments of our third generation. We posed on the porch steps, on the lawn and nestled close together under the huge cedar tree in the front yard. A loving ambience existed that day—-warmth prevailed as we enjoyed Rolanda our first grandchild!

While Marty served in the Air Force, Bryan remained in Fayetteville, soon to be discharged from the Army. And I, I lived in a large Victorian house, alone, but not lonely. I had peace. I had my God. I had my cat, Kelly. No one insulted, cursed, demeaned or humiliated me.

After I'd slept in the den downstairs for eighteen months I decided to return the upstairs to the apartment, as it was when we first purchased the house. It had three bedrooms, kitchen, bath plus access to the attic.

The partition separating the foyer from the living room was replaced. During that week the *700 Club* called and asked if I wanted prayer for a special need. I asked for a tenant. The guy who installed the partition knew a lady who needed an apartment. God's *always* on time: *"Ye have not, because ye ask not."* James 4:2

Whenever I gave God my problems and *waited on Him,* everything turned out fine. But once I became impatient and tried to solve them myself, I suffered.

Beverly Harris, my tenant was unable to install a phone when she moved in, I allowed her to use mine for a month. The telephone company said they couldn't disconnect my upstairs line until she was ready to install hers. At first it didn't bother me when she received calls.

"Hello."

"Yes, can I speak to Beverly?"

"Yes, just a moment please, I'll see if Beverly is home. She lives upstairs."

"Oh, I'm sorry; I thought this was Beverly's phone."

Soon she received more calls than I did. I always answered the phone even though I left my phone in the kitchen for her. Several times I inquired as to when she'd get a phone.

"I don't have the money now, but I'll have it next month."

Next month never came. After waiting *six months*, I called the telephone company again, about disconnecting the upstairs telephone line.

"Yes, we'll be glad to do that for you."

"You can? I was told six months ago that you could only disconnect my lines when she was ready to get her own line."

"Oh that's not true. That line could have been disconnected then."

Shocked but elated, days later, it was disconnected. Beverly returned home from her short vacation during my absence. As soon as I got in the house, she knocked on my door.

"Hi Beverly, how was your trip?"

"It was fine. Dawn did you know something is wrong with the phone?"

"No, there's nothing wrong. I had it disconnected. Now you can have your own telephone line put in."

"Disconnected, why didn't you tell me before I left?"

"I didn't know I could until a few days ago. Besides I've asked you for six months. I think I've been more than fair, don't you? Also I never charged you for using my phone.

"Ye-s, I gu-ess so."

Her eyes penetrated mine like a knife piercing raw meat! She jerked around and marched upstairs. A few days later she asked to receive only important calls on my phone until she got paid. I said yes. Two weeks later, her phone was installed. She'd taken advantage of my kindness, like my former husband Arnold had in using my car when he could have bought one.

Trouble waited around the corner. It lingered, hiding for the right moment to leap out at me!

Every week I mowed the lawn, wearing shorts and a halter top on hot humid days. I edged the sidewalks with scissors, trimmed the hedges, lopped off plants and cut back tree branches. The yard was striking. I'd sprawl out on the porch's chaise lounge, admire the radiant floral blooms and their fragrances that graced the freshly cut green lawn. I'd earned that long-awaited rest.

School opened. I settled quickly and smoothly into my new teaching environment as usual. I'd never taught sixth graders. What a delightful change, to see little children seated, waiting for me to start my lesson. In addition to my darling sixth graders were the rambunctious seventh and eighth graders.

Once again I started a modern dance group. The young girls were as eager to learn good dance techniques as my older girls in high school. The school didn't have an auditorium, so practices and performances were held in the gymnasium or multi-center rooms. Student's art was exhibited in the halls, the library, the cafeteria, and in hall showcases. Everyone praised their artworks.

The assistant principal asked me to design a special display in the teacher's dining room for monthly *Teacher's Perfect Attendance* that would encourage teachers to improve their attendance. Many teachers weary from student's disrespect, teacher overload and crowded classrooms would often miss a day or two for mental resurgence. A monetary gift was awarded each month to the teacher with the best attendance. Its goal was accomplished.

As one principal once said, "All of *that* comes with the job." All of *that* meant: dedication, early and late hours, humiliation swallowed and digested in the classroom from students even when *society* forgot who educated them in the first place for their high paying jobs. Perhaps *that's* why more teachers had mental problems than any other profession! Overworked, overlooked and underpaid, they were still required to have two or more degrees. They earned meager salaries for the hours of mental strain endured for thirty to forty years in the classroom, from some parents and administrators. But still their love in helping children to learn satisfied their need to teach. Many teachers taught including lawyer's wives, not for the money but for an inner need, a desire to motivate children to excel.

The steps on my life's ladder became more difficult to climb. Each step represented another hurdle cleared and additional ones to conquer. Each step was a challenge, an opportunity to grow mentally and spiritually. Each step rose above the obstacle, to move on and upward. Each step said, "I made it, *yes I made it!"* Yes, I reflected on the step taken the last year before Beverly moved into the apartment.

Labor Day picnics, and swim parties ended. September rolled in calmly with children returning to school to new classes, new teachers, in new outfits. Nardia, Bryan's girlfriend also returned to her last year in high school.

Bryan's call in August explained Nardia's severe problems with her mother who had put her out! Nardia, tired of babysitting her siblings while her mother worked or gambled, rebelled. Every date they had included her siblings and older brother Lamar, acting as chaperone. She loved the children, but sometimes yearned to date without them. Free from burdens after having been put out, she bunked with Bryan who lived and slept on his friend's living room sofa.

"Mommy, can Nardia and I come to Baltimore and stay with you while Nardia finishes school there?"

"What, what's wrong now, Bryan?"

"Well, Nardia refuses to go back home, and Barry's apartment is too small for the three of us. If you let us come up there, I'll get a job as soon as I get there."

"I do-n't kn-ow Bryan. You know I won't allow you and Nardia to sleep together in my house unless you're married."

"I knooow you won't. I already told Nardia you wouldn't."

"Well, what do you expect me to do about the situation young man?"

"I'll only need your help for a while."

"Let me think about it." Two days later Bryan called back.

"Bryan I understand your predicament, but you can not stay in my house and not be married."

"Mommy we are going to be married, but later."

"I'm sorry, if you want to stay in my house it would have to be now, not later."

"We don't have any money for a wedding Mommy and all those others things you have to get. I can't even get her a ring."

"If you want to get married, I'll help. Ask Nardia to tell her mother your plans and see if she and her husband can help in any way?"

Bryan called the next day. Nardia's mother agreed with the plans. The following week they arrived in Baltimore. *One* week later a beautiful fall lawn wedding was performed—at *my* expense.

As many weddings as I had had I certainly could plan one for them. In one week I'd invited everyone by phone, ordered the cake from my personal cake *lady*, the flowers from a personal florist and also contacted the minister for the ceremony and counseling sessions. In addition, I made arrangements for tables and chairs, shopped with Nardia for a wedding gown, rented white tuxedos for Bryan and his best man, contacted a photographer, cooked all the food and selected the music.

The wedding was gorgeous! Mama's birthday party and Bryan's wedding were combined. Seventy people attended and were amazed that I'd accomplished so much in only a week in addition to working everyday. My next door neighbor offered me the use of the white folding chairs he'd rented for his daughter's wedding. He even set them up. A rented arch decorated with white ribbon and pink and blue flowers waited for the bride and groom on the green lawn under the huge oak tree. The white plastic runner ran from the porch steps out onto the green lawn, then up to the arch.

Nardia's family arrived a day before the wedding. The morning of the marriage ceremony, Nardia's mother allowed her two smaller children to participate. How interesting that she'd packed a long light blue dress for her four-year old daughter and long pants for her two-year old son. An *hour* before the wedding, the children practiced as flower girl and ring bearer. What a pleasant unplanned surprise! Both children were apprehensive at first but soon adjusted and practiced walking slowly down the steps, out to the lawn, then up to the arch. Soon they were professionals; two gorgeous children, having a Thai mother and African-American father, like Tiger Woods.

Theon (husband #4) took pictures of the wedding. Maurice (husband #1) managed the music. Mr. Heeth, our family friend, brought a whole sliced ham and helped in the kitchen. My dear friend Laurennette started the clean up process after the wedding ceremony ended, on her own. Other friends joined in and helped.

"Girl you've done enough. You prepared everything for this wedding by yourself and even cooked most of the food. Please, stay outside and enjoy your guests!"

I obeyed, delighted to have a break! Romantic music flowed across the lawn from the Magnavox stereo on the porch. The sun's soft silent rays warmed our attentive guests as they sat on white chairs and covered benches lined up in rows like church pews. They watched Nardia and Bryan repeat their vows under the waterfall of flowers over the white arch in front of Pastor Winford, a handsome but self-centered man.

God didn't seem to preside in him or his service. One of my friends said, "Dawn, *where* did you find him!"

Embarrassed, I notified him at a later date of the guest's comments. He stated he didn't care *what* my friends thought or said about his ceremony.

I remember the Sunday morning I attended his church. I sat in the back, absorbing the insulting remarks he hurled out to certain non-participating members in a monetary drive. He didn't specify names; but they knew who they were. The congregation appeared to be untouched by his remarks. However his words struck me as being harsh and inappropriate coming from the pulpit. Days later I mentioned my concerns. He replied:

"Dawn I'm not interested in what you think! I know what my congregation needs to hear and I *do* know how to handle them!"

"But you're a minister, a man of God! I believe, if you must fuss, it shouldn't be in the pulpit where guests might be attending the service."

"Well since this isn't your church, and you're not the pastor, what you think and what you believe really doesn't matter." He was an outspoken rude man!

His enormous new church was being built on the same spot where the old one once stood. Sunday services were held across the street in the junior high school until the completion of the sanctuary. Adjacent to the new church was a high rise apartment complex for senior citizens also being built. Every day he'd check each site's construction and craftsmanship, a mammoth task!

Days following the wedding, Nardia enrolled in high school and Bryan got a job. I moved my clothes and other belongings downstairs where I'd slept since my separation. They lived upstairs—rent free. October and November weren't pleasant months.

Since Bryan's marriage he thought he was grown and didn't have to answer to me any more. *Bi—g* mistake! One quiet Saturday morning, as I lay in bed, I spied a roach crawling down the wall near the bathroom. Soon another one ran down and another. I killed them then went upstairs to find the source.

Bryan and Nardia were asleep and didn't see my anger when I stepped into their kitchen. I scanned the table, sink and stove inhaling the stench of garlic and garbage. The garbage can so full, had spilled over on the floor. I stared at that filthy kitchen: dirty dishes and pots stacked in the sink, left open pots with food, dried meat smelled of garlic in a frying pan. I was *so angry* with that girl! Bryan knew better. He hadn't been raised like that. Mad and disgusted I returned downstairs and got plastic garbage bags and disinfectant.

As I washed the dishes, I became *madder* with every wipe. I thought, "How dare they disrespect my house like this. I'm not charging them any rent. The least they can do is keep the apartment clean. Minutes later I went to the bathroom. Leaving I noticed several baby roaches climbing up the side of the bathtub from the blue bath carpet. I stooped down, yanked back the carpet and *screamed*! A nest of roaches ran in every direction! It seemed like hundreds. I stood motionless. Bryan rushed from his bedroom to see why I had screamed.

"*Roaches, roaches everywhere!* Look don't you see them?"

"Yes I see them, so what?"

"So what? What do you mean so what?"

"It's just a few roaches. I don't see why you're so upset over some roaches."

"Well young man, you know very well why I'm so upset! If you and Nardia would clean up that nasty kitchen and carry out that trash, then the roaches wouldn't be up here in the first place!"

"Yeah Mommy I heard you up here washing the dishes. You don't have to do that. I thought this was *our* apartment anyway."

"Yes it is your apartment, but it's *my* house and I don't like roaches in my house! I don't like roaches period! They are dirty and they carry disease. This isn't new to you Bryan. Remember what happened when your grandmother was eating in her bedroom and left food out all night? I don't want that problem repeated again."

"I know that Mommy. All you had to do was tell me and I would have cleaned it up myself!"

"Tell you? I shouldn't have to tell you anything. You know how to clean up after you eat. You've been doing it since you were five. I think you need to teach Nardia and help her."

Often between 11 p.m. and 1 a.m. the phone woke me up. Bryan knew his friends weren't to call after 11 p.m. Bryan, being Bryan didn't understand why *he* couldn't have calls past eleven.

"I don't know why you don't unplug your phone at night then my phone calls won't bother you."

"I don't want to unplug the phone. I pay this bill, not you!"

A week before Christmas, the phone rang after midnight. Tired, sleepy and disgusted for having been awakened, I picked up the receiver.

"I have it Mommy." Bryan said.

I said, "Young man, has Bryan told you not to call here after 11:00 because I'm asleep. Only call if it's an emergency?"

"No Ma'am he didn't." As I talked, so did Bryan.

"Man, I told you what I have to go through! Can't have any phone calls after 11:00, can't do this and can't do that. It's just like being in the Army!" I hung up the receiver, jumped up from my bed, and rushed up the steps and confronted Bryan.

"Bryan I want to talk to you!"

"I'm on the phone!"

"Yes I know you're still on the phone but I need to talk to you now!"

He told his friend goodbye and stepped out into the hall where I stood. As he screamed foul language, my heart pounded! I was *scared* and *terrified*! I trembled, frightened of my own son! This was the second time I'd feared him. I turned away, *startled* and hurried down the steps to my apartment. Just as I reached the bottom landing, a glass of water *flew* by my head *crashing* into the wall! My head spun around. Bryan stood in the middle of the staircase waving his arms, yelling and screaming hateful words. I couldn't believe this was my son. His diabolic facial expression could kill.

"*Leave me alone!* You just *leave* me alone! You treat me as though I were a child. I'm eighteen years old. I'm a *man!*"

I thought, *a man huh? You think having sex, being married, stealing, smoking pot and cursing your mother makes you a man.* A man respects his mother, pays his rent, doesn't steal and has his own telephone!

"*Get out Bryan! Get out of this house now!* You can't live here anymore. Nardia can stay, but I want you *OUT NOW! Right NOW!*"

I rushed inside my bedroom, closed the door, flopped down on the bed and cried softly in my pillow. I remembered Audry's words years earlier.

"Dawn, Marty won't be your problem. Your *problem* will be *Bryan.*"

What was wrong with my son! I hadn't seen him like that since we lived on Northwood Drive. He ached to harm me, his mother, because I denied him his wishes. I assumed he must have smoked marijuana. Marty said he'd smoked it when he'd kicked and broken the fan. I guess he also smoked it the night he cursed me at Aunt Betty's.

As I lay on the bed, Bryan *yanked* open my door then walked over to the dresser.

"I'll *take* my clock back. Since you want me out of your house, you don't *need* this anymore!"

He returned upstairs with the alarm clock he'd given me for my birthday. That was Friday night. He left the house, cursing as he slammed the door. Nardia stayed.

Saturday afternoon he returned. A drapery client and I sat in the living room when I heard a knock on the door.

"Yes, who is it?"

"It's me, Bryan. I want to see *my wife!*"

"You can't come in here Bryan. Please leave."

"*I ain't goin' no where 'til I see my wife!*"

"You can't come in this house, *now leave!*'

He banged and kicked on the door repeatedly. I was humiliated. My customer, a young Caucasian male was concerned but not too alarmed.

"Bryan I'm calling the police if you don't stop banging on my door. *Leave!*"

He left, I thought. I apologized to my customer for his behavior. Mr. Jusom assured me these problems were no surprise to him. He said his brother was a recovering alcoholic and had similar behavior that had humiliated his mother for *many* years.

About five minutes later I heard banging sounds of *splitting* wood. Bryan had returned. I looked out the living room window and saw him on the front porch with the sledgehammer breaking the baluster railings and making holes in the wooden porch floor. He'd already broken the block glass windows under the house. I called the police! I waited. I prayed.

"Dear God please forgive me for calling the police on my son, but I can't let him destroy my property. Please help him! Please help me!"

When Bryan saw the police car driving up the lane he ran down the steps and into the woods. I explained the problem to the officers. They assured me he would return and when he did, I was to call them immediately. Against his wishes, Mr. Jusom left. As I walked him to his car, I spied Bryan hiding in the woods. Mr. Jusom, a kind, soft-spoken highly intelligent scholar wanted to remain until everything was over but I assured him I'd be fine.

Ten minutes later, Bryan returned. When he started kicking on the door, I called the police. In minutes they arrived. As they walked up the porch steps, Bryan never stopped banging and kicking the door.

"Young man, why are you kicking on that door?"

"I want to see my wife. She won't let me in!" I opened the door to talk to the officers. With the door open, Bryan pushed past the policeman to enter the house. The officer grabbed him!

"Where do you think you're going! Your mother doesn't want you in the house!"

Bryan tussled with both policemen! They had a hard time handcuffing him but finally succeeded. Nardia was in the living room crying. My neighbor who lived behind me ran across my backyard yelling!

"What's wrong, what's wrong! Dawn what are they doing to Bryan? What has he done?"

The officers answered, "Everything's alright sir. Everything's alright."

I watched the policemen walk Bryan down the sidewalk, handcuffed. Bryan kept turning around staring at me. Just before they put him in the patrolman's car he yelled.

"You *B——*, I *hate* you! I *hate* you!"

I glanced at the policeman, who stood next to me behind my car, shaking my head in shame and wonder.

"Why, why? What have I done so wrong to be treated like this?" I said.

"Ma'am I see this every day. Don't blame yourself. You haven't done anything. It's the times. Young people don't respect *anybody* today."

He cited recent cases he'd encountered worse than mine. Lord, what have I done to my son, for him to say such words to me? His mother, who three months earlier, had given him such a beautiful Lawn Wedding, who made three trips to Fayetteville to keep his butt out of jail and who loved him so much!

As I recall that devastation, I hurt. "Had I done too much?" A mother's love is so different from a father's. Every time he got into trouble I bailed him out while his father turned his back. Since his youth, he could depend on me. I recalled his words just three years earlier ringing in my ears.

"Mommy I try to do right, but I can't. *Something always* makes me do wrong."

I remembered those times before he went in the service when we sat on the sofa in the den he'd put his head in my lap. He needed that extra attention. I'd rub his hair and pray. I'd quote scripture to him from the Bible and let him know that everybody did wrong things sometimes but as we got older, we learned *not* to listen to those evil thoughts but to do what was right.

I returned to the house and tried to console Nardia. She loved him so and couldn't understand why he acted the way he did, especially toward me.

"Mom you do so much for him and he talks to you so bad. What makes him do that?"

I reflected on Exodus 20 and one of the Ten Commandments that said, *"Honor thy father and thy mother: that thy days may be long upon the land which the Lord thy God giveth thee."* I knew as long as Bryan disrespected me he'd not succeed no matter how much I prayed. God kept His promises. Bryan had to alter his life style if he wanted to live a long prosperous life.

Nardia had made arrangements to spend her Christmas holiday in Fayetteville. Her relatives were arriving in Baltimore in a couple of days to carry her back. When Bryan was released from jail, he stayed with his friend Melvin and his family for the next few days. Nardia prepared for her trip.

"Mom, where is Bryan going to stay while I'm in Fayetteville?"

"I don't know Nardia, and I really don't care where he stays because he *won't* be living here anymore!"

She packed all of their clothes and other belongings. When her aunt and uncle arrived, they loaded the car and left. I was unaware Bryan was in Fayetteville until Christmas Eve when I called Nardia to wish her a Merry Christmas.

"Have you heard from Bryan Nardia?"

"Yes, he's right here."

"He's there? He's living there with you in your parent's home?"

"Yes. He didn't have anywhere else to go, so we stopped by Melvin's and brought him with us. I'm staying down here to finish out the school year. Bryan has a job."

The court date was set for February. As I sat in the courtroom waiting for our case, I overheard a familiar voice seated behind me. It was Bryan's. He and Nardia were seated in back of me. He spoke loud enough to let me know it was they who occupied those chairs. I did not acknowledge his presence. When his case was called, he went up front. The judge reviewed Bryan's problem and summed up his statement with these words.

"Young man you're not here for what you did to your mother's property. You're here for what you did to the police officers. You resisted arrest. That's a serious offense. I *never* want to see you in my courtroom again! Do you *understand me!*"

"Yes sir Your Honor, I understand."

After the case ended, we left the courtroom, and walked out into the hall. Nardia came over to me and said a few kind words while Bryan strolled down the hall, out the door and down the pavement and never opened his mouth. Nardia said they'd driven to Baltimore in their *own* used car purchased from a friend in Fayetteville.

At the end of April, my thoughts of Bryan were heavy. One Sunday afternoon after Church, as I watched a golf game on television, the phone rang.

"Hello."

"Hel—lo Mom—my, this is Br—yan." His voice was low; his words were dra-wn out like a rubber band stretching out to infinity.

"Well, how are the newlyweds getting along?"

I hadn't contacted him since he'd moved. I knew he'd call when he was ready, when he realized how wrong he'd been. That was his nature. I also knew that that would *not* be the last time we'd *clash*!

"We're doing fine. I called to see how you're getting along and to let you know I'm working."

"That's fine Bryan. Where are you working?"

"At Domino Pizza, it's a fast food business and is growing so fast. There are chains opening up all across America. One day I plan to have my own store."

"Is Nardia working?"

"Yes Nardia works part time at Taco Bell. When school is over next month she'll be working full time as assistant manger." He discussed their visits with Aunt Betty, his car, his job etc. I finally asked Bryan the big question.

"Bryan, we've been talking over fifteen minutes and you haven't apologized to me yet for your past conduct." Slow, sad and sorrowful, he answered.

"Mom—my, you kn—ow I'm sor—ry for what I did." He answered slowly.

"I don't know anything, Bryan. All I know is how I felt and how *deeply* you hurt me. It's been four months now, did you remember that?"

"Ye-s I kn—ow. I think about you everyday and what I did. You know I'm sorry."

"No I don't know; you have to tell me how you feel." There was a long silence. "I'm still waiting Bryan. Are you there?"

"Yes I'm here—I'm sorry Mommy, I was wrong. I'm too embarrassed to discuss it anymore."

Bryan a sensitive proud person didn't like to be embarrassed. Yet he'd shame others whenever he became angry.

"That's okay. You've apologized and I hope it doesn't happen again. Remember you only have one mother and one father. The Bible says, *'Honor thy father and thy mother: that thy days may be long upon the land which the Lord thy God giveth thee.'* If you continue to dishonor your parents your days won't be long and you won't be happy."

"That's one of the Ten Commandments isn't it?" He said.

"Yes it is. I see you remember; now put it into action. If you don't, your days will be filled with misery, overwhelming you from every direction."

"Of course, I'll remember. Nardia and I will have our own apartment by the time you come down this summer."

With Bryan settled I felt relieved, but not for long.

33... A NEW BEGINNING

Marriage resembles a pair of shears,
so joined that they can not be separated;
often moving in opposite directions, yet
always punishing anyone who comes
between them.
Sidney Smith: Lady Holland's Memoir.
Vol. I, Chap. 11

Our school year ended the third week in June; always the last public school system in the nation to close. Snow days extended the preset date to meet the 180 day requirement.

After July 4th Marty, his wife Renata, and daughter Rolanda, who'd arrived a few days earlier and I headed south in my blue Ford Landau (named Betsy) to visit our small family.

Scenic trips always lifted my spirits. Driving on the highway placed me in another dimension; another world of quiet and serene beauty. God's gifts of clouds, myriad colored trees, flowers, birds, crops waiting to be harvested, roaming cattle, horses and green grassy slopes were spectacular. To behold wide open spaces, to float on highways, to leave the city behind was more splendid than eating ice cream, my favorite dessert! We left about six a.m. and arrived around noon.

We cruised into Fayetteville headed toward Haymount Hill, the elite section, then to Oakridge Ave: my secluded, tranquil home in the midst of towering trees that provided cool summer breezes. Terrific mid-eighties temperatures made the drive more pleasant. Aunt Betty, who lived alone since Daddy's passing, was overjoyed at our arrival.

That evening we visited Bryan and Nardia in their cozy apartment. Bryan noted various projects he'd completed to improve its livability.

"Mommy you know I can't live in dirt. My landlord gave us paint and anything else we needed to spruce it up. You know, to make it look slick! Of course he deducted our labor from the rent."

We praised the facelift they'd given their first one bedroom apartment. Bryan's love for his wife and home implied to me—he was maturing. He accomplished what I'd done repeatedly: clean and renovate houses. My sons learned how to paint, mow lawns, clean yards, cook, keep house, wash and iron clothes, even though they fussed and complained. They learned to sew by hand and used the sewing machine from watching me. They also helped to make and install draperies. Each wife *thanked* me for teaching them.

During our one-week stay, Aunt Betty tried to poison Marty and Renata's minds with negative events of my past. She cornered them in the guest bedroom where they slept to carry out her vicious plan. She didn't succeed. By diverting their love from me she'd monopolized *all* my affections and monetary gifts. I loved my aunt, but disliked her selfishness. She often admitted:

"Yes I'm selfish! My husband gives me anything I want. I ain't thinkin' 'bout these *n*—. I don't give anybody anything unless they give me something!"

That was definitely *true*. I lived with that mentality until her death years later.

The following summer Marty was stationed in the Azores. Located in the North Atlantic Ocean they're composed of nine major islands 740 miles from their mother country, Portugal. The United States had maintained a NATO airbase there since 1951.

Marty's job required him to supervise twenty-five men. Somehow he managed to resolve any problems he incurred. I'd plan to visit them during their two-year stay but changed my mind. They stopped in Baltimore for a week before flying to the Azores. Renata was pregnant with their second child Marvis, who was born in the Azores where the cattle had free reign in the streets.

Two days before their departure they left my home, without any notification while I attended my Bible study class, and went to Marty's father's house complaining I'd hit Rolanda. They objected to my hitting her. When they approached me about the smack on her leg, I explained why.

"Yes, I smacked her on her leg. The pop was to save her life."

Rolanda rode with me in the front seat of the car when I returned my dog to its previous owner. As we rode round trip she insisted she'd lean on the door. Tired of telling her to get off the door, I reached over and popped her on her thigh. She cried a little and said.

"I'm gonna tell my Mommy and Daddy you hit me!" After we got in the house she ran straight up stairs. Seconds later her parents rushed down and confronted me.

"Mom why did you hit Rolanda!" Marty yelled.

"Yes, I popped her on her leg. Did she tell you why? I got tired of telling her to get off the door because she could fall out, and get killed, if it opened." I said.

"Well Mom I don't *want* you hitting her. I remember how you used to spank Bryan and me when we were little!"

"You deserved it. But you were boys and I didn't spank her, I just gave her a light pop on her leg."

Renata interrupted in an angry voice, "It wasn't light because that section of her leg turned *red*!"

"*Red!* Her skin is brown. How could you see a red mark on her thigh?"

"I don't want anyone hitting my child, not even *you*!" Renata's anger soared.

By this time I was *real* angry! Their child had stuck a fork in the back of my open weave dining room chair and had started to twist the fork to widen the holes. Had I not stopped her in time my chair would have been ruined! Their child dropped food on the velvet seats of those chairs and smeared it with her fingers. On one occasion their child climbed up the painted radiator. I asked Renata to tell her to get down.

She said, "She's already up there now."

"Yes and I want her down!" I rushed over and lifted her off the radiator. Had it been winter she wouldn't have climbed it. She'd gotten burned!

"Well I'm telling you now, when my grandchildren continue to disobey me, I will correct them even if it means a pop on the leg. I didn't kill her. I only smacked her on her thigh. I'll not watch them do wrong while I do nothing."

They continued expressing their disapproval, then hurried upstairs. When I returned from Bible study, I sauntered upstairs to share my lesson with them and discovered they had left without leaving a note. The next day Marty's father called. He said they'd stopped by his house that night to borrow money for a motel. He gave them the money rather than have Rolanda stand inside his refrigerator trying to reach the top shelf as she had done previously, while they watched and said nothing. He understood my reactions to the child's behavior and agreed with me.

Bryan and Nardia were happy in Fayetteville. Both worked, enjoyed their apartment and young marriage. Marty and Renata survived the dampness in the Azores with their two children. Sometimes Bryan and I borrowed money from each other and returned what we borrowed. Our relationship was great. He called often, sometimes twice a week simply to check on me.

In October 1984, Bryan's phone call revealed Aunt Betty's illness. I called and assured her I'd be down the next week when school was out Thursday and Friday. I'd have four days rather than just a weekend. Bryan promised me he and Nardia now four months pregnant with their first child, would care for her until I arrived. Two days later Bryan called again.

"Mommy Aunt Betty is very sick I think you need to come as soon as you can. Her night bucket is running over. She's not able to get to the bathroom and there's a bad odor in the room."

"I'm leaving tomorrow morning. Tell Aunt Betty I'll see her around noon."

When I turned right at the little white mailbox off of Oakridge Avenue, pleasant childhood memories blinded my vision. I drove slowly down the bumpy dirt road checking the enormous height the pine trees had grown in the thirty-nine years since I'd lived there. Bryan was in the yard. He rushed toward the car to help me. He squeezed me so tight I had to gasp for air. I was home at last.

A sad mirthless feeling grabbed me as I walked in Aunt Betty's bedroom. She had fortitude of steel. She'd never complained about the arm she'd carried in a sling over forty years. Seldom did she get a cold and when she did, it passed quietly. Now she lay helpless in her twin bed close to the wall with her left resting on propped pillows as usual, while roaches raced across her night table and on the wall behind her bed! I leaned over and kissed her smooth cheek, soon to be cared for by someone else.

I emptied the *pee pot* that had run over for the second time since Bryan had spoken to me. Her two friends I'd called rushed over. They were shocked to see her that sick. We all begged her to go to the hospital, but each time she refused. She did agree however, to visit her doctor. I called his office several times before I got through. The doctor wasn't able to see her that day. I don't remember why. I became angry with the nurse who wouldn't understand how ill my aunt was. Had I known what the future held, I *would* have taken her to the hospital anyway!

"I've driven six hours from Baltimore to care for my aunt and you can't see her. She can hardly breathe. I don't know what to do. She's a regular patient of Dr. Matts couldn't you please see her." I said to the nurse.

I begged repeatedly. I became enraged with that woman! She refused to understand how sick my aunt was. I told her Aunt Betty *would not* go to the hospital. Finally I accepted an appointment for the following day.

That night Aunt Betty refused my urging to bathe and change her nightclothes. I'd never seen her in that condition. I was afraid she'd die before seeing the doctor.

"*No* you can do it tomorrow. I don't feel like getting up now. Just sit down and keep me company."

I should have bathed her and took her to the hospital anyway, but I didn't. She wanted my company so I sat next to her bed and talked until she dozed off to sleep.

I knew I'd made a bad impression on the phone while I talked to the nurse. I reacted almost like the mother did in the film *Terms of Endearment* when she demanded medication for her dying daughter's excruciating pain. I needed help for my aunt just like she needed help for her daughter. The only difference was she got help. I didn't!

Aunt Betty shouldn't have been living alone, but it was her decision. For years I begged her to sell that house and move to Baltimore with me. She refused. Now she'd consented. In fact she insisted I quit my job and move down there and care for her. When she discovered how sick she really was she decided to move. I'd told her years earlier that day would come. Now it had.

"Aunt Betty *please* sell the house, move to Baltimore with me and we can buy a larger house where you'd have your separate living quarters."

"I—don't—know. Let me sleep on it."

"You're getting older and you don't need to be living alone. Please don't wait until you get sick and then decide to move."

"I've been thinking about it because it's so much to do around this house and yard. And I can't do it anymore."

"Please, *please* don't wait too long now." I'd even had a real estate agent in Baltimore show me several homes with in-law quarters to help change her mind.

As she slept, I mulled over the possibility of life resembling a disposable sheet of paper: used up, balled up, and then thrown away; as though it never existed. Her body inhaled oxygen to exist but that process alone did not sustain life. I made her as comfortable as I could but her spirit was low. She ate very little, only a few spoonfuls of food but wanted me in the room to keep her company constantly. Bryan had made daily visits when he realized how sick she was. He and Nardia fed her and did whatever was needed.

That night my sleep was broken every few minutes as I lay in the adjacent twin bed and listened to Aunt Betty's heavy breathing. After an hour I moved to the front bedroom. My switch in sleeping arrangements didn't alter my concern and frequent visits to her bedroom. Every time her heavy breathing stopped I left my bed and rushed to her room.

"Dawn, I'm alright. Why don't you get some sleep and stop worrying about me."

"That's why I'm here, to worry and care for you."

"Well, go back to bed, I'm alright."

The following morning Mrs. Redmond and Mrs. Wright returned to help me get her ready for the doctor's appointment. Mrs. Wright, who was younger than Aunt Betty, owned a small carry out restaurant. They'd been close friends for years. Her jovial personality paralleled my aunt's. Mrs. Redmond had known us since I was fifteen. I had babysat her four precious children who were now grown successful adults.

With constant persuasion, Aunt Betty relinquished, and allowed us to help her to the bathroom on the back porch. She permitted me to undress and bathe her. As I undressed her I understood why she had remained in her bed. After she sat down in the warm bubbly bath water, feces floated immediately to the surface. I reassured her she was a very sick lady and accidents like that happened. She observed me staring, at her breast as we removed the bra. One breast was missing. Surprised, I asked her in a low voice, "What happened, Aunt Betty?"

"Ah, that breast was taken off over forty years ago. There was a tumor so the doctor removed it."

I remembered Aunt Betty wearing padded bras, but I thought she was trying to make her breast larger. There were times when she was dressing and the rubber pad would slide down from under the bra and I'd laugh silently, not knowing the truth. *All those years* and I never noticed anything unusual. Had I not bathed her, I still would not have known.

With almost no sleep the night before and after driving from Baltimore, I was weary, worn-out and worried about Aunt Betty's condition. In addition I was disgusted that the doctor would not see her the previous day. Had I known *all the problems* that lay ahead, I would have had an ambulance carry her to the hospital against her will. Since her doctor's office was located on Haymount Hill it only took minutes to get there.

I helped Aunt Betty, seventy-four years old, 5'3" tall around 125 lbs. walk slowly into the Federal Period architectural building and onto the doctor's office. Once she was seated I walked over to the receptionist's counter and signed in. I was told to have a seat and wait for the doctor. Fifteen minutes later a nurse called me into the office. She motioned for me to have a seat and to explain my aunt's problems. Tired, worried and irritated with them, I became snappy in answering their questions. I explained as I had the previous day about my drive down, lack of sleep during the night and how exhausted I was. She wasn't concerned about my feelings, she didn't care. Why should they care about me when they didn't care about my aunt!

"I'm mad because you didn't see my aunt yesterday? She's a very sick lady."

"If she's th-at si-ck why di-dn't you ta-ke her to the hos-pital la-st ni-ght?" Both nurses had a *de—ep* Southern drawl.

"I told you yesterday, she wouldn't allow me to take her! She's a strong willed woman. When she says no, she means no! What kind of office are you operating here anyway that regular patients have to wait another day when they're that sick."

My temper flared and angry words spilled out. i was reminded where I was when the nurses continued their conversation in their defense. I *forgot.* I *was* in *the South!* Not in Baltimore! And my aunt was *colored!* Had she been white, they *would have* seen her. They didn't care about *her* or her health.

"How do y-ou kn-ow how si-ck she is? Are you a nur-se or do-ctor?"

"No I'm not a nurse or a doctor but I've known her all my life and I've never seen her in this condition before." My voice squeaked. Tears formed in my eyes while my body trembled. I was *soo* mad with those two women! Why didn't they understand what I was experiencing? They were nurses, or were they?

"Your au-nt is not Dr. Matts only pa-tient and if you don't li-ke the way w-e do things he-re, you can take her to a-nother doc-tor."

"With the doctor's permission I do intend to carry her back to Baltimore with me, if he thinks she can take that six hour trip."

I apologized for getting so angry with them. Again, I reminded them of my long drive down the day before, no sleep that previous night plus being very upset about my aunt's condition. They assured me that everything would be fine. It wasn't!

Soon we were asked to follow the nurse down the hall into an examining room. I helped Aunt Betty onto the white-sheeted table. Minutes later, the doctor, a tall middle aged man walked briskly into the room. The two nurses stood in the hall near the door. He greeted my aunt then stepped quickly toward me *raising* his voice as he spoke.

"I understand that you're not satisfied with my medical practices and the way I run my office!"

"I apologized to your nurses and they understood why I was so upset. I drove down from Baltimore yesterday and I didn't get any sleep last night. My aunt's breathing was terrible and I was *so* worried about her."

"You take her to another doctor!"

"I'm not carrying her anywhere! Look at her, she's a sick woman. You're her doctor, you have her medical history and I want you to care for her as you have all these years!"

We argued as Aunt Betty sat on the table and observed the feud. He leaned forward, pointed his finger in my face and yelled!

"You—you get out of my office right now!"

"Don't you talk to me like that!"

"I'll examine her, but *you* have to leave!"

"I'm not going anywhere. I have a right to stay and I'm going to stay!"

When I refused to leave he grabbed my arm and tried to *push* me out the door! My body trembled, urine ran down my thighs. I was scared, so scared! That doctor yanked my arm back and forth trying to shove me out the door. I screamed!

"Get your hands off me!"

"You get out of my office or I'll call the police!"

Suddenly my eyes shifted to Aunt Betty seated on the table watching us. I realized I was fighting a losing battle. I was in this *white* man's world where he was king and *did no wrong!* The two nurses who stood at the door wouldn't tell what he'd done to me even it he'd knocked me down on the floor! Slowly I backed off—I knew I'd lost.

"No you won't have to, I'll leave! You had no business putting your hands on me." Again urine rushed down my legs. The nurses saw the entire episode. One of them spoke to me in a low voice.

"Mrs. Albens I think you better leave."

"Yes I'll leave. I don't know what you told him about me. But whatever you said caused this confusion. He's more concerned about me than he is about my aunt!"

I *forgot* where I was. Again, I'd forgotten I was in the *South* the prejudiced biased *South* where colored people were hated by many. It was the *South's* obvious discrimination why I *lived* in the north. Dr. Matts thought he had that right to push me out that door because I had inherited that drop of black blood. No one stood in my defense. Once again my mouth, the truth, had gotten me into trouble. Once again a man resented a woman speaking up to him. Once again my truthfulness was ignored. The nurses saw the incident. Of course they'd never speak against their employer!

I left the examining room and sat in the waiting room. The doctor examined Aunt Betty. Within minutes I saw him *rush* back and forth in his office, talking *anxiously* on the phone using medical terminology about my aunt's condition!

Suddenly the doctor appeared in the hall. He looked perplexed. His voice absorbed my attention. His concern emerged in his slow but firm utterance of words directed at me.

"Mrs. Garnett has to be put in the hospital right now. I've called the emergency room. They're ready to admit her. Do you know how to get there?"

I expected what I heard. She could have died sitting on that examining table! Had he spoken kinder to me I would have left without any problem but I resented him yelling at me those incriminating words, *"You get out of he-re right now!"*

"What's wrong with my aunt, Dr. Matts?

"Her heart is failing; take her to the emergency room right now. They're waiting for her."

I drove to the hospital; they were ready. My prayers eased the anxiety as I sat alone in the waiting room eager to hear something. Later, a nurse called my name and asked me to follow her down a hall and into another wing. Aunt Betty had been admitted and placed in a private room. She was alert but didn't want to be there. I felt relieved knowing she'd get the proper attention. Before I left she asked me to take her black shoulder bag home.

"Aunt Betty it's alright, I'll just put it in the closet."

"No, I want you to carry it home."

"Okay I'll take it with me. I need to get six roach bombs to release in every room tomorrow morning before I visit you. I don't have enough money for that."

She didn't respond. She insisted I take her pocket book home so I did. Her close friend Mrs. Wright called the moment I walked in the house. I informed her that Aunt Betty had been admitted to the hospital. She agreed it should have been done days ago but Aunt Betty refused to let *anyone* carry her. I mentioned I wanted to set off roach bombs in the morning but my money was low.

"Why didn't Mrs.Garnett give you the money?"

"She said she didn't have any money."

"That's not true Dawn. Mrs.Garnett always keeps three to four hundred dollars in her pocketbook."

"*What*! Three-four hundred dollars, where is it." I said.

"She keeps it in that black pocketbook. I'll hold on while you look." I got the shoulder bag, opened it on the bed and started to search.

"I'm looking but I don't see any money."

"Keep looking. Look in all of those separate small compartments."

"I checked them all and they're empty." I said.

"Well, look behind the pockets because she hides it well. I know because I saw her digging in there one day when she was at my house."

"I found it! I found it!"

"I knew it was in there somewhere. How much is it?"

"I'm counting it now. I see one—two—three—four one-hundred-dollar bills! You mean she watched me squirm in that hospital and had four hundred dollars in her pocket book?"

"Yeah, that's Mrs. Garnett. The lady hates to spend her money."

"Yes I'm *well* aware of that. Remember she raised me. I know how tight she can be. How could she live in this room with these roaches? All that candy and cookies she kept on her night table kept them real healthy and fat."

Mrs. Wright chuckled. "Sure did. Mrs. Garnett would just laugh. You know how she laughs whenever she's enjoying herself. I'd mention it and she'd smash one with her hand every few minutes."

I thanked Mrs. Wright and went to the store. I took one bill and bought what I needed. Before leaving for the hospital the next morning, I set all six Roach Bombs. The directions stated not to ventilate for two hours, I waited over eight before returning home.

Before I left for the hospital Monday morning the phone rang.

"Hello."

"May I speak to Mrs. Albens, please?"

"Yes this is she speaking."

"This is a nurse calling from the hospital's Intensive Care Unit. Your aunt was brought in here minutes ago. We knew you'd want to come as soon as possible."

"What happened!"

"She's resting now. You'll be able to talk to her doctor after you get here."

Not sure what condition I'd find my aunt, I prayed all the way. The Intensive Care Unit was quiet as usual. I announced myself and the nurse took me to Aunt Betty's bed. I held back the tears from a strained weary body. Tubes ran everywhere as she slept!

I stared at her limp body, a body that had worked so hard in years past. A body that cared for her husband, whose leg and foot had been amputated because of diabetes. A body that attended to her home; worked in her flower and vegetable garden and cared for my sick father for the three years prior, while having the use of *only one hand.* She did everything with that one hand and *never* complained. As I left her room, I saw her doctor waiting for me several feet away. While he explained her declining condition, I broke down and cried on his shoulder. He didn't respond to my broken heart. He had no compassion for my hurt. My eyes ached from the lack of sleep and my face was drained from worry. He did manage to touch my elbow with one hand. I raised my heavy hurting head from his shoulder and returned home.

Bryan and Nardia visited Aunt Betty that evening and then brought me dinner. They'd decided to give up their apartment and move into the house and take care for her once she'd left the hospital. The few roaches I saw moved—real—slow. The bombs did a fantastic job! I intended to have everything tidy and bright when she came home. The kitchen cabinets had to be cleaned and painted to hold the vast amount of mismatched dishes, pots, pans and canned goods. The bedroom had to be stripped, painted, including the rug. Those worn out thirty-five year old stained and bumpy mattresses were ready for the *dump.* I needed money for all those repairs and replacements. There wasn't much I could do with the ten dollars I had in my wallet. My paycheck was just enough for my bills. The four hundred dollars would have to supply the finance we needed.

When I returned the next day Aunt Betty was awake and glad to see me. She couldn't talk due to the tube in her throat but she smiled, mostly with her eyes. I kissed her forehead and held her hand. She pointed toward the tube. She wanted it out!

"No, I can't take it out Aunt Betty. It's in there for a reason." Tears rolled down her smooth cheeks, as the discomfort of the tube was facially evident.

Now I realized why she hadn't gone to the hospital earlier. She'd anticipated the severity of her illness and was fearful they'd keep her. For two nights I barely slept. As I lay in bed and prayed for my aunt's healing, I also prayed to sleep all night. Exhausted, depleted of energy, I prayed for emotional and physical strength; suddenly I stopped crying. That still quiet voice said, "Look at the foot of the bed."

There at the foot of the bed was the family Bible; the large Bible, that laid on the seat of the coat rack in the hall. Now it lay on the cedar chest waiting to be read. I realized *that* was the *spiritual* power I needed. God opened my eyes, to read His Word. His Word supplied everything I needed. I lifted the heavy Bible and read passages in the New Testament. My spirit calmed. I dropped off to sleep, grateful for the inner peace with the Bible cradled in my arms. We slept together undisturbed, all night.

After visiting Aunt Betty in the hospital the next day and unbeknownst to her I'd pressed charges against her doctor for pushing and treating me the way he had. I knew nothing would happen to him but I filed a complaint anyway. South or no South he had no business pushing me, yelling and screaming at me the way he had, especially in front of my aunt and in a condition unknown to him. Two days later his office called. The doctor wanted to have a conference concerning my aunt's condition. I knew he'd been notified about my complaint. Two nurses sat in on our conference and took notes on everything I said.

During our conference I apologized for my actions caused by my extreme fatigue. I expected one from him. He gave none.

"Dr. Matts are you going to apologize to me as well?"

"Apologize for what? You caused the problem. I did nothing."

I said nothing else but shook my head in total disgust. We discussed Aunt Betty's condition then I left. Why get upset, it was in vain. That night I contacted one of my high school classmates, who'd become an attorney. I explained the problem while he listened.

"Dawn it's useless to hire me because the man is *white* and has too much clout in this town. You'd be driving back and forth to Baltimore for nothing. Besides those two nurses would stick to their word and say they saw nothing."

"I guess you're right. Thanks for the advice. I'll let you know what happens in court."

I remained in Fayetteville for ten days. During that time Bryan and I removed everything from Aunt Betty's bedroom. The dirty blue walls received two coats of white paint. The woodwork was painted salmon. The room's new look was stunning! Bryan and I removed five layers of rugs and linoleum. We cut the new linoleum outside on the lawn to fit the floor. Years of experience enabled me to measure the floor with my twenty-five foot tape and cut the new linoleum without any difficulty. We both agreed the room should have another coat of white paint.

I'd called my assistant principal and explained my aunt's condition. I also asked if she'd sign my paycheck and deposit it in my checking account because I wasn't sure what day I'd return. She agreed to help me anyway possible. She was a *jewel*!

Aunt Betty was still in Intensive Care. I needed power of attorney to handle her affairs. When I first explained to her what I needed, she frowned. The tube still in her throat disallowed any verbal response. Her eyes widened as I justified the feasibility of her giving me power of attorney. She wanted no one, not even me handling her money, everything remained secretive. I knew nothing about her Will, her insurance, her bills etc. She remained silent and divulged nothing. Years earlier I'd questioned her about her affairs.

"Gal, when I die all you have to do is call my lawyer. He has my Will and knows everything. Besides you get everything I have anyway. I don't want to talk about it anymore." We never did.

The hospital's social worker said I needed a lawyer for the procedure. Procuring a lawyer meant money. My change of clothes had run out. I fitted an old *A-line* designed purple dress of Aunt Betty's I found in her closet. It was not my taste but at least it was a change.

As I browsed the attorney's palatial office I'd hired by phone the previous day, I compared it to my plain and unattractive purple dress. The secretary's deep southern drawl reminded me how I too had acquired the same accent after living in Fayetteville for only one year.

Summer of 1948, in New York City, found me a focal point of laughter each time I spoke around Sister and her friends. The accent remained for twelve years until I married and moved to Baltimore. One of my art department's instructor's teasing was ruthless. His humiliating mocking made me determined to rid myself of that accent at any cost. I spoke faster and faster. I became more aware of conversations with others and their reaction to my speech pattern. In doing so, people often asked me where I came from. I'd created my own accent; some southern, some northern. Many people thought I was a westerner.

Mr. Bracket, the lawyer, a tall white southerner appeared in his doorway and called my name. He ushered me into his office and pointed to a seat. Possessing the same cold persona of my aunt's doctor, he reviewed the contents in the document, examined my plain inexpensive dress then asked a direct cold question.

93

"Do *you* ha-ve $50.00?" His insulting look and tone of voice was a put down.

"Yes I have $50.00 but I'll have to give you a check because my bank is in Baltimore, Maryland."

"That's al—right, as long as you ha—ve the money. Baltimore's mo—ney sp—ends too."

Days of worry showed in my face. The extensive house renovations had affected my hair. I looked the way I felt, tired and worn out. I guess it was to my advantage because the social worker had quoted an approximate attorney's fee of $100-$150. That night I retired early; determined to free my face of that drawn look. I also rolled up my hair, something I'd not done since I'd been there. The following day I returned to his office wearing one of *my* outfits and noticed his look of approval. Sad but true, clothes and hair do make a difference.

The social worker and I stood at the foot of Aunt Betty's bed. Mrs. Perot explained the contents of being the power of attorney. Aunt Betty listened with doubt and uneasiness. Usually patients weren't allowed to sign over the power of attorney while in intensive care but since my aunt was fully coherent Mrs. Perot accepted hers.

I remember Mrs. Perot's significant question.

"Do you trust Dawn to handle your money?"

My heart flipped! Aunt Betty trusted *no one* to handle *her* money! My aunt stared at me, turned her head to the left and then back toward me. Mrs. Perot explained I had to pay her bills, take care of her house etc. which required me to sign her checks, with a statement showing I had the legal authorization. She finally nodded *yes*, slowly and reluctantly. I was shocked! For the first time since I'd known my aunt she allowed *me* to share her life, her *private* life. Her little *old lady* was finally trusted. I said to her:

"Aunt Betty, *don't* worry; I'll take care of everything for you." I leaned over, kissed her on the forehead then left with Mrs. Perot.

The next few days were arduous! So much work needed to be finished before she returned home. I'd explained to her the mattresses on the twin beds needed replacing. She agreed and signed a statement from Kimball's Furniture Store where she'd been an excellent customer over thirty years. Now she had a newly painted room, new linoleum on the floor plus new linen on her new mattresses and pillows. That was something I'd been trying to do for many, *many* years. Now with her in the hospital Bryan and I were able to accomplish our labor of love, uninterrupted. The room was absolutely gorgeous! I stayed in Fayetteville ten days, until she was transferred from intensive care to a private room. During those days, I spoke to Mama often. She kept asking me, "When are you coming home Dawn? Can't somebody else do something other than you?" I tried to explain that Bryan had helped with extensive work in the house but I had to handle the business aspects. She understood but missed my visits to the nursing home.

Finally, I returned to Baltimore; to my job. My students were *soooo* pleased I was back. Someone had printed on the blackboard:

"WE'RE GLAD TO HAVE YOU BACK MRS. ALBENS, from your sixth grade students."

When they arrived to class they rallied around me like I was a celebrity! Tight hugs from my little babies lifted my spirits! They were dolls.

I remember a student asking me one day, "Why do you call us such sweet names Mrs. Albens?" I'd call them honey, baby, darling, sweetheart, doll baby, etc.

"Well aren't you sweet children?"

"Yes, Ma'am."

"Since you're sweet children, then you deserve to be called sweet names."

One day at the end of a new lesson I'd demonstrated, and before I turned around from the blackboard, that class clapped! I'd never had a class do that before. They chimed in:

"That was a *great* lesson Mrs. Albens." I couldn't believe the compliment I'd heard had come from my sixth graders. I stood dazed; amazed at their appreciation and applause. But that happiness was short lived.

34...THE END OF THE ROAD

Let me live in the house by the side of the road,
Where the race of men go by;
They are good, they are bad, they are weak, they
are strong,
Wise, foolish —— so am I.
Then why should I sit in the scorner's seat,
Or hurl a cynic's ban?
Let me live in my house by the side of the road
And be a friend to man.
Sam Walter Foss: The House by the Side of
the Road, Stanza 5

Two weeks later Bryan called. The social worker wanted to place Aunt Betty in a nursing home since she lived alone. If they did, they'd take *everything* she owned. One early November Friday morning I drove to Fayetteville once again to save her money and home. I pulled into the bank's parking lot around one p.m. Aunt Betty had saved $1000. The bank manager understood my predicament and agreed I should withdraw the money and pay off her two outstanding bills. I did. He added he'd seen too often whatever savings an ailing relative had, go to the Social Service Department and the *relatives* were left with the bills!

After greeting Nardia, now five months pregnant, I called Lawyer Stevens to inquire about her Will.

"Oh yes I remember Mrs. Garnett, how is she doing? I haven't seen her since she was in court. I believe it was a couple of years ago with an older gentleman. Was that her husband? I remember Mr. Garnett dying some years ago."

"Yes, my uncle passed over twenty years ago with diabetes. I'll never forget that sad week. My baby Marty was nine months old and couldn't be taken into Uncle Dear's hospital room. He never saw my baby. The man with Aunt Betty in court that day was my stepfather. She's not well Mr. Stevens. She's in the hospital suffering from heart failure." I explained in detail and the reason I'd called.

"Mr. Stevens she may be admitted to a nursing home. If so, they'll take everything she has."

"You're right, that's their usual procedure. However, Mrs. Garnett never made out a Will with me. Are you sure she said me?" He said.

"Oh yes! You're the only lawyer she had. For years she's talked about her great friend Lawyer Stevens. What can I do to save her property?"

"That's quite simple. I'll draw up a document that says she's selling the property to you for $1.00."

"$1.00! And what's the charge for your service?"

"Just $26.00. What time can you meet me in the hospital today?"

"You set the time, I'll be there." I answered.

We met in Aunt Betty's room at six p.m. I arrived an hour earlier to alert her I knew she didn't have a Will. Also the danger she had of losing her property if she ever went to a nursing home. The property would go to the state and not to me.

"How do you know all that?"

"I've talked to the social worker and asked her questions—indirectly. I've also called Lawyer Stevens. He told me you've never made out a Will with him."

"What *difference* does it make you'll get everything I have anyway."

"Oh no, that's not true. It does make a difference. If you're ever admitted to a nursing home, your property and your savings go to the state," she said nothing but turned her head toward the window to grasp what she'd heard.

She was delighted to see Lawyer Stevens. He'd been her attorney since she'd had that terrible accident in 1944. She signed the paper that sold me the property for $1.00. I handed the lawyer a dollar bill plus a check for $26.00, his fee.

The following days I darted in one building after another finalizing her business. Aunt Betty knew nothing. She only knew Bryan and I had cleaned the house, not redecorated! Fast food fed my overworked body as I discarded junk, in the house, day after day and painted the kitchen cabinets inside and out. The reality of this task appeared insurmountable. My prayers soared and carried me through each mental and physical chore every day. Without God

I could *not* have made it! When weariness tried to beat me down into the ground—I cried out for help.

"Oh *God* please help me! *Please, please help me!*" He did!

After everything was completed, I returned to Baltimore. Aunt Betty left the hospital a few days before Thanksgiving. That night she had Bryan call me.

"Dawn I can't believe what you've done to this room! I thought I was in a different house! I like the color of the walls and woodwork. You even changed the linoleum. Everything is *soooo* beautiful! Thank you for everything!"

"How does the new mattress feel? You slept on the other one for so long."

"It's great. Everything is just fine and the sheets are simply gorgeous!"

"I bought several sets so your room and bed would stay beautiful. Remember—I know how much you love pretty things."

"I lie in this bed and can't believe this is really my bedroom. How did you know how to do all of this work Dawn? I *really* appreciate everything you've done."

"Don't forget I'm an artist and an interior designer. It could have looked like that years ago had you given me some reign. The important thing is that you're happy and you're feeling better. I'll be down for Thanksgiving."

Two-three times a week I'd call to check on my aunt and Nardia. Nardia, five months pregnant had to be careful. Early Thanksgiving morning I packed, including the Thanksgiving dinner I'd cooked and started another trip to Fayetteville. Only the turkey had to roast in her oven. I arrived early afternoon and found the house freezing! The only heat was in Aunt Betty's bedroom. I greeted everyone then put the turkey in the oven. When Bryan came home I inquired about the lack of heat.

"The other two stoves won't work and I don't know anyone to fix them. We stay in Aunt Betty's room most of the time anyway," he said.

"But Bryan, Nardia is moving back and forth between hot and cold rooms. She could become very sick from that sudden change in temperature."

He stared at me, "My *wife* doesn't complain, so why are *you*!" His nasty side resurfaced. The amount of responsibility he had, didn't justify his rudeness.

"Don't forget to whom you are talking, young man. The cold draft isn't good for Aunt Betty either. Did you ask her about someone who could repair the stoves?"

His tone of voice lowered, "Yes I did Mommy but I've had a lot of overtime so I forgot to call anyone."

"Have you lit the large oil burner in the living room? It'll heat the entire house."

"Yes I know but it burns too much oil and it still smokes sometimes."

I called several of my aunt's friends. The following day one friend's husband brought over a stove we could use while he repaired the other two. One he repaired but the other one needed new parts. The petite white stove in the bathroom on the back porch worked, but needed oil. Often Bryan forgot to fill the tanks that fitted in back of the stoves before going to work. They were too heavy for Nardia to carry even though she did on several occasions. Therefore—the house remained cold.

Nardia *never* complained. She loved Bryan and did anything to maintain peace. But I was his mother. I knew him well. He was wrong but refused to accept the blame.

I drove home Sunday and to work Monday. One and a half weeks later I returned for my court case concerning her doctor. I spied a vacant seat at the end of the center aisle row toward the rear as soon as I entered the courtroom. Moments later I examined the head and profile of the man I sat behind, it was Dr. Matt, Aunt Betty's doctor, what an odd coincidence? The random chance seating, reminded me how Bryan and Nardia had sat behind me the year before. I recognized the man walking down the aisle toward us. It was Lawyer Stevens. As he got closer he spoke to the doctor.

"Hey, what are you doing in here?" He didn't slow his pace but continued to talk and walk never noticing me.

"It's nothing that serious." The doctor answered.

"I sure hope not."

That instant, I thought, *why didn't I call Lawyer Stevens about my problem? But then I remembered he was no longer practicing law.*

Minutes later a man leaned over me and whispered, "An attorney would like to see you in the hall."

"Me, he wants to see me, for what?"

"Just follow me please." The young man and I walked down the hall and made a left turn into a small corridor where the tall thin young attorney stood waiting for me.

"Are you Mrs. Albens?"

"Yes, I'm Mrs. Albens?"

"I'm representing Dr. Matt. I have a few questions to ask you. Is your

99

attorney with you?"

"I don't have an attorney."

"I understand that you did not leave Dr. Matt's office when he asked you to, is that true?"

I attempted to tell him how upset I was and why I didn't leave. "He was yelling at me and pointing his finger in my face. I didn't think he had the right to talk to me like that. When I tried to defend myself, he started pushing me toward the door. As I resisted, he pushed harder."

He leaned over, pointed his shaking finger in my face and said in a low but condescending voice:

"I would have pushed you too if you'd refused to leave my office! Who do you think you are pressing charges against Dr. Matt! He's a well-known person in this city. You just go on back to Baltimore *where you belong!"*

"I'm a human being just like you. He knew I hadn't slept the night before and how concerned I was about my Aunt who sat on the examining table observing everything." As I talked, he talked over me, twisting his head and mouth while still shaking his bony finger in my face. He made sure he wasn't heard by anyone walking past the end of the hall. His grotesque growling mannerisms terrified me! I realized *then* why we conversed in the most secluded corridor in the courthouse.

"Do you and Dr. Matt make it a practice treating patients and clients like this, people you disagree with and can't defend, themselves?"

He leaned over, put his face as close to mine as he could with an intimidating look and responded. "You'll *never* get in that courtroom, today or any other day! Those charges will be dropped! Now you can leave and go back to Baltimore and stay there!"

I didn't see the judge and never dropped the charges. I was a scared helpless woman, in a prejudiced Southern town with no money to hire a lawyer which would have been useless anyway. As he subdued my spirit I felt defeated. I turned with urine easing down my legs and walked slowly down the hall and outside to my car, holding back tears as hard as I could. In the car I cried nonstop thinking *if only I had had a lawyer then everything would have been different.* He'd won without ever uttering a word in court. But he still has to answer to God—in the higher court.

Reality surfaced when I recalled a conversation I'd had with Lawyer Stevens weeks earlier about becoming an attorney myself.

"Rethink your decision Dawn. Women are *not* accepted in this profession, *anywhere*. You'd have to be as hard as nails to survive, especially in the

South. I've had a hard time myself."

"A hard time; how?"

"I'm Jewish. It's taken many years for me to earn the money that other lawyers do. Clients avoided me for years and fellow attorneys only dealt with me when they had to. It has been a *long* hard road."

"Why did you stay here? Why didn't you move to another town?"

"Move where? Every town or city was the same. I'd lived in two other cities and decided I wasn't moving anymore. Eventually things improved. I really liked your aunt and uncle. They sent several clients to my office. Mr. Garnett was a fine and funny gentleman. He always found something amusing to laugh about."

Betsy (my car) and I returned to Baltimore leaving Bryan and Nardia to care for Aunt Betty. The house was in my name, her bills were paid and I had power of attorney. Everything was in order if and when she passed.

The second week in December Aunt Betty was readmitted to the hospital. Nardia, now six months pregnant, could no longer care for her. She required oxygen and assistance from bed. Thanks to God, for two weeks she'd *savored* her elegant new bedroom. She slept on a new mattress with new floral sheets without her companions, the roaches. Unknown to my aunt the hospital's social worker called suggesting I come down and make arrangements for a nursing home.

Farm and forest scenes that once excited me were unnoticed as I drove on Highway 95. Foremost in my mind were visions of my aunt in a nursing home; something *neither* of us wanted. Once again I couldn't keep a family member at home, how distressful. Now Mama and Aunt Betty would live in nursing homes against their wishes.

After I arrived at the hospital Friday afternoon, I went straight to the social worker's office. We reviewed the list of nursing homes. The one where Daddy resided was suitable; convenient for Bryan, and her friends. She also informed me Aunt Betty's assets would be assigned to the state.

"Whose name is the house in?" She said.

"It's in my name." She stared at me. In October it was in my aunt's name.

"When did that happen? I thought it was in Mrs. Garnett's name."

"In November Aunt Betty turned it over to me." She was *not* pleased. After our meeting, I visited my aunt.

"Hi gal. Where have you been! I thought you were supposed to be here earlier?"

"I was here but I had to attend to some business."

"What kind of business? Was it about me?"

"Yes it was." I disliked telling her the truth but I suspected she already knew the inevitable was approaching.

"Your social worker called me." My voice trembled as I spoke those stinging words. "You're not going back home because Nardia's unable to give you the care you need because of her pregnancy."

"So I have to go to a nursing home, right?" She said abruptly.

I lowered my eyes, embarrassed the day had arrived that both of us dreaded. Now the last member of my family would live in a nursing home against her wishes.

"Yes. I'm sooo sorry Aunt Betty. I've done the best I could but we just don't have the funds to provide you with twenty-four hour care at home. I'm *soo* sorry."

She turned her head toward the window, stared in the distance and remained silent. I knew her thoughts. Like Mama, she disliked nursing homes. I too was troubled but, with only my salary, I had no other option.

Late Sunday afternoon, I headed back to Baltimore. The further north I drove, the colder it got. It started to rain. The rain/hale mix transformed the highway into a sheet of ice. I eased into Washington, D.C. taking no chances and observed the cars closely. That treacherous trip was the worst driving condition I'd ever experienced! Traffic inched. Disabled cars, parked on both sides. Even I pulled over one time.

Uncertain of school openings the next day, I eased out and rejoined the creeping vehicles—remaining in the right lane. Stalled cars were turned in all directions, as Betsy and I crawled into Baltimore. God protected us on that sheet of ice, while my prayers filled the silence.

Schools reopened a *week* later. Each day I shoveled more and more snow; three days passed before I reached Betsy and cleaned her blue body. We were friends, Betsy and I. We'd traveled thousands of miles. We'd fought the cold, the rain, the snow and ice and the heat. She was my sanctuary. In her comfortable interior I listened to music and talked to God.

Since I'd spent Thanksgiving with Aunt Betty, I spent Christmas with Mama. The day after Christmas Aunt Betty was transferred from the hospital to the nursing home. Two days later, I returned to Fayetteville during my one-week Christmas break. Nardia and I visited Aunt Betty everyday. Bryan's workload denied him daily visits.

The second week in January I returned for a weekend visit. During those months Mama's jealousy increased.

"I don't see why you have to keep going down there. Bryan and Nardia can visit her. Who's here to visit me?"

"Mama, Aunt Betty considers me her daughter. She raised me for nine years and expects me to be there."

"Yes I know all that. But it's too hard on you to keep driving up and down that road all the time. It's just too dangerous Dawn in all this cold bad weather. She just thinks about herself and no one else."

"Yes, I know that's true, but I do have an obligation. Bryan and Nardia can't make major decisions about her care. Since her doctor dropped her as his patient after the court episode, I'll be there as often as I can."

After forty-seven years, the tug of war continued between Mama and Aunt Betty over me. Each one vied for my love, *all* of my attention. Their envy often made my life miserable. Caught in the middle, I questioned where I belonged. I shared my love between them but neither one was ever satisfied.

Aunt Betty once said, "I didn't save any money for your college education because all you're gonna' do is help your mother anyway. You ain't gonna' help me."

And Mama said, "You don't love me. You only love Mrs. Garnett! You ain't never cared nothin' for me."

Each time she'd utter those words, I'd cringe. I loved my mother. Because I didn't pity her arthritis she thought I didn't care. I avoided discussing her aches and pains. Instead I talked about her flowers, her TV shows, the children, my job and anything, except arthritis. All the years I'd known my mother I'd never heard her say one time, she had a good day. Any suggestions I offered to improve her condition were rejected.

On February 1, 1985, 12:30 a.m. the phone rang. Half awake I struggled to reach the phone.

"Hello."

"Mommy this is Bryan. I hate to wake you up so late but I have bad news. Aunt Betty di-ed a few min-utes ago."

I expected this moment. Aunt Betty ate less everyday. She said she'd lost her appetite. She also disliked being in that home. Bryan waited until my crying was under control.

"I do-n't have any mo-ney Bryan. I ha-ve to w—ait until the Credit Union opens at 7:30 to get the-the few dollars I think I have, it might be $60.00. I don't—even have the $2.00 I need for the par—king ticket after I le-ave the

Cre-dit Union. Oh we-ll, I'll get it so-me wh-ere. I'll ca-ll you when—I'm leaving."

Bryan and Nardia cared for Aunt Betty until the very end; even though she spent the last five weeks in the nursing home. I remembered my last visit with her as I sat on the foot of her bed. All attempts to comfort her had failed. Instead, in her usual humor, she made me laugh! She knew how to redirect my worry. Now at peace, she awaited death and accepted her future.

"Dawn you still have those cute little hands I always loved."

"Yes I do, and these cute little hands have worked very *very* hard."

"Well soon you won't have to work so hard, you'll have everything you ever wanted."

"Don't say things like that Aunt Betty. You're going to be here a lo-ng time."

As I talked, I remembered my stepfather's death a few years earlier in the same nursing home. Friends brought her there every day to visit him. She sat by his bed hour after hour even though he was unaware of her presence. She too remembered years past as he slept for two weeks.

I don't think he knew I was there as I stood by his bed several minutes.

"Daddy, it's Dawn, I'm here." I shook his arm gently. When his eyes finally opened, both hands quickly covered his face, as he cried softly. His soft whimpering resembled that of a child's. Aunt Betty said he cried several times a day never opening his eyes. He'd then drift off to sleep. That was the *second* time I'd seen my father cry. The first time was at Uncle Dear's funeral, twenty-two years prior.

Now I sat in the same nursing home reliving the lives and deaths of two family members whom I had loved!

35...A LIGHT THAT LEADS

Death comes to set thee free;
Oh, meet him cheerily
As thy true friend,
And all thy fears shall cease,
And in eternal peace
Thy penance end.
Boron De La Motte Fouque: Sintram and His
Companions, Pilgrim song, Stanza 3

Eight a.m., I called Aunt Lorna my dear neighbor who lived behind me. Everyone called her Aunt Lorna because she disliked her real name

"Good morning Aunt Lorna this is Dawn. I saw the family room's draperies drawn so I knew you were up."

"Up, yes indeed I've been up. You know Laddie boy won't let me rest 'til he's had his morning walk."

"Aunt Lorna I need a special favor from you. My aunt in North Carolina died at 12:15 this morning."

"I'm *sooo* sorry to hear that Dawn! I know you've made *so* many trips down there since she got sick in October."

"Yes I have, seven, to be exact. I need to borrow $2.00 until I go to the Credit Union this morning. I need it for the parking ticket. If I'd had money I'd left hours ago."

"Of course I'll let you have the money; I'll be right over."

"Oh no, no I'll come over and get it myself."

"No, you stay right there. I'm already dressed. It's no bother. I have to walk Laddie anyway. You know how he enjoys his walks. Stay put, I'll be right over."

Lad, a gorgeous adult Collie was her granddaughter Laura's dog. He and

Laura, now fourteen, had grown up together. Aunt Lorna's daughter, her only child, had died of Lupus the previous year. Since her daughter's death she stayed several days during the week caring for her son-in-law and granddaughter. Aunt Lorna was a beautiful lady with a precious love for our Lord. Seventy years old, she looked *fifty-five!*

She and Lad walked across the back yard. Her radiant smile lifted my heart as she squeezed me tightly and handed me a twenty-dollar bill!

"This is for your trip. You owe me *nothing* except to go and come back safely. Isn't this weather awful? I don't remember when I've seen so much snow piled up like this before. Will it ever melt, I wonder? You take your time "Sweet Girl," and drive carefully." She always called me her "Sweet Girl."

After I left the credit union and cashed the $60.00 check I drove to the nursing home to let Mama know about my aunt.

"Mama—Aunt Betty died early this morning."

"Mrs. Garnett died this morning?"

"Yes at 12:15. Bryan called me around 12:30. I haven't shut my eyes since. I knew she'd die soon but I wasn't prepared to hear it. I'm leaving for Fayetteville after I stop by to see Handel. He has $75 to help me with the expenses." As soon as I said leaving for Fayetteville, she jerked her head to the side.

"But Dawn tomorrow is your birthday. You won't be here for your birthday?"

She looked disappointed and spoke as she looked away. Yes tomorrow was February 2nd, my forty-seventh birthday. But I was stunned! How could she think about my birthday when the lady who'd raised me, had just died!

"I can't Mama. I told Bryan to have her body sent to Silas Sherman's Funeral Home; but nothing else can be done until I get there. I *don't* have any money as usual; so I have to wait 'til I check her insurance policy. You know how secretive she was. She never told me *anything*. She'd known Mr. Sherman over forty years. Maybe he'll work out an arrangement with me. Today is Thursday. I guess I'll have the funeral Saturday."

Mama reached under her pillow and pulled out a large pink envelope and said, "Here's your Birthday card since you *won't* be here tomorrow."

She didn't hide her hurt about me not being with her on my birthday. I opened the lovely card, she'd gotten her favorite nursing aide to buy for her, and saw a $20 bill tucked inside.

"Thank you Mama. You always have more money than I do and you're not even working. The lovely verse says exactly what you feel."

"Yes it does. I'm sorry you have to leave, Dawn. Are you sure you can't wait one more day?"

"Yes Mama I'm sure. I have to leave today."

I hugged her and kissed her cheek. Mama had never hugged or kissed me that I remembered. She wasn't an affectionate person, but wanted affection and lots of attention. I often wondered how she dealt with men.

My friend Handel's small antique shop wasn't far from the nursing home. He and Mama worried each time I traveled during hazardous weather. This was my *seventh* trip in three and a half months.

As I crossed the North Carolina state border line, I noticed a blinking light in my rear view mirror. I'd seen several cars stopped on the opposite side of the highway by patrol cars but didn't pay it much attention. I thought about Aunt Betty not the traffic. Betsy and I pulled over and stopped. The young handsome firm Afro-American Officer asked for my driver's license. He returned to his car, and asked me to follow him. After getting in his car, I started a conversation to ease my nervousness.

"Oh, I see your car is just like mine. How do you like driving this Landau?"

"It drives fine. Ma'am, do you know how fast you were traveling? I followed you several miles before I caught up with you."

"I wasn't driving that fast. I wasn't speeding."

"*Speeding*! It was hard trying to catch you. You were traveling over seventy miles an hour!"

"*Seventy miles!* No, I wasn't either, I wasn't driving that fast." The officer turned toward me and glared as he raised his voice.

"Ma'am, are you arguing with me! I saw you speeding when I was on the other side of the highway miles back!"

I cringed—and remembered this was a highway patrolman no matter how young and handsome he looked.

"Oh no *Sir*, no, no, no I'm not arguing with you."

How could I know the accurate speed, when the speedometer was broken? Of course I didn't mention it. I'd planned to have it repaired my next pay. Until then I guessed my speed. I knew I wasn't doing seventy but couldn't disagree? I calmed down and explained the purpose of my trip and why I was trying to get there before the next snowstorm.

"I haven't heard about a snowstorm heading this way."

"Well it is. It was announced on the news this morning. I left Baltimore with plenty of snow piled ten feet high in some places. Look, I still have snow on my boots if you don't believe me. I'm going to Fayetteville to bury my aunt who died early this morning. Call this telephone number at Sherman's Funeral Home. They'll tell you."

"Oh I believe you Ma'am. It's just that if you don't slow down, your children will be preparing for *your* funeral!"

"I understand. I'll drive slower. Have you ever been to Fayetteville?"

"Yes, I've been to Fayetteville."

"Ohhhh, then you've heard of E. E. Smith High School, my Alma Mater. I'd lived in Fayetteville for nine years before attending A&T College and then moving to Baltimore."

The officer avoided conversation as he wrote his ticket and looked up at me from time to time. I shared my aunt's recent death and the many times I'd traveled Highway 95 since October.

"Ma'am, I'm going to give you a warning ticket this time if you promise *not* to drive over sixty-three miles an hour and stay on the right side of the highway." My heart leapt with gladness!

"Yes sir, I promise! Thank you!" I kept my promise and thanked God for helping me through *another* ordeal. After that my foot remained *light* on the accelerator.

Once I entered Fayetteville's city limits, I drove straight to the funeral home. Mr. Sherman watched as I strolled over to the brown casket displayed in a private room. I stared down at a body now resting in peace. Her soul was in heaven with her husband, my father, her parents, family and friends. She didn't resemble herself. She looked better. The last three years had taken its toll. She'd lost *so* much weight caring for my father. Using only one arm to care for Daddy was a tremendous strain on her. Aunt Betty had persuaded Daddy to leave New York after he retired and move with her since both of them were alone. Mainly, she wanted his money, for *things* she didn't need.

Mr. Sherman and I sat in his office and recently built funeral home. I changed the casket to white, and trimmed with gold. He reminded me to bring the items, Bryan had forgotten. Finally he approached the topic I feared the most, payment. I suggested paying on time.

"No, I couldn't do that! I don't know you that well!"

"But you were friends with my aunt and uncle over *forty* years Mr. Sherman."

Exhausted, embarrassed and distressed, I refused to discuss finances at that moment. I hadn't slept for eighteen hours. I'd driven over six hours half-awake in and out of falling snow, almost gotten a speeding ticket and now he told me he needed all the money right now! I rose slowly from the chair, too weary and too hungry to contest his decision.

"Mr. Sherman I'm going home now to get the other things you need for Aunt Betty. When I return I know you will have solved our problem, since you've been in this business over forty years."

Nardia now seven months pregnant was elated to see me. She needed no additional stress. Bryan was still working at Domino's Pizza. I returned to the funeral home. Mr. Sherman had made arrangements with the First Union Bank to co-sign a loan for me to pay the funeral expenses the following Monday morning after the funeral.

"I knew you'd think of something because you're such a *gooood—* entrepreneur."

I could have said shrewd and stingy; but I didn't. It was a well-known fact, he *overcharged* for everything. The funeral was scheduled for Saturday. We finalized the paper work then drove to the cemetery, the *colored cemetery,* the unkempt cemetery to locate Dear's or Daddy's burial plot. We found neither. Records of the burial plots were unavailable. For half an hour we walked back and forth on the cemetery grounds; in and out the small dismal cemetery office in *cold* rainy weather trying to find at least one plot. We found nothing. Neither one had a monument.

The small umbrella I held over my head was useless. Rough winds blew it wrong side up and almost snatched it away. As rain poured I waded through puddles of water without boots and sloshed from one side of the cemetery to the other. We passed monuments that leaned, while others stood tall as I started sneezing.

The attendant apologized for not being able to locate the gravesites. We returned to his office. I paid $171 for Aunt Betty's plot, knowing next week she'd have a monument on *her* gravesite. No one would have to battle bad weather looking for *her* memorial marker. As soon as I returned to Baltimore, I promised to contact the Woodlawn Cemetery near my home and get a family plot in case something happened to Mama. I didn't intend to experience again what I had encountered that dismal day.

We left the cemetery. Mr. Sherman drove to an impressive floral shop where I ordered a casket spray of red roses. Of course the cost was added to my existing bill with Mr. Sherman to be paid on Monday. Aunt Betty *loved* flowers, any kind was fine, but *roses* were her favorite, red roses. The casket I had admired most and wanted to get was encircled with roses at the top and bottom edges, but exceeded my budget.

Mrs. Redmond came to the house everyday after my aunt's death. She and friends brought food and other items to help us through that stressful time. Again it was a lot for one person to handle. But as usual I turned to my God for help. I called Aunt Betty's friends in New York but many had passed. I called her nephew in East Orange, N.J. and her niece in Cheraw, S.C., both attended the funeral. Even Lawyer Stevens came. He'd seen the death announcement in the Obituary Section of the newspaper. The following day several of my former high school teachers came to visit. They too had seen the announcement and connected her name with mine.

The small intimate funeral was held in the funeral home's chapel. It was well attended considering the few friends who remained alive. Several people came forward to pay their respects. Aunt Betty had lost all contact with her church. The Haymount Presbyterian Church had relocated to a new site. I doubted if anyone knew she existed. Her best friend advised me not to have the funeral there because the few people attending would be swallowed up by the church's large interior. I followed her advice but later wished I'd seen the pastor anyway. Everything was done in such a hurry—at times I couldn't think.

Lawyer Stevens came forward and paid his respects.

"Dawn, people down here aren't used to seeing *red roses* used for a casket spray. On that white and gold casket they are stunning! You've really put your aunt away *royally*."

"I loved her Lawyer Stevens. She raised me to have good taste. Besides she deserved to have a beautiful funeral. I gave my sister, who lived in New York, a lovely funeral also but of course when she passed, I couldn't afford roses."

"It's good to hear you say that Dawn. Most children, who move north, and return to bury a relative, spend as little as possible on their loved ones."

"That's sad. I'm glad I'm not like that."

Monday after we made the bank loan, Mr. Sherman treated me to lunch. I guess he'd figured that was the least he could do after overcharging me for everything. During our lunch he had the *nerve* to make a pass! I reasoned *this is why he asked me to have lunch with him?*

He lived at the funeral home because his wife had put him out! She no longer tolerated his open adulterous affairs, flaunted in her face. She continued working for the business as they lived separate lives. In his earlier years he was a tall striking man. Now he'd changed! Rich and handsome was all he needed to turn the heads of women in former years.

I returned to Baltimore with a terrible cold! Bryan rented a house with central heat and air conditioning because her house had neither. In the south many homes still used oil stoves, window fans, or window air conditioners. Bryan checked the house daily. He cleaned and removed unneeded items as often as he could, depending on his working schedule.

Baltimore greeted me with piles of snow and freezing temperatures. Distraught over the past days, I attended various movie theatres for three consecutive days, alone. The movies and restaurants meant nothing; only an attempt to soften my hurt. I saw six films, ate out and got home as late as possible. All three movies consumed my thoughts. Every night I cried myself to sleep.

The first evening I saw an eight Academy Award movie winner, *Amadeus.* For 158 minutes Mozart's incredible music and actions replaced my sorrow; if only temporarily. Three people sat in the theatre including myself. When I stepped outside, the cold weather attacked my face like needles piercing my skin! I believed we must have been the only three weird souls out at 11:00 p.m. in those freezing temperatures going home from a movie. After my three-day *pity party* I visited Mama. Unaware I was back her face beamed when I stepped over the threshold.

"Hi Mama, I'm back? Did you miss me? I leaned over and kissed her cheek."

"When did you get *back?*"

"Thr-ee da-ys ago."

She couldn't comprehend the torment I'd experienced since leaving Baltimore; the pain I felt? It was I who loved Aunt Betty, not she. It was I who ached, not she. It was I who was drained, mentally, physically and emotionally, not she. She'd never understand my agony.

"Where have you been Dawn since you got back? Why didn't you call me? I've been *so* worried."

"I know you have Mama, but I've been hurting, *really hurting.* I just didn't feel like talking to anyone about the problems I've been through these past few days. I decided to see you when I felt better."

"I guess you have been through a lot. How long have you had that terrible cold?"

"Since the first day I got there. It poured down rain the entire time I was walking in the rain without any boots on. Mr. Sherman, the cemetery attendant and I searched the grounds for Dear and Daddy's monuments. We never found them."

"Well you could have called and left a message at the desk."

"I'm sorry Mama I just couldn't talk to anyone. I haven't seen or talked to Handel either. No one knows I'm back, not even my job." Again she had that somber look and turned her head away.

"I brought you a television to put on your night stand. Now you can watch your own private shows." She turned her head slightly.

"Isn't that the same television Mrs.Garnett used to have in her kitchen?"

"Yes ma'am it is." She stared at the TV then jerked her head away. She didn't want it. Why, it had belonged to Aunt Betty. Even death had not resolved their feud. It lingered like blood stains on a rug, unseen but never gone.

Bryan persuaded me to rent Aunt Betty's house when a guy on his job said his mother needed a place to live, immediately. He explained my aunt's passing; that the old frame house needed some repairs, the bathroom was on the back porch, and it required oil heaters. The lady saw the house and was more than satisfied. Bryan suggested $150 per month for rent. I agreed. It would cover the monthly note to bank for the $5000 loan I'd made.

My students were as happy to see me as I was to see them. The days weren't too bad, but the nights hurt. Living alone allowed me too much time to think. I visited Mama every other day but she wasn't her usual self. Two weeks after my aunt's death the nursing home called my school and asked to speak to me.

"Mrs. Albens, your mother refuses to eat or take her medicine. She says she doesn't want to live anymore. We've rushed her to the hospital.

"What hospital? I'll be right there!"

When I arrived at the hospital, Mama was being rolled down the hall into the emergency room. I rushed over; walked alongside the rolling bed while the attendants pushed it down the corridor.

"What's wrong Mama? Why won't you eat or take your medicine." I rubbed her forehead gently.

"I'm tired. What's the use anyway? I'm not getting any better, so why bother eating and taking medicine. It ain't helping none."

As they rushed her into the emergency room, I stood in the hall stunned! I prayed, "Oh, my Dear God *please* don't take my mother too!"

Alone again: no sisters, brothers, aunts, uncles, cousins I had to share my pain. Only two sons: one in Oklahoma and the one in North Carolina. I sat in the waiting room among other dismal faces waiting to hear news about our loved ones. I prayed for Mama's quick recovery.

Soon a nurse appeared and motioned for me to follow her into the intensive care unit. Tubes were everywhere. They ran from Mama's body to the heart monitor. Dear God I thought, I just have one family member left, please don't take Mama yet. I stood close to the bed rubbing her twisted arthritic hand as her weak eyes stared into mine.

"Dawn—you've been—a good daughter—to me. I want you—to know—how proud I am of you—and how you sent—yourself to school. You've done—so much for me—and everybody else." That was the *first time* my mother had *ever* mentioned how proud she was of me.

"I knew how you felt, Mama. Don't talk anymore, just get some rest." She soon drifted off to sleep. I left her bedside and went to the waiting room until her doctor appeared.

"Mrs. Albens your mother is resting and her signs are very good. I see no reason for you to stay any longer if you have something you need to do."

I did. I peeked in on Mama. She looked so peaceful, as she slept. The monitors revealed her vital signs were normal.

My car had a serious problem. I left the hospital and drove to the shop and let it remain over night. Handel came and drove me home. But first I went to the Woodlawn Cemetery. I'd neglected to order a burial plot as I said when I returned. Visiting another cemetery was too soon; the reason I procrastinated.

I signed the application and paid the $25 deposit on the $1,400 plot. After the check had cleared, only monthly payments of $25 were required.

At 9:00 p.m., I called the hospital. The nurse said Mama had had a few complications but it wasn't anything to worry about. I called Handel; he wasn't home. I called a taxi. As I waited on the taxi I called Bryan and explained Mama's condition. He said he'd see me the following day. Bryan was Mama's *heart*. She'd raised him and had spoiled him since his birth. He *loved and respected* his grandmother!

Marty, stationed at Tinker Air Force Base in Oklahoma, had to wait for payday, two days later.

"Marty your grandmother may not live three-four days. Can't you borrow money from someone and pay it back later?"

"Mom the few friends I have are in my predicament, we're all broke. This is the service. No one has any money near payday, especially if they're married."

I sighed and thought *you don't have to be in the service to be broke. I stayed broke. The house and the car were my albatross.*

"We—ll come when you can. Make sure you call me before you leave."

"I will and you try not to worry too much Mom, things will be alright. Have you called Bryan yet?"

"Yes I have, he'll be here tomorrow."

When I arrived at Bon Secures Hospital that night, Mama was awake. As we talked I noticed her eyes were a dull yellowish color.

"How do you feel Mama?"

"I feel a *lot* better. I just want to get well." Her voice was stronger and she appeared to be more alert.

"You will Mama, you will."

I sat in the adjoining waiting room and prayed. Ten minutes later the chaplain came to comfort me. I told him that God was first in my life. Pleased to know I was a devout Christian, he soon left to help others who didn't have God as their main source of strength. I remained all night in a most uncomfortable chair. A nurse brought me a blanket and a pillow, but I still couldn't sleep. Around 7:00 a.m. the doctor walked in.

"Mrs. Albens your mother is doing a *lot* better! You can go to work if you want to. There's no reason for you to stay here all day unless you just want to."

"Are you *sure* she's getting better?"

"The machines that monitor her vital signs indicate that she is doing fine."

"Well—if you think it's alright—I'll call someone to come and get me." I watched Mama as she slept, her breathing was normal. Everything appeared natural just as her doctor said. My assistant principal knew of Mama's illness because I'd left school early two days prior when she was taken to the hospital. My students were concerned about Mama being hospitalized. I refuted the worry and tried to concentrate on my job. About an hour before school ended that day, Mrs. Spendoll appeared at my door.

"Mrs. Albens you have an important phone call." I rushed to the main office.

"Hello, this is Mrs. Albens." The voice on the other end spoke hesitantly, with a stutter.

"Mrs. Albens this is Doc—tor Young, you—r mother's doctor. Your mother has had a heart attack. I did eve—rything I could."

"Mama had a *heart* attack? I'll be right there." I hung up the phone and couldn't stop crying. Mrs. Spendoll grabbed me and comforted me. She asked if I wanted her to drive me to the hospital. I said no.

As I drove *all the way* across the city I kept prayed.

"God please take care of my mother. Please let her get well. Please don't let her have another heart attack."

I parked the car after finding a vacant space, scurried to the building, through the lobby, then onto an elevator. When I got to the Intensive Care Unit I didn't look for anyone but walked straight toward Mama's bed, which was surrounded with a curtain. I moved slowly around the privacy curtain. The room was unusually quiet. I saw and heard no one. There she lay, a human body silenced, her soul passed on to God. Her eyes were closed. Trickled blood from the corner of her mouth had dried. However it didn't mar the sweet peaceful smile on her face. Without crying I moved closer and stared down into her face. Without a *doubt* I knew she was with God. Her pains were gone. Now she rested in peace with family and friends.

As I stood there I realized I'd misinterpreted the doctor's statement. When he said, "I did everything I could," I should have known Mama had died but that thought never crossed my mind. I cried softly as I thanked God for taking her home to be with Him. Seconds later a nurse walked in.

"I didn't know you were here Mrs. Albens." She stared at the dried blood. "I'm so sorry you weren't supposed to see that. They forgot to clean her mouth." She cleaned it herself.

"That's alright. It won't bring her back, will it?" As a Christian Scientist I was taught not to acknowledge the corpse but to know the soul had gone to God.

"You can touch her if you want to. Her body's still warm." The nurse said.

My fingers ran over her soft gray silky hair that always refused to hold a curl. I touched her face, her smooth satiny skin and wept. She'd never used anything on her face and now it was as radiant as ever. While I spoke and cried softly, Bryan appeared at the foot of her bed. He'd arrived earlier but had gone to the lavatory to cry in private. He put his arms around my shoulders as I cried gently on his.

"When did you get here Bryan?"

"Just a few minutes after she died."

I recalled how he and Nardia had taken care of Aunt Betty weeks earlier and watched her die—day by day. Now he faced death again, two weeks later. The nurse reappeared.

"Mrs. Albens, who will be handling your mother's funeral?"

"Marshall's—Funeral—Home—Bryan—would you call them, the one on North Avenue, and ask them—to take care—of everything. God bless you for coming right away. I don't know what to do next. I'm all confused. Let me sit down a minute—and get myself together."

The following day I met with Mr. Marshall the owner of the Funeral Home and finalized the arrangements. In selecting a casket I was able to get Mama the same one I'd seen in Fayetteville, with the roses around the top and bottom edges for a *$1000* cheaper! I increased my credit union loan to bury my mother. She had a small $1,500 policy but not enough to cover everything. I reflected a moment—*at least I don't have to pay the $1,400 for the interment* since I'd obtained that plan last week.

Once home, Bryan notified my friends of my mother's passing. I drove to the cemetery to make the burial arrangements.

"My mother has died and I'd like to make arrangements for the opening of the burial site." The secretary eyed me strangely before revealing her thoughts.

"Mrs. Albens I'm afraid you'll have to pay the entire amount, $1,400. Your check hasn't cleared. It's only been two or three days."

Exhausted, still in shock I felt warm tears roll down my face. I explained to the secretary I'd just buried my aunt two weeks earlier and I didn't have all of the money.

"I understand your position but there is nothing I can do about our policy. We must have the entire amount before preparation of the ground can begin. The policy isn't in force at this time."

I thanked the secretary and said I'd return later. As I drove downtown to the credit union, my dependable finance helper, I prayed to get what I needed. Had I gone to the cemetery as soon as I returned from Fayetteville, I wouldn't have needed the entire $1,400 but only a monthly payment of $25. But it *never crossed my mind* that Mama would die, especially *two weeks* after Aunt Betty's death!

The time I sat and waited to be called by a loan officer helped break the *rushed* cycle of the past few days. I reflected on the past four months of illness, deaths and despair. Upon completion of the loan application, I drove uptown to my three co-signers' homes and then back downtown and turned in the form. I deposited the check the next day.

I ordered a monument that was paid off three months later. Mama's plot was near a stream of water that flowed into a lake, where ducks walked and swam, where flowers bloomed from spring to fall. She'd loved the setting, mainly the color spectrum of flourishing plants. Woodland was a huge, beautiful well-maintained resting place.

Rev. Darius Mears presided over the service in the funeral home's chapel. During the Wake, I cried non-stop. I kept thinking *Mama you're gone and I still don't know who my real father is. How could you do this to me? Who am I? I have no knowledge of my father's family. Maybe I have sisters, brothers, aunts, uncles, cousins, grandparents existing somewhere.* Years of hurt and disappointment escaped through those tears. I also cried for Aunt Betty's death, two weeks earlier. Two deaths in two weeks; the *last* of my family!

Rev. Mears started his sermon. He and his wife had been friends of mine for several years but I'd never heard him preach. My crying eased, as my eyes, ears and mind concentrated on Darius' sermon. I thought, *Darius can really preach. Why haven't I heard him preach in all the years we've known each other?*

Surprisingly, the *only* flowers at the funeral were the miniature pink and white roses painted on Mama's casket and my pink rose casket spray. My friends gave me money, totaling $350 rather than sending flowers. They understood my financial situation. As friends, Rev. and Mrs. Mears accepted no money for their services.

I'd met the Mears through my friend Vallis. She recommended me to them to make their draperies. They lived in a huge house on a quiet street in a Jewish neighborhood. From the time I met the Mears we hit it off. Darius loved art, antiques, house restoration and decorating. He kept me laughing!

They gave me free reign in most decisions for their draperies. His wife, Carol, was the most patient person I've ever known. She embraced her husband's unusual personality. I didn't understand how she accepted his spontaneous and unplanned decisions. His keen eager mind had him buying and selling antiques almost daily. I'd visit them one day, admire an old dining room set and the next day, Darius would have sold it and bought something else. He spoke as quickly as he thought and acted. His reactions to situations were most comical. He was one of the funniest persons I'd ever known!

Besides the Mears' own church and school, they had two more churches: one in England and one in Florida. At one point they sold their home and moved to Africa for a year, returned to America, then traveled west for various Christian workshops. He had no apprehension about getting up, moving on and doing what he wanted to do. His trust was always in the Lord.

They had one son.

After the service ended I told him how much I enjoyed his sermon.

"Darius, or should I say Rev. Mears you *really are* a preacher, an excellent preacher. In all these years we've known each other, this was the first time I've heard you preach."

"Thank you Dawn. It's all from the Lord."

His 6' frame looked down into my face as if to say, "I've invited you to my Church many times but you've never come."

Marty and his family arrived the day before the funeral. The six of us including Mr. Heeth rode in the family car that followed the hearse. It was indeed a gorgeous February day. Coats weren't needed. As we approached the burial plot the ducks spread their lofty white wings and lifted toward the sky, leaving the grounds to us. They landed on the calm lake at the bottom of the embankment. What a beautiful spring day it was for Mama's funeral. Cold temperatures returned the next day.

Friends came to the house after the funeral. Mr. Heeth, our family friend busied himself in the kitchen. He was an excellent cook and didn't mind helping. He *loved* my mother and used to call her Mama as I did. Whenever he visited they'd talk for hours. Mama loved him best when he brought turtles he'd caught near the marina where his boat was docked.

My family had disappeared. They weren't available to assist in serving the food. Since no one volunteered to help Mr. Heeth, I started placing items on the table. One friend remarked.

"Dawn you're not supposed to be doing that."

"I know, but no one else is doing it and Mr. Heeth needs help." She didn't offer to help. No one did.

After a few minutes I sat down and let the company help themselves. I was *worn out; totally exhausted*! Earlier that morning I'd set the table as I had for Mama's annual birthday parties: a lovely tablecloth, sterling silver candelabras, my best China, sterling flatware, stemware and cloth napkins. That was her *Going Home Party*.

After the guests left my family reappeared. I cleared the table, put away the food, washed the dishes and cleaned the kitchen. Nardia, over seven months pregnant, arrived the day before the funeral, *unexpectedly*. Dubious, why Bryan had to attend the funeral, she traveled almost 400 miles on a Greyhound Bus to the man she loved but did *not* trust. A male friend of my sons who'd paid his respects invited them to go *out*. Nardia and Renata, overly jealous of their husbands, *objected*!

With drained eyeballs, feet and body, I flopped down on the white antique sofa in the living room and listened as wives protested being left alone. Marty and Bryan, now on the porch, were ready to leave. Renata followed. Nardia stayed inside. Minutes later, loud foul language exploded between Marty and his wife. As they pushed and shoved each other, I rushed to the porch!

"*Look*, my mother was just buried today! *Don't* you two have any respect! Stop all that cursing; and *no* fighting! Do what you like in Oklahoma, but *not* in my home!" They tried to explain but I refused to listen.

"Either you stop this now or go somewhere else to fight and argue. How *dare* you act like this after I just buried Mama!"

They stopped. The men left; the women remained. I climbed the steps to my bedroom and fell into bed half dressed. My family left a few days later. Peace and quiet resumed! In silence I realized *throughout my life Mama and Aunt Betty entangled me in a Tug of War. The same mania occurred when they died two weeks apart.*

Sunday, the next day, I attended my church, but sat in the hall. Only three church members had shown for Mama's funeral; no one came to my home. I was *so hurt*! I felt abandoned by my church members! I never returned again.

Instead, I attended and finally joined a Pentecostal Church near my home. The new service was directly opposite what I'd been used to, however I felt God's presence and soon adjusted to their vocal approach in serving God. For two weeks I wore black to school everyday. An observant student questioned my attire.

"Mrs. Albens, why do you wear black everyday?"

"I wear it to respect the deaths of my family."

"My mother said that was the reason but I just wanted to make sure."

Bad nerves, saddened spirits influenced my negative reactions toward mischievous students. The first few days back weren't so bad. But soon I sent more students to the main office. The assistant principal, Mr. Green placed a note in my mailbox. He'd requested we meet with the principal, Mr. Todder. Already disgusted with the man for having a meeting, I held nothing back during our conference.

"Mrs. Albens, Mr. Green has brought to my attention that you are sending too many students to the office."

"Yes I have. Since my family's deaths, my patience *is* short. I sleep little

119

at night, so I'm tired the next day. Mr. Green didn't experience burying his last two relatives, two weeks apart plus making all the arrangements and financial expenses."

"I think you need to see a doctor, Ms. Albens if your nerves are that bad." Mr. Green said.

Mr. Green's statement was cruel and sarcastic. He shook his head frantically and stared at me as though I were a maladjusted person

"No, I haven't seen a doctor because I don't need medicine." I said.

"Well you must do something about those bad nerves of yours."

I spoke to my principal rather than answer him. "Mr. Todder, in the past weeks I've buried the last two members of my family. I'd think Mr. Green would be more understanding had this happened to him or his wife!" By this time my voice had escalated.

"I've never seen a human being as insensitive as he! I've made *seven* trips to North Carolina since October to care for my aunt. And now two weeks after her death, my mother dies. How much does he think I can take?"

Mr. Green attempted to defend himself in a softer voice.

"Mrs. Albens, why don't you take some time off?"

"More time? I've already missed sixteen days. I can't afford to miss anymore. Besides my students need me and I don't want to sit home day and night feeling sorry for myself!

"I also noticed Mr. Shaw was welcomed back after the death of his mother on the intercom this morning. Why wasn't I treated the same way? Nothing was placed in the bulletin about my mother's death. I do a *lot* of extra work for this school, Mr. Todder. The least the *school* can do is acknowledge my return. *I've buried two family members in two weeks!!* Think how awesome that has been for me without any financial or moral help. In two weeks I've borrowed $7,000 to cover funeral costs. I think I *deserve* to be a little upset, *don't you!* I live alone. I must endure the problems of my job and then go home and grieve."

Now my principal, Mr. Todder tried to defend himself.

"Mrs. Albens I thought it was common knowledge about your mother's death."

"Not so. It's only common knowledge if everyone knows, and everyone didn't know. A teacher asked me yesterday, where I had been? When I told her about my aunt and mother's death, she was shocked that the deaths hadn't been *placed* in our school bulletin! Since a couple staff members attended the services, I assumed the school had been told."

Mr. Green avoided me in the future. After lunch that day a teacher's aide came to my room.

"Mrs. Albens, Mr. Todder wants to see you in his office. I'll watch your class."

When I entered the main office I saw a huge majestic arrangement of flowers on the secretary's desk.

"Mrs. Albens these flowers are for you. I *apologize* for the oversight from the office. Will you accept our apology?" Mr. Todder spoke in a slow—sincere tone.

I stood speechless! Not since Theon sent that one dozen roses to me at my former school had I been so overwhelmed! I'm sure he discussed our heated conversation with the assistant principal, who confirmed my hurt and feelings of neglect were *absolutely* justified.

"Yes I accept your apology. Thank you for the gorgeous flowers. You have *certainly* brightened my day."

He handed me the vase of brilliant blossoms; I inhaled its aromatic fragrance and floated to my classroom. The teacher's aide smiled as she left; she'd known all along.

The Bible verse, *"You have not because you ask not,"* appeared before my eyes. I hadn't asked for flowers but for consideration and respect. I got *both*. The adage, *"Evil flourishes when good men do nothing,"* also surfaced.

My honesty and outspoken personality were admired by few. Perhaps my lack of tact might have offended several people but the truth is the truth no matter how it's spoken. Wrong is wrong; right is right. I stood up for what I believed was right, whenever I was wronged.

During spring break I drove to Fayetteville. Briana, my second granddaughter was born on April 4, 1985. Bryan, a new father, beamed with pride! He loved children. I knew he'd make a good father. Ever since he was young; he always played with and watched out for smaller children. I also met Mrs. Grimes, the lady who'd rented Aunt Betty's house. She'd been living there over six weeks. By now she'd made the necessary adjustments, I thought.

36...ANOTHER PHASE, ANOTHER MOVE

We are not weak if we make a proper use of
those means which the God of Nature has placed
in our power...
The battle, sir, is not to the strong alone;
it is to the vigilant, the active, the brave.
Patrick Henry: Speech in Virginia Convention
Ibid

Months passed before Mrs. Grimes complained about sewage backup in
the toilet. I paid for the septic tank's cleaning. The problem improved but
soon returned. I stopped her rent for two months until she relocated.
Replacing that septic tank would have cost me a fortune; money I did *not*
have!

Bryan checked the house often. Human traffic flow meant it wasn't
abandoned. After a scrupulous cleaning, it was up for Sale. Before an offer
was made Bryan decided to open his *own* Domino Pizza business.

A year after my aunt's death, I drove to Fayetteville again, only this time
I mortgaged the house for $25,000 to help finance Bryan's business. A big,
big, *Big mistake!!* He'd never asked me. I thought of it *all by my little self!*
Lists of people waited to pay the $20,000 franchise fee for partnership. But
now we'd keep the money in the family. The additional $5,000 helped with
living and traveling expenses while he searched for the right location.

Beverly, my apartment tenant was moving closer to her job. Bryan and his
family would occupy the apartment, rent-free again.

They packed Aunt Betty's furniture in a U-Haul-It attached to the rear of
his old car. I trailed them in mine. He drove too fast, pulling a trailer packed
with heavy furniture. During a rest stop I pleaded with him to slow down.

"Ah, my car is *just* fine. You *worry* too much, Mommy. Old cars can haul trailers better than yours."

"Mom I've been telling him to slow down but he wants to get there before dark. He won't listen." Nardia said.

"Yes, I know what I'm doing, *I'm the Man!*"

"That's not the point Bryan. It's too much stuff in that trailer for your car to be pulling on this highway."

"Let me handle this Mommy. I rebuilt this car. I *know* what it can take. You and Nardia worry too much," he said.

"Alright, *Mr.* Bryan, it's your car, have it your way. You never listen to anybody anyway."

He thought as a typical man. "What did women know about cars?" I knew enough to see it was headed for trouble, *serious* trouble.

Two hours outside of Fayetteville Bryan turned off at an exit. His tired, worn out car crept into the service station as steam *spurted* from under the hood!

The attendant raised the hood carefully and waited for the steam to escape. I watched Bryan's sunken expression. He avoided my look. *Three* hours later plus $327, we left. Thereafter he maintained a sensible speed. I thought *some people never learn until it's too late.* Once again, Bryan did it *his* way.

When we arrived home Beverly was still loading her truck. Parked on the adjacent road, we waited and waited and waited! Still owing a month's rent, she left. Three months after my persistent calls, she finally paid.

"Dawn I'm sorry it took so long to pay you the $400 I owed. You were *such* a good landlady. I didn't want to leave with any hard feelings."

She revealed she wasn't as satisfied with her new apartment as she had anticipated and realized how fortunate she'd been renting from me. I knew I'd been fair, that's why I persisted in *calling* for my money. Bryan's friends continued to check on the house in Fayetteville and maintained the yard at my expense.

One Friday evening Nardia and I attended a Mary Kay Show given by one of my friends. So impressed with the cosmetics, she booked a show of her own. At her show held in my dining room she decided to become a representative. Skeptical about his wife working, Bryan took Nardia to the meetings when he wasn't on the road looking for a business location. She yearned to earn her own money. She signed up. Bryan paid the $300 for her starter kit. I gave her first booking. My friends came, making her first show a great success. Bryan didn't mind her first few shows but later complained about taking care of the baby when she wasn't home.

"A wife should be home with her baby, not running around from house to house at night." He protested so much she stopped. I often felt he thought she just might surpass him in her business. She had started to earn her *own* money.

Bryan's numerous trips to New York, New Jersey and other states searching for a suitable business location put a terrible strain on his old car. Compounded problems influenced his search for a new vehicle. He found the car, a dazzling burgundy sports car, one of the hottest on the road, an I-ROC. His negative credit rating kept him from purchasing the car without a co-signer. His father said *No!* A *smart, smart* man! So I co-signed, a decision I *lived* to regret! He used $3600 of his $5000 expense money as a down payment.

After two months of location disappointments, he quit looking and took a job offer as manager to open a brand new Domino Pizza in Pasadena, Md. By *that* time the $25,000 had *decreased!* Paying $500 bank loan, $360 car payment plus $136 for car extras totaled $996 a month. In three months he'd spent over $6600 just on the car and the bank loan payments. His traveling and living expenses also weakened the till. I agreed with him, to take the management position. I took $5000 of the remaining balance and paid off some bills.

Later he and Nardia rented an apartment in Pasadena, closer to his job, for $600 a month. Nardia stayed home with the baby. Bryan worked 31 consecutive days without a day off to get that store opened on schedule. Before the store's official grand opening, Nardia left Bryan and returned to Fayetteville. She was tired of being alone.

She said often, "When he *is* home he sleeps all of the time. He never spends any time with us Mom. I understand what he's trying to do, but I'm by myself most of the time."

Bryan explained that all his hard work was for her and their daughter; in the future he'd have more time. Young and lonely, she missed her family. Thai people very family-oriented, *always* helped family and friends. She loved her family but knew no one in Baltimore.

Weeks later, she returned. They smoothed out their domestic problems but she still remained lonely.

"Mom, I get tired of staying in this apartment everyday. When Bryan *is* home, all he does is sleep."

"Nardia he's tired. He doesn't get home until four, five or sometimes six in the morning. I've talked to him about taking you out but he says he's too tired to go anywhere and when he has that one day off he just wants to be home with you and the baby."

"Yes I know all that, but what about me. When am I to have any fun? I'm tired of this apartment. One day when he comes home I won't be here. Briana and I will be in Fayetteville with my family." She left again, but returned two weeks later. This travesty of little time spent together had no end.

Bryan began hanging out in our large city park with his buddies on Sunday afternoons; time he could have spent with his family. His excuse was selfish as usual.

"Mommy I work hard all week; why can't I have some time to myself?"

"What about your store? You're the manager. Who takes care of it when you're in the park?"

"Oh, I have *everything* under control."

"Is that right?"

"Yeah that's right. I've trained my personnel well. They know exactly what to do when I'm not there."

"Yes Bryan I know that, but what about your family?"

"Like I *saaaid*—I need time to myself!" His attitude had changed. The *chip,* large as a boulder, perched on his shoulder had no intentions of moving. Whenever he came to my house to wash his I-ROC in the driveway, he parked behind my car. Every time I asked him the same question.

"Bryan why didn't you wash my car when you finished, washing yours?"

"I didn't have time. *Look* Mommy, I'm in a hurry, gotta' get back to work. I'm a *working* man you know. Come on Ace, let's go. Let's get outta' here!"

He'd leave, with his friend whom he'd recently hired, weighted down with that monstrous chip on his shoulder having forgotten who helped get him that car in the *first* place. Before he and Nardia moved to their apartment in Pasadena, he allowed Harrel whom he called Ace, and two other friends to move in my home without getting my permission.

One day Harrel greeted me at the door when I came home. I'd known him since he was a small boy and certainly didn't mind him staying there for a while but still, no one had consulted me. He stayed in Bryan's bedroom while Bryan slept downstairs on the sofa in the den. Two weeks later two more unexpected tenants arrived, Gary and his brother Juan. Bryan hired friends who'd worked with him in Fayetteville. Being the manager, he controlled the hiring. The two brothers slept on the floor on palettes in the den with Bryan.

"Fellows you are welcomed to stay here but I *hate* to see you sleeping on the floor like that."

"Oh that's alright Mrs. Albens, don't worry about us, we're just happy to have somewhere to stay. We've slept on the floor before. After a few paychecks we'll be able to get our own apartment."

They were from Peru, well-mannered young men, eager to work and get ahead. I felt I had a rooming house. Rarely did I see the three tenants. They worked 'til three, four or later in the morning. When I left for school they were asleep. When I got home, they were at work, unless it was someone's day off. Bryan, a firm employer, required the best from his employees, sometimes, *too* much.

Gary once said, "Mrs. Albens I'd rather be Bryan's friend than his employee. He demands too much. He wants everything done just right." I thought *I guess the apple doesn't fall too fall from the tree.*

When Bryan got the two-bedroom apartment in Pasadena they all moved in together. This time everyone slept on the floor; no one had a bed. Bryan, Nardia and the baby did sleep on a mattress. I remember Nardia's telephone conversations.

"Mom, I'll be glad when I can have my apartment to myself. I'm tired of stepping over people sleeping on the floor. I can't watch television when I want to. I can't use the bathroom at special times and when Bryan *is* home he's always asleep or at the park with his friends."

"Be patient Nardia, I know it's wearisome for you now in these early stages of the business, but later he won't have to work so hard."

"I understand Mom but all I do is stay in this apartment or take Briana for a ride in her stroller. He says their rent helps to pay our rent but we still *never* have any money. I *don't* know what he *does* with his money." She left again, only this time she didn't return. Gary and Juan soon got their own apartment; Harrel remained with Bryan.

Later, Sgt. Banner (Benny) the man who encouraged Bryan to steal in the service, moved in with Bryan. Benny's wife had left him due to alcohol and drugs. So my kind son, like his mother, offered him a place to stay until he was mentally and physically ready to leave. After several weeks, Benny visited his wife in New York. He *never* returned leaving his furniture piled in Bryan's apartment plus a trailer, parked on the lot, stuffed with his life's memorabilia.

I relished summer, peaceful moments sitting on the front porch early in the mornings when time permitted. The woods facing my old Victorian home shared its chirping birds and cooing doves. I'd rise early put on a sweat suit and run the mile down the hill from my house, around the park then back up the hill home. I ran and caressed God's provided beauty; inhaling sweet aromatic fragrances from blossoming trees and flowers in neighbor's yards.

Later hours were filled with making and hanging draperies for happy customers. Window fans and two small air conditioners cooled the humid Baltimore heat as I worked long hours, everyday. I prayed for the time when I wouldn't have to work all summer, but I had expenses that had to be paid year round and one salary wasn't enough. So while I worked I planned for the forthcoming school year.

In addition I mowed the huge lawn. Twice a week I moved manual sprinklers every two hours to water the lawn. Years of hard work had paid off. The yard looked terrific: luscious green junipers, flowering shrubs and variegated hosta lined the sidewalk nestled close to the house while some slept under a few shade trees. Aged lilacs planted next to the house sweetened the air every spring. Indeed the yard had taken shape. The pear and apple trees in the back yard, flanked by the black grape arbor invited us to dine. We did.

Each summer guests sat under the yellow flowered white fringed umbrella. They ate broiled chicken, succulent corn on the cob, zesty crab soup, mild potato salad, spicy baked beans etc. on the round redwood picnic table covered with the yellow tablecloth. Cool breezes helped settle the evening, as twilight sauntered in and took a seat. My friends *were* my family.

Marty was still stationed in the Azores with his wife and two children while Bryan struggled in Pasadena with an apartment piled high with furniture, somebody else's furniture. After Nardia's third abandonment, multiple job problems, Bryan visited me less. The house and yard, the business and my adorable calico cat, Kelly occupied my time. The word lonely didn't exist for me. I attended the Pentecostal Church three times a week and loved every moment. With two Bible classes on Wednesday night, a Friday night service, Sunday school plus Sunday morning service, I was contented!

Kelly had *little* time for me. Her time was spent caring for *litters* of kittens. A great little mother she was too. I recall one time while her four babies played on the basement floor; she came down the basement steps with a mouth full of baby mice she'd stolen from a mother's nest in the attic. Kelly spent a great deal of time in the attic so she knew exactly where to search. I wondered how she could steal babies from another mother to feed her own. I watched her bathe them. In time they bathed each other and themselves. She taught her kittens how to use the cat box, how to drink milk, how to eat and how to kill for their food, a natural instinct.

The devil envied my contentment and whispered to his companions, the evil ones,

"No, *no* we can't allow her to be happy. We must arouse her temptations. We must rattle that haven then she'll be tormented again, the way she used to be before all that church nonsense stole her from us. *No, no* we won't allow her to be peaceful!"

37...I MARRIED A CAR, NOT A MAN

...Give me your tired, your poor,
Your huddled masses yearning to breathe free,
The wretched refuse of your teeming shore,
Send these, the homeless, tempest-tossed to me,
I lift my lamp beside the golden door!
Emma Lazarus: The New Colossus
(Inscription on the Statue of Liberty)

The men I met were either selfish, two timers, liars or married. Some of those tired poor excuses of masculinity—I dated. I broke from romance until I met Lenard Winters, an auto mechanics teacher at the school where I taught. The campus had two buildings. I taught in the original building, the academic section and Lenard taught in the vocational section, previously a department store and a cafeteria. The city bought the adjourning buildings and converted them into a magnificent vocational school that combined with my school.

When my car's annual Auto Emissions test failed I had our school's auto shop check it out. Mr. Wardell, the same teacher who selected my first car, eighteen years earlier, assigned Mr. Leonard Winters, his assistant to locate the problem. Later Mr. Winters and I drove the car to the testing station. It failed again. Mr. Winters became highly irritated!

"*No car* can make a fool out of *me*! I'll find out what that problem is; I'll find out *today*!" He did.

He'd injured his foot (still in a cast) on the job several weeks earlier but nothing stopped him from coming to work, unofficially, a few days a week. The strange man loved his students and his job. He should have been off that foot. The following morning I saw his car moving toward the shop entrance.

"Mr. Winters, what are you doing here? You need to stay off that leg."

"I came back to locate that problem with your car. It'll be ready after school today. The foot's all well now. The cast comes off in two days."

"Well that's good news."

After school we returned to the Emissions Station. Betsy passed, thanks to Mr. Winters's persistence. As we returned to school he asked me a question.

"Mrs. Albens, why don't you let me take you to dinner sometime?" I stared at the man young enough to be my son. Intelligent, well mannered, well groomed, handsome and muscular, he was still not for me. Just recently divorced from a younger man, I'd *not* travel that road again.

"Why do you want to take me to dinner? I'm too old for you, probably old enough to be your mother."

"I like older women and you're not much older than I am anyway."

"How old *are* you?" He hesitated before giving me an answer.

"I'm——thirty-seven."

"What took you so long to answer? Did you forget your age?"

"No, not really. My birthday was yesterday. I had to think about it for a second."

"Oh, happy belated birthday! What did your sons give you?"

"Nothing. Nobody ever gives me anything."

"Don't feel bad. I don't get anything either."

He discussed why I should have dinner with him. I insisted I was too old. He insisted I wasn't. I rationalized *what's wrong with having dinner? I haven't been on a date in several months; what harm could it do?* So I relented.

"Let me think about it then I'll let you know. I really need to rest, I'm exhausted." He called that night. We discussed various topics, including religion. I informed him I would not date another man unless he was a Christian and attended church on a regular basis. He said he was a Christian, but didn't attend any church. And added my company would influence his return. He then asked me why I was so tired.

"Why are you so tired? It's Friday. There's no school tomorrow. You need to get out and relax yourself, have some fun. Life's too short to stay in the house all the time!"

"Relax, I guess you're right, but what about just plain ordinary sleep. Mr. Winters tonight ends a long, strenuous two weeks of not sleeping! My daughter-in-law Renata and my granddaughter Marvis were visiting me from the Azores. I thank God they returned yesterday!"

"The Azores, where are they? I've heard of those islands but didn't know what ocean they were in."

"They're Islands in the mid Atlantic owned by Portugal. My son's in the

Air Force; he's stationed there for two or three years. His wife's trip was for business. She came to buy beautician chairs and supplies and have them sent back there to set up a business. *Every* night the baby woke up around 2:00 a.m. *crying* for her bottle and didn't go back to sleep. After a few nights, I realized her time schedule for the Azores had not changed. There's a five-hour difference in their time zone from ours." My body cried for sleep, plain old everyday *sleep!* Everyday students asked how I felt.

"Mrs. Albens did you get any sleep last night?"

"*No*! There won't be any sleep for me until they leave."

Everyday I went to work drained! My eyeballs felt as though they'd drop from their sockets! I loved Marvis but I wished she'd known how to tell time.

Renata spent $400 in beauty supplies. Four large beauty shop chairs occupied much of my dining room and blocked my foyer. When I received my telephone bill that month, I discovered Renata had made *$300* worth of long distance phone calls without my permission to the Azores! *I—was—furious!*

First they weren't to my son. Second I already had a $200 bill of my own. Now it exceeded $500! One call she'd made lasted for *144 minutes!* She'd talked over two hours!! They were all made during the night when Marvis was awake. After I called Marty he tracked down the numbers. Most were to *her* boyfriend's number; a few were to Marty. She had the *audacity* to call her boyfriend on *my phone*, in addition to leaving me with her *$300* phone bill to pay! She had *some* nerve!

"I refuse to pay that bill! Let them cut it off!" I said to my closest friend, Lily.

"No Dawn, you need your phone! Go downtown and discuss it with the telephone company. They'll work out arrangements with you."

I rethought my decision and took Lily's advice. They agreed to send copies of the bill to Marty, and highlight all of her calls. I agreed to pay $100 every two weeks until the bill was paid, if I wanted my service to stay on. Three months passed before Marty *sent me* anything. He did send the phone company $155 toward his $300 still owing me $100. Renata never contacted me about the furniture that crowded my dining room and blocked my foyer. I looked at those large beauty shop chairs for months. They weighed a ton! Since I refused to move them, they remained in place as though they were family members.

Mr. Winters met me at church Sunday morning. I sat down front, second row on the left side. I avoided distraction if possible. My eyes concentrated on the service and nothing else. He arrived a few minutes into the service, but nevertheless he showed, dressed in a blue suit, white shirt and tie. He reminded me of a little boy. When the minister spied him sitting next to me, his frown depicted absolute dissatisfaction. Again he was displeased about my selection of a companion. He knew more than I did.

After church we went to dinner. When Mr. Winters pulled into the parking lot, I soon realized where I'd have my Sunday dinner. Surprise, surprise, *surprise*, we were dining at *Chuck-E-Cheese's*! I gazed straight ahead as though I were in a trance. I considered the man and the moment—*you mean this man brought me to Chuck-E-Cheese's? Is he out of his mind? He's definitely missing a few marbles!*

He said, "I thought we'd eat here and watch the children as they play the games. They also have great music. Have you been here before?"

Never in my life had I been more bewildered, more shocked! Here I, a *forty-nine year old woman*, was having dinner with a man fourteen years my junior, at Chuck-E-Cheese's! In one way I felt let down; in another way I felt enamored. During dinner, I realized his lifestyle did not parallel mine. This person was unique; a man I'd soon understand. After dinner we drove to the park after stopping at Baskin Robbins for ice cream. Since I didn't drink anything alcoholic, we did more *exciting* things like walking through the park admiring the trees and landscape. Mr. Winters revealed much of his past life to me; the positive fragments; the quiet elements he thought I should know. Later I soon discovered the negative traits; not too far in the future.

About two a.m. a few nights later my phone rang. I answered half asleep, "Hello."

"Hi, this is Mr. Winters."

"Why are you calling me so late at night? Is there something wrong?"No it's nothing wrong. I just wanted to talk."

"You can talk to me tomorrow, not two in the morning."

"I miss you. I want to see you." He sounded like a little child yearning for a mother to comfort him in the middle of the night.

"But you saw me earlier. I have to get my rest, call me back tomorrow okay? You go home and get some sleep. Goodnight."

I hung up the receiver and returned to my interrupted dream. An hour later I heard my doorbell. I raised the shade a little and saw Mr. Winters's car parked in the driveway behind mine. I said out loud *this man is crazy coming to my house this time of morning.* Before I put on my robe to go downstairs, he rang the bell again. As I reached the bottom step he started knocking. I opened the door.

"Mr. Winters, why have you come to my house so late at night?" He stood there like a lost child.

"I just wanted to see you Mrs. Albens. I was walking around the streets where I live thinking about you. I just want to be with you."

"Why were you walking the streets this time of morning?"

"Because, that's the only time it's quiet. Can I come in? I'll sleep on the floor just as long as I'm with you."

I stared at this muscular confused man and felt sorry for him. He held something in his hand that was touching the porch floor.

"I guess so. Come in." As soon as he entered the living room he sprawled out on the hardwood floor clutching something in his arms like a baby.

"I can sleep on the floor if you just let me stay the night"

"I don't know about that."

"I won't be any trouble; I just want to be near you." I felt sorry for him. Very soon I'd learn about his emotional problems.

"Come in the den. You may sleep on the sofa." I went upstairs, got sheets, a pillow a blanket and made up the sofa for him. He thanked me. I returned upstairs to my bed and to sleep. Later when I was in a deep sleep I heard tapping on my bedroom door.

"Yeees. What is it?"

"Mrs. Albens I want to be married. I want to marry you."

I sat up *briskly* unprepared for the words I'd just heard. I yanked on my robe and opened my bedroom door. There stood Mr. Winters wearing his *pajamas*! I thought, "Where did he get those pajamas? He'd come prepared to spend the night. Indeed he *was* ready for marriage. Then I remembered; that's what he dragged in the house and was clutching onto when he sprawled on the floor.

"Mr. Winters lets go downstairs where we can talk." He followed me downstairs. We sat on the sofa and talked for several minutes.

"You can't marry me. You don't even know me."

"I know all that I need to know. I know I want to spend the rest of my life with

you. Isn't that enough?"

"I'm afraid there's more to it than that. People date first. They find out whether or not they're compatible. You're fourteen years younger than I am. My last husband was twelve years younger. It just wouldn't work."

He grabbed and hugged me—and placed his head on my shoulder.

"I need you. I feel so lonely when I'm not with you." My heart softened for this warm and affectionate man.

The night's stillness soothed the moment. That man's gentleness touched my heart. He raised his head from my shoulder, kissed my lips and caressed my body. I fell limp. I took his hand then led him upstairs to my bedroom where we made passionate love. He spent the night while we slept clutched in each other's arms.

Our next date was a disaster! When he arrived, he'd been drinking. I knew by his slurred speech, his walk and his mannerisms.

"I'm not going anywhere with you. You're drunk!" His English was perfect, even though he spoke fast, until he drank.

"No I'm nooot. I've had a fe-w dri-nks, but I'm not dr—unk. Come on. Tomorr—ow is Mother's Day. I want to buy you so—mething then take you— to see so—me of my friends." He begged. I relented. How could I resist that boyish manner and those *gorgeous* eyes! Eyes were my weakness; his eyes twinkled like brilliant black diamonds!

His auto mechanics shop, a rented garage of a retired college art instructor, was across the alley from his mother's back yard. His shop was immaculate; so was he.

He stopped at a client's house and picked up $50 owed to him. Within fifteen minutes the money was gone! He bought flowers for his mother and me, paid on his liquor store bill, bought two-carry-out dinners and was broke! I was shocked! In *fifteen* minutes with three dollars left he drove to see another customer.

"I know there's another customer that owes me some money. Let me think a minute. I'll drive down this street and maybe he'll come to mind."

"Lenard, in fifteen minutes you spent $50. Is that the way you usually handle money." He picked up my small hand with his large rough hand and raised it gently to his mouth and kissed it.

"Dawn you worry too much. You must learn to relax and enjoy life."

"Yes, you're right but I also have to live and pay my bills. How do you feel about money? Do you spend it this way all the time?"

"Ah, yes, why not? I have no respect for money. When it's gone I'll make some more. Money was made to spend not keep. I make it. I spend it."

"Boy, you scare me! You'll never have anything if you spend everything you make." I knew he'd spent his last dollar, but kept stopping at different liquor stores. After each stop his behavior worsened. He left Baltimore driving on backcountry roads, in outmoded places I never knew existed. He drove that car like a crazy man, jerking and yanking on the steering wheel, pressing his foot hard on the accelerator and then on the brake! He acted insane!

"*Take me home!* I want to go home now, right now!"

"Are you afraid of a little excitement, Dawn?"

"No, but you're *drunk*. I want to *go home!* Take me home *now*!!"

"Allll—right, allll—right I'll take you home."

He drove me home, in silence. I had nothing else to say to him. As we approached my house I made a firm statement.

"Lenard I can't see you anymore. You have a *serious* drinking problem. I've had one alcoholic marriage and an alcoholic boyfriend. I'm not getting involved in another one."

"You're right I do change when I'm drinking but I promise to stop. Please go to the auto races with me tonight. I'm sure you'll enjoy the track. Have you ever seen auto racing before?"

"No! And I don't plan to see one tonight! Go home, Lenard. I'm very tired and you need to sleep off that alcohol."

This was a man that *refused* to take *NO* for an answer. He stood on my porch until I agreed to attend the auto races with him that night.

He returned several hours later, sober; an entirely different man! Was this the same person I'd watch stagger to his car earlier? Lenard was a kind generous appealing person. His broad shoulders filled out his yellow long sleeved shirt while his fast jerky walk said, "Let's go." He was comical and delightful company until he drank.

We walked through the parking lot to the racetrack. Lenard placed his arm around my shoulder and talked as though nothing erroneous had ever happened earlier that day. As he relished our time together, I wondered what was wrong with me. Did I realize what I'd gotten myself into? He was a *determined* man. He wasn't easily insulted nor did he hear the word *no!* Besides he was an alcoholic. Yes, but I liked him. I really liked this man. He was funny, kind and thoughtful; traits I needed from a man."

Our third date was worse. Always neat and clean Lenard showed up at my door a bit tipsy.

"You've been drinking Lenard. I'm not going out with you." I was closing the door when he started to apologize.

"Dawn I've only had a few drinks and the country air will make that

135

disappear. Please come with me. I'm going to see a friend in the country about a car part. I know you'll enjoy the ride." I watched his innocent smiling face, his robust body stationed firm on the porch, and his tilted head with those beautiful eyes that begged without speaking one word. How could I say no?

We rode miles outside of Baltimore until we slowed down in front of a trailer home in a remote part of the county and parked the car. Weeds and junk were piled high around the trailer with dogs barking non-stop. Lenard opened the door for me to get out. Afraid to move because of what I might step on and the yapping dogs, I stood motionless. Lenard's Caucasian friend stepped from inside the trailer, his mouth packed with snuff.

"Hey Len! I'd just 'bout give you up. Lawd have mercy you showed done gain plenty weight since I seen you last. Wha's you been do'in since to yo self man?"

"Nothing much Brad, same O, same O. I brought my girlfriend along to keep me company. Is your mother home?

"Yeah, Ma's home. Take her to da house Len."

The dogs stopped their ruckus and scurried to other parks of the property. They'd done their job so now they scampered into the woods for more mischief. Lenard walked me to the house about twenty feet from the trailer. The three-year-old home had been well maintained. His mother stood at the door waiting to welcome me inside. Lenard remained outside with Brad. The car part he needed was somewhere in the area among the yard's junk: clutter, trash, litter, broken bikes, old cast iron bathtubs etc. My head spun as my eyes perused the mass of debris that encircled the house and trailer. His mother was friendly.

"Len tells us that you're an artist. Maybe you'd like to look at some of my pictures hanging on the walls and give me your opinion. My son did some of those in the dining room, but he died in the Vietnam War, God Bless his soul."

I stepped inside the house, into another world! There was *nowhere* to sit! Her adult daughter rushed to one chair pushing back clothes and boxes, leaving a little corner for me to sit on. Every chair, sofa, stool was stacked with something: books, toys, clothes, groceries, filled paper bags, boxes etc. Everything *imaginable* was in that house! In *all* my life I'd *never seen anything* like it! Things overflowed from the mantle piece, all of the tables, every counter top; *not an inch* of surface was visible! I walked from room to room as his mother talked from the kitchen about her son who'd died. She was preparing dinner.

"Dawn I'm in here trying to get dinner on."

I walked through the dining room shaking my head in pure amazement at the turmoil until I entered a kitchen, *total* chaos! I stepped backwards to catch my breath, another disaster area, only this one was *worse!* The large beautiful kitchen was well designed. The major problem was only the fronts of the appliances and cabinets were visible. Everything else was *completely covered!* The counters were stacked with all kinds of food, boxes, potatoes, unopened staples etc. Cabinet and appliance tops were piled high with more stuff. Even parts of the stove that surrounded the burners had stacked items. With all of the clutter, the house appeared clean. I dared not see the bedrooms. The mother was cleaning a chicken on the counter. She'd pushed back enough stuff, the size of a hand, just large enough to place the chicken on the edge of the counter. I was *flabbergasted, speechless* and *outraged* that people could live in such disorder, total, *total* confusion!

Foodstuffs were piled so high where she worked I wondered how she managed to keep them from falling over! I excused myself from the entangled maze and returned outside where at least I could see the sky. *Whew!!* I needed air. Maybe not fresh air considering the confusion outside, but at least it was air. I looked up to the sky, the peaceful restful sky; the infinite open space where *no* junk existed.

After Lenard found the car part, we left. But he left with something other than the car part. He left almost inebriated! His search had not included alcohol; he needed help, help I could not provide.

"Lenard you don't look well" I said.

"I'm fine Dawn, I'm fine."

"Let me drive Lenard. You're in no shape to drive."

"*No,* I'll drive. I'm taking you to that thrift store on Charles Street you've wanted to see. I know exactly what I doing so let me do it!"

"*No, no* Lenard not today. I'd rather go home. I've had *enough* for today!"

When he drank, his determination increased. That warm, funny, cuddly teddy bear personality disappeared. We drove to the thrift shop. He remained in the car, napping. Fifteen minutes later as I waited at the counter to pay, I glanced over to the large decorated store window and saw Lenard's face pressed against the glass, peeking inside like a child. Minutes later he staggered in the store.

"Are—n't you re—ady yet?"

"Go back to the car Lenard. I'll be out in a minute." The cashier stared at Lenard then at me. Lenard tossed his head up to the side, turned around and staggered toward the door and to the car with those quick jerky little steps of his.

"Is that your son?" The cashier said.

Embarrassed, unable to speak I answered her as calmly as I could, considering how crushed I felt.

"No he's a friend." As soon as I got into the car I broke down in tears. Lenard drove to the park. We sat in the car and talked for a *long* time.

"Stop worrying about what people say about us. I love *yooou*! I wouldn't care if you were ninety years old. It's you I love; not a number."

We got out of the car and strolled around the park as Lenard tried to ease my pain. With all the walking, talking and fresh air, he sobered up. He was the *kindest* man I'd ever met, but he needed treatment. His entire personality changed after one drink, not to mention four or five!

He did *anything* he could for me: cut my lawn, wash my car, and pay for car parts required when he worked on the car, within reason.

I recall the first day Bryan met Lenard. Bryan was still managing the Domino Pizza and had stopped by to pay a visit. Their paths crossed on the sidewalk by the porch when Lenard was leaving the house.

"Mommy don't you marry that man! That man's *crazy*! He was out there talkin' junk to me about his son being just as good as I am. And just because I managed a Domino Pizza doesn't mean that I'm any better than his son. Something's wrong with him! *Don't you marry that man Mommy!"*

"Bryan I'm not marrying Lenard, I'm only dating him. Who said anything about marriage? I didn't."

"Yes, but I know you Mommy. You date and the next thing I hear is marriage. *Please* don't marry that man!"

"Bryan, Lenard is a kind person. You met him on a bad day. He's really a very nice guy."

"Well from what I saw today I've written him off my list. I know you get lonely Mommy but please listen to your darling son, date him, don't marry him. He has more problems than I have!"

"Okay Bryan, okay, since you want to be my father I'll check with you first. Is that alright with you?"

He shook his head in doubt, opened the door and left. He and I spoke openly, honestly while Marty and I could not.

One afternoon in school, I noticed a young man standing at my classroom door. Both hands were held close to his chest holding a small blue stool with a lovely floral arrangement placed on the top. I motioned for him to come inside.

"Are you Mrs. Albens?"

"Yes I am."

"Mr. Winters asked me to bring this over to you."

I had to restrain from laughing. That boy held the stool and vase of flowers straight out in front of him like Frankenstein held his hands when he walked. I spoke, after regaining my composure.

"Why are you holding the stool like that?"

"That's the way Mr. Winters told me to hold it. He told me to be very careful while I walked over here and especially when I walked up the steps."

"Well you go back and tell Mr. Winters I said thank you very much." That sight was *so* funny I almost choked holding in my laughter!

Lenard explained later, he'd asked someone in the carpentry shop to make the stool so I could reach the *blackboard* better! A student in the floral department arranged the flowers. He was an unusual, amusing thoughtful guy.

Once on my lunch hour he came unannounced with lunch for both of us. I detected he'd been drinking, not much but enough to notice a change in his attitude and speech.

"Lenard it's not professional for you to come over here as you do. Wait until school is over."

"I don't see a problem with me visiting you sometime."

"Sometime? You're here every other day." He smiled, finished his lunch and laughed.

"Dawn you worry too much. I just want to have lunch with you. By the way have you seen my son today? He wanted you to see his report card." Lenard's two sons lived with his former wife. Since his sons attended the same school where we taught; he saw them everyday.

His trial date for delinquency of $12,000 in child support payments was set in mid May. I should have offered to go with him but I didn't think it was necessary. Late that afternoon I was called downstairs to the main office for an emergency phone call. When I walked in the office I saw his younger son Earl, standing at the counter. As soon as he saw me he rushed over.

"Mrs. Albens my father is in serious trouble. He's on the phone, waiting to talk to you." I picked up the receiver, but he'd hung up.

"He hung up Earl, what's the matter!"

We moved over to the far side of the office for more privacy and sat down. Speaking as low as possible Earl struggled to tell me everything he knew.

"I took my father to the courthouse this mornin' and waited for him outside in the car. We got there real early. Daddy said he'd go inside and wait. After I waited a looong time, I went inside to find out what happened. They told me he didn't show."

"Didn't show? Have you found out anything since then?"

"No ma'am. I don't know where he is." Earl was distraught.

"Mrs. Albens I wish my Daddy was the same way he was before he started teaching. He didn't drink the way he does now. Mr. Wardell's no good for him, 'cause they drink all day on the job. Only thing is my Daddy acts so crazy when he drinks. I just wish things could be the way they were before."

I listened and ached for Earl, as tormented troubles tumbled from his trembling lips about the father he loved. As soon as I returned to my classroom another intercom message stated I had a visitor in the main office. When I started down the steps I met Lenard coming up. Head dropped, clothes disheveled and his light blue shirt hanging halfway out of his pants, he looked horrible! When he recognized me he shook his lowered head in shame. We walked quickly to my room and closed the door since it was my planning period.

With bloodshot eyes, smell of alcohol, and frightened, Lenard unraveled the morning's hectic event. I listened as he explained.

"I, I, I messed up Dawn, I, I, I really messed up this time." His rapid babbling words ran together as usual when he got upset. Today he was a nervous scared wreck; I barely understood a word he said.

"Slow down Lenard, I can't understand a word you're saying, what are you talking about? Ple—ase slow down and tell me what happened." He waited a few seconds then started again. This time his words were more coherent.

"After I left Earl and went into the courthouse, I was so scared; I left through another door and got a drink at the corner bar. By the time I got to the courthouse I guess I'd had too many."

"You mean—you went into the courthouse *drunk*? You *know* you had *no* business drinking and then returning to the courthouse." Once again he reminded me of a little boy trying to explain why he stole cookies from the cookie jar.

"I was scared. I told her years ago I wasn't working and that's why I couldn't pay the full amount of child support."

"Did you go to the office and tell them yourself?"

"No. I thought she'd tell them."

"No Lenard that was *your* responsibility."

"Yeah, I know now. I was too disgusted about not having a good job and didn't go."

"So what happened this morning that you didn't show for your case?"

"I was there. But since I'd been drinking I knew I better not go inside."

"You mean you were there and didn't go inside?"

"I waited in the lobby for Melody and her lawyer to come out so I could talk to them together. When her lawyer wouldn't listen to what I had to say I *punched* him in the face! He fell on the floor and I *ran!*"

"Oh Lenard, Lenard, Lenard how could you *do* such a thing?"

He continued expressing his inadequate feelings and insecurities. I listened and wondered how he could have gotten himself into such a predicament.

Weeks passed. Two weeks before school closed, a young man stood waiting at my door. I excused myself from my students to see what he wanted.

"Do you want to see me?"

"Yes ma'am. Mr. Winters asked me to give this to you. He said for you to keep it for him until he sees you." He handed me a *wad* of bills, held tight in his hands.

"Where is Mr. Winters?"

"I don't know. He left school in a hurry and said he'd call you later."

The young man walked away and down the long hall, while I stood holding a hand full of balled up paper money, and curious about Lenard's emergency. I knew something was wrong, but how wrong puzzled me. I stuffed the money into my purse, in my coat closet and returned to my students.

After school, Lenard stopped by my house. His facial expression confirmed my suspicions. He'd been drinking, but not enough to slur his speech this time.

"Did you get the money from the boy?" He said.

"Yes here it is. I flattened out the bills and put a paper clip on them for you."

"No, you hold on to it for me until I need it."

"What happened in school that you had to leave, so early Lenard?"

"These kids today just don't have any respect for nobody! I knew one day

141

I'd blow my top and today I did. A substitute teacher in one of the classes was having serious problems with a boy. I knew the kid, 'cause I've taught him before. One of her students came to my shop and said Samuel was giving Mrs. Landers a hard time and would I come and give her a hand?"

"So what happened?"

"As soon as I walked in the room that boy hauled off and *slapped* her in her face! Without thinking I grabbed him and slung him around the room like a rag doll! He hit the blackboard then bounced off landing on the floor."

Lenard's grandparents had raised him; they demanded the utmost respect. He didn't like any child disrespecting an adult. I wasn't surprised at his reaction.

"Where did you go when you left the building, Lenard?"

"After I realized what I'd done, I got scared and rushed from the building. Before I left, Samuel kept yelling, 'I'm gonna' git you fo this! I'm gonna' git you fo what you did ta me you s— of a b——! My buddies will fix you up gooood!' I came back before school let out and went to the principal's office to hear the verdict."

"I'm so sorry Lenard. I know how you felt because I've felt like doing the same thing when students have cursed me and said such horrible things for no reason. What did your principal say?"

"He put me on a week's suspension because I was drinking on the job. I'm not to return for the remainder of the year. That's only two weeks so I'll manage. I don't think it's fair because Wardell drinks everyday and sometimes he sleeps in his chair right in front of his students."

"Yes, but you must remember Lenard, he's the department head; you're a teacher. Besides he didn't do what you did today, even though he might have wanted to."

The following day Lenard attempted to see Wardell but was alerted by some students that Samuel's friends were waiting, with guns. As he approached the entrance to the auto mechanics shop he saw the gang and *fled*! They screamed obscene language and charged after him as he ran for his *life*! He didn't attempt to see Wardell at school until several days later.

Even though school had ended customers' cars in the shop still had to be repaired and delivered. Since Lenard had contracted the jobs, he was responsible for finishing the work. Mr. Wardell had a summer job. Three cars had to be reassembled. The owners had paid a deposit but still owed a balance.

When Lenard delivered one of the cars, he'd been drinking. Overworked, tired and disgusted for the week's troubles, he parked the lady's car on part of her lawn. While he stood at the door arguing with her son about how he'd parked the car on his mother's lawn, the son threatened to knock him out if he didn't move the car immediately. When the guy raised his arm to strike him, Lenard raised his arm in defense. When he lifted his arm, his pants *dropped* to the floor! His belt was unfastened.

Embarrassed and humiliated he pulled up his pants, ran down the steps and rushed from the neighborhood. His son waited in his car but Lenard had run from the scene and hid. Hours later his son called me in search of his father. No one knew where he was.

After I'd gone to bed I heard the doorbell and knew it was Lenard. When I opened the door he stood, shaking his dropped head in disgust.

"Dawn, how do I keep getting involved in all of these problems?"

I placed my arms around him and said, "It's the drinking Lenard. You must stop drinking. The alcohol changes your entire personality, can't you see that?"

"Yea, I know but I *just* can't stop."

My principal, Mr. Dextall a small man in statue but a giant in mentality appeared in court for the hearing. Lenard said when the lady's son mentioned the incident when his pants dropped to the floor, Mr. Dextall lowered his shaking head in shame, as the courtroom *roared* in laughter!

School was over, summer had begun but peace was not in sight for Bryan. Overworked, stressed out with job problems, wife and child in another town, Bryan decided to quit his job. I sympathized with his struggles and persuaded him to stay.

"Mommy I'm having a tough time meeting my expenses. Since Gary and his brother moved, I have no financial help. My rent's behind and I have a $300 gas and electric bill. Is there any way you can help me?"

"Bryan you know I don't have any money. I'll call Valarie. Maybe she can help you. Meanwhile ask your friends perhaps they can make you a loan."

"Friends, a loan? They don't have anything either."

My close friend Valarie loaned me the $650 for Bryan's rent. My close friend since college always bailed me out of financial situations. However I *always* paid her back. The Salvation Army paid his $300 utility bill. The following month he called again, this time under dire stress.

"Mommy I have to leave this job. I can't take these pressures anymore!"

"What pressures Bryan? Why are you so upset?"

"I'm upset because during the time I was on vacation the manager in my place raised sales so high, I've been pressured as to why I couldn't have done that myself."

I listened as he spilled out the promotional methods and how they were bound to drop after a certain point of increase. As I heard his explanations I recalled the numerous days he wasn't there; how he allowed his assistant manager to take charge. I admit he'd trained his staff well but was absent far too often.

He'd said, "Mommy they have to learn how to operate when I'm not there. They're in management training and must learn to run the business alone."

"Have you explained to your supervisor the outcome of her over advertising?"

"He knows what'll happen. That's why I told Tanya not to use as many coupons as she did. Now she's caused a cramp in my position. If I don't bring up my sales to the level she had them, I'm done."

"Well do what you have to do. Remember you have many obligations to meet and getting another job that pays your same salary may not be available right away."

The next day he called.

"Mommy I quit my job last night."

"You quit your job Bryan, without having another one?"

"Oh I'll get another job. I can always get another job. I was getting tired of the pizza business anyway."

So in July of 1987, Bryan quit Domino Pizza! My problems soon escalated to *unimaginable heights!* Several days later he was hired by a construction company, cleaning up debris behind carpenters and workmen. At first, his complaints were few but I knew my son. They increased with each desperate phone call.

"Mommy I was wondering if you'd let me move back with you until I get myself together?" What could I say? I had the space and I couldn't see him in the street when he was in trouble. Only I didn't know the truth, the basis of his trouble.

"Well I guess so. Your room is still vacant."

He moved everything back by himself. I never knew how he did it.

"Mommy whenever my friends ask me to help them I always do. When I need help they're never available."

"Join the club Bryan, I understand perfectly. I have friends exactly like that. I've been there for them but when I've asked for help to pack a few boxes, they *never* show."

Benny's furniture and stuffed van followed. His furniture and belongings were stored in the basement, under the house, and in the attic. Since Lenard had loaded those massive beauty parlor chairs one by one in the wheelbarrow, and rolled them out to the shed, little space remained inside the shed.

What a mess I'd incurred? My home had become a storage facility. Benny's sofa covered with colorful vinyl stayed on the side porch until it joined Gary and Juan in their apartment. For *three years* Benny's van was parked on the side of my yard before being vandalized. Lenard soon hauled it away. Benny's drug addiction settled him in a world of horror and eccentric behavior thereby, ending all contact with his family.

38...DETACHMENT!

This house is to be let for life or years;
Her rent is sorrow, and her income tears.
Cupid,'t has long stood void; her bills make known
She must be dearly let, or let alone.
Francis Quarles: Emblems. Book II

The school year ended with more spirited students. Lenard, a Vietnam Veteran had suffered multiple problems which altered his behavior severely. He'd already shared his childhood and early life experiences with me.

First, his mother gave birth to Lenard at fifteen. She'd climbed on the back of a motorcycle with a good-looking light-skinned guy her age, rode out to the country. She felt enthralled when he offered her a ride on his bike, unaware he only wanted her innocence. He never bothered again, not even when he knew she was pregnant with his child. So Lenard knew of a father who had no interest in him *whatsoever*.

Second, his grandparents raised him from birth so his mother could finish school.

Third, his maternal grandfather, a master mechanic spent his evenings and days off in the alley outside his garage repairing cars. A huge old-fashioned wrought iron belly pot hung over a fire cooking their meals. While the men repaired cars, the women entertained them with music, drink and laughter. As a child Lenard loved cars. He inherited master mechanic skills from both grandfathers. However, his father's father, an Indian, couldn't handle alcohol.

Lenard's days after school were spent in a dirty alley with cars, not playing with other children. He liked working on his little cars and trucks, his only recreation.

Fourth, the family was poor. I mean pooor! He wore ragged clothes and shoes to school and often didn't have any lunch. Everyday he volunteered to wash his teacher's blackboards or do other things to earn extra milk and cookies. She continued her daily treats even after he'd passed from her to the next grade. One afternoon we visited his beloved elementary teacher.

"Lenard was a wonderful child." She smiled as she looked at him. "I knew how poor he was as were many of my other students, but there was something special about Lenard. Even now he stops by occasionally to visit me after *all* of these years."

Lenard said, "You *never* knew how much that milk and those cookies meant to me. Many days that's all I had for lunch."

"I knew Lenard. That's why I continued giving them to you after you were promoted to the next grade."

Lenard worked everyday after school. His fifteenth birthday was a turning point in his life. Problems with his mother's boyfriend increased and he was asked to move. He rented a room and continued school. His clean clothes were usually spotted with grease marks from the mechanic shops. His girlfriend became pregnant his senior year in high school so they got married. After graduation, he joined the Army. His wife and two sons followed him after he was stationed.

Fifth, the Vietnam War was the catalyst responsible for his uncanny future. Unaware of Vietnam's negative influences mentally, he returned to America expecting to continue life as usual. Not so!

The mess hall food added poundage to the thin frame that had enlisted three years earlier. Lenard returned to Baltimore proud of the hefty muscular frame underneath his striking military uniform. Family and friends marveled at his new physique! Indeed he was not the same skinny young man that signed up to defend his country! Separated from his wife, he stayed with his mother for two weeks. Later he slept in his car two weeks before being able to rent a room. Adults in his family *didn't* live with family members, except for a short time. Lenard pulled his own weight, he'd been taught that early in life. Eventually he and his wife reunited, but once again unsolvable problems split their marriage.

When I met Lenard, he'd been divorced several years. He'd dated but had no inclination of remarrying until he met me. I wondered how I'd earned the privilege and honor to be his wife; a person destined to save his life from total destruction.

After working for the construction company two weeks, Bryan and the I-Roc left for Fayetteville in July and joined his wife and daughter who lived with her parents. In August his creditors called me for his delinquent payments. I tossed the reminders aside. I knew Bryan would pay. Calls from the mortgage company in Fayetteville, the Chevrolet office in Baltimore, plus the bill for extras on the car, increased!

By September, bombarded with close to *$1000* a month of Bryan's bills, I prayed! "Dear God *please* help me! I can barely pay my own bills, where am I going to get $1000 more a month to pay Bryan's." Actually they weren't his—they were *mine*. Why? They were in *my name* not his. He left Baltimore, and those bills!

Words can *not* express the torment I experienced the next *four* months! I'd shift bills or not pay some at all. Now *my* creditors were calling for late or unpaid bills! Lenard helped me some, but he had his own expenses. Besides he wasn't teaching and his small automotive business was his only means of survival.

Soon Nardia informed me why Bryan left Domino Pizza. His former Sunday afternoons at the park with his friends had introduced him to *crack cocaine!* His *habit* consumed his time and money, not his family. His move to Fayetteville was to break the obsession, but he was *hooked*. Ashamed to tell me himself Nardia did. He worked for other pizza companies as an assistant manager but used most of his money on *drugs*. Because they argued so much, her parents asked them to leave. They moved to her aunt's home. Requested to move again they rented a small trailer, just what they wanted.

Bryan tried to stop *using* but couldn't. Nardia, now pregnant with their second child, wanted it aborted. Bryan said, "No."

"I want my child." He said he was doing better. Nadia told the truth.

"Mom, why should we have more children? We barely have enough food for the three of us now? If it weren't for me working, we'd starve!" In tears she explained her pain.

"I do work. I work everyday!" Bryan's yelled in the background.

"Yeah, you work. You work to pay the drug dealer. He gets all your money, not Briana and me."

He pleaded with her not to abort his baby. He called and revealed his pain.

As I talked to them I recalled an assignment in my Creative Writing class.

…Soul Confession…
I sat glued to the seat, hunched over in pain, as I felt life yanked from my

body. The plop/splash sound that hit the water said *it's over*. I rose with caution from a firm wooden oval white set, now spotted with red, and turned around. As I kneeled down, the room's heaviness anchored my body to the floor and my head dropped closer to the spotted seat. My eyes burned with tears shed for my baby, my aborted baby deep down in the well of that toilet.

"It wasn't time to have children," he said.

My selfish, self-centered husband had our baby murdered! I gazed, cried and gagged at the bloody lifeless sight. Visible and clear were his facial features, tiny hands, arms, legs and feet in a big glob of bloody mass. A two-month fetus, completely formed human being lay in the neck of that commode. Death's smell consumed the air. I breathed the stench and inhaled the foulness of my sin. I was a sick, sad, tormented soul. We were told at two-three months the baby had not formed. They lied! Lied! Lied! I saw eyeballs begin to bulge. I saw a nose and mouth take form. That blob of blood had lived a few hours ago!

Twenty-one, immature, crazy in love, I married Maurice my college sweetheart. He couldn't wait one more year 'til I finished school. Twenty-two, married seven months, in my last year of college and pregnant. We used the rhythm method, you know that fail proof method approved by the church.

I wanted my baby. He wasn't ready for children. I begged for my baby.

"No, no, not *now*!" He said.

We'd planned to have children five years later. But Maurice refused to use protection. Every time I complained he'd say:

"It's not the same feeling if I use protection. Besides, all you have to do is rush to the bathroom." His climax, his high, his orgasm, his selfishness caused this torment and anguish. It wasn't his agony to bear!

A week earlier we met with a woman, a former nurse and made an appointment for the procedure. Forty dollars we could afford but two hundred dollars for a doctor was out of the question! I cried alone in the darkness and the light, the next few days. I knew some women died from abortions even when performed by a doctor. I risked my life, to kill my baby. We knew abortions were illegal and aware of the penalty involved. I cared. He didn't care. He slept. I didn't sleep at all!

We arrived at the former nurse's home after her family had left, an early cold November morning. I stared at the newly painted white glass-paned door and thought, "Behind that door, is death for one and help for another." My confused mind, cold and frightened body shut down the guilt feelings when the door opened and I walked under the lintel. We removed our coats. The woman, of slender build, attractive and middle-aged, hung them in the crowded closet next to the front door. Maurice' tensed body relaxed in a recliner in the living room. I climbed the blue carpeted row house steps behind the woman and dragged the heavy load of guilt behind me. I wondered what Maurice thought while I was upstairs having his baby butchered!

My heart grieved and my soul drowned as I lay on a covered ironing board top, placed on a long, strong wooden table, with my legs bent and covered by a sheet. I watched the woman as she sat relaxed in her chair at the end of the table. With wrinkled brow and squinted eyes she inserted the firm metal speculum into my vagina, the same instrument used by a doctor. Next she picked up a reshaped wire coat hanger, already sterilized for her death surgery and inserted in through the speculum. I watched her mouth twist and her head shift from side to side and listened to her concern for my pain. I felt the poking, twisting and turning of that coat hanger inside of my body. How ashamed I felt!

My opened hands covered a drenched face as I cried silently. I a married woman was having an abortion because of my selfish egotistical husband. How could he do this to me? How could he do this to his unborn baby? I prayed for forgiveness. Tears streamed down my face as I envisioned a life being cut from his mother's womb. Too young to cry, I thought, did he feel any pain, I wondered?

The soft blue walls with white sheers at the long windows kidnapped my thoughts, thoughts that the wall color was perfect for my baby's room.

The worst of the ordeal was over. I was padded and helped down from the sheeted ironing board top placed on the long table. The lady explained what would happen later but assured us that everything would be fine.

I passed out at the commode after I saw my dead baby! Maurice revived me and carried me to our small bedroom. Guilt consumed my mind and death blinded my sight. I lost my appetite, lost weight and almost lost my mind! The physical and mental emptiness consumed my entire being. Maurice cooked and cared for me. We sat in silence at the kitchen table. He begged and pleaded with me to eat. I refused. So he started feeding me and wouldn't leave 'til I had two or three spoons of soup. I got weaker and weaker and knew I would die. Worst of all the grief was as ever present as the oxygen we inhale. I ate nothing when he worked. He called every day. He forced me to eat more each day and promised this would never happen again! He lied!!!

We couldn't go to the hospital but depended on the *surgeon's* advice. She was worried! I returned to her home to be examined and received suggestions on making me eat. Our worry subsided after my appetite increased each day. I had lost ten pounds in two weeks and looked like death! My life was spared but the Bible says "You reap what you sow" and so I did.

Dreams of my sin seem to have no end. Even now those horrible memories resurface, reminding me they are still alive. My mind, as my body ages, reveals unique insights of my past with each new eventful year.

I became quite depressed as I started this last assignment. Several days passed before I was able to resume writing the paper. I had fallen in a pit and couldn't climb out. My fervent prayers to God lifted me from that well of darkness.

* * *

Nardia did not abort her gift from God. The baby girl grew strong and beautiful with long thick black hair which passed her waist. The quiet, kind, loving but still strong small girl had been given my middle name, Elyse. Neysa Elyse Jennings, now Bryan had *two* beautiful daughters.

Nardia possessed wonderful qualities of motherhood. She worked as long as she could and tolerated Bryan whom she no longer understood. She'd visit her mother more often than usual for meals since Bryan spent most of his salary on drugs. After two months and no car payments, Lenard and I drove to Fayetteville and drove the I-Roc back to Baltimore and parked it next to Benny's van on the side of my yard. My, my, the house was filled with my son's belongings and now the yard was crowded with cars.

Less than two weeks later Bryan returned to Baltimore; he said to get a job. I knew better. After begging a week, I returned the car along with a list of obligations he intended to keep. He understood it was I who paid his bills of $995 every month. He promised to send something every month. He *never* did!

My teaching salary, making draperies seven day a week plus help from Lenard and shifting bills around, I scraped up enough to pay my bills. Still, everything was behind. My creditors understood the dilemma and worked with me. Delinquent payments still doomed my credit record.

Lenard and I planned to marry in November, only if he'd stop drinking! He'd stopped, I thought. During the two months we planned for our wedding everything happened that could happen. I saw and heard the warning signs but chose not to acknowledge them. Instead I plunged forward; straight into hell! God worked through his people. I ignored His signals. I chose Dawn's way, the wrong way. Her way that led to misery, to grief—a mosaic of sorrows.

A friend revealed her prayer, the *first warning signal* that I wasn't to marry Lenard.

"Dawn I've prayed to God to do everything possible to keep you from marrying Lenard. He's not the man for you."

"How could you do such a thing Tanya! I'd never do a thing like that if you were planning to marry."

She spoke to me in her soft quiet manner while I got angrier by the moment. I thought, *how dare she say, whom I should marry. This is my life, not hers. She has her fine husband, why can't I have mine.* After that conversation our once warm relationship cooled for a while.

Lenard and I were scheduled to meet my pastor for counseling sessions. Lenard didn't show; his car nearly caught on fire en route to the church. As steam escaped from under the hood, he pulled over and located the problem in time. No matter what he wore, he'd stick his hands and arms inside the workings of a car never thinking about the grease that remained on his clothes. Every white shirt I bought was ruined! Eventually I gave up and bought all dark shirts.

After the pastor and I waited almost an hour we left. I returned later and parked some distance from the church. Lenard's car was parked in front of the church. He *banged* on the hood while steam spurted from underneath! He straddled the hood with both hands in agony. Another church minister tried to console him. Unaware of my presence, Lenard entered the church with the minister and prayed in the sanctuary.

"Why am I having all this trouble? This car was fine 'til today. I don't understand what's happening."

That was *the second signal* I ignored.

One Saturday, unannounced, I went to Lenard's shop behind his mother's house. I saw his car parked in the alley but he wasn't in his shop. I opened the backyard's chained linked gate to his mother's yard and walked up the sidewalk to her back door.

"Ms. Winters, have you seen Lenard, I see his car but I don't see him."

"He was there a few minutes ago. I guess he went to see a neighbor. Try next door."

I went next door but he wasn't there. As I walked out of the neighbor's gate I saw Lenard across the alley standing on a back porch talking to a lady. The heavy lady had her hand on his shoulder and pushed him slightly inside the house in jest as they both laughed. I walked across the alley, opened the gate to the backyard and walked up the steps to the back porch. The house needed painting; the yard was a mess. In this poor neighborhood all the houses looked the same. I knocked on the weather-beaten door. A child pulled back the curtain and opened the door.

"Would you tell Lenard that Dawn is here please?"

The young girl invited me inside the kitchen, pointed to a chair and offered me a seat. She left to get Lenard who returned immediately.

"Who told you I was here?"

"Your mother said you were visiting a friend and I saw you come inside this house."

Just then the heavy lady I'd seen pushing Lenard walked in the kitchen.

"What are you doing in my house!"

"I came to get Lenard."

"You came to *my house! Get out of my house, now!!"*

I walked slowly toward the door as the angry woman poured out profanity! I couldn't understand why. Once I stepped on the porch, she reached out to *push* me down those rickety steps! That *instant*, the reason for her hatred surfaced. Lenard must have dated that woman. As she hurled profane language, Lenard stepped in front of her while I walked quickly down the steps. I was *scared*!! I was *angry*!! I was humiliated and embarrassed! Silently, I questioned Lenard's mother's judgement in allowing me to walk, into that dangerous situation. His mother relished confusion, I didn't. Leonard had flaunted me in front of a former girlfriend. She had a right to be angry, but not with me, with Lenard! That was the *third* signal I ignored.

I left him standing in the alley, awestruck, shaking his bowed head as usual when anything went awry and returned to my car. I sat terrified, trembling, and tattered by the overwhelming past twenty minutes! Lenard walked over to the car slowly. I stared straight-ahead ignoring his presence not wanting to hear his words of defense, yet I listened to his *sorry pitiful masculine* explanation.

"Dawn you had no business going into that lady's house."

"No business what! What are you talking about? You had no business doing what you did. You disrespected her and endangered my life. You *are* crazy! Leave me alone. I'm going home!"

I started the car. He placed his hand on the car door and asked me to hear his side. Humiliated, tired and still trembling, I paused and listened.

"Dawn let me explain. Yes, we used to date. Every time she sees me now, she wants us to get back together. I keep telling her no! That's why I was in her house today, she wanted to talk. She knows I'm seeing you and she's seen you in the alley with me. That's why she got so mad."

He moved toward the passenger's side. As he walked around the car, I almost pulled off; then I thought, *that's exactly what she wants me to do.* The instant I saw her peeking through her kitchen window I changed my mind. I refused to satisfy her anger. Lenard got in the car and we left in silence. His pathetic reasoning continued as I drove home. With that problem resolved, new ones waited close by, eager to spring forward.

I don't know why, but on November 14, 1987 I married Lenard A. Winters. I guess I loved him. Even then with all his irrational decisions and behavior he was the *kindest* and most *considerate* man I'd ever met. He needed me and I needed him; I thought.

The day before our small church wedding I discussed my awful financial problems with the church organist, a devout Christian. We knelt before the altar and prayed together. She was a *praying, praying* lady! The sound of her prayers penetrated the church walls and my heart as we knelt before God. The silent sanctuary and her urgent petition for help brought tears to my eyes. After her prayer she said in sincerity:

"Sister Albens why didn't you tell me you were having those problems? You're to tell the church so we can pray. God *will* get that house sold for you in North Carolina!"

One week later I received a call from my real estate agent. He'd found a buyer! Our closing date was near the end of December. The house was sold. Alleluia! I thanked God for the buyer and was eternally grateful. I was finally, free from the house and its payments; still the stunning burgundy I-ROC remained. Four more years of car payments, pain and tears remained plus the other bill totaling $495 a month faced my future. Nevertheless, $500 less was a great help. The property sold for $31,000. After deducting the bank's balance, the agent's fee etc. I left settlement with $1000 which paid *delinquent* bills. So Aunt Betty sold me her property for $1.00. I profited *nothing* thanks to my kindness to Bryan in volunteering to mortgage the house in the *first place!!* I'd learned my lesson, or had I?

An old adage says, "A man never knows how unimportant he is until he attends his own wedding." Most men don't want to be involved, while a few do.

The oversized Sunday school room wasn't available to decorate for the reception until after 6:00 p.m. the evening before the wedding. Lenard had the mauve satin fabric pressed and brought it by the church that evening.

He said, "I don't know why you're working so hard. Why you are down on the floor cutting paper; all that's not necessary." His concern wasn't church beautification but only automotive repairs.

"Not to you, but to me. See, I'm covering those bulletin boards with paper and Biblical Scriptures. Look over there; see how pretty it looks."

"Yeah—it looks pretty but you *don't* have to wear yourself out the way you do."

"Everything will be finished tonight then I won't have to do anything tomorrow."

The bridal and cake tables had draped mauve satin fabric and added touches of greenery. The guests' chairs were lined on one side of the room in twos or threes. A church member catered. The three-tiered wedding cake with stairs leading up to the second and third layers had the wedding party placed on the steps. I'd requested a two-layer cake but my personal *cake lady* added the rest.

"Dawn this *will* be your *last* marriage that's why I added the *rest* as a gift to you." I'd met Elvira as a drapery customer. We became friends and sent each other customers.

My fantastic, cream, lace, silk, sequined wedding gown purchased two years earlier was set aside, just in case I needed one in the future. With my marriage and divorce record, anything was possible. Rather than sell the gorgeous princess styled wedding gown, I kept it. Later I planned to cut off the short train and use it as a gown.

Previous cold winter weeks had snow piled high in some areas. Our wedding day however was *heavenly*. Sparkling fallen snow and leafless trees sent messages of winter while sunlight shined through lacy tree branches. Coats weren't needed so we took several wedding pictures outside amid God's winter scene as friends surrounded us. Only two of Lenard's large family attended. Later I questioned his family members who had previous engagements. Their absence left me thinking I wasn't accepted in the family, although I'd never witnessed any dislike during my visits. Those buried thoughts surfaced months later.

Both of my sons were out of town: Marty still in the Azores and Bryan, well Bryan had dates with the drug man and had to work to finance his habit. He'd work all week *clean*, then every weekend use his paycheck on *crack cocaine!* So as usual my close friends (my only family) and church members made our wedding and reception a happy spiritual occasion.

With low finances, a honeymoon was impossible. So we planned to stay home that Sunday and return to work on Monday. My husband however, up at six a.m. Sunday morning prepared to leave for his shop.

"Where are you going Lenard, today is our honeymoon?"

"Well I can't make any money staying in the bed."

"I hadn't planned to stay in the bed. We'd planned to have dinner out then spend the

rest of the day together. Isn't that what we said?"

"No, that's what *you* said, I just listened?"

Since our courtship only entailed daily phone calls and personal contact two-three times a week, I was unfamiliar with his morning and daily routines. However, I learned *real, real* soon! After expressing my deep concerns about him working on our one-day honeymoon (the first month after marriage should be sweet as honey) he relinquished and spent the day with me. In fact that was the *only* whole day we shared during our entire marriage unless we went out of town and even then he yearned to return to Baltimore.

Two weeks later was Thanksgiving. I looked forward to spending another full day with my husband because I'd seen *more* of him when we dated. Everyday Lenard came home one or two a.m. After he labored half the night many customers never—even paid! His kindness won their hearts but kept his pockets somewhat empty. Sooner or later they'd pay something. A gifted mechanic, he'd listen to a car and determine the problem almost instantly.

Since I sewed or attended church after work, having two days off meant a lot. Early Thanksgiving morning I rose and started dinner. While I dressed the turkey, Lenard came downstairs to the kitchen.

"I'm going out for a while, I'll be back soon."

"*Out!* Out *where* Lenard?"

"Down in the country. Every Thanksgiving I have breakfast with my older friends in the country. They cook all that pork I love to eat, all that heavy country food *you* don't like."

"I thought we were going to spend the day together. I'd cook while you'd keep me company, watch television and get some rest."

"Rest, I rested last night."

Lenard left to visit his friends and didn't return until the following morning, late morning the day *after* Thanksgiving! As he walked up the steps, I sat in the den waiting, waiting to hear his lies. He went in our bedroom and flopped down in the chair. Later I strolled in the bedroom.

"And why are you in this bedroom?

"This is my home."

"Oh no, this is *not* your home. Your home is where you spent last night. I don't want to know where you were. I could care less. But I'm telling you now if you stay out another night, this marriage is *over*! In fact you may take *all* of your clothes and leave right now if it's too hard for you to come home! Married two weeks, our first Thanksgiving and you spend it with other people. You're not a single man anymore Lenard, you're married or have you forgotten. Married men come home at night. They come home to their wives and families. I am your wife. How would you feel if I didn't come home all night? You never even called. I will *not* go through this again with *another* man *Lenard!!* Do you understand what I'm saying? Have I made myself clear or do you want me to repeat what I just said!"

His bewildered and confused look said, 'Do you really mean I can't stay out all night.' I explained his alternatives.

"You mean if I stay out another night you'll put me out?"

"That's right. Staying out all night tells me you don't want to be here. And if you don't want to be here, live where you spent the night. Isn't that a simple solution?"

He didn't know what to say. He stared down at the floor, then up at me, then down at the floor again, then up at me, speechless. I'd given him an ultimatum. I left the room after expressing my anger and disgust, went downstairs and ate my breakfast.

Who did he think he was anyway? Did he think he was still single and could come and go when he felt like it. For *months* he rang my phone all day and half the night because he wanted to be *with* me.

"Dawn won't you let me stay the night. I want to be *with* you. Why won't you let me stay?"

"No Lenard, wait 'til we're married then you can stay every night." Now married, he *stayed* somewhere else.

Christmas morning I knew Lenard was going to visit his family and friends while I again prepared dinner. He *said* he'd return early afternoon. After 11:00 that night he walked into our bedroom dangling a plastic bag in my face as I lay in bed.

"Here, this is something I bought you for Christmas. I knew I couldn't come home if I didn't have you a gift. It's not wrapped; I didn't have time to wrap it."

I looked at the store's plastic bag dangling in my face and felt like knocking it out of his hand. I thought *why did I marry this man? He's rarely home.* He spends his holidays with his drinking, cursing and festive friends that love that fattening food. He knew I did none of those things when he met me. He changed his address but not his habits. On several occasions he'd say:

"Why don't you come down to the shop sometime while I work? No, you can't do that because you don't want to see the rats. You think you're too good for the rats. I've slept in the cars many nights and they didn't bother me." He meant every word.

"Lenard after I work all week I don't want to spend my Saturdays sitting in a dirty alley surrounded with trash, garbage, old mattresses, broken furniture etc. I do visit you sometime. Every time I show up you tell me I shouldn't have come. Make up your mind what you want."

"I want you to show interest in my work. I want you to keep me company sometime while I'm working."

Lenard needed someone to ride with him, talk with him and keep him company while he worked on cars. As a child he was involved with cars every single day in an alley while his family and friends socialized. I wasn't spending my leisure time sitting in an alley.

As soon as Lenard entered anyone's home he used their phone. He needed to talk constantly by phone or in person. He kept a pocket full of quarters for his daily calls, making the telephone company richer! I responded to his statement.

"Well I could say the same thing. I want you home with me sometime. You're never home before eleven or twelve at night. I never know when you come home unless I see you sleeping on the floor."

"You know why I sleep on the floor. I come home so dirty and tired; I don't feel like taking a bath so I sleep on the floor 'til I feel like getting in the tub."

"Yes I know and understand your reason but you could still come home like normal men come home from work before dark. I ate alone every night before we married, I didn't think I'd still have dinner alone and spend all my evenings by myself after we married."

"When it's light, Dawn, I have to work. It's too early to come home. When it's dark I come home to sleep."

He meant *every* word. When I begged he'd come home early. He'd shower, eat dinner, flop down on the sofa, and fall asleep. I was still alone even though his head rested on my lap.

After weeks of watching television all alone, I was intrigued by an appealing commercial, advertising Kim's Karate. I watched in amazement as young children jumped, leaped, sparred and yelled!

39...LONELINESS FULFILLED

Deceive not thyself by over expecting
happiness in the married estate. Remember
the nightingales which sing only some months
in the spring, but commonly are silent when
they have hatched their eggs.
Thomas Fuller: Of Marriage
Ibid

In January at fifty years old, three weeks shy of turning fifty-one, I signed up for martial arts classes at Kim's Karate Studio. Their intriguing commercials triggered my curiosity and dire interest to enquire if I qualified for classes. I was tired of staying home alone. I needed an outlet; something to fill my loneliness without my husband. So I called their studio.

"Hello, my name is Mrs. Winters. I'm interested in taking karate lessons. What's the age limit for adults?"

"Ma'am how old are, you?"

"I know I'm too old to start those classes even though I've taught modern dance for many years. I sprained my right ankle some years ago. It doesn't flex as well as the left one when I try to do a grand plie. Would karate help that problem?"

"Oh *yes*, in time it'll be back to normal." What great news to my ears.

"You mean I'll be able to dance as I once did?"

"Oh yes. It sounds like you're in pretty good shape to me. There is no age limit to take karate Mrs. Winters. A few months ago in another state we had a lady sixty-seven years old get her Black Belt. It took her five years though rather than our regular three."

"You mean I could get a Black Belt in three years?"

"Yes, but it all depends on you and your ability. How old are you?"

"Next month I'll be fifty-one."

"You don't—*sound*—like—you're fifty-one."

"I am, but I don't look it either. I've been very active *all* of my life."

The following day after school, I visited the karate studio. I watched astonished, as small children practiced and young Black Belts rehearsed their forms! I signed up that day! Mr. Bun, a Korean instructor for Tae Kwon Do was impressed with my agility and concentration. His awesome performance dazzled me! I'd only seen karate performed by Bruce Lee and Chuck Conners in films. Now I witnessed Mr. Bun's vaulted leaps, swift turns and precise transition in motion as he progressed from one space to the next. His brilliant timing was captivating as he dominated the floor through his masterful and powerful moves. He was *magnificent*! I never tired of watching him execute his powerful moves!

Along with developing physical and mental coordination martial arts developed a sense of self-esteem needed by so many timid withdrawn children.

Beginner's class was held every Tuesday and Friday at 5:00 p.m. Five years later I'd reached my brown senior belt, next to a Black Belt. Several medical conditions not related to karate prevented me from attending numerous classes during that fifth year, until I was forced to stop altogether. Extreme dizziness required I walk to the side of the room. Or the arthritis in my right leg became active. Sometimes I simply forgot my form. I felt cheated. I'd worked *so* hard to earn all those belts; got so close and then had to quit.

Mr. Bun promised he'd be there when I got my Black Belt but he left after two years. He and his American wife, also a Black Belt, opened their own karate studio separate from Kim's Karate. He was missed by everyone, students and staff.

Karate added a new dimension to my life; it filled my loneliness; it offered me new challenges while my ankle improved drastically. I looked forward to classes. They helped release the built up stresses I'd endured all day. The co-ed class had students of various ages: beginner, intermediate and advanced. Each class' routines started with exercises of arm and leg movements, kicks, jumps, turns and combination of all the forms and self-defense techniques for each belt level. Belt ranking was selected by a multi-colored belt system:

Beginner: no belt, white belt, yellow belt and green belt
Intermediate: blue and purple belts
Advanced: red belt, brown junior belt, brown senior belt
Black Belt.

Even though I was unable to complete the brown senior belt, I enhanced my mind and body through struggles endured earning each belt. Pride enveloped me each time the instructor placed a new belt color around my waist as I stood before our class. It was phenomenal! Indeed, a momentous occasion for me at ages fifty-two through fifty-six. I felt like an Olympic Gold Winner!

Lenard never attended any of my classes. Once he carried me but sat outside in his car rather than come inside.

"Why are you taking karate classes? That's for men. You should be home tending to the things of the house, not out somewhere fighting."

"Lenard, I'm learning it for many reasons: first to keep from being alone all the time. Second to improve my ankle that doesn't bend, third to keep my body fit and in shape and fourth for self-defense. I've learned ways to protect myself if anyone attacks me. You want to see what I've learned?"

"*No* I don't want to see nothing."

"If you were home more often, I never would have enrolled in the first place. Do you understand!"

With all eight belts I'd earned, not one family member or friend, witnessed any tests! I'd watch other class members being showered with hugs and praises as I went home and thanked God who'd given me the strength to pass my test. There were guests however that congratulated me on several occasions on breaking my boards with kicks or the success of my forms. The students' parents always uttered supporting words for my tenacity and perseverance. Their encouragement in addition to my instructor's positive critiques kept my candle aglow.

Lenard and I made an emergency trip to Fayetteville to help Nardia. The new baby was two months old and they were two months behind in their trailer rent.

"Mom I hate to ask you again to help us but Bryan uses all his money on drugs and sometimes we don't have any food in the house."

"Oh Nardia, *I'm so sorry* Bryan is putting you and those babies through this! Is he there now? Can you talk?"

"No he's not here. I haven't seen him in three days."

"Three days! Where is he, do you know?"

"Yes I know. He's hanging out there with his cocaine friends. Four days ago we got our Income Tax check for $800. He told me to hold on to the check and not to give it to him no matter what he said. Hours later he came home high, wanting *his* money."

"Give me my money Nardia! I want my money now!"

"Half of this money is mine Bryan. You can waste yours on drugs. I have to feed and take care of these children. You forgot about them didn't you?"

"No I haven't! I just want my money! Give me my money now!"

"Mom he acted like a mad man, yelling and screaming all over the house! Briana started crying when she saw him push me against the wall. Then Neysa started crying. We all cried while Bryan threw books, shoes, and anything in his way around the house. So I gave him the money. Three days later he came back *broke!* Every penny was *gone*! I had to get money from my parents for food. They've given me *so* much money for food and rent I just can't ask them for anymore!

"Where's the car Nardia?"

"He has it. It sounds bad."

"I'll help you on one condition; that you put Bryan *out*! When I get there I don't want to see him! I'll bring you $300 for your past and present rent and food."

"Al-right Mo—m I really appre—ciate what you're do—ing."

She cried agonizing tears! I was *mad, mad, mad* with Bryan for mistreating his wife and those innocent babies. It didn't take much for Nardia to cry. Poor girl, she'd been through so much dealing with my addicted son! I would *never* see them evicted or not have any food due to his stupidity! With no money as usual I'd renew my credit union loan to help my darling daughter-in-law and my precious grandbabies.

"Lenard and I will leave early Saturday morning and come back Sunday. Do you have somewhere for us to sleep?"

"Of course I do Mom. You and Lenard can sleep in our bedroom. We'll sleep out front in the Living Room."

"Nardia remember I *do not want to see Bryan!* Have him park the I-ROC at your trailer. Lenard will drive it back home where it will stay *permanently*! He's not making any payments; he's not taking care of it so he doesn't need it!"

We left early Saturday morning and arrived at one p.m. Bryan's car was parked outside the trailer. Nardia greeted us warmly and held the door open while Lenard carried in the $50 worth of groceries I'd bought. I hadn't told her I'd bring food but that I'd give her the money. But to make sure she had food I bought some and delivered it myself. I gave her the $300 for the rent and an extra $50 for whatever she needed. She was *sooo* thankful. She deserved far more than that for how my son treated them.

She didn't look well. Worrying about her children and her no count husband had taken its toll on that young woman.

"Mom thanks so much for helping us, *again*."

She grabbed and hugged me *real* tight as tears rolled down her face. Proud of her small but comfortable home, she showed us the trailer and the various changes she'd made to improve its appearance. It was small but nicely decorated and enough room for them. As soon as I walked into their bedroom there was *Mr. Bryan* sprawled out in the queen size bed, leaning up against the headboard playing with my two gorgeous grandchildren!

"What are you doing here Bryan?"

"I came to see my mother."

"Oh you did huh? I don't know why because I *didn't* come to see you!"

"And why may I ask?"

"Why! Because, you're *not* taking care of your *family*! I shouldn't have to come down here to pay your rent and buy food. That's *your* responsibility. You spend all your money on drugs. How can you stay here knowing that your family is hungry? What's *wrong* with you Bryan!"

"I work everyday."

"For what! To pay your drug dealer and keep him rich! You're home every night but take your paycheck on Fridays and disappear 'til Monday morning having wasted your family's money on drugs!! You need help my dear son or you will die and leave your children fatherless. Is *that* what you want?"

After unleashing my anger, we all went out for dinner at my expense then took the children to the local annual Fair. We returned to Baltimore Sunday morning with Lenard driving the I-ROC.

With Lenard's increased drinking plus the Special Education children I taught, my life was *miserable*! Some days I didn't want to live. I went to work only because I had expenses. Life was depressing and I was getting blown away a little more each day. Without God I could *not* have made it! I *would not have lived!*

I taught two Special Education Classes at the same time. They were *terrible*! I'd begged my assistant principal to separate them but he refused.

"I don't have anywhere to put them Mrs. Winters."

"You don't! Why do I have to teach two classes when the law states only 10 to 15 students per class? All of their other teachers only have one class. I have two and they fuss, argue and curse each other everyday! I'm tired. I can't take anymore. You must find a way to separate them, *please*!"

Rather than separate the classes he called my art supervisor and asked her to give me alternate suggestions for their lessons. I didn't need suggestions. I knew how to teach! I needed the office's cooperation in separating the two classes. She came. We both knew they needed to be separated. She empathized with my situation as we reviewed alternatives for peace between the two emotionally hyperactive classes while they worked in the *small* crowded art room. Once again I pleaded.

"Mr. Boman, would you please separate those classes! Why must I have two! I have almost *thirty*! That's unfair and illegal."

"We only have one art teacher Mrs. Winters and the schedule doesn't provide another slot to put them in. Please try to understand our predicament."

"Understand your predicament; what about mine? What about my sanity, while you're in your office? Remember I'm in the classroom *every* other day with them. *Please* help me! I can't teach under these circumstances. You're aware of the problems. They curse each other, throw things at each other when I'm helping another student, run around the classroom, play and hide under tables and bang on the tables rather than work on their projects. The list goes on and on. I don't have these problems in my other classes. Besides, whenever one of the classes doesn't show the other one works very well. That's the answer, they can't work together."

I had suffered enough humiliation! One Friday afternoon I left a letter in my assistant principal's mailbox stating I would *not* return until he separated those two classes. My head ached; I refused to teach them anymore. He called Monday morning asking me to explain my letter. Of course he thought I was being unreasonable.

"Mr. Bowman as I stated in my letter, I will only return when you have separated those two classes. I can't take any more disrespect. Some of those students want to learn; they're being denied an education. Are you thinking about them or just somewhere to stick the class because your schedule doesn't have a vacant slot?"

Home four days on sick leave provided the time I needed to call the Board of Education, my art supervisor, the supervisor of Special Education and The Baltimore Teacher's Union. *"The squeaking wheel got oiled."* Thursday afternoon I received a call from Mr. Bowman.

"Mrs. Winters, would you *please* return to work."

"Only if you have separated those two classes."

"We have." Those were the words I'd longed to hear.

"Where is the other class?" There was a pause then he answered in a bitter offensive tone.

"I don't know where they are!" I'd won; he'd lost. He resented his defeat.

The school missed me. I was the best art teacher they'd ever had. They didn't want to lose me but had—for that week.

Meanwhile, back in Lenard's alley he was experiencing major quandaries with his customers. Problems to him meant more drinking which incited more trouble.

After two months of marriage Lenard arrived home late one night as usual but not drunk. I was in bed. He stood in the middle of the doorway sober with an enigmatic look that surfaced each time he experienced a serious decision.

"What's the matter Lenard? You don't look well."

"I think I need a break."

"A break from what?"

"A break from marriage." I looked at the sick man I'd married. The man I loved.

"But why Lenard?"

"I don't know. I guess I was too hasty in getting married. I need time to think."

I wasn't surprised at his statement. He possessed a free spirit. He resented having to come home *every* night. When he was too drunk or too tired to drive, he spent a night at his aunt's house. Or he might flop down on his mother's sofa, sleep at his uncle's house, snooze in a friend's chair or curl up in the back seat of a customer's car in the alley and spend the night. It never mattered where he slept when he was drunk or excessively tired. No, he shouldn't be married. It's what he begged for and it's what he got.

"Lenard, do whatever you think you have to do."

I knew something was wrong and now he'd revealed his problem, at least part of it. The man turned, walked down the steps and out the door, a free man!

With business so slow he got a full time job at a paper company where his sister worked. He said he'd worked there before, driving their delivery truck whenever his business was slack. Lenard called often to check on me.

One day I paid him an unexpected visit at his new job. He hadn't returned from his last delivery so I parked next to his car on the parking lot—and waited. Needless to say, he was not glad to see me. He walked toward me slowly with his head dropped as though he'd lost his last friend.

"What are you doing here Dawn?"

"I hadn't heard from you in a few days so I thought I'd stop by and visit."

While I'd waited for him, I sat in his car for a short time. On the passenger's side was a brown paper bag that held a large purple plum wrapped in a Bounty floral blue and white paper towel. I stared at the paper towel and knew it wasn't his selection. Neither had he taken time to fold the top of the bag that neatly. He said he rented a room after he left me, with kitchen privileges and the older gentleman used that brand of paper towels. I asked him to come back home. He said he needed more time. I was hurt and disappointed. I saw signs of his instability before we married but I ignored them.

Two weeks later he returned. Standing in the same spot about the same hour he'd left while I lay in bed.

"I'm back. I guess this is where I'm supposed to be."

I'll never forget those words. Did he think he was doing me a favor by coming back? During that two-week period he called often to see how I was doing and share his confused feelings about having to come home every night. Again I reminded him that married men come home.

"Dawn when I got married I didn't think you'd mind if I didn't come home sometimes."

"Well I didn't discuss it because I thought it was *obvious* Lenard."

What did I marry? We discussed his problem on the phone. I kept reminding him to do what he thought was best. We'd dated for seven months and then married. The length of time wasn't the problem it was his alcoholism, insecurities and restlessness. He was a sick man, extremely sick. Besides, I'd seen the problems. They struck me hard in the face every day! But I thought I could *change* him by helping him to accept another life style, *my way of living*. I thought a stable and different environment would have a constructive influence on his life and help to stop his drinking. Having had an alcoholic husband and a boyfriend previously should have taught me a lesson but I was still trying to save the world. Why, because I was sick myself and didn't know it!

I recalled when Lenard mowed the lawn like a wild man! A normal person would cut in a back and forth motion, but not Lenard. He'd cut in *all* directions! Rocks, stones and anything in his way flew through the lawn mower. I saw the maze, the entanglement from my second floor window and rushed downstairs to complain. He ignored me.

"I learned how to cut grass very well in the Army. You're just too hard to please."

Bryan stopped by one day while Lenard was mowing the lawn.

"Mommy have you seen what Lenard is doing to your lawn! Rocks and sticks are flying everywhere and he *never* stops! He pushes that lawn mower in every direction! The lawn looks terrible! What's wrong with him?"

"He's drunk."

As Bryan complained about the lawn, I recalled the day a year earlier when his friend Harrell was cutting the lawn while he was in the house using the telephone. I stood and watched Harrell the few minutes he did cut.

"Ms. Dawn I'll cut the grass for you. You have no business cutting all this grass." My grateful smile acknowledged. He understood it was a man's job. He'd only cut about five minutes before Mr. Bryan rushed outside.

"Come on man, we gotta' go!"

"But Bryan, Harrell volunteered to cut the lawn."

"Not today; we have to go *now*! We have *more* important things to do."

Harrell cut off the lawn mower, got in the car with Bryan and left. I resumed cutting the huge lawn as usual.

Weeks later the lawn mower refused to be abused anymore by Lenard— it died! He carried it down to his shop for its final surgery. I knew I'd never see it again. I begged him to return it because the lawn needed cutting.

"I'm still working on it. Don't worry about your *precious* lawn! It *will* get cut!"

After I'd rented a lawn mower twice I visited Lenard's shop, unannounced. Lifting a lawn mower in and out the trunk of my car was not a woman's job. I parked in front of his mother's house; then walked to his alley shop. The garage door was open. Things were in order as usual, but where was Lenard? I noticed the lawn mower placed far back in the right corner of the garage, untouched. I pulled it out and into the alley. As I started pushing it toward the street, Lenard *leaped* from behind a parked car in the alley, enraged and drunk!

"I told you not to come down here! What are you doing with that lawn mower!"

168

He rushed toward me and *yanked* the mower from my hands! I gazed at his blood-shot eyes, hair mangled with dirt, dust and grime, and *filthy* clothes. He looked and acted like a wild man who'd been living in a jungle for weeks! I was *scared*! I'd never seen him in that condition. Was this the same man I married? What happened to him? Then reality surfaced and jolted my brain. *This was the alcohol*, not Lenard.

I watched him *sling* that lawn mower up and down the small narrow street of old row houses in front of his mother's home! He'd lift it, then *slam* it on the ground, lift it again, then *slam* it on the ground! *Snapper* mowers were the best you could buy. As I watched Lenard hurl and jerk the man-made machine I thought, *it's his inner rage coming out on that poor innocent lawn mower. Doesn't he know he needs help?*

"Go home!" He yelled. "*I told you not to come down here! Go home where you belong!*"

I stared scared trembling and prayed for my sick, suffering husband. He acted like a maniac, only worse! He yanked open my car door on the driver's side and yelled, "*Get in and go home!*"

Neighbors peeked from their living room curtains. They were used to Lenard and his mother's drunken rants and rages! He never hurt anyone. Neither did his mother. The poor but decent neighborhood survived its blight and emotionally disturbed mother and son alcoholic tirades. As I slid behind the steering wheel and pulled away from the curb in front of his mother's house he yelled, "*And don't come down here anymore!!!*"

I drove down the small street Lenard had cleaned earlier and saw him in my rear view mirror still tossing and throwing that broken banged up lawn mower around in the street. What a pitiful sight to witness. Even worse, *he* was my husband. I cried uncontrollably as I drove home. I didn't understand how alcohol could transform a kind, sweet humorous person, into a raging maniac!

Lamar was just the opposite. He'd stagger off somewhere and go to sleep. Nat however was nasty, but not violent. But Lenard was the worse alcoholic I had known. The next day he called as usual and apologized. For some reason he thought his apology would excuse his abominable behavior. He'd always blame it on the alcohol.

I thought, *I'm* the one who's crazy for constantly dating and marrying alcoholics. I realized that moment; it was *I* who needed help! Something was *definitely wrong* with me! I kept marrying the same type of man *over* and *over* and over again!

Lenard's sons moved in with their Grandmother, Lenard's mother. Since they refused to obey their mother—she put them out! He didn't want me burdened with the boys, so he found them an apartment for $300 a month. Of course after Lenard paid their rent bought food and paid the utilities nothing was left for our household. Their mother wanted him to shoulder the total care of his sons. She had that right. I'd raised two sons; I knew the headaches involved. This new liability increased his drinking which added to my stress.

The grimy furnished apartment had cracked plaster walls, torn dangling wall paper, a dirty stove and refrigerator etc. In a poor neighborhood, what he could afford, all three of them lived there. Actually they did; I saw him less and less. They had no phone and no electricity at first. The neighbor next door allowed Leonard's son to run a heavy duty electric cord from his apartment to theirs for a fee. Lenard told his son to disconnect the cord but he didn't. The electric company found out and charged the neighbor extra for the illegal use. Lenard was forced to get his own electric sooner than he'd anticipated.

Often two to three days passed before I'd hear from Lenard. He'd *say* he didn't have access to a phone. After weeks of calling his mother to relay messages to him, she asked me a direct question.

"Dawn do you have Lenard's telephone number?"

"Telephone, he told me they didn't have a telephone." There was a lo—ng pause; later she'd revealed the truth.

"Well he does. They've had it for two weeks now."

"Two weeks and he didn't tell me. I wonder why?" I said.

"I don't know Dawn—I don't know." Her slow answer revealed the opposite. She gave me the phone number with my promise not to divulge the source. I called the next morning bright and early.

"Hello, may I speak to Lenard please? This is Dawn." There was a pause—then the son called his father.

"How did you get this number Dawn?" Lenard said.

"Why didn't you give it to me Lenard? Why did you lie and tell me you didn't have a phone when you had one all the time?"

"I didn't want you to have it."

"You what? You didn't want me to have it. Why? Why didn't you want me to have it? I'm your wife or have you forgotten?"

"Well you'd be calling here and asking all kinds of questions."

He avoided my questions and talked around them. He'd come home for a few nights; then stay at the apartment a couple of nights so the neighbors could see him coming and going. A week later I called again at 11:00 p.m.; he wasn't home. Early the next morning I called at 5:00; he still wasn't in.

"Mrs. Dawn my father isn't home right now."

"Where is he this time of morning?"

"I don't know I haven't seen him since yesterday. I thought he was with you."

"No I haven't seen him either maybe he's with another woman. Is he seeing another woman?" He dragged out his words in hesitant syllables.

"I—don't know. I ain't got—nothin'—ta do—wid-it."

I thanked him and hung up the receiver. He confirmed my suspicions. I returned to bed, slid under the covers and thought—oooh how I thought! 'Something was rotten in Denmark' I knew I'd solve this mystery yet.

Since school cutbacks eliminated elective teachers first; a music teacher and I were transferred from the senior high school. My transfer had been to the middle school that involved *my four-day-home-retreat.* My supervisor knew I wanted to teach senior high so one evening she called me at home.

"Dawn I knew how intent you were about returning to senior high. Are you still interested."

"Interested! Of course I'm interested Tess. When do I leave!" She laughed.

We'd known each other over twenty-five years and open conversation was easy. She was *beautiful*, well dressed, older, and more experienced. We'd both been through many husbands and didn't tolerate foolishness.

"Not until September. You still have a month left in school so start getting yourself together to leave."

News spread that I'd be returning to senior high in September. The principal and teachers *begged* me to reconsider! The parents were the *crème de la crème.* Every holiday teachers were treated royally with tokens of appreciation.

I included two field trips for my students every year. These were student paid trips and parents were welcomed to go if they desired. Washington, D.C. our nation's capital was number-one. The president of the P.T.A., Mrs. Hart stopped me one day in the hall with an alarming surprise.

"Mrs. Winters we'd like to help you with your trip to Washington."

In all my years of teaching I'd never had any help from a P.T.A. or school. I said, "Would you like to help with collecting money or as chaperones?"

"Well we could do that too, but we thought we could pay for the bus."

"*Pay for the bus!* That would be great, but the bus is over $700." I couldn't believe her words!

"Well, what about half of it?"

"You mean you'll pay *$350* toward the bus!" I was shocked. I didn't know what else to say.

"Yes we will. That'll help reduce the cost of the tickets; then more students can afford to go."

She stood there so calm as though she gave away money every day. The tickets *were* moving slowly and we *really* needed help.

"Mrs. Hart, please forgive my excitement but in my, entire, let me see, twenty-six years of teaching no one has *ever* helped *me* with a trip! I *thank* you so much!"

"We were told the seats weren't moving that fast so we decided to offer our help. Let me know when you'll need the check and the name of the bus company."

"Oh I'll write that down for you right now. It's The Monumental Motor Tours. Their slogan was *Travel to Learn and Learn to Travel.* Thank you *so much* for your *help!*"

The P.T.A. enabled us to avoid the trip's cancellation. Students and parents reported raves for their fantastic day! As usual I took pictures. What joy I experienced as I saw their elation and enthusiasm in every new site we visited.

I knew Baltimore youth *must* tour The White House, The Capitol, The Lincoln and Jefferson Memorials, The National Art Gallery, The Ford Theatre, etc. We saw as many sites as possible. The statue of *The Awakening* at Haines Point Park, where they had their picnic lunch was the highlight!

Other trips included The Tomb of the Unknown Soldier and the Changing of the Guards in Arlington Cemetery, an *unforgettable* sight! Many parent's work schedules or financial problems denied their children those visits. I felt it was our duty as teachers to expose our students during their twelve years of public education to see some of America's historical sites. Therefore I exposed my art students to as much art history and architecture in our national capitol as possible. On every trip I was as excited as my students—I loved to travel, to see God working through man.

40... ERUPTED EMOTIONS

I must abjure the Balm of Life, I must,
Scared by some After-reckoning ta'en on trust,
Or lured with Hope of some Diviner Drink,
To fill the Cup—when crumbled into Dust!
Omar Khayyam: Rubaiyat, LXII

Lenard arrived home late one night—sloppy drunk! He smelled *bad.* He looked awful! Strong whiffs of gin and beer mixed with foul underarm odor combined with days of greasy perspiration stained clothes, churned my stomach. I ran his bath water as he stumbled up the steps. I helped this drunkard, this pitiful man—my husband of one year. Happy to see my spouse, I folded back the comforter and sheets. The bed was ready for his tired, alcoholic body.

After he finished bathing I helped him out the tub, into his pajamas and to our bedroom where he fell onto the bed. He weighed twice as much as I did, so I helped him as best I could. Only half awake, he managed to pull the sheet slightly over his body. Neither his head nor his arms were covered.

As usual in August, Baltimore had hot humid nights. Our cool room was the only room in the house blessed with an air conditioner. Lenard asked me to call one of his customers.

"Da-wn, before you ca—ll Mrs. Hestan, would you get me a cold gl-ass of water from do-wnsta-irs?"

As I walked down the steps to the first floor kitchen for the water, I wondered why he asked me to go *downstairs* when there was an upstairs kitchen. Before I returned I decided to call Lenard's client. When I lifted the receiver I overheard him talking to a woman. Their conversation was a total surprise.

"I've been too tired, Sina, to drive all that distance," he said.

"I *told* you, Lenard, if you have to wait a week to come and see me then don't bother," she said.

"I promise to see you tomorrow night."

My body stiffed with anger. Instantly I relived the numerous nights he'd not come home; other nights he didn't bother to call; the two weeks a telephone was in the boy's apartment—unknown to me. Was I dreaming or was this really happening to me *again! No, No, No! Not Again!* Oh Dear God *not again!* How could this kind generous man, who *begged* me to marry him a year ago, have the *nerve,* the *audacity* to call his woman in *my* home, while sleeping in *my bed!*

He hung up his receiver. I replaced mine slowly, still stunned! Hurt, nerves raced through my body as I trudged toward the staircase. Disgusted, humiliated and devastated, I paused on the steps to resume control of my insides that churned in turmoil. Before I reached the second floor and my bedroom, I paused and thought—*that lousy bum! That dog!* I shuddered—thinking how I'd just helped bathe his filthy stinking body and then he called his woman on *my* telephone!!

The staircase lifted me as though I were floating. Unaware of planting my feet on the steps, plans to expose his adulterous affair unfolded. I had to be more careful this time than I was when I'd learned about my first husband's affair.

He was asleep. I whispered softly in his ear, "Who is Sina?"

He mumbled something. I asked again softly, "What is her phone number?" He mumbled a telephone number clear enough for me to understand. Wrong number, it was her mother's. Pretending to be a friend, the mother gave me her number.

"Hello, may I speak to Sina."

"This is Sina, who'd this?"

"Did you just talk to Lenard a few minutes ago?"

"Yes I did. Who is this?"

"I'm Lenard's wife and who are you to Lenard?"

"*Wife!*" she yelled. "I *told* him not to get married on me. I *thought* he was seeing somebody else."

"We've been married over a year. How long have you been seeing Lenard?"

She explained they'd been living together on and off for *ten* years. Everything he owned was there.

By now Lenard was wide, *wide* awake, listening to our conversation. He stared at me then dropped his head in shame.

"Excuse me a minute, Sina." I leaned over and slammed the receiver against his head, his arms, his legs, everywhere I could, as I yelled and screamed, "How could you do this to me! What kind of a man are you!" Sina was still on the phone *yelling*!

"Tell Lenard to come and get his things and leave my *house key!!*

She hung up her receiver. I'd broken mine banging it on Lenard's head and chest. While I cried and screamed, I punched him all over his body again until he grabbed my hands. He held me tight while I cried and tussled to get lose. He'd never hit a woman. Aching, I cried tears that rolled down a weary, worn face and crushed heart! He released me slowly while stabbing pains pierced my chest! I dropped to the floor. Warm agonizing tears soaked the carpet while my limp body curled up into a tight ball. I wanted to *disappear*!!

God please, *please* help me! I keep doing the *same dumb* thing over and over again. At that moment I heard the still quiet voice say, "I did. I will." Yes He had. He'd opened the book. He'd revealed the problem. Now He'd guide me step by step through the problem with His omnipotent love.

Minutes passed as I cried. My chest ached! I couldn't stop the pain or the tears. I had to stop before the severe strain I felt caused physical harm. I recovered slowly—enough to get up off the floor—enough to call my best friend, Lily who'd been my maid of honor, who'd gone to the beach with us on several occasions when I was able to drag Lenard away from the alley and who listened to my hurts as she always had. It was one a.m.

"Lily this—is—Dawn, I'm so—rry to call— you so l—ate." I could barely speak.

"What's wrong, Dawn! What's wrong!"

"I just found out about Lenard's girlfriend. He's been living with that woman on and off for over *ten* years! I'm hurt Lily, I'm so—o hurt. My fifth husband and the same thing all over again! I can't believe this is happening again Lily. Can you believe it!"

"Oh Dawn I'm *so* sorry, I'm *so* sorry. Stop crying and get yourself together otherwise you'll make yourself sick." I couldn't stop crying so I handed the receiver to Lenard. Lily asked him.

"Which one do you love Lenard?"

"I love both of them." He tried to explain in his stupor how all of this happened. Too drunk to drive, I told him to leave the following morning. I felt sorry for that dumb drunk. He laid asleep in our bed at my mercy, my pity and my sympathy. I stood and watched him sleep and wondered *how, could he sleep with that woman, then come home and sleep with me.*

The only word I saw was *dog, dog, dog!!* He was fortunate I was a Christian. Another woman would have *wiped* him out while he slept. Then I remembered what he'd told me about his grandfather, who'd done the same thing. When Lenard was a little boy he'd leave him in his car while he visited his girlfriend in her home. He said he slept for hours before his grandfather returned! He used Lenard as an excuse for his absence. Of course Lenard was told not to tell where they'd been. There were other times he'd mentioned. Lenard actually thought it was okay to have a girlfriend and be married. As a child every man he knew did the same thing; therefore he believed it was normal.

I packed his belongings in green plastic bags and stacked them by the front door, took my house key off his key ring and cried myself to sleep on the den sofa downstairs. Before he left he came in the den stared at me stretched out on the sofa and shook his head.

"I'll call you. It's not the way you think."

"*Don't* call me. Just *leave* me alooone. You've hurt me enough."

He left. I cried. He called two days later. I hung up! Everyday he'd call, I'd hang up. His persistence won. At last I listened to the bum's reasons for committing adultery. During those agonizing days, I'd talk to Lily. Ears and heart open, she listened to my cries and felt my pain. Nearly everyday before and after school, we'd talk.

"Dawn you don't deserve this. You've been too good to Lenard. I just don't understand how neither one of you noticed anything was wrong for over a *year.*"

"I was suspicious but I pushed those thoughts aside. Remember Lily, I've told you my husbands' adulterous acts are always made known to me. After I talked to his son that morning, I asked God to reveal the truth to me. He did. It hurt. The pain cut deep as it usually does, but I hold on."

"Yes, you do go on Dawn. You always have. You're a *strong* woman. You've been through so much with these *no good men!* You don't deserve to be treated like this, you deserve better."

"Well—I saw the drinking problem and thought I could help. He told me he was easing away from Sina. That she'd been so good to him a few years ago when he'd lost his job he felt obligated to her."

"You mean obligated to sleep in her bed!"

"In every way! She loves that man and he loves her. They've been dating on and off for *ten* years. When he gets into trouble, she's always there. When the automotive business fell into a slump, his employer closed his service station and Lenard was out of an excellent job. He stayed with Sina 'til he was back on his feet. He's been back and forth with her ever since."

"Please tell me how *did* he manage to keep *both* of you from finding out about each other?"

"Easy. She lived in Terrytown. She only came here when she hadn't seen him in a while or when he insisted she visit him at his shop. He was slick. He had no scruples about what he did. He didn't care about our feelings. Everything was about *him*!"

"Well Dawn, aren't most men that way? They connive, lie and evade issues to see just how many women they can get."

"I know that Lily all too well. It'll take me a while to get over *this* hurt. I'll never understand why men mistreat their wives the way they do. It's *not* fair!"

Lenard left; Bryan returned from Fayetteville. He returned in search of a better job. Every time I mentioned medical help for his problem, he'd turn me off.

"I don't need any help. All I need is a job. I have a family to support. How can I provide for my family while I'm in a hospital? Are you going to take care of them?"

"I'd do what I could to help you, as long as you do your part."

"And what's that?"

"Check yourself into a center for addicts."

He didn't seek any help but instead returned to work. Bryan slept in his old bedroom upstairs next to mine and worked as a delivery person for the same Dominoes he'd opened as manager. Of course he resented working under another manager, especially a woman! He complained everyday about the way she ran the business; about all the work he'd done to open the store and now had to watch someone else do the job that was once his. He'd remind me, that one day he'd again be a manager.

Three weeks before school opened, I received a welcome letter from the new high school. I made an appointment to meet with the principal, Dr. Dupont the following day. The enormous three-year-old contemporary building set on the top of a steep hill. After a short meeting, Dr. Dupont escorted me down the hall to the art wing consisting of two large classrooms, four smaller classrooms, and an office and storage area contained in the center of the complex.

Total disaster greeted us as we entered the *worst* art rooms I'd ever witnessed in my entire teaching career!! As Dr. Dupont and I wove in and out each room my heart pounded so hard I thought it might *explode*! I kept quiet until we reached the last room, the epitome of filthiness, the ceramics center!

Dear God why, *why me!* Dried clay from June's projects remained on the tables, *walls* and *blackboards*. It looked as though a clay battle had occurred the last days of school! The cabinets and drawers had entangled papers, threads and dirty ceramic tools. Torn plastic bags contained dried balls of clay. I was appalled that an art teacher was allowed to leave a room in that condition!

"Dr. Dupont how could these art teachers leave their rooms in this condition? This place is filthy! I've never seen a maze of dirt and neglect like this in my entire life!" He answered in a composed unassuming manner.

"Well Mrs. Winters I didn't get up here the end of school so I wasn't aware of its condition. If you need some help the custodial staff will help you."

Dr. Dupont's calm demeanor clearly stated, *he- did- not- care— one bit!* I asked for the large room next to the art chairman's office—he said no. He assigned me another large room; the room that had belonged to Mrs. Maurice. She was the same *dirty* art teacher whose room I cleaned years earlier when I became art department chairman at another school.

She was teaching a summer art program downstairs on the ground level. She never acknowledged my requests to see her. So once again I cleaned *her filth*! It *took three to four days* to remove dried up sandwiches, half pint milk cartons, candy wrappers, balled up paper, discarded art materials and supplies inside the students' work tables and desks, in addition to cleaning the rest of the room!

When I opened the first set of vertical cabinet doors, roaches *flew* everywhere! Smaller cabinets under the sink and counter were infested with roach and roach beds, mice feces, turned over paints, supplies knotted with yarns, spilled bags of plaster of Paris etc., etc. Everyday I cleaned that nasty room I said, "Why me, Lord? Why me? Was I put on earth just to clean other people's dirt?" Three large trash cans were filled and removed daily by the cleaning ladies as they marveled at the gradual drastic change! The day I started cleaning the art office Dr. Dupont paid me an unexpected visit.

"Mrs. Winters I changed my mine and decided you may have the other room, the room Mr. Collier had." Mr. Collier was the previous chairman who retired.

Completely dumbfounded at his words, I stared at this, intelligent human being and wanted to scream, *"Man, are you crazy!* I just spent three agonizing days cleaning that nasty room and now you tell me you have changed your mind!" While I slaved and cleaned on *my* time, during *my* summer vacation, he sat in his office in his comfortable chair getting paid to *change his mind!*

"Dr. Dupont I've worked for *three days* cleaning Mrs. Maurice' filthy, filthy room, so I'd rather stay here. Why did you change your mind?" He looked at me in an apologetic manner.

"I thought, since another high school will be sharing the building with us this year I decided to keep both of their teachers on the other side. They could use those three rooms and you may have these three."

Later I found out, it was not he who made that wise determination but rather Mr. Colliers the former art chairman.

"Well, that makes sense. I'd planned to clean all the rooms anyway before school opened so I'd better get started on my new room right now."

Dr. Dupont eyed me curiously. "Why don't you let *them* clean their rooms themselves?"

"Dr. Dupont those teachers have enough to worry about. They're already being uprooted from their school for a whole year, while asbestos is being removed from their building. Why should they come here and clean *this* school's dirt? I don't think that's the way to treat company, do you? Scripture says to "treat people the way you want to be treated."

"Do as you like Mrs. Winters. Remember the custodial staff will help."

"There's not much they can do. I have to separate, throw away and remove all our supplies, spread around in six rooms before the other art teachers arrive. They need that space for their *own* materials."

For *two and a half weeks* I cleaned cabinets, scraped paint and glue from stainless steel sinks, scrubbed dirty tools, discarded junk and debris, sorted materials and various types of paper etc. I removed *everything* from the cabinets in my two rooms and stacked them on tables. After I cleaned the dirty cabinets the piles and piles of paper and supplies from all the other rooms were placed in my clean cabinets. Every morning I arrived around 9 a.m. and left 6 p.m. or later.

Everyday I complained and prayed. Soft Christian and Classical Music which flowed from my radio helped ease my stress. Each day I drove home exhausted and *mad, mad, MAD!* For dinner everyday, I ate fast food or leftover pizza (Bryan brought home from his job). I'd shower, flop in bed and not wake up 'til morning. Toward the end of August my energy slowed to a trickle. One day I thought *did I earn these Degrees to clean art rooms or to teach art?* My spirit lay flat on the floor— suppressed, smashed, squeezed tight, *unable to breathe!*

A week before school opened, Mr. Grayson, an art teacher from our guest school, brought in some materials. He took the first room I cleaned, the immaculate room. The other art teacher, Mr. Weldon, used the two smaller adjacent rooms, as one large room. He arrived *two* days before school opened and was outraged because his accommodations weren't any better! After all of the work I'd done to get his room partly in order, he refused to finish the rest.

Had I listened to Lenard and Bryan *nothing* would have been cleaned and he *really* would have been *mad!* They thought I was a fool for doing all of that cleaning anyway. Had he come a day later I'd have finished his room. I'm glad I hadn't done anymore than I had because he was a most unappreciative person. When Lenard and Bryan brought my teaching visuals from Lakeland Middle, I took them to see the ceramics room, Mr. Weldon's room. They were appalled.

"Mommy *why* are you cleaning this room for someone else!" Bryan said.

"Because I've asked the custodial staff *three times* and they haven't shown. They said they had too much other work to do since two schools would be using the building this year."

"Well I still wouldn't clean it. Look at those walls and these tables are the pits! How could a teacher leave a room this way?"

"Well Bryan since I'm the chairperson, I feel responsible for this department. The two former art teachers who left were *filthy*. I'd taught with one before and was her chairperson. The other one was *the* art department chairman; he retired."

"*He* was in *charge* of this department and left it *looking like this!* " Lenard chimed in with disgust because his small garage for repairing cars was *always* clean!

"Yes he did. When he stopped by a few days ago to meet me, I asked him about its condition." Bryan and Lenard listened intently.

I said, "Mr. Collier, how could you retire and leave these rooms in this condition?"

"Ahhhh, they were worse than this." He answered with a smile.

"*Worse*! How much worse could they have been?"

"Much worse, believe me. This office was packed with everything and that small room next to your room was blocked off."

"Blocked off, what do you mean?" I said.

"I mean the door stayed closed. The room was filled with all kinds of junk."

"You mean just like the room in the back, still packed with junk?"

"Yes but worse. It was so jammed no one could walk through to the back room. You should see my garage. My wife's always after me about getting rid of some of the junk I keep inside."

I listened and stared as the tall, handsome, even tempered man described the former junkyard he'd created in his art department. I thought as he talked, I'm glad I wasn't here during his time. I'd have *stayed* on him to the point he'd retired earlier just to flee from me. The staff loved him though. He really was a kind person.

Mr. Weldon was the most *ungrateful* person I'd ever met. He was nasty and rude, obnoxious and crude, mean and backbiting! He complained about everything while Mr. Grayson was just the opposite. He understood the unpleasant situation and made the best of it as I did. One day, I overheard them talking in Grayson's classroom.

"Man you have a real nice large, clean room. My room is the pits. Two rooms that were opened up and used together"

"But Weldon, Mrs. Winters cleaned both of our rooms. They were terrible man! And your room was horrible! All the tables were covered with dried clay. Man there was even clay on the boards, the floor and dried up in the sinks. It was everywhere! Besides she's still cleaning her office and storage room. Have you seen that back room with all that junk! This place was a *wreck!*"

I shouldn't have but I sometimes thought my supervisor assigned me that position because she knew I'd clean up that pigpen!

Their conversation had no effect on Weldon. He never changed and had absolutely no respect for me! I was told he didn't respect anyone, especially women. I *did* not and *would* not allow him to walk over me!

School had been open about two weeks. The smaller room adjacent to my classroom had a folding door that opened all the way back giving the illusion that my room was enormous. So I used both rooms as one. There'd been dried up enamel paint in the sink. Again roach and mice feces in the cabinets, opened and spilled over bags of plaster of Paris left under the sink, ruined paint brushes etc. I'd worked *hard* cleaning that small room but it was worth it, my students would have additional working space.

One afternoon in the middle of my lesson, Weldon paraded his students through my smaller room. Amazed, I watched him walk along side of them and look over at me as if to say, "And you can't do a thing about it either!" I rushed toward his parade.

"Mr. Weldon, why are you walking your class through my classroom?"

"It's closer than walking all the way around the hall to the other side."

"But I'm having a class. If I didn't have a class I wouldn't mind. Besides you never even asked me."

"Why should I have to ask you? It's not your classroom. Your classroom is on the other side."

"I beg your pardon; this *is* my classroom. My students work in here *everyday*. The rooms are separated, by a folding door that stays open just like yours. It's a permanent part of my classroom just like yours."

We knew why he was so angry. Mr. Grayson and I had the better classrooms. Had he arrived at school weeks earlier, as I did, he could have had the back room, which was the *largest* one in the suite. But he chose to come two days before school opened.

I refused to argue with that inconsiderate childish man and returned to my students. The next day I spoke with his school's principal. He didn't bring them through my room anymore. Friction between us lasted the entire school year.

On another occasion I noticed his students carrying large boards and other items down the hall from the back room. I approached him once again, only this time we almost came to blows. Had I been a man he would have struck me, I'm sure. While they carried the boards, boxes etc. down the hall, he strutted beside them.

"Mr. Weldon, why are your students carrying these things to the trash?" I asked him.

"Who said they're going to the trash? I'm just getting them out of my way."

"Yesterday I saw some of these same things on the trash pile and asked the custodian to return them when he was able."

"Well I don't want them back in *my* room."

"Mr. Weldon, that's not your room. That's my room."

We wrangled back and forth! My students listened from their seats as we bickered like two children, over trash! He rushed toward me and stood, stared and cursed me with his eyes. I never budged or advanced one step. We exchanged more angry words before his students *returned everything* to the room. The following day I saw his principal again. By this time he'd already spoken to Weldon. Someone on his staff evidently had alerted the principal to what had transpired. Needless to say he never used the room again.

On several occasions however he'd use the telephone in my office. I didn't mind because the three of us shared the office. I *did* mind however that he'd lean back in the swivel chair and prop both of his legs and shoes on my desk even when I'd left unfinished paper work in view. If I walked in while he was using the phone, he *never* removed his legs and shoes!

The third week of school I stood at the front counter in the main office waiting for the secretary. My principal walked over in front of me to review the sign-in book.

"Good morning Mrs. Winters." He never bothered to look up.

"Good morning Dr. Dupont. I'd like you to stop by sometime and see what I've done to the art department."

Without raising his head and a non-committal tone of voice he said, "I've already seen it Mrs. Winters."

"You've already seen it. Why didn't you tell me or at least say, 'Thank You' for the three weeks of work I've done." His small eyes bored through me like a hawk ready to attack.

"Mrs. Winters, you'll get your reward in heaven."

His *callous* remark dug deep, it hurt beyond words! I stared at that so called educated man with a Doctorate Degree, who didn't have the *courtesy* to say *Thank You* Mrs. Winters for all the hard work you did in that *filthy* art department on *your* vacation time. Head lowered in shame, so hurt to reply I left the office, *wounded* to the core. My former principals had appreciated my cleaning efforts. I cleaned, ten times more dirt, and never got a *Thank You.*

Other administrative staff and teachers who'd been there during Mr. Collier's time marveled at the obvious change. Their favorable remarks lifted my spirits. God sent them to ease my pain. I remember Mr. Perkins one of our assistant principal's, first visit. He walked briskly to where I was standing. Before he reached me—he stopped suddenly. His body made a complete turn, as his head jerked from side to side!

"What's the matter Mr. Perkins?"

"Oh, nothing's the matter. I was wondering if I was in the right classroom. This *is* the room Mr. Collier had, isn't it?"

"Yes this was his classroom." I said.

"Well what happened to it? For some reason it looks much larger than it did before."

He kept staring at the small room I'd opened next to mine. The man was dazed. He eyed the bulletin boards; the students busy on their assignments. The room's clean organized environment was more than the bewildered man could handle. The man complimented me on the grand job. He left smiling still shaking his head—amazed!

The administrative staff had a wide awakening from their new art teacher. The enormous, spacious building that housed two separate schools that year would override the vastness of the institution in future months.

Once again I formed a dance group at the high school and had our first performance in December. The music, dance and art departments presented, a spectacular Christmas pageant days before our Christmas holiday began. Various students and I decorated the huge stage with the gigantic *Merry Christmas* banner I'd made that stretched across the entire back curtain along with other items that enhanced the theme. There were twelve dancers. Boys volunteered to play Joseph, the Wise Men and Shepherds. Students brought in as many old sheets as possible to drape the Nativity Scene cast. Their response was tremendous! Art students made the shepherds' staffs and I used *all* my costume jewelry for the Wise Men.

After two complete rehearsals with the music department, we were ready. During dance practices several girls complained the audience would laugh at them. I assured them that wouldn't happen. The school choir stood on risers placed in front of the decorated back curtain and banner that hung above their heads. Soft lighting circled the stage as the girls shortened their steps and moves to fit the small area left in front of the risers. Still afraid, only *three* of the dancers showed! Since there weren't enough girls to complete the choreography of the last dance, The Nativity Scene with the voice of Mahalia Jackson singing *What Child is This,* I filled in at the last minute when one girl refused to go on stage in fear of students' remarks.

The curtain opened. Mary sat on the right side of the stage facing the audience, holding baby Jesus. Joseph stood close to her, looking down at them. A student stood at the podium on the left side and read verses from the Bible in the second chapter of Luke describing the birth of Jesus while an instrumental version of Silent Night played softly. As the narrator read, the Wise Men and Shepherds moved slowly from behind the wings, inching toward Mary, Jesus and Joseph down stage, in front of the choir.

The reading of scripture ended as Mahalia Jackson's voice started with

What Child is This? The dancers and I entered. We made our historic journey to see Jesus with ease, as our arms waved and bodies swayed to the music. We danced in and around the standing Shepherds and Wise Men using the small area left to *exalt* our Lord's birth. I cherished every single moment! As soon as the audience realized that one of the dancers was a teacher, I heard whispering and then silence. The Wise Men, Shepherds, Mary and Joseph draped in sheets with colored fabrics trimmed with my costume jewelry looked quite authentic. We received a standing ovation! After the curtain closed, the girl too ashamed to dance expressed her regrets. For several days the participating students were praised for taking part in the production. One teacher made a negative comment to me during our lunch period.

"Mrs. Winters, the Christmas program was lovely but I just don't see how you could *do it.*"

"Do what?" I said.

"*Dance* on stage in front of everybody and a *teacher* too!" She voicing her sarcasm and disapproval.

"Ahhh, I've been dancing all my life Mrs. Neuman, I'm used to it. One of the dancers backed out at the last minute, afraid that the students would laugh at her, so I filled in because we needed a third person. Other dancers also backed out. I love to dance—that's why I teach it. I've had years of professional training so that's why I share it with my students. Dance enables the body to express so much emotion. Besides, it's just another art form. Members in every dance group I've sponsored during my teaching career have always asked me to dance with them if possible.

"I know all that but I couldn't do it. I just *would not* dance in front of my students."

"I don't know why. The teachers at The Peabody Institute always dance on stage in their students' annual dance recital. Students love to see their teachers perform. Besides, the parents and the audience will understand why that teacher is qualified to teach. You're not an artist, Mrs. Neuman. Artists *are* different. We're not afraid to express our feelings in public. Dance is an art form just like music and drama. Teachers act, recite poetry, sing, and play musical instruments. They also teach ice skating, sports, swimming, gymnastics etc., so why can't they perform a liturgical dance in their school's program?"

She'd *never* understand. She was a traditional teacher and ultra conservative.

Marty's Air Force duty in the Azores was ending. He'd asked if he could stay with me a while until he found a job and got an apartment. He and his wife had separated. Several months prior he'd come to America on a hop (an Air Force military plane) for $10.00, to buy a part for his car. During his two-day stay his wife Renata had a marijuana party in their apartment. Neighbors called the military police. Marty was notified he had to return immediately! He was held responsible for his wife's actions. When he returned, he was given two alternatives: to divorce his wife and remain in the service or to stay with his wife and leave the service. They separated. Renata returned to America and lived with her mother. Marty returned at the end of his tour duty and lived with me.

He'd mailed very few resumes to the United States. His friends however mailed more and had good jobs waiting for them when they left the military. Since Renata had ruined his chance for a government job he returned home unemployed.

So Marty slept in the den downstairs, paying $50.00 a week as his brother did for room and board. He managed to find space in the stuffed basement and attic for his footlocker, boxes and luggage. When they arrived I couldn't believe he'd stored all that stuff in his barrack's room.

"Mom, my room was piled high to the ceiling with all these boxes. But there was a small corner left for my bunk and TV."

"Well what's in all those boxes anyway. There are sooo many!"

"They're filled with parts I'll use to repair VCRs, TV's, car radios etc. They're parts that I won't have to buy later on."

I listened. I understood perfectly. Being an artist and teacher I too had saved all kinds of materials for my students and myself over the years. But my junk was not obstructive. It was organized; tucked away and out of sight, for the most part.

So now both sons were separated from their families and back home living with Mom. Bryan still worked in pizza businesses and Marty drove for a limousine company that made numerous overnight trips to Atlantic City. At first he slept in the car all night, since renting a motel room exceeded his funds. Soon he started visiting the slot machines and gambling tables. A *big, big* mistake! He got hooked! He squandered *all* his money every time. In addition he found local gambling places on Friday nights and dropped his salary at their feet! Now I had an alcoholic husband, one son on cocaine and the other one a gambler!

I thought *what had I done to encourage such negative behavior in my children?* I'd raised them in church; they knew right from wrong; were taught good morals; so what happened? Where did I go wrong? I knew five marriages had some influence on their behavior. Yet I didn't resort to drugs, alcohol or gambling. I prayed for my family. I asked God to change their paths in life—to seek Him and clean up the mess the devil had instigated.

Bryan's two beautiful little girls visited us that summer. One day I arrived home and found him seated on the steps, holding them in his arms. As I walked toward them I saw him and the girls crying.

"What's wrong Bryan? Why are you crying?"

"I-I-I can't li-ve like this anymore. I've ru-ined my l—ife; I've lost my wife and my ch-ildren. They aren't with me and I don't want to live anymore."

When he first returned from Fayetteville, I urged him to seek professional help.

"All I need is a job. Who's going to take care of my family if I'm cooped up in some halfway house trying to get rehabilitated?"

Zackary, a family friend, once a counselor for addicts, managed to squeeze Bryan into a rehabilitation program. Bryan refused to go. He *insisted* he'd control it himself. I knew better; so did he. I knew the intensity of his problem! Nardia had revealed the truth during our numerous phone conversations. He needed qualified help. I was scared for my son! Thus far, drugs controlled his life! Had he surrendered his life to Christ, he'd have been saved.

"I don't need any program; the doctor said I could stop any time I wanted to because I don't use it everyday." He always rationalized his use of drugs.

He'd work all week supporting his weekend crack cocaine habit, making other people filthy rich while his *wife* and *children suffered*!

"Zackary got you in a program but you refused to go. But today *I'm* taking you to the hospital myself. I'll *not* sit by and watch you destroy your life!"

The girls sat quietly in the back seat while Bryan's drained body sat next to me. Nervous and scared, I drove to the hospital praying all the way. After waiting two hours, he was seen. They refused to help him! I was furious! I knew their experience with drug rehabilitation sustained their decision. The doctor insisted he could stop whenever he chose to. After two weeks my grandbabies returned home to their mother while Bryan continued his drugs.

Bryan never came home on weekends. His manager called often about his absence. He was fired. The manager at his new job called; he'd not turned in

$52 receipt money and had not returned to work. She stated she'd press charges unless he paid the money and was sending someone to my home to retrieve it. I promised to write a check.

I heard a knock at the door. Bryan had come already come home. I opened the door. A tall policeman held the bill.

"Is this the home of Bryan Jennings?"

"Yes it is." I said.

"Are you Mrs. Winters his mother?"

"Yes I am."

"I have a bill for $52.00 from the manager of the Domino Pizza. She said you'd give me a check for the amount due."

"Yes I will. Why did she send a policeman? I told her I'd pay the bill."

Disgusted, angry and humiliated my hand trembled as I took the bill. It shook worse as I attempted to write. Finally I walked over to the piano to fill out the check. My left hand steadied my right hand to keep it firm as I wrote. I felt shamed and degraded by my son. I hadn't been that nervous since I signed the Driver's License form after passing my driving test twenty years prior—another awesome day I'll *never* forget!

"Bryan, come here!"

He appeared from the den, face drawn, downtrodden and disgraced for another problem he'd caused me. He listened as I read his rights.

"This is the *last* time I'll pay my hard earned money for *your* stealing. The next time this happens you *will* go to jail! Do you understand me! Have I made myself *clear!*"

"Yes ma'am I understand. Thank you."

The officer left. I closed the door and my mouth for the rest of the day. I crept up stairs, lay down across my bed and cried softly into my pillow. The same pillow that held tears from other men that had pierced my heart!

"Dear God please help my poor sick son. I give him to you. I *don't* know what else to do." Hired at another pizza company, Bryan still *hurled* his money to drug dealers!

41...THE FALSE ALARM

Labor not as one who is wretched, nor yet
as one who would be pitied or admired.
Direct yourself to one thing only, to put
yourself in motion and to check yourself at
all times.
Marcus Aurelius: Meditations

Lenard called me almost every evening. One night his slurred words were difficult to understand.

"Co—me pi—ck meee up at—the barrr."

"Who is this? Is this you Lenard?" I barely understood him.

"Ye—a it's meee. I'll wa—it for y-ou ouuut—-side."

"I'll be there shortly." I said.

I drove to the Bar, several miles away that he frequented daily, if only to talk with friends. When I arrived, I didn't see Lenard. I searched the curious faces staring at me in the I-Roc. When I got out, I spied Lenard lying on the dirt and gravel ground about seven feet from the car. Stunned to see my pitiful sick husband sleeping on the ground I walked over, knelt down and shook his shoulder.

"Lenard get up, it's Dawn, let's go."

He grunted something but couldn't get up. I returned to the car and drove it closer to him. I guided his crawl to the car, helped his limp, drunken body in the back seat, then drove, to his mother's home. Reluctant to take him in, she helped me walk Lenard in her house. Later that night he called to thank me. A week later he called again.

"Co-me and ge-t me. My ca—r won't st-art. I'm at the hos-pi-tal."

"Lenard, are you crazy? Do you know what time it is? It's 1:00 in the morning? You expect me to drive across town this time of morning? Call your *girlfriend*! Let her pick you up!" I hung up the receiver and tried to go back to sleep. But the phone rang again.

"Are yo—u com-ing or *not*?"

"*No* I'm not coming anywhere! I said to call your girlfriend? I helped you the last time. Let *her* help you this time."

"You're my wi—fe! You're sup—posed to he-lp me any ti—me I ask you!"

"You're drunk Lenard. Call somebody else because I'm *not* coming!"

"Yea, so wh-at! I had a fe—w dr-inks. That do—esn't me-an I'm dru—nk. You do—n't kn-ow what yo—u're tal-kin' 'bout."

I hung up the phone, waited ten seconds then removed the receiver. As soon as I drifted off to sleep I was awakened by *harsh banging* at the side door downstairs. I pulled on my robe, rushed downstairs to inquire about the thunderous banging at the door.

"Who's there?"

"It's the Police, *open the door!*"

"Police. I didn't call the police you must have the wrong address?"

"Is this 56 Daleview Avenue!"

"Yes it is."

"That's the address we were given. *Now open this door!*"

I opened the door. The officers *pushed* through running in every direction! I stood behind the door as it flung wide-open backing me up flat against the wall, hands high above my head! Dazed by fright as the policemen raced through my house: upstairs, downstairs, in the attic, in the basement and outside around the house! The pounding of heavy boots reminded me of a cattle stampede! I leaned flat against the wall in my black velvet bathrobe and white satin shawl collar—and hair in rollers. I was embarrassed for the hair rollers and horrified by the policemen's actions!

"What are they looking for?" I asked the policeman who stood guard at my side.

"The body! We had a report that somebody was killed here tonight."

"Not here! I live here alone. Who made that report?"

"We don't know. He didn't give a name."

"I have an idea who it was, my drunken *husband*! We're separated. He called about thirty minutes ago asking me to pick him up at the hospital. I refused. So *this* was his way of getting revenge!"

The other two officers finally came downstairs into the living room where I still stood plastered up against the wall, astounded!

"It's nothing upstairs, nothing in the basement and nothing outside. Somebody is playing games."

I knew then, it must have been Lenard and voiced my opinion.

"Yes and I have an idea who that somebody is, my dumb drunken husband."

"Charges could be placed against him for this. False alarms are serious business."

I was furious! Why did he do something that stupid? Was he *that* deranged? I stood by the door as the policemen started to leave.

"Ma'am we're *sorry* for this inconvenience and getting you so upset but we had to respond to the alleged murder phone call."

"I understand—is that a carrr—I see parked—in front of my hedges?"

"Yes it is. It's a white car parked under the tree."

"And I know whose car it is. It's Lenard's car. He has his nerve coming to my house after all the trouble he's caused me tonight! Excuse me please, I'm going out to see what he wants."

"Do you want me to come along?"

"No he's not violent, just stupid!"

As I approached the car I noticed Lenard seated behind the steering wheel; his head leaning back on the headrest sound asleep. I stuck my hand through the rolled down window and shook him vigorously!

"Wake up Lenard! Wake up!"

"Uh, uh wh—at y-ou w—ant?"

"I want to know why you're parked on my property after all the torment you caused me tonight."

"Le—ave me a—lone. I'm not bo—thering anyone, I'll leave."

"I will not! Why did you call the police and tell them someone was *murdered* in this house?"

"You wo—uldn't co-me to the hos—pital and get me. Yo—u're my wi—fe and you did—n't come, th-at's whyyy." By this time one of the four officers was standing next to me and to Lenard's car.

"Sir I advise you not to drive in that condition. If you do I'll have to lock you up."

"We-ll she w—ants meee to leave, so I'll leave."

"I'm warning you sir; if you drive away I *will* lock you up on DWI charges."

I realized Lenard was too drunk to drive.

"You may sleep here tonight but *leave* in the morning."

The officers left; I returned to the house; Lenard slept in his parked car next to the hedges all night. The following morning I walked down the sidewalk toward my car inhaling the sweet fragrance of lilacs. The strap Lenard had tied around the large tree trunk was gone! At last he'd removed it. It was the chain he'd used for Baby Face, his pit bull he kept at the shop. On occasion he'd bring the dog home before we separated and tie him to the tree.

I shall never forget our first meeting. I left my car and rushed up the sidewalk to the side door as usual but didn't see the dog when he ran out from behind the tree. He lunged at me barking as though, I were a stranger in my own yard! Terrified, I ran back to my car screaming and locked myself inside! Seconds later Lenard appeared, laughing.

"Why are you screaming Dawn? That's only Baby Face, the puppy I keep down at the shop. He won't bother you. He only barked because he's doesn't know you."

"Know me? *Puppy*? He doesn't look like a puppy to me. He looks like a *vicious dog* trying to make *me* his meal!"

"Ah no, he's a fine puppy! Dogs are what their masters make them. If they are agitated they will attack. They've gotten bad raps but really they're not bad dogs."

I examined his mean face, muscular body and saw nothing fine to me! What I read about the pit bull's past wasn't pleasing. He was a crossbreed between the powerful, bulldog and the rat killing badger baiting English white terrier; now extinct. The cross of breeds created a fighting dog. When he latched on to his victim he *never* let go! Even though he was intelligent, I thought; *why would Lenard want that dog, then name him Baby Face.*

"What made you name that dog Baby Face anyway? His face does not resemble a baby's face to me."

"I have no idea. It was the first name that came to mind." The strap was gone, the dog was gone and *so was Lenard.*

Several weeks later I received a call from Lenard's grandmother.

"Dawn this is Sarah. I guess you already know Lenard drew his shotgun on some children in the alley."

"What, what was that Ms. Sarah! I told Lenard to leave that shotgun here in the attic but he kept calling and worrying me so much, I left it on the porch three nights ago."

She continued, "Rumor has it that he threatened several children in the alley that kept vandalizing his customers' cars: slashing tires and breaking out windows. He got tired of paying for the repairs and blew his stack!"

"I knew something like this would happen one day. I just *knew* it! Did anyone get hurt?"

"No, no one but Lenard. It took several officers to restrain him. They threw him on the ground and put their feet on his back. He was drunk and helpless. We don't know where he is. Would you find out Dawn?"

Lenard's intelligent family spoke very well. Alcohol was *their* downfall. It ruined their financial and social progress: excellent minds, thrown to the dogs, devoured. It's hard to stop loving someone overnight so I called the closest police station in that area.

"Hello, my name is Mrs. Winters. I'd like to know if my husband, Lenard Winters is there." The officer told me to hold on while he checked.

"No ma'am he isn't. He's gone to the hospital for evaluation. Call over there and they'll tell you where he is." I called the hospital where he was taken.

"Hello, I'm Mrs. Winters. I want to know, is my husband waiting to be evaluated?"

"Yes he is. He's with a police officer in the waiting room."

"May I speak to the officer please?" I said.

"Oh yes, hold on; I'll get him." I was frightened for him but thought, *now he'd get the medical and mental help he needed.*

"Hello, this is officer Burland. How may I help you?"

"I'm Mrs. Winters, Lenard Winter's wife. We're separated but I'm still concerned about him. What happened?"

"Well ma'am earlier this afternoon, three children were running down Baltimore Street yelling, 'He's gonna' kill us, he's gonna' kill us! He's got a shotgun and he's gonna' kill us!' They ran over to our parked car and explained everything that happened. We rushed to the alley. He didn't have the shotgun in his hand but he was drunk, yelling and cursing. He resisted arrest so we had to restrain him by force, bring him down to be handcuffed."

"Was he injured?"

"No he wasn't. He's just mixed up. He's sitting quietly next to me in the waiting room."

"Officer, *please* don't hurt him. He's a very sick man. When he's not drinking he's a totally different person. He wouldn't have hurt those children. He's never hurt anyone, except himself."

"Yes ma'am I believe you. I know he's a sick man. After we got him into

193

the car he broke down and cried, begging for help. That's why we brought him here to be evaluated."

What a pleasant April Saturday afternoon it was when I drove to the hospital and parked my friend Zackary's tan car across the street from the hospital; the same car I'd used after my car was totaled. The psychiatric evaluation ward was on the second floor. I strolled upstairs nervous and anxious for Lenard.

"I'd like to see Lenard Winters please, I'm his wife."

"Have a seat in the lounge Mrs. Winters. We'll get him."

Seconds later Lenard appeared in the waiting lounge where family and patients met. He was dirty, clothes torn, hair disheveled and eyes reddened from drinking. He looked a sight! I walked toward him slowly. He lowered his head, then grabbed me with one of his bear hugs and cried softly on my shoulder.

"Dawn, I'm so sorry for causing you all this trouble. I need help. I need a lot of help." I hugged him as I would have my child and rubbed his back gently.

"Don't worry Lenard everything will be alright. I brought you some clothes so you can bathe and get cleaned up. How did the policeman treat you after I spoke to him in the hospital?" He raised his head, rubbed his eyes and started walking toward the window.

"His attitude changed after he talked to you. He said how concerned you were about me. We talked a while after he found out how much I knew about cars. Things were fine after that."

"Tell me Lenard, what actually happened."

"Remember I told you how those bad children kept bothering my customers' cars and I couldn't catch them. Well I caught them today, got the shotgun from the shop to frighten them. They flew out the alley yelling and screaming, 'He's gonna kill us, he's gonna kill us.' The next thing I remember, policemen grabbed me and threw me on the ground."

"Did you have bullets in the shotgun?"

"No! It wasn't loaded. I was only trying to frighten them. They've cost me *plenty* of money breaking car windows and puncturing tires. I was fed up. I used to give them money to leave me alone and when I stopped they started on the cars again. I guess the combination of the alcohol and Dexatrim made me go off."

"Well, I told you to stop taking those diet pills and of course you wouldn't listen."

"Yea, I know but I like that little buzz I get from alcohol. And when I take those pills I feel even *greater*."

"Yes we all know that. That's why you're in here now because of alcohol and pills. Where's the shotgun now?"

"I don't know. I do know that I'm not making any money in this place. Some customers think I can work for nothing. I repair their cars. When they finally come to get them they have only part of the money or *no* money at all. Some pay later. And some never pay me at all!"

"Try not to worry about that now. Work on getting well."

"I'm sick of being played for a fool Dawn. When I get out of here I'm gonna get a job working as a mechanic in someone else's shop and let *them* have all the headaches."

"That all sounds good but first you must get well."

"Yeah, I know. I see you're still driving that guy's car. When will you get the I-Roc fixed?" He said as he eyed Zackary's worn out car.

"I don't know. It's still parked in the yard. I don't have the money to get it repaired anyway. So it'll stay there until I do."

Lenard looked great the next day. Well groomed, clean clothes and *no* alcohol! The poor man needed rest. Bit by bit he was killing himself on alcohol, diet pills, little food and nearly zero sleep.

After two weeks he was released. The doctor said he wanted to return home and asked how I felt about his decision. I complied. So my husband came home and again we tried to work on the marriage. His birthday was two days prior to leaving the hospital. At his request I gave him a small party. He'd *never* had a birthday party. It lifted his spirit. In addition other patients enjoyed the festivity.

For thirty days he came home every night. I thought he was well. One night my friend Valarie called to inquire about Lenard's progress.

"Oh Valarie Lenard's doing fine! He's been coming home every night for thirty days!"

Lenard said in a soft sad voice, "It's not what *I* want though" as he lowered his head and stared at the floor. I pretended I'd not heard his unhappy utterance.

Misery, stress and military mental baggage did not allow him to sleep in the same place. Old wandering habits returned in addition to drinking. My happy days were over and life's roller coaster of adversities resurfaced to greater more formidable heights! Finally he stopped coming home altogether but did call daily. I tossed him to the wind where he wanted to be and concentrated on my other parasites: Bryan's addiction, Marty's gambling and *most of my* money being wasted on the I-Roc, the car I never should have helped Bryan get. Little time remained to mourn over Lenard.

All attempts to get that stunning burgundy piece of machinery reliably mobile were pointless.

Memories resurfaced of how I became a *car-less* woman were unbelievable! One day after school, at Lenard's request, I drove my car to his shop after filling the gas tank. His jalopy with each door painted a different color was my vehicular mode home. Humiliated to be driving such a wreck, I avoided the stares of other motorists as they drove by. As I approached Church Lane and made a right turn, the door on my side *flew wide* open! As my right hand guided the steering wheel, I stretched my left hand out as far as I could and grabbed the door handle yanking the door shut! I thanked God another car wasn't in the opposite lane when that door flew open!

I related my shocking experience to Lenard. Of course he found it quite amusing, as usual. Two hours after I got home the phone rang.

"Dawn this is Sarah. Do you have a blue Ford?" Sarah was his mother.

"Yes you know my car is blue. Why?"

"Because it's on *fire!*"

"*Fire! My car's on fire!*"

"Yes it is. The fire department just arrived. They're putting it out."

"Is it the whole car or just one part?"

"I can't tell with the firemen squirting that foam every where. Look; don't tell Lenard I called you. He'd get *real* mad with me if he knew. Just wait 'til he calls and tells you himself. You know how easily he gets upset."

"Is the fire, out yet!"

"Yes they just finished. It doesn't look too bad from my kitchen window."

Fifteen minutes later Lenard's younger son, Earl called.

"Mrs. Dawn, I have some bad news for you. Your car caught on fire while my father was working under it."

"How's Lenard? Is he all right? Is the car burned real badly?"

"Yeah, he's all right. Only some of his hair got burned. The car isn't too bad."

"Tell me what happened, Earl! How did the fire start in the first place?"

"My fa-ther had the drop coord light under the car. Some—how it fell. Sparks from the broken light bulb set fire to the gas, the gas that overflowed from the gas tank when we filled it up earlier. I thought my father was on fire but he got out just in time!"

"I thank God Lenard is all right. The car can be repaired."

"Mrs. Dawn the fire inspector wants you to come down here. You have to sign some papers 'bout the car and your ownership."

"Well you'll have to come and get me because I will not drive that wreck of Lenard's ever again not after what happened today."

Earl came after me. We rode downtown as he described in detail the unfortunate disaster. Everything happened so fast that it was difficult for him to explain. We parked in front of Sarah's house. I walked slowly down the alley on the left side of her row house with my hands plunged deep into my tan trench coat pockets avoiding the early night chill. The fire truck was parked in the middle of the alley behind my burned car. Several men stood around with their hands also into their pockets as they observed and discussed the hapless accident. I stood quietly by, gazing at my former beautiful blue *paid for* car.

I recalled the many times I'd stood at my dining room window staring out at the car thanking God because it was paid off! What a great feeling that was even though making those payments the last five years were difficult. Now the car was *gone*! Its rear exterior was burned badly; also the inside rear. I stared sadly, thinking how would I pay for another car in addition to paying for Bryan's I- Roc. My thoughts were interrupted by Lenard's voice.

"Dawn I'm so, so *sorry* for what has happened to your car. I just can't do *nothing* right anymore. Even though it was an accident I *still* feel responsible."

"Well we know 'when it rains it pours'. Too bad it didn't rain today."

We moved toward the fireman who held the papers I needed to sign. He reminded me to contact my insurance company. Also, I'd be *billed* for the services rendered by the fire department. I thought *no transportation, and now another bill.* I felt lost; violated. I felt cheated and entrapped, caught in a web of always owing somebody my money, just for the necessities of life. Days later the insurance adjuster came and reported it as *totaled.* The $900 check arrived. Lenard's grandfather bought the car for $500. His masterful hands repaired it over several months. Within two years it looked great! He *loved* that car. I loved Betsy too; we'd shared many happy moments together while I prayed on icy roads, snowy streets and long drives to Fayetteville. I missed my car.

Co-workers gave me lifts until school closed. My friend Zackary, an author who'd attempted to help Bryan, let me use one of his older cars. It was ruddy tan in need of a paint job, jammed door on the driver's side and one window that wouldn't roll down. Since the front axle was out of line the front tires were turned slightly to the right. On occasion the windshield wipers came on by themselves and didn't stop. I remember stopping at a red light one day in ninety-degree temperatures. The gentleman in the car next to me made a remark, I often heard.

"Lady your windshield wipers are on."

"Yes I know. They're broken. Thank you."

Did he think I was blind? Of course I saw the wipers swishing back and forth in *front* of my face? For two months I used Zackary's car. For two months I was grateful, yet unhappy for having to drive another problem. But it took me where I needed to go and I didn't have to bother anyone. Late one night driving home from a friend's home the car stopped as I was ascending the steep hill of Northern Parkway. I managed to pull over on the side of the highway just before it cut off. I sat and *prayed*.

"God please help me. I don't have much money but I do have my AAA Card. As I prayed I noticed a van pull up behind my car and stop. The man got out and walked over to my car.

"Excuse meeeee. Dawn—is that you! What are you *doing* out this time of night by yourself!"

"Oh hi Nathaniel, I was just praying for help and God sent *you*!"

"He sure did. I was on my way home from work when I saw this car stalled on this side of the highway. Before I got to the light something kept telling me to turn around, drive back and see who was in this car," he said.

"Of course that was God telling you someone needed help. You have no idea how *glad* I am to see you!"

We talked a few minutes before he left to phone AAA. An hour later a tow truck arrived. The driver checked the car then suggested it be moved the next day. Nathaniel drove me home where I called Zackary. My dear God heard and answered my prayers at that moment. He's *always* on time!

Mrs. Firwell the physical education teacher at school informed me about a summer job, teaching modern dance at the Community College. For six-weeks she provided my transportation to the college. Of course I paid my way. What a long, *longgg* hot summer. We experienced stifling gym temperatures *every single day!*

For *eight* months I depended on transportation from other sources. Useless attempts to get Bryan's car on the road became frustrating. Every time I attempted, it misfired and frizzled out. Five sets of tires in three and a half years revealed Bryan's outrageous neglect in maintenance.

Shortly after my car burned, I drove the I-Roc to the closest Chevrolet dealer. It turned off while enroute. I waited a few minutes, pressed the accelerator then the engine turned over. I continued to the dealership. They couldn't locate the problem and suggested I check with the original dealership. Returning home, it cut off three more times. I parked *it* on the side of our gravel driveway, its home for the next several months since the $600 required for repairs weren't available. A week later, distraught and weary, over not having my car I called AAA to tow the sports car to the original dealership.

As the truck came down my dirt/gravel road my heart leaped with joy. Finally I'd have my own transportation again, I thought. The driver got out and stared at the car.

"Ma'am I can't tow that car."

"What do you mean you can't tow that car? Why?"

"This is the wrong truck, you need a flat. That car has to be placed on a flat; it's too low for a regular tow truck." Disgusted and tired I asked another question.

"How long will it take to get one here?"

"Oh, I guess about one to two hours?"

"Another two hours, I waited for you over an hour! Will you call the company please?"

"No ma'am I'm sorry but you'll have to call them yourself. It's company's policy."

He left. I called AAA again, this time for a flat. An hour later the flat arrived. I greeted the man as pleasant as I could.

"Sir, I'd like you to carry this car to a dealership." I handed him my AAA Card.

"I'm sorry Ma'am I can't use this card. My boss only wants cash for flat tows."

Choked to the point of tears, I stared at the card held in my trembling hand turned around and walked about six feet away so the driver wouldn't see my strained wet face. I prayed silently, "God please help me. He needs cash. I don't have any cash. The other man had the wrong tow truck. I don't know what to do. *Pleaseeee* help me!" The still quiet voice said, "Do nothing." I did nothing. After regaining my composure I turned around and walked toward the driver.

"Thank you but I don't have the cash so I'll have to call you another day."

The truck pulled away. And I, I dragged my tired, weary body up the sidewalk, up the side porch steps and into the house that awaited my agonizing cry. Tears, tears and more tears. Sleep overpowered my dismal thoughts. Days later the same towing company returned with a flat while I rode with a friend in her car to the Chevrolet Company. The car was removed, rolled into the shop and checked. Minutes later a mechanic appeared.

"Ma'am we couldn't find nothing wrong with your car."

"What! It wouldn't start for me."

"Well it did for us."

I drove out of the garage then home without any problems, an incredible, but welcomed feat. The engine's response was unbelievable. I do believe they corrected the problem because that was where it was bought.

The following week as I drove on a scenic county back road, admiring the homes and their simplicity I embraced the countryside's peace and its pastoral quiet that eased my sorrows. *Suddenly*, a stream of mist interrupted my vision and idyllic thinking. I leaned over the steering wheel and looked closer at the unexpected. Yes there it was a stream of steam oozing out from under the hood! An Exxon Station was straight ahead. I crept into the station. The problem was obvious. Parts were ordered and three weeks later I retrieved the car for $562. Three *days* later I traveled the *same* road and saw steam escaping *again* from under the hood near the *same* Exxon Station.

"Oh dear God *not* again, *not* again! I don't have the money to keep fixing this car. *Help* me Lord, *please* help me." I pulled the car into the same service station, watched the *same* faces I'd seen three weeks earlier stare in disbelief as steam spurted from the hood. Mrs. Hansom, the owner's wife, a smart and personable woman, shook her head and slammed the palm of her hand on her forehead in astonishment. I stepped from the car and handed her husband the keys.

"I'm back." I waited in the office while her husband checked the problem. Minutes later he announced the verdict. Since I'd just spent $562.00 a few days ago I knew it couldn't be over $50-60 dollars.

"The water hose needs replacing ..."

"The water hose. How much will that cost?" His hesitant response said to expect a large sum spill from his lips.

"It'll cost $349.50 to repair." Is he *crazy* I thought? Does he think I'm made of money?

"Excuse me please." I went to the ladies room closed the door and *screamed as loud as I could!* After my crying ended, I opened the door gently and returned to his office to finish our sad conversation. Customers gawked at me as I re-entered the office as though nothing had happened. I didn't care *what* they thought. They couldn't *imagine* the problems I'd had with that automobile, *that I-Roc*, that *albatross*, that burden, that shackle around my wallet!

Weeks prior to these problems while I traveled across the city, in a well-to-do neighborhood the car stopped in the middle of the street. I drifted over to the median, out of traffic. As cars and trucks zoomed by on both sides, I rushed across the street, then up to one of the stately brick homes on the hill and asked for help.

"Excuse me, my name is Dawn Winters. My car just stopped and I'd like to use your telephone to call AAA?"

"Why certainly Mrs. Winters, come right in. The phone is back here in the kitchen. I noticed your car outside and wondered what was wrong."

She was such a kind lady. We talked extensively while I waited on the tow truck. Minutes later I saw a police car parked behind mine and an officer writing a ticket. I rushed from the house, down the long driveway, to my car.

"Why are you giving me a ticket officer? My *car* stopped here. I didn't park here. I went to that house on the hill and asked to use their phone to call AAA."

"You're not supposed to be parked in a median. Why didn't you leave a note on the car? I thought it was abandoned?"

"I didn't leave a note because I could see the car from the lady's window."

"Well you didn't see me and I've been out here over fifteen minutes."

"That's not true officer. I just called AAA about five minutes ago."

"Are you calling me a liar Ma'am?"

"No I'm not. But I *am* telling you that you haven't been out here for fifteen minutes because Mrs. Gywnn and I were right there at the window."

"Well why didn't you see me when I pulled up?"

"I don't know. I was on the phone and I guess she looked away for a moment. Please don't give me a ticket. This is my son's car and it's already caused me *so* many problems. My tow truck will be here soon."

"You might as well cancel that order because my tow truck is already here."

"Yours! You didn't tell me you'd called a tow truck?" I looked up and the truck was nearing the intersection where we were parked.

"I called when I realized the car was abandoned," he said.

"Abandoned, what made you come to that decision?"

"I looked for some kind of identification in the glove compartment and didn't find anything."

I opened the door and looked in the glove compartment myself. When I saw the pictures of Bryan and his friends, I realized why he'd been so hasty in calling for a tow truck. He assumed the new gorgeous burgundy sports car was owned by a young black male. Surprise, surprise it was owned by the son's mother who needed help!

The towing fee was $75. At my request the driver stopped at a bank for me to withdraw his fee. The police officer was unfair! He delighted in giving me a ticket! His harsh attitude was typical of the city's policemen, at least the officers I'd encountered.

Several weeks passed. The car had to be repaired. I depended on friends to take me to the market, to church, and to my summer job. *Never* in my life had I felt so *helpless!*

Mrs. Firwell and I left our summer job between three and three thirty. Many days I arrived home after six p.m. especially on Fridays. My friend had a crowded agenda. She'd complete her list of places to go; then carry me home. Most of the time, I didn't care. Since I lived alone, why hurry. Besides, that time allowed me to unwind from the hectic week's *hot* weather and busy blessed children!

Lenard had a friend who worked at an auto repair shop where he formerly worked. Forced to *refinance my mortgage* I needed $1,800 to replace the car's harness, a new set of tires and a right front fender. In addition, the house and property needed: new gutters, sidewalks repaired, septic tank removed, city sewage connected and $5000 to pay Theon for our divorce settlement.

Months earlier Bryan had skidded into a pole during a terrible rain. My insurance company paid but I postponed the work and paid my mortgage and Bryan's car payments. *Now* the fender *had* to be repaired. The rusted area had expanded my financial problems.

In addition to using my AAA card, it cost $85.00 to have the car towed on a flat from Baltimore to Glen Burnie. Lenard met me at the shop and drove me home. Two weeks later on July 21, 1989 my girl friend Lily drove me twenty miles to Glen Burnie early that morning to get the car. After I paid the bill, I got in the car and drove it a few yards from the office. Just before I got to the highway the car cut off! My head dropped on the steering wheel. I cried out, "Oh Lord *not* again, *not* again!" By this time Lily had stopped; parked her car and rushed to my driver's window. She knew the *eight months of pain* I'd endured with that car because she too had shared my anguish by phone.

"What's wrong Dawn? What's wrong with the car now?"

"I don't know Lily! I don't know! I'm just *sick and tired* of this car! If my car had not burned, this car would *still* be parked. I can't take much more of this!"

"Don't worry Dawn I'm not going to leave you out here by yourself."

"Thanks Lily. I'll go back to the office and ask for someone to check it out." I walked the few yards to the office and explained my problem to the manager.

"I'm sorry Mrs. Winters, once the car leaves our lot we're not responsible anymore."

"Not responsible! What do you mean, you're *not* responsible? I just paid you almost $2000 and you can't send a mechanic to see why my car stopped in *your* driveway?"

"I'm sorry but I don't make the rules, the company does."

"Well what am I supposed to do now?"

"I don't know Ma'am, I don't know." His lack of concern was obvious.

I was so *maaad* with that man!!! I stood in his office, looked at my car parked just a few yards from his office door and they weren't allowed to check the problem. It was absolute madness! I refused to use their phone to call a tow truck. Instead I ran across the highway and used a pay phone. Had I been a man they wouldn't have treated me that way. Later a highway patrolman pulled up behind my car.

"Ma'am you can't park here." I explained my problems as he listened in disbelief.

"I understand your problems but you simply can't park here. I'll call my office. They'll send a special truck to move your car farther off the highway."

Lily and I waited over two hours before my flat arrived. Because I needed a flat, it took longer. The driver checked under the hood and detected the battery was dead. The company had recharged the 350volt battery knowing it *wasn't* the voltage required for that car.

I walked briskly back to his office—furious! The manager saw me but didn't *want* to see me.

"It's the battery. I can't believe you did all that work to my car and didn't check the battery? What kind of business are you operating here anyway?"

"Ma'am you weren't having trouble with your battery so why should we check it?"

I stared at that insensitive man and shook my head in *disgust, turned* and rushed out of his office back to my car. Even *I* knew a new harness in the car meant a more powerful battery was needed. Lily stayed until the tow truck and I pulled away.

Her true friendship was unveiled in my time of distress *that morning.* We prayed as we waited in her car. We paced back and forth on the highway to relieve built up tension. I realized an evil force activated my unnecessary torment. How could *one car* cause so many problems?

Once again the car was taken to the same Exxon Station, another $75 towing fee. The replaced battery, coolant overflow container with the large hole, flushed out radiator and new belts totaled another $234!

Two weeks later it cut off *again*! Smoke escaped from under the hood. Because another company had installed the $1800 harness, the Chevrolet Company refused to work on the car; therefore I was responsible for another $75 to have it towed back to Glen Burnie. After a few days the company informed me the speedometer cable needed replacing in addition to something else totaling $205. Another phone call stated $900 worth of work had to be done: new valve seals, the intake gaskets were leaking and his list continued.

"I'll just pay for the work you've done and get back to you later."

Once again $75 towing fee returned the car. The mechanic was shocked that JBA had quoted me on items that *weren't* needed. A Cadillac converter, adapter and tune up totaled $275, a *giant* drop from $900!

Most of my paycheck and credit union *loans* covered the monumental debts incurred by *that I-ROC!* The $350 payment was made *every* month even though I didn't drive it for over seven months.

While I paid heavily to get the car repaired that Bryan had totally neglected, he paid the drug dealers dearly for his highs! Only my *strong, strong* belief in God kept me from falling apart. *His* strength sustained me because mine had diminished.

How could I forget the time the I-Roc was stolen from the yard in between shop visits? As usual before I left my warm and comfortable bed to prepare for work, I'd look out the window behind my bed. As I stared out the window I noticed the car wasn't there. Had it been stolen! Not believing what I witnessed, I ran downstairs and opened the side door. It really wasn't there; it *had* been stolen! After I notified the police, I got a ride to work. Thanks to my principal's recommendation, I rented a car for a week. They delivered the car to my school and transacted business in the main office. What a blessing!

Mixed emotions about the thief bounced back and forth. The car presented me too much sorrow to care about its immediate return. I didn't care whether they located it or not. On the other hand I needed transportation. I knew the insurance company wouldn't pay off the balance. So I'd end up having to buy another car plus these car payments. Either way I couldn't win.

So I drove a *problem free* rented car two weeks and lived happily, thinking only occasionally about the missing *headache*. After two weeks a policeman phoned.

"Mrs. Winters we've found your car. But I have good and bad news for you."

I sat silent; stared straight ahead before I spoke.

"You did; where did you find it?" My sullen response didn't express joy of an elated person.

As the policeman delivered the details I sat numbed in my kitchen chair hearing only parts of his conversation and thought *Sorrow had returned!* During that two-week period I imagined: maybe I'll never see it again; maybe someone took it out of state; maybe it was painted another color and resold; maybe someone had an accident and it was demolished. Maybe, maybe, maybe *it will never ever* return! All kinds of erroneous thoughts flooded my mind, negative hopeful non-Christian notions. The unwelcome male voice proceeded with his unwanted message.

"Mrs. Winters, there's a $165 impounding fee, plus an extra $10 per day that it's parked on the lot. I'd advise you to get it as soon as possible."

He relayed the necessary information and wished me good luck. I didn't need good luck. I had God!

My close friends La Raine and her husband Vincente drove me the long distance to the impounding lot outside of Baltimore, far into the country. They were a *blessing*! It took us *five* days (three business days) to get that car. Two tires were flat, it wouldn't start and the lot's office was closed on weekends. It also needed new tags because those had expired! The thieves drove that sports car until the poor thing was drained of all life! It rejected any more human abuse.

After we made several round trips to Glen Burnie, I was able to get the new tags. Each time Vincente made the drive I felt guilty, angry and ashamed! Upon completion of one task, a clerk would inform me of another. Finally, after days and days of mental stress, I broke down and cried in my house all alone. I suppose crying did ease some of the pain. Better I let it out than keep it inside to fester even more.

"What's going on here La Raine? Why am I having all these problems? My car burns, then I spend a *fortune* trying to get this one fixed, someone steals it and now I'm going through hell trying to get it out of impoundment. It isn't fair! *It just isn't fair!* I helped Bryan get this car for business purposes and now it's my albatross."

La Raine reached over and consoled me.

"Albatross? What's that?"

"Ah, it's a bird, a bird in Samuel Coleridge's poem, *The Rime of the Ancient Mariner.* The poem tells of mariners, seamen stranded in a boat, lost at sea when an albatross befriends them, an omen of good luck. It flew close and around the boat everyday eating the food they offered. Delirious from lack of water a mariner shot the albatross with his bow and arrow. The crew believed they and the ship were cursed by the bird's death."

"How do you remember all that stuff Dawn? There are times when I can't remember anything when I was young."

"I love poetry La Raine! I read and teach poetry in my art classes. Many students *love* it. I've written several poems myself. Our teachers taught me to appreciate great poets and authors from elementary to senior high. Our twelfth grade English teacher, Ms. Daniels had us learn excerpts from *twenty-four poems* in order to graduate. Many, I've never forgotten."

"Let me hear something from the poem about that bird."

I felt honored she'd asked me and recited what I remembered.

It is an ancient Mariner
And he stoppeth one of three.
"By thy long gray beard and glittering eye,
Now wherefore stopp'st thou me?

"La Raine that's the first verse of that long, poem. It has 144 verses!"

Vincente chimed in, "144 verses! I never heard of a poem that long."

"Oh yes, there's one even longer, Longfellow's *Hiawatha.* The poem *is* the book. Would you like to hear a few more verses?"

206

"Go on. Recite what you know, Dawn."

I continued reciting the poem while my friends listened. "That's one of my favorite poems. It made Coleridge famous. Sick and unhappy most of his life, he died at sixty-two. That *I-Roc* like the albatross once a blessing has now become a *burden*."

"Dawn none of these problems are your fault. You tried to help Bryan. How would you know he'd get hooked on drugs? Stop blaming yourself. You've done the best you could."

La Raine a sweet, precious lady reminded me of myself, always helping someone in need. Her husband, Vincente's hard exterior, breathed gentleness within. They too had experienced similar children problems. They sympathized. They understood my pain.

Only prayer sustained me, pulled me through the muck and mire and saved my sanity from the heartbreak I-Roc! God protected me *again*! As I pulled out the impounding lot onto the highway, my devoted friends smiled and waved as I passed them in the night's darkness. I waved good-bye, just as I had to the $300 in my checking account and hoped I'd never have to see that place again!

The battery was replaced and the car ran in tip-top condition! I actually enjoyed driving it. Every time I'd get gas or use a car wash I'd get a question from the young guys.

"Ma'am is that *your* car?"

"No, it's my son's car. He couldn't make the payments and since it's in my name, I *had* to. Sooo, I guess it's *really* my car."

The car couldn't handle the snow. Schools closed often due to falling fluffy flakes, and refused to melt but hung around for weeks. Heavy accumulation let schools out early one Friday. The low sports car skidded through the snow. It frightened me so that I parked on a side street and started my long walk home. Trudging through blocks of almost knee deep snow with a heavy leather bag, the untouched white mounds of beauty began taking a toll on my legs. The physical strain slowed my pace to a sluggish, slothful walk. Just lifting a leg up and putting it down, required tremendous effort. Cars drove by while passengers glanced my way. No one stopped.

I wondered about the onlooker's insensitivity toward the lone woman, trudging through snow, carrying a heavy leather bag. Finally, I reached the corner where I'd turned. I thought *if I could only sit down for a few minutes*

207

and rest, I'd feel better. But there was nowhere to sit except on a mound of snow. Straight ahead I saw a sheet of white silent still loveliness. Previous car tire treads left tracks that provided ample place for me to walk as I prayed.

Sounds of crunching snow, vehicular tires searching for direction intruded my thoughts. The navy blue van slowed down, then stopped.

"Ma'am would you like a lift? You're the only person I've seen walking; brave enough to *tackle* this snow!"

"*Yes* I certainly would! You're the only person to stop and offer me a ride." I stepped up into the van and thanked God!

"Ma'am did you abandon your car?"

"Absolutely, it's at least a mile back. It's a sports car and couldn't handle this snow."

The young, articulate man worked at Social Security, several blocks back.

"At first I was hesitant about stopping, but then I thought about my wife. If she'd been stranded I certainly would appreciate someone giving *her* a lift."

"You have *no idea* how happy I was when you stopped! Your compassion saved my legs! Since there wasn't anywhere to sit I had to keep walking whether I liked it or not."

A Christian, he drove me home and accepted no money, my *angel* in a blue van!

I created my own problems when I signed for Bryan's car, the I-Roc. *Never, never* did I think he'd become an addict and I'd be left with his payment! As I trudged through the deep white maze I reflected on *Betsy* and how she'd *never* let me down during inclement weather. I missed her; my dependable, paid for, blue Ford Landau.

As Edgar Allen Poe said in his poem *The Raven:*

…Nothing farther then he uttered—not a feather then he fluttered—
Till I scarcely more than muttered, "Other friends have flown
before—
On the morrow he will leave me, as my Hopes have flown
before."
Then the bird said, "Nevermore."…

The excerpt from Poe's poem—spoke to me—it said, "Nevermore, never anymore would I, become so deeply involved in another person's life as I had in the past and the present—to the point I'd injure my health and my wellbeing. I prayed for guidance to handle my immediate situation: Lenard's alcoholism and Bryan's drug addition before something tragic happened to me!

42...LENARD'S MAJOR PLIGHT

For though we are made especially for the
sake of one another, still each of us has his own tasks.
Otherwise another's faults would harm me,
which God has not willed, in order that
my happiness may not depend on another.
Marcus Aurelius: Meditations

Lenard's visits to my home and job increased during each drinking spree; also his irate phone calls continued late at night.

"It's meee. Coome oo-ver to the bar and pick me up. I want to coome hoome."

"Lenard you don't live here anymore. Go where you live."

"I *do* live there. You juust woon't let me come home."

"No I won't! What do you think I am anyway? You're sleeping with another woman and expect me to let you come and go when you feel like it? You're out of your mind!"

"Well I got to sleep with somebody, 'cause you won't let me sleep with you."

"You got *that* right!"

His calls continued. Often I left the receiver off all night. Finally I relented. He came back. He improved for a while then his bizarre drinking habits returned. One night as we drove home, he cursed and complained so much I wondered whether he was possessed. Yes, he was possessed, by *alcohol*! That demonic drink had ruined *countless* lives.

Stopped at a red light in a residential neighborhood, Lenard opened his door and ran from the car! I turned the corner, parked the car and ran after him. He was dirty and drunk. He jerked away each time I got close.

"Go home Dawn! Go home to your precious house where you don't have

to see rats and cats running all over the alley!"

He withdrew each time I reached out my hand. After minutes of begging and pleading he surrendered and climbed back into the car. On the way home he curled up on my shoulder and went sound asleep.

Several days later he called, I thought from his job. We talked a few minutes and then I asked.

"Lenard where are you? I hear water splashing."

"I'm taking a bath."

"Taking a bath, in whose bathtub?"

"I'm at Sina's. She's not here so I thought I'd stop by and take a bath."

"You mean you're in Sina's bathtub and have the nerve to call me!"

"Oh it's just a bathtub Dawn, it's just a bathtub."

The man was crazy! I was even crazier for putting up with him. The following week I received another call of desperation.

"It's me. Please come and pick me up."

"Where are you Lenard?"

"I'm at Sina's."

"Sina's! You called and ask me to pick you up at that woman's house! What is *wrong* with you Lenard?"

"It's not what you think. I came out here to get some money she owed me and my car stopped."

"She said she'd leave the money but she didn't. I want to come home. I'll meet you three blocks from the house on a corner."

He gave me detailed directions. I drove forty-minutes to get a man I loved. He needed help. How could I reject a person so mentally confused? The sober times we'd spent together were magnificent. His jubilant laughter and radiant smile had stolen my heart, along with other positive qualities. I prayed that his straying would end. Actually he *was* a child in a man's body. Lenard patterned his manhood after his grandfather. Exposed to his grandfather's adulterous affairs as a child; he assumed adultery was the norm. One day his grandfather admitted his faults to me.

"Dawn I'm sorry for all the problems you're having with Lenard. I guess I just didn't raise him the way I should have. You're the best thing that's ever happened to him. I wish he'd get himself together. You've got him going to church and he's dressing sooo well. I've never *seen* him look so good." His apology meant nothing. He'd disrespected his wife with no remorse.

One night as soon as I arrived home and walked in the kitchen Lenard gave me the telephone.

"Here talk to Sina." I slammed the receiver on the hook!

"Lenard what's the matter with you, giving me the phone *to talk to your girlfriend?*" He was too drunk to realize what he'd done.

Days later on a dreary afternoon, behind his favorite bar, Lenard approached a parked policeman's car, drunk.

"Of-fi—cer do youuu have an-y tic—kets for Le-nard Winn- ters?" The officer eyed Lenard; then checked his dispatch. Known as a harmless drunk, the officer saw the warrant for his arrest since the previous year. It was the warrant issued when he didn't show for his hearing and punched the lawyer in the courthouse lobby.

"Yes I did find a warrant: for not appearing in court last year in May. I have to take you in."

The officer handcuffed Lenard, put him in the back seat and drove him to jail. An hour later he called me at school in my office.

"It's meee. I'm in jail."

"Jail! What are you doing in jail Lenard?" In his drunkenness he relayed his pathetic story. I promised to see him after school.

The police precinct was down the hill from my school. The aged brick building was across the main street in a low income neighborhood. I entered the room which was empty except for personnel seated behind the counter. My 5'2" body barely saw over the counter top. Standing on the tips of my toes I spoke to the policemen seated behind the counter.

"Excuse me please, I'd like to see Lenard Winters, I'm his wife." They ignored me and continued what they were doing. Again, I spoke to the idle desk clerk.

"Excuse me sir, I'm here to see my husband, Lenard Winters."

He raised his eyes from his newspaper and glanced at me as though I'd said something offensive.

"Ma'am I'll be with you in a minute!" He spoke abruptly; returned to his newspaper and ignored me. I watched the other officers behind the desk laughing and talking while I waited patiently. Finally someone came over. His demeaning voice was intimidating. He treated me as though I were a criminal!

"Now what do you want!"

"I'm here to see my husband and to find out what will happen to him."

"And *who* is your husband, somebody Winters!"

212

"Lenard Winters, he was brought in earlier this afternoon."

They searched their files on the computer. "We can't find anything about him. He *was* here but I don't know where he is now."

"You don't know where he is! What do mean you don't know where he is?"

"Exactly that! He was here and now he's not here and the computer doesn't say where he's been transferred."

"Well I'm not leaving until you tell me where he is. I have that right."

A female officer rushed over to the counter. "Miss whatever your name is you'll leave whenever we tell you to."

"Who are you talking to? Are you addressing me? Why, I pay your salary. I'm a city employee just like you. You can't talk to me like that. I teach at the high school at the top of the hill. Everyday I remind my students to respect the law. Now I understand why some of them don't! You don't respect the citizens who pay your salaries. Oh no! I'll leave after you tell me where my husband is and not before!"

The female officer stared at me all huffed up in her police uniform waiting to get a word in while I spoke so fast I could barely get my words out!

"Besides you don't know who I am. I could be a spy sent to check your precinct to see how it runs. You really don't know who I am, do you?" They all stopped what they were doing and stared at me, then at each other. A cough broke the silence.

"We're doing what we can Mrs. Winters. We'll find out where your husband was sent. Would you have a seat?"

"Noooo thank you, I'd rather stand!"

Their hostile attitudes changed instantly! They spoke to me as officers should have in the beginning. Several men busied themselves with the search while the others left through various doors. Minutes later the search ended.

"Mrs. Winters we found him. It takes a while for the information to hit the computer after admittance to the main jail." He gave me all the particulars.

"Thank you. May I see the person in charge of this precinct?" He stared at me and his mouth hung open, as did the other officers.

"Ma'am he's not in at the moment, but I'll be glad to give him a message."

"No, I'd rather talk to him myself. May I have his name please and also your names?" They muttered out their names and the name of the lieutenant in charge.

Once again I'd been disrespected by the Baltimore City Police Department. I'd experienced too many unpleasant occurrences with them in the past. But today was the *worst*! Higher authorities *would hear* from me!

Every day I called the precinct, the receptionist asked who I was and what I wanted. Of course he was busy or not in. Finally I disguised my voice and gave another name and got him. I explained why it took me so long to reach him to file my complaint. We set a meeting date.

As soon as I arrived, I was shown *graciously* to his office. Lieutenant Parker knew why I was there but he needed more details. I expressed my dissatisfaction about the manner in which his officers treated me the previous week and didn't omit *anything*!

"Mrs. Winters I apologize for my officers' conduct. I want you to know that what you experienced is not the typical manner in which we transact our business. We try to represent our best to the public."

"I do understand that you must speak and handle lawbreakers firmly but not someone who comes to your office to locate a relative. I wasn't a criminal; yet I was treated like one. I would like to have in person, apologies from those people." He avoided responding to my last request.

"Again I apologize for the officers' unprofessional disrespect toward you and I repeat it is not our typical precinct policy."

"I certainly hope it isn't. From what I've witnessed with local police officers I would say the rude behavior *is typical* throughout the city. Is it possible that I could receive a verbal apology from them?"

"I understand that one officer in particular offended you more. Would you please give me his name?"

I named the officer. The lieutenant promised to reprimand him and would place a complaint letter in his permanent file. The following week I received a formal letter from Lieutenant Parker stating the steps taken in reprimanding the ill-mannered officer.

Lenard was incarcerated for twelve days. Overwhelmed with concern about how his confinement would affect his nerves, I prayed daily. His free spirit rejected being caged in. Sunday was visitation day. I'd put a change of underwear and toilet articles in a bag and carried them to the jail. My first time visiting anyone in jail, I felt my privacy had been invaded as I drove downtown because of Lenard's drinking sprees.

I recalled the last time he'd been locked up. His car had stopped on the highway late one night outside the city. He left his car and staggered on the highway's shoulder in search of a telephone. A lighted window in the rear of a building encouraged him to inquire. He walked onto the property, ignoring the large sign. The door was ajar so Lenard just walked in.

"Is any—body here? I ne—ed to usee the phooone." He staggered around looking for someone to help him. Boxes were stacked almost to the ceiling. He wove in and out the stacked aisles calling for help. Finally a night watchman appeared with a gun pointed straight at him!

"Why do yoou havve that gun poi-inting at me? All I wan-ted was to use yoour telephone. The door was oo-pen so I just waallked in."

The angry security guard answered, "You mean you didn't see that sign posted outside this building that said, *"Do Not Enter! Private Property!"*

"No I ne—ver saaw a sign."

"I guess you didn't! You're too drunk to see anything in your condition!" At that moment the police arrived.

"You didn't ha—ve to call the police. I only wa—nted to use the phone 'cause my car is stran—ded up the road." The officers seemed a little sympathetic.

"Is that your car we passed parked on the shoulder of the road with the hood up?"

"Yes, that's my car. I was on my waay home and the thing just stopped. I'm sick of dri—ving these old beat up pieces of junk!"

They took Lenard to jail. He spent the night sleeping off his drunk and was released the following morning. No charges were sited. He was stranded in unknown territory and without transportation. He had enough money to get a local bus back to the city.

Another time on that same country road, in a different section, his car stopped again. He tinkered and fooled around with it for a while but quit after all efforts failed. A car part he'd placed carelessly on the edge of the front fender fell on the ground and rolled away. While he crawled around looking for the part he suddenly spied the shiny disk in the ditch. The bright moonlight had reflected a glitter. Lenard staggered down the grassy ditch. For some reason the ditch felt comfortable. Since he was so tired and sleepy he curled up and went to sleep in the ditch!

Lenard slept anywhere: on the ground, on the pavement, in deserted cars, in the alley, on the floor etc. It mattered not to him. But this time I think he picked the wrong place. The ditch already had boarders!

Soon he was awakened by something pulling at his shoes and butt! He jerked around and was terrified when he saw an opossum's grinning pointed white face, beady black eyes, stout body and long rat like tail! He jumped up!

He ran as fast as he could with the possum on his heels! Unaware, opossums were harmless marsupials, and considered nature's little sanitation engineers, he ran and ran without looking back! Eventually he hopped up above the ditch, back onto the road and continued his run until he was far away from the possum's territory. Fright sobered him *real* fast! He *never* napped another night in a ditch or outside his car!

Once again on a hot afternoon when he and Baby Face, his pit bull were riding on a main highway in 90 degree temperatures he noticed steam spurting from under the hood. He pulled over, stopped, raised the hood of the old car and waited for the radiator to cool. As the radiator cooled and the cars zoomed by he and Baby Face started walking with hopes of hitching a ride. They walked and walked. He signaled with his thumb, no one stopped. He couldn't understand why no one offered him and his dog a ride.

Days later a friend asked me, "Dawn why were Lenard and his dog walking on the highway Monday, as hot as it was?"

"Because, he's *crazy*! If he'd been alone someone might have picked him up had he stayed close to his car. But he did not stay still long enough to get help. Besides, *only* Lenard trusted his puppy, his vicious looking pit bull!"

"He was walking fast, as usual, bouncing along with his head high in the air as though he didn't have a care in the world. The dog, held on a leash, seemed as happy as Lenard."

I said, "Yes I'm sure they were. They were meant for each other; two carefree spirits."

I parked the car two blocks from the jail after circling block after block in search of a parking space in the residential neighborhood. As I walked swiftly toward the jail I met his sons Earl and Lenard, Jr. walking toward me.

"Ms. Dawn we've already seen our father."

"You have, how is he doing?"

"Oh, he said he's doing okay, but we know how he really feels. You'll have a long wait because there's a *real looong* line over there."

When I reached the corner and saw the *long* line, I was tempted to turn around, but instead, I walked over, stood at the rear in total disgust. Intimate conversations were expressed from irritated men and women. Wearied family members stood in line for an hour or more. Most of the visitors were women: mothers, wives and girlfriends. They rationalized as I did. Why were they visiting these men in the first place? I listened and related to the unusual explanations, as the line lengthened behind me.

Reflection on his recent phone call explained how an inmate had made sexual advances. He reported it to the guard but was ignored. Because he'd lost so much weight due to taking Dexatrim and not eating enough, he felt incapable of defending himself. Every time he went to the lavatory the guy eyed him waiting for the right moment. Lenard was well prepared for the pervert.

At one point I thought, why am I standing down here, at a jailhouse door, waiting in line to see a man who repeats the same stupid mistakes over and over again? Is this why I worked so hard to finance my college education? Is this why I've struggled to raise two sons, take care of a sick mother in addition to working part time jobs all my life? Have I accomplished so much yet allowed a man to bring me down to this state that I'm standing in a jail line to be a mother and fool to an overgrown child? What's wrong with me? I promise I'll *never, never* stand in another jail line.

I shared the environment with visitors who cursed, used terrible English, possessed cut marks on their faces and arms, exhibited tattoos, told awful dirty jokes etc. I asked God, how I allowed myself, to get involved, with a man who'd have me exposed to this awkward, situation.

Love! Oh yes it was love I sought, human love. I craved the attention, the warmth and closeness from a man. My soul, lost to a human being, forgot that the Lord's love was always present without harm.

Preoccupied with my little pity party, I ignored the inching movement of the line. Soon it was I who faced and stared at the main gate. I was next! After a forty-minute wait I walked through the gate, up to the booth and announced the person I wanted to see.

"I'm here to see Lenard A. Winters."

He checked his list carefully. "I'm sorry Ma'am he's had his two visitors for today."

"But I'm his wife and I've been waiting in that line a long, long time."

"I understand that Ma'am but there's nothing I can do about that. He's only permitted to see two people, I'm sorry. Come back next week." I handed him the paper bag with Lenard's underwear and toilet articles.

"Would you please see he gets these few items?"

He took the bag and promised Lenard would get the package. He was kind but there was nothing he could do. I left defeated and sauntered back to my car. I'd allowed weak emotions and low self-esteem control, my life.

Lenard called collect, daily. The jail ministry he received regarding his drinking and marital problems opened his eyes for in-depth self-evaluation. He yearned to know, what made him drink since he didn't like the "taste of the stuff anyway."

Just before his release, Sina revealed he'd slept with her the eve of our wedding day. Also he'd spent his Thanksgiving, Christmas and New Year's holidays with her and her family. He certainly had; he wasn't with me.

Lenard's next call was the last one I accepted.

"Lenard how *could* you have sex with Sina the night before we were married!"

"Ah, that was only sex. It wasn't anything to it."

"Only sex! What's *wrong* with you man! You spent the night with that woman, made love to her and married me the next day! That's downright dirty! You're *crazy!* And I am just as *crazy* to keep helping you!"

"Ah, Dawn that didn't mean nothing to me. I married you, didn't I?"

"How *could* you do such a thing to me?" I cried and yelled at him! He'd broken my heart again. "You've caused me nothing but misery ever since I've known you."

"Don't say that Dawn. We love each other."

"Love! You don't know the meaning of love man!" I hung up the receiver and refused any future collect calls.

Two weeks later he called *begging* to come home after his release. He pleaded with me to understand when he drank he did stupid things. Also he was going to the VA hospital for help. I listened to his rehabilitation agenda and decided to let him try his plan. I was to pick him up at his shop at 8 p.m. Reluctantly, I drove downtown, parked in the alley as he requested and waited and waited. After an hour passed, I decided to leave. Just before I left, he showed, staggering down the alley, drunk! The man was just released from jail and was already drunk. I thought *this man is driving me insane.* I'm stupid to be out here in the first place. *I don't know what I'm doing anymore!!*

Sina had met him at the bar to carry him home with her. He wouldn't go because he wanted to come home with me. Caught in an emotional web, he got drunk, sent Sina home and staggered to his shop where I waited. He decided in jail he wanted to be with his wife. Nevertheless, he still felt an obligation to her for helping him during those years after his employer died and work was scarce.

"I can't drop the girl just like that. She was *too* good to me when my family turned their backs."

"Well why didn't you marry her instead of me since you felt so obligated?"

"I wanted to years back but she said I couldn't take care of her. Her husband had died a year before we started dating. She and her daughter were getting Social Security and the job she had didn't pay much. If she remarried her benefits would stop. I wasn't making enough money to make up the difference. Besides, work in my field during that time was not reliable."

"Well, when I met you Lenard you were teaching and working in your shop. Why didn't you marry her then?"

"Over the years we drifted back and forth. With her living in Peadmont, and me in Baltimore, the distance was hard on the relationship. I dated another lady for a while but she drank more than I did, so we split. When I met you, a nice Christian lady who didn't drink I knew you were the one for me. I had some clothes at Sina's, but really I had clothes everywhere. I wasn't there that much. I was sleeping everywhere and left clothes wherever I slept: at her house, my aunt's house, my grandparents', and my mother's or in a car in the garage when I was too tired to go home."

"And where was home Lenard?"

"Wherever I fell asleep." He laughed at himself; that chuckle I admired. When he wasn't drinking he was a wonderful guy. He laughed, joked, and was quite respectful to ladies. An old fashioned young man, in his thinking, he was warm and caring and would give you his last penny and think nothing of it. He often said, "Dawn you know I don't care anything about money. When it's gone I'll make some more." He was truly a free spirit.

He didn't like ladies to wear too much make-up, tight skirts, fancy hairstyles or extreme fashions. His idea of female dress was a simple blouse and a pleated skirt; a taste *too* extreme for me.

Lenard increased the telephone company's wealth! Quarters filled his pockets for unnecessary calls. Even in the hospital, he called daily using money his sons and I supplied. The itinerant auto mechanic was constantly on the go.

We remained separated. He rented a room. At least that's what he told *me*. His non-verbal visits continued. I noticed he'd lost more weight since his release. He'd knock on the door. When I answered, he'd just stand there, well-groomed, wearing immaculate work clothes and his little hat that covered the small expanding ball spot and remaining black curly hair. Still a handsome man with broad shoulders and an easy smile, he'd drop his shaking head, then walk down the steps quickly back to his car. I often wondered why he bothered to come. Later he admitted he was too ashamed and couldn't speak. So in his sadness he left. He knew how much he'd hurt me, but didn't know *what* to do with his life.

Early Good Friday morning, Lenard called and asked me to take him to the country to collect money owed to him. I agreed. As I drove, I sympathized with his conversation concerning his deadbeat customers as relaxing music soothed the strain. Music eased his stress during his soberness, the time he experienced most of his grief. We finally pulled into a well-maintained apartment complex where all the buildings were on one level.

"Dawn wait here, I'll be right back." He left the car with his cute little bouncing walk and went half way down the group of apartments. Minutes later he returned and handed me $50.

"Take this. It's your Easter present. Buy yourself something real nice to wear on Sunday."

"Lenard you don't have to do that. Your customers haven't been paying, as they should, so *you* keep it and pay your bills."

"No I really want you to have it. I'll get more money next week."

We sat and debated back and forth about the money. Just as I started the car, a heavy set, dark-skinned lady appeared at my window. It was rolled up to an inch, just low enough to hear her conversation.

"You mean you brought *her* to *my* house Lenard!" She didn't curse but she made some strong statements that perked his ear!

"Who is this woman Lenard?" Shocked that Sina came to the car, Lenard sat speechless.

"You, yoou know who s-he is."

"You, you brought me to Sina's house? How *dare* you have me drive you out here!" The man's mind was *gone*! He took me, his wife to his girlfriend's house to get money she owed him. *Wow*! What nerve, what audacity he had! Sina yelled at him!

"Give me my key Lenard, *now*!"

He pulled the keys slowly from his pocket and removed her key from his chain. She hurried around to the other side of the car and snatched her house key from his hand, threw him a devastating look and headed back toward her apartment. I drove back to Baltimore in silence while Lenard's words of defense revealed his hurt. Nothing this man said convinced me, *he was sane!*

The next night, the night before Easter, Lenard called. He wanted me to come to his shop. I explained it was entirely too late for me to be driving downtown.

"Dawn I need your help. Sina came by the shop this morning and dumped all my clothes and everything else I had at her house on the ground in front of the shop."

"Where were you?"

"Sleeping in a friend's basement; up the street from my mother's house. Since Sina took her key and you put me out, I slept in the shop 'til last night. Ben stopped by and saw me sleeping in a car and offered me his basement for a while. I'm dirty from working on cars all day and hungry because I don't have any money."

I heard my heart pound as ragged nerves race through my exhausted body! I prayed, "Dear God please help this child of yours. I've done all I can. I don't know what else to do for him."

"Lenard I'll come down tomorrow after church."

"*No!* I want you to come down here right now!

"I'm not. You go to sleep and I'll come down tomorrow after church."

"*No!* Why can't you come now? You're not doing anything."

"Good night Lenard I'll see you tomorrow."

I hung up the receiver and lay thinking about how I could get him to the hospital. The phone rang again. And again I told him I would not come down until the next day. He was a *very* persistent man. He called again. After that call I kept the phone off the hook all night and finally got a little rest.

The following morning I called a police precinct and asked if they could pick him up and take him to the Veterans hospital.

"Ma'am I'm sorry but we can't pick him up unless he's committed some type of an offense." I explained to the officer my problems and *begged* for his help.

"Ma'am I understand your problems. I see them everyday and I sympathize with you but there is nothing I can do. Can you get him to go on his own?"

"*Oh no!* He wouldn't go. He'd say he has to work."

"That's your only recourse. Call the hospital and explain your problem, I'm sure they'll tell you how to get him there."

I called the hospital, explained in exasperation my heartbreaking problems. They understood and told me if I got him there they would give him the care he needed. All I had to do was—*get him there.*

After church I changed clothes. When I arrived at the shop dark green plastic bags lay on the dirty grease-spotted ground. More clothes were spread around where Sina had thrown them. Lenard, nasty drunk in his used-to-be white shirt I'd bought the previous year, staggered toward the car carrying an armful of things. That sight reminded me of the film, *The Jerk* where Steve Martin shuffles along while his pants are down around his ankles as he carries his chair, thermos, paddle etc. after having lost all his wealth.

"What tooook you so loong? I drank something else affter I talked to you. I guess you're mad, 'cause I ruuined your Easter but I need soomewhere to put alll this stuff. Some of it's noot worth keeping annnyway. Go through this junk and throw away anything that's not any good."

I thought, what am I, doing here picking up his life stuffed in plastic bags. I need as much help as he does! I'm just a maid cleaning up his dirt.

The I-Roc didn't have much storage space because of the hatch back. As Lenard tossed his belongings in the rear seat all mashed together, I noticed a framed certificate sticking out an opened section of one bag. It was his Army Discharge Papers that he couldn't find. *God answered my prayer.* Lenard's healing process had begun. I took his Discharge Papers and hid them in my purse. I thought, now I'll return to a normal person once he's hospitalized. Somehow I *had to* think of a way to get him admitted *that day!*

As I pulled away from the shop, Lenard drunk and dirty, reeking of foul body odor from past days of not bathing, said:

"I'm hun—gry. Get me somethi—ng to eat."

"What do you want Lenard? He pointed to McDonald's. I pulled up to the Drive-In Window and ordered. As I drove away, the attendant stared at the piled up clothes in the back seat and the stinky, dirty drunk talking out of his head seated next to me. Lenard opened his sandwich then *threw* it out the window!

"I dooon't wa—nt thi—s mess! Why did y—ou order this junk for mee any—way!"

"You said you wanted: a quarter pounder French fries and a vanilla milkshake. That's what you ordered. I don't appreciate you throwing my money out the car Lenard. You can throw yours away, but *not* mine!"

I stopped the car to pick up the food he'd thrown on the ground. Before I got out, Lenard opened his door and *ran* down the street, *yelling and complaining!* I felt sooo sorry for him. There I was on Easter Sunday, running down the street after my husband. He stopped, turned around and stared at me. Customers gathered outside McDonald's to see the commotion. After they saw Lenard had calmed down and was walking back toward the car, they returned to their cars.

I managed to get him back into the car peaceably. He fussed, complained acting maniacal. My nerves were shot! My head felt tight. Thoughts of getting him to the VA Hospital were prevalent. I prayed, "Dear God please let me get him to the hospital before he realizes where I'm *really* going."

His arms flung in the air as he moved restlessly in the seat. I checked the door slyly as I prayed he wouldn't open the door and jump out again at a stoplight. I kept answering his questions to keep his mind off the direction we were traveling. I'd promised the hospital I'd get there and my promise *would* be kept.

"*Take* me to my cusstomer's house! He owes mee money. Are you gonna' take me or nooot! If not, just sttop the car; I'll get theere on my oown!"

"Oh stop talking silly Lenard; I'm going to take you there as soon as I pick up a drapery deposit." I promised myself, when I got him back into the car, he *would* be admitted to the VA hospital that day! And if he didn't, somebody would have to commit me! I *couldn't* take any more! Lenard recognized the section of town because he'd installed rods for me in that area the previous year.

"Ah, I knoow you're going to that laady who has that oold house like yours; who had a car accident last year."

"Yea, that's where I'm going."

He calmed down as he relived the difficult time we had installing the traverse rods on her aged cracked walls. His ingenuity saved the job! The plaster started to crumble while he was installing the rod. But Lenard improvised, saving the client hundreds of dollars to get the wall rebuilt. His fantastic inventive mind was being destroyed everyday by alcohol.

As we neared the hospital I trembled, fearing he'd refuse to go inside. Lenard remembered the hospital was in that neighborhood.

"We're not too faar from the VA hoospital, Dawn. It's about two bllocks away."

I stopped in front of the hospital. The security guard out front was directing visitors and patients.

"Wait here Lenard, I'll be right back." I rushed up the steps toward the guard.

"Sir I have my husband in the car. He doesn't know I've brought him to the hospital and he might cause some problems. Would you please help me if he refuses to go inside?" I shook all over while my voice cracked as I talked to the guard. I couldn't believe we were actually there after years of hurts and tears.

"Yes Ma'am I'll be right here if you need me."

I returned to the car and asked Lenard to get out and come with me. He got out hesitantly but followed me up the steps to the landing where the officer waited and observed us moving in his direction.

"Here we are Lenard." He looked up and saw the name on the building and surprised me with his answer.

"Well I guuess this is wherrre I need to be. But I don't haave my Discharge Papers."

"I have them. They're right here. They were mixed in with your clothes." Amazed at his willingness to be admitted to the hospital, we moved closer to the door. "Dawn, I had noo idea wherre those papers werre, and you found them toodday. That's strraange."

I knew God placed them there to keep me from going insane. The officer escorted us to the main desk. I told the clerk who I was.

"Oh, yes Mrs. Winters I spoke to you this morning. I see you *did* get him here. You *said* you would." Lenard looked at me.

"You tri-cked me; but th—at's all right. I ne-eded to be here any-way. Tha-nk you Dawn for bri-nging me."

As we waited in line at the desk, Mr. & Mrs. Otis, former drapery customers approached us. I stepped to the side without Lenard noticing and explained I'd finally gotten my husband to the hospital. It was on their living room floor that he'd curled up in the corner and napped. Mrs. Otis had seen him sleeping.

She said, "Do you think he'd sleep better on the den sofa?"

"Oh no he'd just fine. He's used to sleeping on the floor in his shop. He's okay, just very tired from working on cars all day." I said.

"We knew he had a problem the day I saw him sleeping on the floor. We're glad he's getting help now." She held my hand, smiled and said, "Now you need to stop worrying and take care of *yourself.*" She saw my tired weary face, *drained* from the day's *unbelievable* events.

Death beckoned Lenard. His weight dropped from 230 lbs. to 158 lbs. The strong well-built man I'd married a year and a half earlier had disappeared. I handed his papers to the clerk. Lenard stood next to me like a little boy, dirty, quiet and obedient. The clerk asked me to sign the forms. My hands shook terribly! They *trembled* so badly I had to *steady* my right hand with the left one, to sign those forms! My whole body *quivered,* my heart thumped in pain!

How long I'd waited for this moment! How I soared with relief! Now he'd be *healed*! Lenard was examined and questioned by several doctors during our *four-hour wait*. At last we went upstairs to his room.

The doctor arrived as we stood at the foot of his bed. His head rested on my shoulder; he clung to me for dear life. His child-like behavior encouraged my comfort. I thanked God for directing me that day, that *heart-wrenching* day!

"Dawn I'm s-o so-rry. How did I manaage to get myself into this pre-dica-ment?"

The doctor asked Lenard to change his clothes in the bathroom. Then he took several steps toward me.

"Stop treating him like a baby!" His demeaning and accusatory tone of voice was totally unexpected.

"I didn't think I was. He asked for forgiveness because he's caused me so much unhappiness and heartache." As I left, the nurse asked me to step in her office.

"Mrs. Winters have you heard of Al-Anon?" Her smug snobby look wasn't typical of a nurse. I guess she thought I was white; married to a black man.

"No I haven't."

She handed me a few pamphlets; thumbed through them unconcerned and discussed the program's effectiveness for spouses of alcoholics. I listened and respected her explanations. "I suggest you find a local group in your area. It *will* help you to understand alcoholism."

I glanced through the material at home but tossed it on my desk to read later. Later was way, *wayyy* down the road. Lenard did remarkably well in the hospital and regained his weight fast after that vitamin shot. He underwent intensive therapy and group counseling. I on the other hand didn't locate an Al-anon group. I didn't think *I needed* anything like that, an enormous error on my part. One I'd soon regret.

During Lenard's stay, family was instructed *not* to give him any quarters for phone calls. He must stop his old habits in order to heal. Every time I visited he looked *soo* good: his eyes weren't red, he was well rested, his skin revealed that ever present smoothness and rich glow as he laughed and talked in his usual humorous manner. Once again the sober half I loved functioned normally.

I knew he had a drinking problem ever since our second date but I thought

I can help him stop. All he needs is a better environment.

Before Lenard's release his doctor asked to speak to me regarding his living arrangements. Once again Lenard wanted to return home. My compassion and love for him said yes. With two DUI's on his driving record, attending weekly veterans meetings was now mandatory plus his weekly AA Meetings.

I attended his first veterans meeting and met his counselor, Mr. Remington. He explained Lenard suffered from Post-Traumatic Stress Syndrome (PTSS). Many vets from the Vietnam War had acquired the disease called Asian Orange. He suggested I have Lenard visit the main VA office because he might qualify for special benefits. While Lenard sat in his group meeting I sat in his counselor's office learning about and how to deal with his problems.

Mr. Remington explained the symptoms didn't surface until fifteen or twenty years later. Lenard's was under fifteen. Some vets never returned home but lived deep in wooded areas, far—away from people. Sleeping in cars, on the ground and on any floor were typical behavior patterns of vets suffering from PTSS. His counselor enlightened me on the causes, actions, reactions and time frame for recovery for the vets that *did* recover. The following week he was interviewed and examined at the VA's downtown office.

His multiple war dreams increased; how often I didn't know since he rarely slept home. Sometimes he'd grab me around the neck as though I were the enemy! Only my *loud* screams and severe punches woke him up! He'd apologize, kiss me on the cheek, hold me tight then drift off to sleep hugging me like a small child. Unaware I was mothering him I thought an affectionate and lovable spouse was part of marriage. Never did I realize I'd influenced his reliance on the bottle. Countless—hectic—days lay ahead, of which I'd soon dread.

43...THE PLIGHT CONTINUES

A little consideration of what takes place
around us every day, would show us that a
higher law than that of our will, regulates
events; that our painful experiences are not
necessary. A believing love will relieve us
of a vast load of care. Oh, my brothers,
God exists!
Ralph Waldo Emerson

Lenard came home from the hospital. Some days were better than others.
His car was disabled so I'd drop him off at his new job; then head to mine. He
attended AA meetings and saw his probation officer. He'd stopped drinking
and came home every night. After two weeks the negative cycle returned. My
nerves were twisted. One by one each nerve unraveled—until the few
remaining, weren't strong enough to carry the load. I cried for no reason;
became more irritable in the classroom; couldn't sleep.

Married five times, I was determined Sina wouldn't take my husband. But
I failed to remember, I *never had him* in the first place; she did. Who was I but
an intruder whose opened eyes revealed the truth: *now* feminine competition
joined the automotive and drinking rivalry! She'd known him ten years. I'd
known him seven months before we married; but I was his wife. He told her
one version of his feelings and told me another.

One Saturday evening I waited in my car for him parked by his shop. He
and his friends were wrapping up a job, due that evening. Lenard walked back
and forth assuring me he wouldn't be much longer, in his humorous non-
drinking manner.

The last time he came, he stood in front of the windshield holding up a
large dead rat by its long skinny tail. I *screamed* and *screamed*! He dangled

that big black fat rat closer to the windshield as I plastered both hands over my face! He roared with laughter while I shrieked! He laughed non-stop! I backed out the driveway, sped down the narrow street and drove home terrified! His actions were heartless; inhumane! Civilized people didn't do crazy things like that. But whoever said he was civilized! I refused his phone calls! He lived with rats! I didn't!

"Dawn I don't know why you got so upset. It was only a dead rat, he couldn't bother you," he said after I finally accepted a phone call.

"Yes I know all of that, but you thought it was *so* funny; didn't you! You watched me, *scream* and *humiliate* myself in front of your friends. I saw you laughing as my car raced down the street. That was a hardhearted prank you performed!"

"I didn't think you'd act like that. But of course I see rats, everyday. They don't bother me and I don't bother them. Some of them are larger than these cats that roam the alley, so the cats leave them alone."

"Well I felt the same pain you did when your brother hit you on your head with his baseball bat last summer, remember?"

"Ah, I was drunk that day. It didn't hurt that much. You know how I act when I'm drinking."

"Yes I know, but you weren't drunk *that day* you dangled a rat in front of my face! So what reason do you give for scaring me half to death!"

"Ah, come on Dawn, you know I was only playing. That was not the *real* me. Can't you take a joke? You're too serious. Relax, that dead rat wasn't going to hurt you."

"But you hurt me—the *real* me! I don't drink, smoke or use drugs so I'm the real me everyday!"

Lenard rented a room (that's what he said) near his new job. Working for someone else was better for him. He'd known the owner of the small auto repair shop for years. He'd offered Lenard a job every time he'd complain about his customers not paying. Lenard, a master mechanic was a poor businessman. Money ran through his fingers like a broken dam!

Many customers took advantage of his kindness. They'd influenced his illness and forced him to shut down his business. Many cars were never retrieved even after he'd invested his own money for auto parts. I'd told him.

"Lenard, I never take a drapery order unless I get half or more of the total amount due, so I've never encountered those problems. You don't give your customer bills. You don't keep records. How do you expect—respect, when you present yourself in such a non-business manner?"

"Ah Dawn these people down here don't need any bills! They just want their cars fixed. We deal on hand shakes."

"Is that right? If that's so, why are you drinking yourself to death? Obviously they don't honor *their* handshakes."

While he was hospitalized, he called the owner of the small auto shop and was hired. His life improved—even his telephone conversations.

I'll never forget the day Sina and I met accidentally at his shop one Saturday afternoon. Lenard had asked me to stop by and get some money. As I talked to him while he worked on a car, Sina strolled into the alley. It was then I learned she'd given him back his key to her apartment. He visited her as he used to, on his terms. We stared at each other. Lenard's head dropped.

"Lenard I thought you told me you weren't seeing Sina any more." I said.

"He told me the same thing that he wasn't seeing you anymore. You must make up your mind which one you want. Who do you love Lenard, Dawn or me?" Sina said.

With his head lowered he gazed at the ground in silence.

"Are you going to answer Sina's question Lenard? Which one of us do you love? Which one do you want?"

He was under tremendous pressure. Two women who loved him; he had to chose.

"I love both of you." He answered; his head still lowered as a child caught in wrong.

Sina spoke up. "No Lenard you don't! You can't love both of us. You love one and like one. Now what is it?"

"I told you I love *both* of you."

Sina stepped forward. "*Give* me my house key! I gave it back to you but you'll *never* get it again!"

Reluctantly he removed her house key from his filled key ring and handed it to her with that guilty smile.

"Lenard, I've told you, when you burn a candle at both ends, it burns out leaving nothing." I turned and walked toward my car.

He called me that night. "Dawn you and Sina really surprised me today. I've never been in such a crisis as that before. The truth is I do love both of you and I want both of you."

"That's not the way it works Lenard. I'm stepping back. Eventually we'll get a divorce and you can marry Sina because you'll never stop seeing her and she'll never stop seeing you! You two belong together. I'm off this roller coaster marriage. I'll be dead or in a mental institution while you and Sina live the way you have these past ten years."

As usual Lenard ignored *no*. Whenever he called, I hung up. When he came to the house, I'd not answer the door. He'd stand at the door sober and deliver his little speeches of sorrow. He always left $20 or more in an envelope with a note. Sometimes I'd open the door and say a few words but most of the time I didn't! He'd call on my job. He even came to my school some mornings followed me in the building and to my classroom. On one occasion he'd been drinking and loud. His constant aggravation affected my sanity!

One evening as I sat at the dining room table with my head in my hands I could not stop crying! I called a psychiatric hospital and asked to be admitted. Between sobs and cries the nurse listened as I explained my problems with Lenard, Bryan, the I-Roc, the house, recent family deaths, working seven days a week to meet Bryan's additional expenses and my job.

"I can't take anymore! I don't know what to do! I'm in so much pain! Please help me! I don't want to live like this anymore. It's not fair to have all of these problems. I live alone. All I want is a husband to love me. Instead I married a man, who broke my heart with alcoholism, lies and another woman. *Please, please help me!*"

She asked varied questions involving my present state of mind. "After listening to you Mrs. Winters I feel you'd get the help you need in our out-patient office. Call and make an appointment. They *will* help you." She gave me their number. I called the next day. Had I known what lay ahead, I'd never called but would have obtained my *own* psychiatrist!

Seven years had passed, since I'd talk to my former psychiatrist. Against his judgement, I taught school and incurred more stress. I moved from a mean husband, to a kind alcoholic husband. I loved Lenard. I also loved an adulterer who was taught as a child that his type of male behavior was acceptable. But now I had to learn to love *myself*. I'd spent my life taking care of *everybody* except Dawn. Everyone I'd helped had moved on with their lives. Now I was left to experience a well-deserved nervous breakdown!

As I waited to see the doctor I examined the art reproductions displayed on the walls in the waiting room. They were abstract, surrealistic or expressionistic on a somber tone using drastic contrasting colors. Some exhibited exciting subject matter while others were miserable and melancholy. Obviously they weren't there to improve a person's thinking.

The psychiatrist listened to my mental mini-series for one hour. I spilled out teary dilemmas of anguish; then she prescribed 50mg of Zoloft daily. In addition I would visit a social worker weekly in the same suite.

The married social worker, Amy Smothers was a tall slender attractive blonde. I related to Amy immediately. She was warm and exhibited genuine concern for my problems. One day, she asked me a poignant question.

"Dawn, why do you look at the wall, rather than at me?"

"I don't know. I guess I think better looking at the wall. I do look at you sometimes, don't I?" I avoided looking because I was ashamed of my life.

"Yes, you do. But you stare at the wall more often."

Amy was *great*! She suggested I find an Al-Anon group and attend its weekly meetings in addition to seeing her. I did. Had I followed the nurse's advice in the VA Hospital months earlier, my healing process would have begun.

I thought I could do it on my own, but I couldn't.
I thought I didn't need Al-Anon but I did.
I thought I didn't need medication, but I did.
I thought I understood Lenard, but I didn't.
I thought my son would quit using drugs, but he didn't.
I thought I could change Lenard, but I couldn't.
I thought, I need to change me; my way of thinking!

Bryan used drugs at his family's expense. He'd lost his wife, children, several jobs, but still insisted he'd handle his problem himself. Every time I suggested drug rehabilitation confinement for a year, he'd refuse.

I thought my payment free Ford would last for years, but it didn't.
I thought my home would be mortgage free when I retired, but it wouldn't.
I thought after four husbands I'd found a good one, but I hadn't.
I thought I'd never put my mother and aunt in a nursing home, but I did.
I thought my life was *over*. It wasn't.

Yes my life resembled a run away train. New dilemmas provided *fuel* to maintain its intense velocity. Fuel zoomed in fast! It wasn't questioned. Getting off the train was a big, *big* enigma! So colossal was my problem my soul refused to respond. It lay lethargic, recovering from past explosive calamities.

I'd say, "Soul, wake up, I'll do better. I'll try to avoid being hurt. I'll stop giving my all to a man and getting little or nothing in return. I'll try! Please wake up! I want to live again. I want to live. Wake up!"

Al-Anon meetings *awakened* my tired soul. However, it was a slow sl—ow process. Other members' problems and reading, *One Day at a Time* by the Al-Anon everyday, I soon realized it was *I, I* who also needed help! I couldn't change the alcoholic but I *could* change myself. *I* had to change *my* reactions regarding his actions.

At first I resented learning it was *I who needed to change* and stopped reading the book. Anger set in! As I attended meetings, listened to situations similar to mine or worse I returned to the book. While the pages offered and revealed changes, so did my biased opinions.

Tears squeezed through walled in hurt, anger and despair. No one comforted me at meetings. I'd cry until the pangs of hurt decreased; then I'd speak. These people had experienced the identical torment and understood my dilemmas. Their injured hearts reached out and calmed mine. They listened, as words poured through my trembling lips. My stammered, sometimes inarticulate, speech soon became silent as I cried softly. Only muffled sounds escaped my mouth. Once I stopped crying, the normal meeting proceeded. Then I listened and started to learn. Oh *how* I learned! And what I learned! The next few months were fantastic! Those meetings were *exactly* what I needed when I was married to my *second* alcoholic husband! Oh, how I needed them during that time!

Alcoholic Anonymous (AA), begun in 1935, has helped alcoholics to overcome their drinking problems. A New York City stockbroker and an Ohio surgeon decided to help other alcoholics by using their experiences, a Higher Power and the twelve step program.

Wives of early AA members met at various homes and discussed ways to cope with their *own* problems. In helping each other they decided to try the Twelve-Step Program of AA, altering it to their needs. Thus the "Al-Anon Family Group" was formed.

In 1957 a young high school boy in California, shared his knowledge with suffering teens. From his sharing and caring, his hurting friends found emotional relief thereby creating Al-Ateen under the guidance of Al-Anon.

"God grant me the serenity
To accept the things I cannot change,
Courage to change the things I can,
And wisdom to know the difference."

Even though Lenard and I were separated, he remained in my life. I still loved the man. I'd rationalize his problems and my actions. Al-Anon taught me how to change my way of thinking, grad—u—al—ly. During that three-year period I realized I had a *serious* problem. I tried to change Lenard. Instead, *I had to change my thinking patterns and allow Lenard to change his.* With prayer, my therapist, the Zoloft, and Al-Anon biweekly meetings, my life cruised down a more sensible, stable sound road of healing.

Marty and Bryan finally moved to their own apartment, with my financial help of course. After I paid Bryan's delinquent gas and electric bill the utilities were turned on. At summer's end, they *returned* home. Bryan spent his money on drugs and Marty couldn't handle the expenses alone. The charge was $50.00 weekly for room and board as before; however, Bryan's payments were sporadic. Marty still drove the limousine and Bryan made pizzas. Marty slept downstairs in the den and Bryan slept upstairs in his former bedroom.

The I-Roc's lease would soon end. Its right front fender still hadn't been repaired. Marty's friend in Glen Burnie replaced the damaged fender with a used one Bryan had located. The guy even touched up the scratches and any other needs. He promised its completion that Friday. That afternoon, I cruised on Highway 95 to Marty's new job, in Glen Burnie. As I waited inside, I prayed:

"God please, *please* don't let Marty have an accident with that car! It's cost me *so much money* and so *many headaches!"*

Marty was late. My nerves danced. I prayed. I walked outside. I paced up and down the sidewalk in the front of the store. At last, I saw the beautiful burgundy glittered car turn the corner, headed in my direction. Elation filled my soul! Marty followed me in his car as I drove the I-Roc for the *last* time to the Chevrolet dealership. When I arrived the guy I'd spoken to on the phone minutes earlier was waiting outside with pad in hand.

"Hi Mrs. Winters, are you sure you want to turn in this *gorgeous* car?"

"Yes I *am!* You *know* all the maintenance problems I've had and the many phone calls we've shared about this car. *How could you ask me such a question!"*

"Just thought, I'd ask."

"Sir, actually I would keep it, but my son is living with me and I'd never get a minute's rest with him around. Even though I've made eighty-five percent of the car payments and all the expensive repairs, he still considers this *his* car. Thank you, but *no* thank you."

He checked everything and totaled the amount due for extra mileage. We stood next to the car as I signed the form he had on the clipboard. Once again my hands *shook* so much I used my left hand to steady my right hand.

"What's wrong with your hands Mrs. Winters?"

"I'm *sooo* glad this day has arrived! You just don't *knowww how happy* I am to give you this car. It has caused *me sooo much pain.*"

"I remember the pressures you've experienced these past years. But we'll still miss having you as a customer." I thought; I *sure* won't miss you!

I shook his hand then got into Marty's car. We returned to his job. I opened my car door, slid behind the steering wheel, turned on the ignition and floated home, relieved of all mechanical burdens, released from pent-up emotions, renewed with strength and vigor. I thanked God for lifting me over the hurdles and easing my pain. He never promised me a *rose* garden but said He'd be *with* me through *all* my trials and tribulations. He *was.* He *heard* my cries. He *soothed* my sorrows. Throughout it all He was there.

Two weeks prior I'd purchased a four-year old Cadillac Seville, the one that resembled a gangster's car with the slanted back. A burgundy beauty, it looked new with its plush maroon velvet interior and white-walled tires. Marty checked it out before I made a final decision. I'd always admired that car but never thought I'd own one. During the test drive I heard a small click, click sound. Marty pulled over on the shoulder of the highway and checked under the hood. He found nothing. Before I signed any papers, the used car owner's mechanic inspected it thoroughly. I withdrew $3000 from my annuity and renewed my credit union loan for the remaining $1500. The night of the purchase I drove home levitating in mid air. I'd wanted to own a Cadillac or Mercedes by the time I retired but this was ten years early.

Two weeks earlier, Bryan sat at the upstairs den window staring out at my car. I knew his thoughts before he said one word.

"Mommy you have a new car and I don't have anything," he said.

"That's a used car and it's paid for. I'm tired of car payments. It never ends. You pay for one then it's time to get another one."

Irritated, Bryan waved his hands in anger as he expressed his annoying feelings about his illogical life style.

"I understand all that, but I just can't seem to get myself together!"

"And whose fault is that? Stop giving your money to the drug dealers. Then you'd have a car. You had a beautiful car Bryan. In two weeks the lease runs out and it goes back to the dealer. Don't discuss what I have. I work *very* hard. I teach, make draperies and attend classes two nights a week."

"I know Mommy, I know. You don't have to tell me, I know my problem."

"Since you know it, what are you going to do about it?" He stared out the window, with no response.

"By the way I was in the attic yesterday and noticed Theon's photographic enlarger was missing. Do you know what happened to it?" He continued staring out the window.

"Did you hear my question, or are you going to ignore me and keep staring out that window?" His refusal to answer implied, he knew *all* about it.

"I sold it."

"You did *what*!"

"I sold it."

"You mean you stole Theon's enlarger and sold it? That *wasn't* your property!"

"Well it's been up in the attic a few years now. I didn't think he wanted it. It was only accumulating dust."

"I don't care how many years it was up there or how much dust it accumulated it still wasn't yours and you had no business selling it. How much did you sell it for anyway?"

"$50."

"*$50.!* Theon paid $250 for that enlarger!"

I knew he'd used the money for drugs. I also knew he'd soon start stealing from me.

"Have you stolen anything else from me Bryan?" He dropped his head.

"Your gold necklace. It's in the pawn shop."

"*You pawned my necklace for drugs!*"

My heart sank. I flopped down on the sofa; he stared out the window. How could my son steal from me, his own mother? I knew addicts stole from anyone: parents, spouse, children, relatives, employers and strangers. They stole for that *high*. They didn't care who provided the finance. He gave me the $50 pawn ticket. The shop was a few blocks from our home.

The following day I retrieved my necklace. I'd seen the shop but had never been there. I had no reason. I informed the owner Bernardo, what had happened. He consoled my hurt and shared the sadness of his past life of alcohol and drugs. Business was slow. His invitation to sit in a comfortable black leather chair behind the counter with him in his small working area was accepted. He related several tragedies he'd encountered. He explained his mental and physical hardships experienced prior to the five years he'd been clean and operating a lucrative business.

"What made you stop?"

"I was tired of being poor; of never having any money and making somebody else rich. I wanted to be rich. In order to be rich I'd have to put an end to my wretched habits. So I stopped. It wasn't easy though. But I was determined and stuck by my convictions."

He pulled out his desk drawer and removed a small green book and began reading certain passages, the ones that guided his healing process. His truthful enlightenment on Bryan's dilemma breathed clean air in my foul environment. He alerted me to change *my* actions otherwise Bryan would steal everything I had!

I explained I attended weekly Al-Anon meetings. We discussed its written material in depth and how AA had helped him. He admitted *he* made the final choice to stop. He wasn't an atheist but he wasn't a Christian either. Bernardo was however a kind, handsome divorced young Italian guy about forty with a ten year old daughter.

He said at first his shop *was* housed in the home where he grew up. After his mother's death, he moved his shop to the building adjacent to his house. As he talked I learned that long before the narrow road had been widened to a major road with two lanes, he'd coast on sleds down the hills during heavy snows! He reacquainted me with the old neighborhood. As he reminisced I too remembered that road before it was widened into a main thoroughfare.

He also revealed how he'd throw stones at my house and broke out many windows whenever Mr. Smith, made him angry. In addition, I learned Mr. Smith had attended Bernardo's Catholic Church, on several occasions.

Before I left, he gave me the reading material that had helped him. He confirmed what doctors had told Bryan; he *could* stop when he was ready. On many occasions I'd visit his shop to pawn my jewelry. Each time, he'd unlock the swinging gate for me to sit in the comfortable black leather chair. I felt honored he trusted me with thousands of dollars in jewelry and money.

Sometimes he'd crawl through his small hidden door in the rear of the large room and into his house while I guarded the shop.

"Mrs. Winters, I'm going next door to check on my dinner. Do you mind sitting here for a few minutes? I'll be right back."

He'd crawl on his hands and knees through the little flip door he'd cut through the wall for him and his daughter, as easy access to both the house and his shop. The first time I saw him crawl though, I was in awe! I thought *how ingenious of him to devise a method of entry between home and work unknown to his costumers.*

His entryway reminded me of *Alice in Wonderland* when Alice follows the rabbit down a long hall and finds a small door. She peeks through the door and wishes she were small enough to get through. In this case Bernardo's opening was large enough. Of course my imagination ran wild as I envisioned multiple events occurring between the two buildings. I'm sure only a few people knew his secret. I felt privileged to be one of those few. He used his passageway on rare occasions when business was slow.

One day his former wife came in while I was seated behind the counter. Their conversation was held out front as though she were a customer. She like her daughter was beautiful, only she had serious emotional problems.

Another afternoon, as a customer waited for Bernardo to assess his gold necklace, ring and bracelet I was seated behind the counter, the guy asked him an interesting question.

"Hey Bernardo, is that your wife?" Surprised by the unexpected question, I glanced at Bernardo and waited for his answer!

I could have been. What other woman would be seated comfortably behind the counter while he handled business? He'd *never* made a pass and was always a gentleman. Being a lady and always getting large amounts of cash, he gave me my money when his shop was empty and escorted me to my car. His customers were mostly men.

"No, that's not my wife. I'm not married." He turned, looked at me, smiled and continued his appraisals of the gold chain, ring and bracelet. His varied age of customers intrigued me. Some wanted $20 while others needed $40 or $50 'til payday. No one requested thousands as I did. His interest rates were lower than his competitors. When his business expanded, so did his interest rates!

44... HABITS, HARD TO BREAK

Sorrows are like thunderclouds.
Far off they look black, but directly
over us merely gray.
Jean Paul Richter: Hesperus

I recall an incident before the I-Roc was returned. A drapery order was due Monday so I rose early Saturday morning to complete it by late afternoon. Pressing draperies, handling yards of fabric, and finishing details in that dreary dismal attic was exhausting! Since my helper had the flu I worked alone. Above the soft classical music of Camille Saint-Saens flowing from the small radio on the old unpainted ladder back chair, I heard Bryan's slow down-trodden footsteps ascending the attic's creaky wooden steps.

"What's wrong Bryan? Your footsteps speak of sorrow." His tired appearance revealed his shame.

"Y-es, you're right Mommy. I ne-ed a fav-or. A guy has my car until I pay him money I owe him."

"If he has your car, how did you get here?"

"I walked."

"Walked from where?"

"The bottom of the hill; that's where the car is. Come downstairs; I'll show you."

I followed him downstairs to the second floor bedroom. He approached the opened window slowly. The lilac's fragrance from beneath the window filled the heavy room with sweetness. Between the open leaf spaces of the huge oak tree, I spied his car parked at the bottom of the hill.

"Bryan I don't have any money. You got yourself into this predicament, now get yourself out. What do you think I am your bank?" He revealed that sympathetic face, an expression hard for a mother to refuse.

"But Mommy you're the only person I have that can help me; I'm your son. Please help me Mommy, *please*."

"How much do you owe this guy, Bryan?" Head down with his hands clasped together in his lap he uttered.

"Eighty dollars."

"Eighty dollars! You know I don't have eighty dollars. All my money has gone to pay *your* bills and some of mine."

"Mommy I really *need* the money! He's gonna' keep my car if I don't give him something." He presented his saddest face—as he pleaded.

"If you could just give me $20.00 'til I get paid on Monday. I know he'll take that." Instantly, I knew it was for drugs. A few days earlier, I'd heard, an addict had beaten his mother to death because she refused to give him her rent money. I didn't think Bryan would go that far but I couldn't be sure. I also recalled how he'd mistreated Nardia when she refused to surrender their $800 Income Tax refund check

"Bryan I don't have any money in the house. I might have $20-30 in my checking account. I knew I had at least $60 but wouldn't tell him. I drove to the bank. Bryan sat by the window but was outside when I returned.

"Bryan I don't believe someone would hold your car for such a small amount of money. Get off the drugs; I don't intend to finance your habit. You have a lovely wife and two beautiful little girls in Fayetteville. *Please* get some help! God gave you a good mind and how do you thank Him? You cook your brain! Every time you use drugs you're killing your brain cells boy!"

"I know Mommy, I know." I gave him the twenty-dollar bill. He thanked me; walked down our gravel/dirt road, then down the hill until he reached the car.

My dear son was committing suicide, bit by bit, with each drug use. I loved him. I'd given him life and yet—I felt helpless in saving his life. I cried on God's shoulder daily. He'd promised he'd answer our prayers; so far He had. I prayed for patience to *wait on the Lord.*

Two weeks later on a Sunday afternoon after church Bryan called. Marty answered the phone. His face expressed fear!

"It's Bryan Mom! He's in *big* trouble! He's in a phone booth! A guy is holding a gun at his head! He owes him money!" He handed me the receiver.

"What's wrong now Bryan!"

"I owe this guy $250. He's holding a gun to my head. *Please* help me, Mommy, I don't want to die." Bryan was *so* high he could barely talk. His repeated words were so slurred, I handed the receiver to Marty.

"Man, today is Sunday. We don't have that kind of money and don't know where to get it." Marty talked to Bryan a few more minutes.

I said, "Marty, ask Bryan to give you the pay phone's number. I'll call La Raine maybe Vincente will lend us the money 'til I get paid." He got the number. I called La Raine. It was *hard* convincing Vincente however he finally agreed to lend me the money with his persistent *wife's* pleading. Vincente, a fine man, held on *tight* to his money! Vincente loved money. Next to his family, *his* money was a strong second!

Marty called Bryan back to confirm we'd gotten the money. He obtained the address where to meet Bryan then we left immediately for La Raine's home.

Bryan's possible burial funds, newspaper scandal and payment to Vincente by using my bill money imbued my mind. Nevertheless, I *was* grateful my son was alive at least for now! Weeks later Bryan confessed that his friend was the victim and not he.

Several weeks prior, my next door neighbor's son, Michael was shot and killed over drugs. He'd dropped out of high school, moved in with his girlfriend and was dealing on the corner near a store. He used the pay phone outside the building for his contacts. Bryan told me after Michael's funeral that he'd seen him on that corner selling drugs and begged him several times to stop. He refused. A drive by gunman shot and killed that handsome, eighteen year old boy *instantly*! Even with the recent death of Michael, Bryan's use of drugs didn't cease. I thought *what does it take? Even the senseless murder of a next door neighbor, had no influence!*

We waited in suspense thirty minutes in La Raine's home, for Bryan's call so Marty could deliver the money. I prayed that nothing would happen to my son. After we got the call we left. Marty drove me home first then proceeded to the drug house, located in a decent neighborhood. Were the neighbors aware of the criminal dealings in that *lovely* home, I wondered.

Marty knocked on the door.

"Who's there?" A deep voice asked.

Marty identified himself; the door opened. A large rugged bearded man inspected him from head to toe; then nodded toward the living room. Marty scanned the limp bodies spread around the room on the floor leaning up against the wall.

"He's over there, against that wall." The man said.

Marty walked into the living room, and saw people all ages, all sizes. He wondered how people could drop to this level. He spied his brother among the weak and suffering... Bryan noticed Marty and motioned to him.

"Tha—nks bro for he-lping me. I o-we you one."

Marty stooped down and helped his brother up off the floor. They moved to another room where he handed over the $250. He then assisted his brother in leaving Satan's drug infested house. Once they were in the car Marty released his fury! Bryan too high to care—nodded while his brother's angry harsh words were unheard.

God directed me to La Raine and her husband; the same friends who had helped me retrieve Bryan's car after it was stolen and impounded.

Weeks later as I sat at my office desk checking test papers, suddenly that still quiet voice said, "Call home." I did. Bryan answered the telephone.

"Bryan what are you doing home? I thought you worked today."

"I am working today. But I had to come home to get something and then I'm going back."

An uncertain feeling entered my mind as we talked. Something was wrong. I detected strangeness in his voice. As soon as I pulled into the driveway that afternoon the uneasy feeling returned. My steps dawdled as they moved closer to the house. Suddenly a frightening thought appeared. I rushed up the porch steps, unlocked the door then ran up the staircase to the second floor den. It *was* gone! Bryan had *stolen* my VCR. Hurt gripped my heart as I eyed the vacant spot where the VCR belonged. I thought *why are you so upset?* You knew this would happen one day. *Put him out!"*

I rationalized, "How can I evict my own sick son? He'd have to live on the streets. If something happened to him I'd never forgive myself. He needed hospitalization. But no one would help him get admitted. I'm—all he has."

I thought with my heart and not my *brain!* Bryan didn't come home that Friday night, Saturday or Sunday. I called his job everyday. They hadn't heard from him. On previous absences he'd lie: he's been out of town or was sick. His manager explained his three-day pattern: always on their busiest days, the weekend.

Monday he returned home drained! Before I voiced a word he explained. Yes I was hurt, but he felt and looked worse! My love and pity covered him as he attempted to explain that initial high's reaction. I listened as he relished his slow insidious suicide. He didn't care about the hurt his family braved while he enriched men's purses who sold drugs. Addicts only cared about themselves. He agreed with me. But admitted he just *couldn't* stop. Drugs had devoured his once bright and intelligent mind. Now he awaited his next euphoric cruise to *hell* at somebody else's expense.

"Did you pawn the VCR or sell it?"

"I paw-ned it. He-re's the ticket." He reached into his pocket, pulled out the ticket and handed it to me.

"How much do I have to pay *this* time Bryan?" He dropped his head.

"Sixty-five dollars. I'm sorry Mommy, I'm re-ally sorry."

"Well Bryan this is the last time you'll have to say those words to me. And where did you take the VCR? I know not at Bernardo's."

"I'll show you the pawn shop. It's on Holland's Road and you don't have to go in the pawn shop, I'll go."

"I had no intention of going in." Days later when I got paid, I drove to the pawnshop with Bryan seated next to me.

"Mommy, remember the day I took the VCR?"

"You mean *stole*! Not took."

"Well, whatever, I was disconnecting it that very moment when you called," he said.

"How could you do that to me Bryan? I understand your drug problem. But to steal from me after *all* I've done for you?"

"That's why I feel so bad. When I'm high I don't think about anybody except me. I'm trying to get that same high I got on the first go round. But it's never the same. Addicts spend hundreds of dollars trying to repeat that same high. I needed the money right then. I'll pay for it when I get paid."

"Is that so? When you get paid? You never come home, remember? And since you've missed so many days on your job, you may not have one now."

"Yea, I know but I promise to come home this weekend."

"Bryan this is the *last* time you'll steal from me! The next time, I'm pressing charges and I'm *not* going to drop them. You need help. If you won't seek help yourself then you'll have to get it in jail!"

He stared straight ahead and remained mute. He knew I meant every—single word. I had him locked up twice in the past: stealing my car and damaging my property.

The Bible states, "If you spare the rod, you'll spoil the child." Bryan had not been denied the rod but he'd been severely spoiled by his grandmother and mother! Daily spankings were a part of his youth. I'd left their father Maurice when Bryan was almost three and Marty nearly five. I never understood why trouble *always* attracted Bryan but repelled Marty. I realized siblings were different but not that different. They agreed on nothing: not clothes, music, friends, education, religion, food or personal hygiene.

Three days before the school's Christmas break while I stood on hall duty, two sharp pains *jabbed* the instep of my left foot! The severe pains returned during the day. Mrs. Sawyer, the main office's secretary, a pleasant lady, recommended her podiatrist, Dr. Segal. I visited his office the same day after school. His examination revealed a bunion, unbeknownst to me and suggested I have it and the ingrown toenail removed as soon as possible. I agreed.

"I have an opening this Saturday before Christmas or the Thursday after Christmas." I listened as he described the various procedures and the estimated healing time. My feet were most important, so the pain had to go!

"This Saturday will be just fine Dr. Segal." I said.

"You don't mind being shut in during the holiday season? You don't have any special plans?"

"Nothing really; oh *yes*, I almost forgot, my Goddaughter, in North Carolina is getting married on the December 30th. I promised to decorate for her wedding."

"North Carolina! Do you think that's wise so soon after the operation?"

"I don't know, what do you think?"

"I don't think you should go, however you'll know how you feel by that time."

"I promised to decorate. I always honor my word. Her family promised they'd do all the work and my job is to direct the placement of everything."

Dr. Segal suggested using the laser technique to remove the bunion and ingrown toenail. Friday after school I finished up everything I had to do before the surgery. Bryan drove me to the doctor's office for out-patient surgery. He returned a few hours later and waited in the lounge.

I hopped on my right foot down the hall out of the office and leaned on Bryan's arm for support. He assisted me to the car without incident. Once home, he helped me up the porch steps, then *up* the staircase to the second floor to my bedroom. It never occurred to me to ask for crutches and neither did Bryan. What were we thinking about as I hopped down the hall in the doctor's office then outside to the car.

Monday I called and spoke to the doctor and returned to his office for the crutches that day. I wondered why Dr. Segal hadn't given them to me in the first place. I asked Bryan to get them but the doctor insisted they had to fit according to my height.

Bryan brought down Mama's bedside potty chair from the attic. It had been on vacation since Mama had entered the nursing home. Even with crutches, it was awkward trying to maneuver my foot without it touching the floor. So I'd hop forward, move the crutches forward then take another hop. That painful process required lots of practice to get to and from the bathroom. It always embarrassed me when he emptied it, although it only held urine. I was an independent woman; used to doing everything for myself. Now my son had to empty my bedside pot. How humiliating I felt every time he did so.

He'd say, "Oh mommy, stop worrying about it. I don't mind. Remember I emptied Aunt Betty's and it was filled to the top."

"But I'm not Aunt Betty and I do mind!"

Years prior when I'd jumped off the embankment and sprained my ankle handling crutches wasn't as painful or as awkward. I surmised that combined surgery was worse than a sprain. Besides getting up and down those steep steps everyday didn't help. Looking back I should have moved downstairs in the den where Marty slept and he could have stayed upstairs in the second den. We never thought of that alternative. Besides, Marty's room packed with *everything* including television, VCR's, computers parts had no space left.

Marty still drove the limousine. Rarely did I hear him come home from work. He left extremely early and returned very late every night. Brainy, Marty learned quickly to maneuver Maryland's roads and highways. My sons later regretted their decision, not to attend college. Two intelligent young men floated from job to job because they ignored my constant pleas. For some *odd* reason they thought they had enough education and *did everything their way.*

Hannah's gorgeous white negligee set wrapped, I'd decided *not* to go to North Carolina. That way I'd have two weeks to heal after surgery before school reopened. Recovery chances were greater, if I remained home, then I'd be ready for work the first of the year. *Wrong!* I was home over *two* months! Multiple setbacks intervened. A so-called minor surgery developed into a *major* recovery. I returned to work, *March 11th!*

Rachel and her family came by the day after Christmas for Hannah's gift and the reception decorations. They planned to leave early Thursday morning. She called first, allowing me time to get down those steps. I slid down each step one at a time while sliding the two crutches down with me. Once I'd gotten to the bottom, which I considered a challenge, I hopped over and sat on the white antique sofa in the living room near the door. The same gorgeous sofa I'd gotten for $125 through Gene and had reupholstered a year later. Minutes later the doorbell rang. I opened it and saw three souls huddled close together braving December's cold.

"Come right in; have a seat." We hugged each other; discussed the weather and the holiday events."

"How was your Christmas, Joy? What did Santa bring you?" Joy was a bright six-year old girl from Rachel's previous marriage.

"I don't believe in Santa Clause Ms. Dawn. My mom and dad gave me many presents but we won't open any until we get to my Grandmother's house. What did you receive for Christmas?"

"Nothing. But I gave presents to my sons and their families. I did receive *lots* of lovely Christmas Cards." I pointed to the cards displayed around the living and dining rooms. Since I'd decorated before surgery, the house looked quite festive inside and outside.

"You didn't get any gifts at *all* Ms. Dawn!"

"No not *one*, but I'm used to that now." Bryan used drugs and Marty never had any money. Rachel interrupted our conversation.

"Ms. Dawn it's traditional in our family, to open our presents together Christmas Eve. We sit in front of the lighted tree and fireplace; read the Bible and sing Christmas Carols before opening our gifts. I wish you'd change your mind about going then you'd see how we have our Christmas? We *really* need your help Ms. Dawn, besides you're Hannah's Godmother and she's expecting you."

"Rachel I'm sorry, I just can't. I'm using two crutches and really don't feel like going. It'll be so awkward for me, plus an inconvenience for everyone having to wait on me. That's a six-hour drive to Rosen Hill and to have my foot propped up that long…"

She interrupted, "But you *wouldn't* have to do anything once you got there!"

"Rachel, my surgery was performed four days ago. Yesterday morning, I came down those steps, by sitting on one step at a time as I did today and cooked Christmas dinner, only to regret it by having *so much pain* last night. My sons didn't come home until late, so I ate alone."

"You mean you spent Christmas Day *alone*!"

"Yes I did. My cat Solace and I spent the day together. Of course he's my devoted baby. He follows me everywhere and even sleeps with me."

"I sure wish we'd known, we'd have come over and shared dinner with you. I didn't cook, so we ate out."

"You knew I had surgery, Rachel. Had you called to check on me and how I felt, you would have known."

"Ye—ah, I gue-ss you're ri—ght, I di—dn't think abo—ut that."

I gave Rachel Hannah's gift and the wedding reception decorations. She took them reluctantly, with that pitiful solemn expression.

"Ms. Dawn, I'm going home and give you time to think about this. I'll call you later, okay?"

"Okay. Call me later."

I thought. Odd she could call encouraging me to go and decorate for the wedding but couldn't call to inquire about how I felt after my surgery or offer to help me in any way.

Guilt haunted me after they left. I promised to decorate weeks earlier for my dear friends Melvin and Lauren Clemons. How could I disappoint them now? They depended on me. I couldn't let them down. Why hadn't I scheduled the surgery after the holiday? Why, because I loved my students. Dedication to my students and my job insisted I go then rather than wait until after the holidays. With me not there, they'd have an excuse not to learn or misbehave. Extreme guilt mixed with commitment changed my mind. I called Rachel and said I'd reconsidered. Of course she was elated!

So early Thursday morning, I sat in the back seat of their car, with my left foot propped up on the armrest between the two, front seats with Joy seated next to me.

My Goddaughter Hannah, a loving young lady, sang like an angel. I first met the Clemons several years earlier during one of my visits at Sally and Handel Caldwin's gorgeous home, nestled in a secluded wooded section in Rosen Hill. Sally had been one of my college roommates. She and Handel married in secrecy. Their close friends and family knew they were engaged. Now, Handel owned a prospering contracting company. His wealth didn't hinder his genuine mirth and generosity with residents of the small college town. Sally, a former teacher was as humorous and forthright as ever.

Sunday afternoons she held poetry sessions in her huge basement with a hardwood dance floor and full kitchen facilities plus his and her bathrooms. I'd *never* seen anything like it! It was during one of those visits Sally took me to see the Christian family that had bought their previous home.

The scenic trip to Rosen Hill was a relief from my day to day routines. For once I viewed farms and landscapes without having to worry about reckless motorists when I drove. *How* my foot throbbed! I didn't complain about the pain since the newly married couple was doing their best. The six-hour ride was fun. We laughed, talked and played travel car games with Joy.

We arrived after dark. Since the car was parked some distance from the back door my walk was awkward on the bumpy ground. That was the second time I'd gotten out since we left Baltimore. I'd only used the crutches a couple of days so my pace was slow and clumsy. Lauren and Melvin rushed out to greet their family and their friend on two crutches. By the time I hopped up the back step and into the kitchen I felt like an old used up rag doll ready to flop down in bed. However my long awaited desire to lie in a bed would not happen until after another prearranged affair had ended.

"Where's Hannah?" I asked.

Lauren was slow in answering. "Ah, she's—lying down…"

About ten minutes later she appeared wearing a pink seersucker robe, bare feet and rolled up hair. She said hi in a dismal tone, to everyone and sat down next to her mother on the royal blue sofa. She was not the same girl I'd met years earlier or the girl I'd taken back to Baltimore with me for a week's vacation. Missing—was her radiant smile; her sweet gentle laughter. I expected her greeting to be warm and pleasant. I wanted to hear words that expressed happiness of her wedding. I needed to hear, "Thank you for coming to decorate for my wedding," instead, I heard nothing. She sat on the sofa staring into space. Later, her mother made excuses to me privately about Hannah's strange behavior.

"Dawn I forgot to tell you how Hannah clams up whenever she's involved in large events. For the past few days, she'd given everyone the cold shoulder. We're used to her moods. But this is the first time you've not seen that happy, smiling Hannah."

"You're right Lauren I wasn't prepared for this Hannah."

Melvin was a fine Christian who tried to keep peace. He lived in a house with five females and coped. Melvin gathered his family in the living room *every* morning holding hands in a circle and prayed before departing for the day.

Lauren stood facing us and said, "It's time for everyone to leave for the bridal shower. I'm not going; I've had a long hard day and I need to rest for tomorrow."

I touched Lauren's arm. "Lauren I'm not going either. I need to rest my foot so I'm just going to bed." She looked agitated.

"Dawn I'd like for you to go. You'll enjoy the shower."

"But Lauren I don't *feel* like going. My foot needs rest and so do I."

"But I'd *appreciate* it if you'd go. I *really* need to be in this house alone for a while." She shook her head in disgust and returned to the kitchen but then stopped short.

"Oh yes I forgot, everyone's on their own for breakfast in the morning. The boxes of cereal will be on the counter."

I didn't respond. What could I say? She'd already made it *quite* clear she didn't want *anyone in the house.* I returned to my room on the second floor and freshened up for the bridal shower.

Yes, my room was on the *second* level of their split-level home. Once again I moved up one step at a time just like I had at home dragging my crutches beside me. Hannah walked up the steps to her room sliding on the opposite wall as she moved up the seven or eight steps toward the second floor, never offering any assistance, not even to carry my crutches. She treated me as though I were a germ. Melvin was the only one who remembered, I used crutches because I'd had foot surgery less than a week earlier. They viewed me with their eyes, but not their hearts.

Less than an hour in the home I *regretted*, I'd come. First, the bride to be, ignored my presence and second the family ignored my surgery, not completely but enough to alert me that my health was of little importance to them. They begged me to come, knowing I wasn't well then treated me as though nothing was wrong.

Against my wishes I attended the bridal shower. Melvin drove us in his spacious Buick. The house situated on a low hill had a steep incline and *no* steps. Rained over soil, left impressions of forgotten steps once started. As I fought that hill I thought, *had I known I'd have to endure this steep incline I'd have ignored Lauren's "command" and stayed at the house.* Melvin assisted me. He braced my back with his hand as I trudged and hopped up the inclined rugged slope to the house. My heavy warm clothes only added weight as I lugged up the hill, reaching the porch *exhausted*! I rested in Margie's comfortable living room before joining the other guests in the family room.

Hannah received many lovely gifts, games were played plus the refreshments were outstanding! Hannah remained calm. She introduced me as her Godmother. Nothing was mentioned about my recent surgery, or that I'd just arrived two hours ago from Baltimore with her family. I sat in *dire pain*, crutches on the floor next to my chair, tired, sleepy and emotionally injured. Again I thought *why am I here? I must be crazy to put Hannah ahead of my physical condition; to come down here and endure such selfishness and ingratitude.* As negative thoughts rushed through my mind, I picked up my crutches and hopped into the living room.

Soon Margie joined me.

"What's the matter Dawn?"

"I'm so tired and weary. I should be in bed resting my foot."

"Would you like to lie down on the sofa until the shower is over?"

"Yes I would. *Thaank you,* thank you so much!"

Margie propped a pillow under my head and elevated my foot with two more; a kind and considerate lady who helped ease my pain. She was the *only* person who'd shown me any concern since we arrived.

"Dawn, why did you come to the bridal shower? You should have stayed at Lauren's."

"I wanted to but Lauren wanted *everyone out* of the house so she could rest."

"*Rest!* You staying there had nothing to do with her resting. Besides you had no business *battling* my hill with those crutches. I don't know how you made it in the first place! I can barely walk up that hill myself, *not* using crutches. We've had several estimates given for installing steps but my dear husband thinks he can do it himself. It's been a *year* and we still don't have any steps." At *last* someone other than Melvin had compassion for me.

Melvin had braced my back with his hands to keep me from falling backwards!

Descending the hill was as dangerous as ascending! I thought I'd topple over any minute due to the steep incline. God heard my prayers and guided every hop I made. Once I got to the bottom I thanked God. Only He knew my pain and the stress I endured. After climbing safely into Melvin' car, we headed home.

Lauren asked everyone to gather in the living room. This close clan waited until they were altogether to open their Christmas presents as a family, their tradition. We sat around the glowing fireplace and the decorated tree. With bowed heads, everyone held hands and listened as Melvin prayed. He thanked God for allowing his family to be together, Hannah's upcoming wedding and our safe trip from Baltimore. Melvin was a *devoted* Christian. He not only *studied* the Bible; he lived it by his *walk*— the way he treated people. After prayer, Lauren read scriptures about Jesus' birth, followed by everyone singing Christmas Carols. The Christmas Eve service was warm and inspiring.

As a child my sister and I got up Christmas morning, opened our presents and then played all day. At nine years old I lived with Aunt Betty.

Before Christmas arrived she announced, "Girl there is *no* Santa Clause. *I'm* the one who buys your gifts, *not* Santa."

So that December I selected the doll I wanted in Woolworth's Five and Dime. She bought it. I wrapped it. Then placed it under the Christmas tree in the cold hall that was only heated on Sundays or whenever we had company. Aunt Betty could have destroyed my Christmas spirit but I refused to let that happen.

Living with my aunt was like living in an isolated world. I ate, slept, bathed, and existed. Being around adults encouraged my maturity. By sixteen I was self-sufficient. I financed my college education and married at twenty-one, too early in search of love I'd *not* received as a child. As I watched the Clemons family, I'd longed for their closeness, their peaceful and loving home. No one used profanity. They neither, drank alcoholic beverages or played cards. They lived in a God-loving environment. Growing up I thought it was normal to live in such a worldly environment. I'd never known anything else. Since my basic needs were provided, I assumed our life style was normal.

The fireplace's crackling flames returned me to the present. Gifts were distributed among the family. I also received a gift, a lovely red scarf, just what I needed for the freezing winter months I'd face in Baltimore.

Up early the next morning, I hopped down the steps then to the kitchen for my morning's cereal. The cereal boxes were on the kitchen counter but not the milk. In the refrigerator was a large glass gallon bottle of milk. I questioned how I would carry that glass bottle *without* a handle and hold on to my crutches at the same time.

I removed the bottle from the refrigerator with one hand trying to use only one crutch but I couldn't! After several failed attempts I replaced the milk in the refrigerator, but did not close the door. There was one choice left, crawl on the floor. I rested my crutches against the kitchen table; got down on the floor and crawled toward the open door. Raised on my right knee I reached for the milk on the top shelf. Very carefully I lowered the gallon bottle held with both hands, then placed it on the floor, pushing it along ahead of me as I crawled back to the table where my bowl of cereal waited. I imagined the cereal chanting, "Push, push just a little far—ther, push, push just a little far—ther." On raised knees, I poured milk over my cereal then made my return trip to the refrigerator. What an awesome ordeal to experience for a bowl of cereal. As soon as I was seated and enjoying my cereal a family member entered the kitchen.

"Ah, Ms. Dawn I see you've already gotten your breakfast."

45...THE WEDDING, THE FAMILY AND ME

But what is wedlock forced, but a hell,
An age of discord and continual strife?
Whereas the contrary blingeth bliss,
An is a pattern of celestial peace.
William Shakespeare: King Henry VI, Part I. Act II, Ibid.
Sc. 5, Line 62

After breakfast we placed the reception decorations in the car and headed for the church. While the family arranged tables and chairs Melvin and I shopped for more elegant glasses, yet not too expensive, for the bridal table. I avoided mentioning how my foot *pained* because I should have stayed in Baltimore anyway. What an awful day! Everything went wrong that could— go wrong. Since I'd had five weddings, I knew what to expect.

The Clemons knew my artistic meticulous side. They also knew my inability to decorate myself would augment my stress. Therefore, my periodic outbursts should not have surprised them. College graduates who could not follow *simple* directions mystified me. Bible verses, I'd hand lettered on pink paper, decorated the bulletin boards. Pink satin fabric was draped on the bridal table, accented with greenery and white bows at the gathered points.

The final touches were left for me to do alone. Tired of my directing their corrections, one by one everyone left. I wanted everything to look right. That was the purpose of my being there, I thought. No one understood.

Eventually Lauren said, "Dawn, I'm going home, you don't need me do you?" I couldn't believe she'd leave me there to finish everything all alone.

I leaned on and pushed a chair that held the items I needed. The crutches helped me hop along. Because I was never satisfied until everything looked perfect, my foot *cried* for rest! I did too much as usual, for a family who didn't appreciate the elegance, the finesse, the refinement of a job well done. When they asked me to *decorate* they weren't aware I was a *true artist*, one who cared about her work and how it was presented to the public. I'd never been a person to *throw* something together and *never* would be.

An hour later someone returned and took me home. I could barely hop the short distance to the house. When I opened the door and hopped through everyone was seated in the living room relaxing. They watched me and *never* said a word.

So I spoke, "Hello, I'm just exhausted. I'll take my bath and then go straight to bed. My foot hurts sooo *bad*. I know I did too much, but it's all over now." Still no one said a word except Lauren.

"Dawn, don't you want some dinner. I cooked spaghetti and made a tossed salad."

"No thank you Lauren. I'm *toooo* tired to eat. I don't have the energy to hold the fork." At that moment I could have curled up on the floor and slept all night. But instead I hopped past everyone in the living room and fought those steps to the second floor, as the family watched. No one offered to help me—in any way!

"But you haven't had anything to eat since noon today and it's after eight o'clock."

"I know Lauren. Maybe after I take a bath and lie down for a while I'll feel more like eating, but not now I'm just *too* tired."

They stared as I advanced toward the staircase on my crutches. Once again, I sat on one step at a time until I reached the second floor, exhausted, out of breath, then stretched out in prone position, on my stomach on the floor! My foot *throbbed* like a toothache! Unable to get up, I dragged myself to the bedroom on my stomach, propped myself up against the side of the bed and undressed. I retrieved my nightgown and toiletries from my luggage on the floor near the bed. I put on my robe; slid up onto the bed, grabbed my crutches and headed for the bathroom at the end of the hall.

Warm water flowed from the faucet into the bathtub releasing a gardenia fragrance from bath crystals, the same brand I'd bought Hannah. The bath helped to soothe unsavory memories of the day. I removed the wrapping from around my foot: one layer, then two layers of stretch gauze. The *swollen foot* must have welcomed the bath as I lowered it into warm water. It pained as badly as it looked; the size of a *cantaloupe!*

Twenty minutes later I returned to my bedroom and was resting in the bed when Lauren appeared in the door.

"Dawn I didn't bother you while you were taking your bath. How do you feel?"

"I feel a little better, but my foot pains *terribly*! I've taken my medication, so I guess the pain might ease a little."

"Are you ready to eat now?"

"I guess so Lauren but I can't go downstairs. Do you mind bringing it up here?"

"Of course not Dawn, all that you've done today you have to be tired."

Minutes later, Lauren returned with my dinner on a tray. I sat on the floor with the lights out.

"Why are you sitting on the floor in the dark Dawn?"

"It's not completely dark. The room has all the light I need. You may put the tray on my lap. Besides sitting on the floor, light from the hall and downstairs provides me with a subtle quiet atmosphere. Don't you agree?"

"If you say so Dawn. Do you mind if I stay up here for a while? I'll lie down on the floor with you."

So Lauren relaxed on the floor with me while we reviewed the hectic day's activities. After she left I listened to their laughter downstairs. They soon retired. But, I couldn't sleep. My foot *never stopped throbbing!* Throughout the night I kept getting up. I sat on the bed or just held my foot and prayed while it throbbed and pained! There were moments I thought my foot would *explode*! I felt like screaming, *"Somebody please—help—stop—this—pain!"* Several times I almost called out when I couldn't hold back the tears. But I didn't. I knew everyone was tired. And I was the *last* person they wanted to hear complaining! I'd ruined their day by bossing everyone around. No one *cared* about my pain. After *hours* of pain I finally dozed off. From my sound, sound sleep, Lauren awakened me early the next morning.

"Dawn I hate to disturb you, but we need your help again. We forgot to order the boutonnieres and bouquets for the maid and matron of honor."

Still half asleep I managed to speak.

"How did you forget that Lauren?" She shrugged her shoulders and shook her lowered head.

"I don't know. I thought I'd ordered them." As usual Lauren was disorganized.

"Why didn't you order them with Hannah's bouquet?"

"Hannah wanted a silk arrangement to keep, so we only needed something small for her to throw away."

"I see. Weeell what do you want me to do?"

"We called the florist this morning but they can't help us. Would you help us Dawn? We need two bouquets, two corsages and six boutonnieres?"

My heart dropped. I was *soooo* tired and my foot still throbbed. I promised myself during the night, not to do *anything else* for that wedding because I had *not* been treated fairly. I could not understand how she parted her lips to ask me to do anything else when she *knew* how I felt? Or maybe she really didn't *care* how I felt!!

"Lauren, I'm sorry. I just can't do anything else. Yesterday got the better of me. My foot pained all night long and I got very little sleep."

"Why didn't you let me know that you were in pain?"

"Why? What could you do? I took my medicine and prayed. Besides you needed your rest and I already felt I'd been a burden to you and your family. I have to rest this morning if I plan to go to the wedding." Lauren walked toward the door, but stopped short, turned around and stood in the middle of the doorway.

"Dawn, we *really* need your help. Melvin and I bought the flowers, greenery, baby's breath, wire and ribbon but no one can make them look as good as you can. Would you *pleease* reconsider?" Once again I heard *pleading*!

I looked at Lauren and thought about Melvin, her sweet kind husband and how compassionate he'd treated me my entire stay. I thought about the money he'd spent and didn't have to spend. *Only because of Melvin* I relented, trying to ignore my throbbing foot and weary body that cried, "Please let me rest!"

"Okay, Lauren I'll make them. I'm not a corsage designer. I worked in a florist for six months and only *watched* the designers complete wedding orders."

"I know all of that Dawn. But I do know, whatever you do, it will look great."

So, with *flattery getting her somewhere* I hopped downstairs, sat at the kitchen table and started work on bouquets, corsages and boutonnieres. A couple of ladies handed me the items needed so I wouldn't have to get up. That was quite the opposite from the *bowl of cereal* the previous morning.

After an hour's work, everyone started getting dressed to leave. As I worked, Lauren rushed in the kitchen.

"Dawn, you're not ready yet? We're leaving in a few minutes."

"Leaving! No one told me to get ready. How can I get ready when I'm still working on boutonnieres? Besides, my gown hasn't been pressed."

"Gown, why are *you* wearing a gown?"

"I told you on the phone I would, to hide my foot, remember?"

"Yes, I remember now. Where's the gown I'll get someone to press it for you. Why didn't you tell somebody earlier?" Voices in the background urged her to hurry.

"Come on Mama! We're running late!"

"Dawn, if I set up the ironing board and set out the iron can you manage to iron the gown yourself?"

"Yes I can Lauren. You hurry your family's waiting."

She set up the ironing board in my bedroom on the second floor then rushed into the kitchen for the last boutonnieres and paused before she left.

"Dawn, after we get to church I'll send someone back for you."

"That's fine. I'll be ready."

Nobody—came—for—me. Much later I heard someone downstairs opening the front door.

"Who's there?" I called a second time.

"Who's that downstairs?" A man appeared. He was as shocked to see me as I was to see him.

"Ma'am I didn't know anyone was here. I was told to pick up some food in the refrigerator."

"You mean you didn't come after me?"

"No, no I didn't. Nobody said anything to me about picking up a lady. They just told me to look in the refrigerator and get the large bowl of turkey salad."

I couldn't believe it. They'd *forgotten* me! If that man hadn't come for the salad I'd have *missed* the wedding and the reception. I'd have missed *everything*! The gentleman helped me down the steps as I held on to the wall and hopped one step at a time. He was indeed a gentleman.

When I entered the church the wedding was nearly over. I sat on a back pew, disgusted, disappointed and *angry* with the Clemons. I was *soooo* hurt! I'd come all the way down there after having surgery on my foot to decorate for my Goddaughter's wedding only to be left at their house and *completely* forgotten! I'd missed the marriage ceremony. Well, I thought what else could happen?

After the wedding, guests flowed into the reception room adjacent to the sanctuary. Hannah and the wedding party remained for *the picture taking session.* Hannah made a beautiful bride. Her elegant white bridal gown, long veil and angelic smile signified her virginity. She'd saved herself for her husband Marcus, a handsome young man, also a devoted Christian. Had he not been a Christian she'd never have dated him. She held her bridal bouquet close to her gown and stared straight ahead. I moved slowly down the aisle, from the back of the church to the front and sat on the front pew in front of the bride and groom. *No one* acknowledged my presence. Hannah didn't smile or look at me. I sat directly in front of her. It was as though I wasn't there. After the pictures were taken, everyone moved toward the reception room including the photographer. Before they left I asked Lauren, may I take a picture with the bride.

"Of course Dawn, why not, you *are* her Godmother." Lauren said.

I rose from the pew, adjusted my burgundy taffeta gown so I wouldn't trip over it, hopped with my crutches up front and stood next to Hannah. The photographer made changes in our pose, which allowed me to lean on Hannah slightly while Lauren held my crutches. After he took several shots I leaned over and kissed Hannah on the check.

"I love you Hannah. I want you to have a happy marriage."

She replied coldly, not looking at me or changing her facial expression.

"I love you too."

What had I done so terrible for her anger to linger, on the happiest day of her life! This young Christian woman had not forgiven me for my bossiness in insisting everything be right for her wedding reception? She'd not grasped the significance of her Godmother's wishes for her precious day? She'd not understood the artistic touch in design. *No,* she had not. Unfortunately she was too young and too inexperienced to comprehend the dedication of one person to another. Again I was hurt. I retrieved my crutches from Lauren and moved into the reception area with the other guests. As we walked inside, I questioned Lauren why no one was sent to the house.

"Lauren, why wasn't someone sent to pick me up?" She answered coldly.

"Someone was sent Dawn."

"No, no one came after me."

"Then how did you get here?" Her words were aloof, unfeeling.

"A man was sent to get the turkey salad and I came back with him. Had he not come I would have missed the wedding." Lauren looked puzzled.

"I'm sure I told someone to pick you up but I don't remember who it was now."

"Well, no one came and I missed the entire marriage ceremony. When I arrived it had ended. The ceremony is what I really wanted to see."

"Well, *you're here now aren't* you! I'm sure I asked someone." Her indifferent tone implied *back off.* I'd learned in those few days the Clemons females were set in their self-centered ways. Not so with Melvin, the only true Christian in that home.

Soft Christian music enhanced the wedding reception while guests circulated and congratulated the newlyweds and their families. Early afternoon sunlight peeked through the windows facing the bridal table providing enough light to create an elegant peaceful ambience. Guests savored their finger food, punch as they mingled. The banquet table consumed most of the space. I sat by the door to the sanctuary, relieved to get off my foot, in one of the few chairs provided. The lady I sat next to commented on how lovely the room was decorated.

"Oh, I've never seen this room look like this before, and the tables, the tables are *sooo* pretty. Do you know who did the decorating?"

"Yes. I did. I'm Dawn, Hannah's Godmother. I came down from Baltimore with her sister and family just for this purpose. What's your name?"

"I'm Cora. *You're* Hannah's Godmother! How wonderful of you to help the family. But how could you do all of this work with two crutches?"

"I had lots of help. I brought the paper, fabrics and lettered signs with me. Marcus and his friends acted as my legs as I told them where to place *everything*. I'm afraid I created a few enemies being so particular. I wanted everything to be just right and raised my voice when my helpers didn't do things the right way. I'm used to doing everything myself. It was difficult sitting and telling them what to do every time I wanted something changed."

"I'm sure everything will be alright. Weddings are always hard on everyone. I've had two already for my two daughters. The Clemons are a good family. Her husband Melvin is a deacon in my church and a *fine, fine* Christian man!"

"Yes I knew he was a deacon and he *is* a fine Christian man."

I noticed several ladies talking to Lauren who stood at the end of the bridal table. Each one pointed to the boards, wall decorations and then to the tables with smiles. On several occasions Lauren pointed in my direction explaining who'd decorated. Not once did she bring anyone over to meet me. Not once did she ask me if I wanted anything to eat or drink. Not once did any of the family acknowledge my *presence*. I felt like a total outsider as I sat by the door all but forgotten except for the lady who sat next to me. Only pride held back my tears. Soon I too stood with my crutches and headed for the refreshment line. Seconds later Lauren approached with a plate of food and a cup of punch.

I said to her, "Hi Lauren, how's everything going?"

"Everything's fine."

"Lauren, after you finish what you're doing, would you please bring me a plate and something to drink, it's hard to carry anything with these crutches."

"Can't you see I'm doing something!"

I was shocked at the way she responded to my request. She was curt, rude and walked away. She didn't return. I was humiliated and embarrassed. How *could* she be so insensitive? I couldn't understand why she was so *mean* to me. I'd only asked for some food. She'd asked me that morning to make all those corsages, bouquets and boutonnieres and I did them graciously. I asked her for a plate of food and she insulted me in front of her guest. That moment I wondered about her *being a Christian.*

After she Hannah rushed away Cora who stood in line behind me offered her help.

"Dawn, why didn't you ask me to get you something to eat? I'll be glad to? Here, you sit back down and I'll bring you some of everything."

I held Cora's seat until she returned with food for both of us. We talked a while until I finished eating. Then I returned to the sanctuary to be alone with God. I spilled out my hurts, my problems in His house and asked to be forgiven for any hurts I'd caused that family. About five minutes later Sally joined me, my close friend who'd introduced me to the Clemons. The friend whose home the Clemons's had purchased. The friend I needed to talk to about this dilemma.

"Hi Dawn, you did a *fantastic* job decorating that room. I've never seen it look that good. How's your foot?"

"Oh Sally I'm so disgusted with this family. Thanks for the compliment. It always makes me feel good when people appreciate my efforts. The Lord gave me the talents, so I try to share them with people as much as I possibly can. However, I think I should have stayed in Baltimore this time. This trip and work was more than I anticipated. I'm weary. The physical, mental and emotional strain has taken its toll."

"I understand perfectly. Weddings are stressful on everybody. I thank God I have three sons and no daughters. My nerves couldn't take the problems I've seen other families endure. I don't understand why you came down here anyway after just having surgery on your foot."

"I decided not to come, but after Rachel reminded me how much they needed my help. I came anyway against my better judgement. I wanted to help the family since their finances were very low. Besides Hannah *is* my Goddaughter."

"When are you returning to Baltimore Dawn?"

"We're leaving around four o'clock this afternoon. Daniel has to go to work early tomorrow morning. I'm sorry I wasn't able to visit you before I left."

I related the previous day's challenges as she listened. We reviewed the unpleasant happenings, which Sally had by this time anticipated. My roommate in college for a year, she understood me. She accepted me. She used to call me her *temperamental artistic friend*. She also knew the female Clemons wouldn't tolerate my artistic nature very long. Why, because they were *too* involved with themselves to understand my personal attachment in making everything charming for the wedding. My innate ability to beautify the room in excellent taste meant nothing to them. My presence was to decorate, not to be overly concerned with aesthetics. They weren't concerned about excellence, as I was, but only with some décor to enhance and lift the room's dreariness.

I waited in the sanctuary until the reception was over. A young man asked me if I'd come in and assist them as they removed all the decorations. I hopped in on both crutches and sat in the chair they provided in the middle of the room. Whenever they asked me anything, I told them, "Whatever you do is fine with me." My remarks and voice were pleasant. Actually, *I didn't care what they did!* At that point they could have *trashed everything*!

That's the way I felt at that moment. However I knew I needed all the materials for future weddings, where I got paid a handsome price for my hard work and creativity. Here I'd donated my talent, time and endowment from God as a gift. There *were* people who appreciated beauty and talent! That family appeared to appreciate neither. They had no idea what I charged in Baltimore for the same service. I vowed that day *never* to do another wedding free, for *anyone!*

The day prior to the wedding I finished the hand lettered 2'x18' banner to be placed on the long vacant dark brown paneled wall behind the bridal table, at the Clemons' home. Most of the Old English blue, brush lettering on a scroll of pink paper had been finished in school before our vacation started. I'd planned to finish the rest at home. The surgery, however, denied me that privilege. Subsequently I finished it on their dining room table. The banner read:

**"Congratulations Mr. and Mrs. Marcus Dotson,
December 30, 1990"**

I rolled up the banner with flowers and vines surrounding the words, that had been taken down so carefully by the young men—and presented it to the newlyweds. Hannah said she planned to display it every anniversary. We returned to Lauren's home and relaxed in the living room. Discussions of the wedding awaited my approval.

"Dawn, you're very quiet over there, we haven't heard from you. How do you think every thing fared today?"

"I didn't see the wedding but the reception was lovely."

"Is that all you have to say?" Lauren said.

"What else do you want me to say? I feel as though I've been mistreated."

They had no idea how much they'd hurt my pride. They were insensitive to my feelings. Their smug and self-centered expressions showed a nonchalant attitude.

"No one mistreated you Dawn. Tell me what you mean by mistreat?"

"Well first Hannah has ignored me the entire time I've been here. She's avoided me as much as possible. I came down here for her and she's really broken my heart." Lauren defended her daughter's actions.

"Dawn I told you how Hannah reacts to large events."

"Yes you did. But there's still no excuse why she *froze* when I kissed her on the cheek while the three of us posed for the picture I had to *ask* to be taken after the ceremony."

"I wasn't aware that Hannah had done that." Lauren said.

"Also I wasn't picked up and taken to the church as promised." Lauren answered.

"I told you I'm sorry about that."

"Sorry? If that man had not come for the turkey salad, I'd have missed the wedding. I came down here in mid winter, four days after my surgery for Hannah: to decorate for her wedding and see her married and *no one* cared enough to see that I got to the wedding."

"I'm aware of that but we tried to make you as comfortable as we could."

"Comfortable? I don't think so. Why was I put on the second floor Lauren when you knew I was using two crutches?" Lauren looked perplexed.

"When I gave Rachel and her husband the first floor bedroom, I'd forgotten about you using crutches." She could have changed the room after I arrived.

"And what about last night? Everyone left me at the church to finish the decorating by myself? Athena was supposed to help me; where was she? She never helped me do anything." Lauren jerked her head toward Athena in astonishment.

"Athena, why didn't you help Dawn decorate?" Lauren was surprised and irritated.

"I didn't know I had to help decorate." Athena, the youngest girl around sixteen, was smart but very *lazy*.

"Lauren I asked her to help me when she stopped by the church hall with her friends. She said she would. They left and *never* returned." I said.

"When I got back Ms. Dawn, you'd finished, and everyone was gone."

"Athena you *saw me* using my crutches to push a chair with my supplies as I decorated. Where was your compassion girl! Did you ever think about my foot! Do you have any idea how much *pain* I endured yesterday? I didn't discuss my pain because I had a job to do and I was committed. I was tired. I'd been there all—day—long?"

"I didn't think you needed any help since you corrected everything we did."

"Yes I did. I wanted everything right for the wedding. Couldn't you understand that Athena! Couldn't all of you understand that the pain enhanced my irritability because I had to rely on other people to do *everything*?"

The youngest child and spoiled, I once overheard Rachel tell her mother, "You *never* let Hannah and I get away with the things that Athena gets away with, Mama!"

Daniel and Rachel started packing the car while my negative conversation with Athena continued until I walked out the door. Lauren attempted to quiet her daughter but Athena never stopped in voicing her opinion until Lauren finally yelled.

"Athena, be *quiet*! Shut up Athena, did you hear what I said!"

Athena never stopped talking. I guess she thought she was my age. I informed Athena of her selfishness whether she liked it or not. We had words until I left. As I walked out the back door I turned and said, "God bless you Athena."

Displeased with my trip, I remained silent as I rode back to Baltimore. When Rachel and Daniel pulled into my driveway about eleven p.m., I thanked them for the safe trip and said good night. Rachel spoke up.

"Ms. Dawn you haven't said a word since we left Rosen Hill."

"I didn't have anything to say Rachel."

They helped me out the car and to the porch. Joy was sound asleep on the back seat stretched out full length. I unlocked the door and Daniel carried my luggage upstairs to my bedroom. Rachel hugged me and said, "We love you Ms. Dawn. Thank you for everything you did." I thought *I needed to hear those words in Rosen Hill!*

"Thank you Rachel. Good night."

46...UNEXPECTED PHENOMENA

I was angry with my friend:
I told my wrath, my wrath did end.
I was angry with my foe:
I told it not, my wrath did grow.
William Blake: A Poison Tree

Malicious thoughts of the wedding impeded the healing of my foot. Day after day, I lay in bed thinking of the negativity I'd experienced those few days. My doctor reminded me at my next visit, why I had such *excruciating* pain!

"Ms. Winters I suggested you not go. But you went anyway. You *said* the family would do most of the work and you'd only direct; that didn't happen, did it?"

"*No* it didn't Dr. Segal! I don't feel like talking about it. That's the only thing I think about *all—day— long!* It was the worst trip I've ever had in my life! Had you said point blank *do not go* I would *not* have gone to that wedding! But I'm always trying to help people when they don't think about me."

My doctor smiled and shook his head, full of gorgeous black hair.

Sunday, a week after the wedding, I called the Clemons. I hadn't heard from them since I'd returned. I had to release the emotional stress I allowed to steal my joy and slow my physical healing. The bottled up anger only hurt me and no one else.

"Hello, may I speak to Lauren please?"

"My Mom isn't here; she and my Dad haven't come home from church yet."

"Hannah is that you? This is Ms. Dawn."

"Yes—I—know. How are you?"

Her cool tone remained. I was glad I had an opportunity to talk to Hannah.

"I'm fair. My foot is giving me a *lot* of trouble. I'm in so much pain. Otherwise, I'm doing okay. How's married life? It's been a week now."

"Oh everything's just fine," she said nonchalantly.

"I'm surprised you answered the phone."

"Yes we rode over from Durham to get the rest of my things. We returned from our Honeymoon two days ago." Her conversation was limited so I initiated the questions.

"Are you feeling better now since the wedding?"

"Better? I felt fine. I wasn't sick."

"Well Hannah you weren't yourself when I was there, so I thought you weren't well. You ignored me the entire time. I went for *you* Hannah. I went on crutches after surgery to help you have a beautiful wedding but instead you weren't happy. Why?"

"Why, because that's all I *heard* before you came down here! How *you* were coming to decorate for *my* wedding—right after *your* surgery; and what a great thing *you* were doing for *me*. *You got all of the attention!*"

"That's not true Hannah."

"It was *my* wedding day. *I* was supposed to get all of the attention, *not you!*" Her voice escalated! My foot pulsated with pain while I listened to her complain—as tears swelled in my eyes.

"Hannah, no one gave me all of the attention. In fact I got very little attention *except* for your father. Besides you walked up the steps when I was on them and never offered me any help.

"I was just trying to *stay out of your way!*"

"Out of my way, but why, Hannah? Why stay out of my way? You saw the hard time I had going up and down those steps, sitting on one step at a time."

"You seemed to be doing alright to me. If you needed help, why didn't you ask?"

"I shouldn't have had to ask. The way you glued yourself to the wall gazing down on me, I felt I had something contagious."

"Ms. Dawn you *ruined* my wedding!"

"What do you mean I ruined your wedding?"

"You know exactly what I mean; the way you raised your voice while we were putting up those bulletin boards. You had no patience with us at all."

"Patience, you have no idea the pain I was in. My foot ached the entire time I was there. Not *once* did you ask how I felt. Not *once* did you say thank you from your *heart*. Yes I was irritable: first, because I'm not used to telling anyone else how to decorate for me; second because those young college men could *not* follow my directions, *simple, simple* directions."

She talked a few more minutes about the way I bossed the guys who put up the decorations. She thought I should have accepted whatever they did since they weren't artistic. I explained the mental stress I endured giving step by step directions for every sheet of paper, every lettered scroll and where to place every staple. It was exhausting and aggravating sitting in a chair telling them what to do. My students understood and followed every direction, whether they were artistic or not.

"Well Hannah that was last year. This is a new year. I want you and your husband to be very happy."

I said good bye and hung up the receiver. The following week I received a thank you card from Lauren and the poster paints I'd carried with me to complete the banner.

There was nothing else to say. I'd been forewarned and did it *my* way, the wrong way. I believed—the family's promises. Now weeks later I remained in bed, *all* day *everyday* in constant pain.

Over two months passed before I returned to school wearing a pair of $100 orthopedic shoes. I could have returned earlier wearing the open flat blue shoe with my crutches but I didn't. I *refused* to have any more setbacks: people stepping on my foot, fire drills where I'd have to walk up and down three double flights of stairs, walking four long corridors from the elevator plus other occurrences.

During the two month recuperating period I depended on Bryan most of the time. Marty was rarely home. When he was home, he *never* came or yelled upstairs to inquire how I felt or if I needed anything. His life was spent working six to seven days a week. Sleep for him was an occasional treat.

My days were spent praying and trying to read. Television was irritating and the wedding events remained foremost in my mind. I prayed for relief from that throbbing pain! My throat pounded as each thump from my foot actually *shook* the pillow it was elevated on! I watched the pillow move with each throb! My little toe *pained* the most! Oh *how* it *pained* and *throbbed*! I regretted having that ingrown toenail removed. Those pains were *worst* than *giving birth!* I cried, and moaned, and groaned pleading with God to *please* remove my suffering!

Recuperating from my illness allowed plenty of thinking time. My thoughts centered on better living arrangements in case I was incapacitated again. So—I decided to *sell* my house. After eleven years, the longest I'd lived anywhere, it was time to go. The inconvenience of having a two-story house and using crutches was enough to persuade me to sell and move to an apartment with everything on one level. Besides my sons stored junk in the shed, basement, under the porch and attic. I lacked the courage to evict them when they disrespected my property. Therefore, *I'd move*!

I'd been told, adult children didn't move into an apartment with their parents. *That* was my answer: sell the house and get a three-bedroom apartment. Why, three bedrooms, I needed a den, an art studio and the bedroom. I alerted my sons. Of course they weren't too elated. But I had to save my sanity! There were times when they became indignant if I asked them to do anything around the house or in the yard.

I contacted a real estate firm. Buyers were attracted but not enough to sign on that dotted line. Others sought a newer styled home or didn't desire to finish the basement and attic.

For two weekends Bryan drove me to various apartment units. Finally an apartment in Pikesville perked my interest. I preferred the first floor but they only had a second floor available on April 1st. The 1400 sq. ft. layout resembled a house: plenty of closet space, French doors in the master bedroom and living room that opened onto a balcony. The apartment had cross window ventilation. I yearned to have that *stunning* apartment, tucked away in a quiet section surrounded by trees. In addition, the new subway station was adjacent to the complex and each resident had a key to the gated fence. Residents who rode the subway to work only had to unlock the gate to the subway's parking lot and walk over to the station. After I filled out the necessary forms, we left.

I thought *would that apartment unlock the door to a new life? Would it bring me happiness or sustain unearned misery?*

On March 11th I returned to work, wearing my unattractive tan orthopedic shoes. It felt *good* to be back and missed by my students. I'd asked Howard Walters, a retired art teacher, to substitute during my absence, so that my students weren't denied their art education. During my absence Howard called often concerning their projects, grades and behavior. He even dropped by twice to chitchat. What a blessing it was to have a qualified person in my field, even though his techniques were different. Of course all of my students weren't that eager to see me return because I required more work. I *wasn't*

Mr. Walters.

The same day I returned, I met the principal as I walked down the hall toward the main office.

"Good Morning Ms. Winters, we're glad to have you back. I see you're wearing *intelligent* shoes now." I looked down at my large comfortable shoes and laughed.

"Yes sir they are really that, intelligent and *unattractive*."

"Ms. Winters, would you stop by my office some time today before you go home? There's something I'd like you to do." I knew he had something artistic in mind.

I'd already promised myself, *not* to do anything for the school right away. My foot was *not* completely healed and the doctor warned me *not* to stand too long. Besides with all the stage designs, yearly elaborate graduation decorations, homecoming banners, and signs for any teacher who asked, I received *nothing* from the school during the time I was home, not even a phone call. Now as soon as I get back Mr. Amos wants me to do *something*!

I did receive a get well card from the hospitality committee after being home for *two* months. My name was written on the envelope in blue ink in one person's handwriting. The address was written in black ink in another person's handwriting and the return address was written in a different blue ink, by a third party. I examined the envelope closely and cried softly. The various colors of ink and different handwriting screamed out loud, *they didn't care!* No one cared enough to address the envelope in the same ink and the same handwriting.

One late afternoon when I'd returned from the doctor's office, I saw a large basket of fruit from a florist at my side door. The card read, "We miss you, hurry back to us, The Music Department." Finally somebody remembered me. It had come from *one* of its teachers. I felt better.

I met with Mr. Amos later, in the main office.

"Have a seat Ms. Winters. I asked to see you because I really need your help. We're having an assembly program the day after tomorrow. Several businesses will give presentations to our students and I wanted the stage to look attractive. Would you make us a banner?"

"I'm afraid I can't, Mr. Amos because my foot has not healed completely."

"You mean you're *not* going to make the banner!" His face flushed! His eyes were demonic.

"No. I can't make the banner because I can't stand on my foot that long. This is my first day back and my doctor advised me to stay off it as much as possible the first few weeks." His anger increased!

"Well I *guess* I'll have to *call* your *supervisor* and see if she can get someone else to make one for us!"

"I think you better because I can't make one tomorrow." I thought, *what would he, have done, had I not returned to school.*

He was *maad!!* His intimidating tactics didn't work. I knew my rights. I recalled the pain I encountered in Rosen Hill. That ungrateful trip had caused my agonizing pain and lengthened my recuperating period. I would *not* allow that pain to return, especially for people who never bothered to call and ask me how I felt! I'd made another enemy: someone who cared about his image, *not my health!* Two mornings later, I escorted my class downstairs to the auditorium. Someone, I guess a student, made a small banner on brown wrapping paper with black letters. I should have felt sad for not making it but I refused to stand on my foot that long. Sitting down as I lettered wasn't feasible because I had to stretch across the table to brush in the *large 36"*
letters.

Nine o'clock one Sunday evening before I returned to work a gentle knock on my bedroom door awakened me.

"Mommy, its Bryan, may I come in?"

"Of course Bryan, come in." He looked haggard and drained. His eyes avoided mine because I read his so well. I hadn't seen him since Friday morning before he went to work.

"Mommy do you have change for $10.00?" I checked my wallet and found no change for a ten.

"No, Bryan I don't have change for anything. I only have three dollars." He thanked me and left, making sure he *closed* the door behind him. Two hours later, after deep meditation, I hopped to the door and called downstairs to Marty.

"Marty did Bryan say anything to you when he was here?"

"Yeah, he asked if I could loan him ten dollars."

"He asked you to loan him ten dollars? And he asked me did I have change for ten dollars. That's strange?"

"When did he come upstairs before or after you gave him the ten dollars?"

By this time Marty was walking slowly upstairs as I balanced on both crutches in my bedroom's doorway.

"He went upstairs after I gave him the ten dollars."

"I see. Something's wrong Marty. Ever since he left I've had a strange feeling. His actions were suspicious, rather sneaky. Marty, look in the desk drawer in his bedroom and see if my bank card is there?" Marty checked the desk drawer.

"No it's not here only the blue card holder."

"That's it! Bryan took my *card!*"

"He did what! He stole your bank card!" Marty was *maaaad*! Whenever he became angry he'd huff and puff, like an angry young child.

"Bryan's going to use my bank card for drugs!"

"No Mom, remember he can't use it without your code. Does he know your code?" I nodded.

"Yes he does Marty. After my surgery, he withdrew money for me after banking hours. He needed the code to handle my business."

"*Mom* you know Bryan uses drugs *how could* you give him your banking code?"

Marty gave me that *I can't believe you did that* look. Interpreted *how could you be so stupid?* Yes I'd made a *dumb, costly* mistake. I held the small empty envelope in my hand and panicked!

"Oh Marty my paycheck was deposited Friday! He could withdraw all my money. What am I going to do!"

Nervous and angry I picked up the receiver and dialed the bank. The telephone teller bank service had closed. I got dressed. Marty drove me to the bank. I slid my card into the machine. I thanked God he'd only taken $245 thus far! With a previous balance and my Friday's paycheck deposit there was still over $1400 left.

We returned home. I heard Marty's snores downstairs as I endured restless hours of worry and prayer upstairs. I closed my eyes several times, but not to sleep. I thought about the peace I'd have in the *future*. Visions and thoughts revealed rains and storms! Suddenly a trickle of light appeared. I was free! Yes I was cleared of all responsibilities, duties and obligations. The optimistic visions ended when I saw it was a little past nine. I leaned over, picked up the receiver from my white pedestal antique phone then dialed the bank.

"Hello my name is Ms. Winters. My son has stolen my Bankcard. Would you please tell me how much money was withdrawn last night?"

"Just a minute please, I'll check." I waited for the representative to locate my file and prayed he'd not emptied my account.

"Ms. Winters, my records show that he's withdrawn $540."

"$540, that's my bill money! Stop the card's use right now before he returns for more of my money!"

I explained Bryan's addiction problem and why he knew my code. She sympathized and cancelled its use! He'd gone to various banks and withdrawn amounts of $20-40 at each transaction. I cried and cried, "Oh Dear God please help my son. I can't prosecute him. He's my suffering son. I don't know what to do. Please help me! I just can't prosecute Bryan, *he's my son!"*

I Marty and told him what Bryan had stolen. He rushed upstairs in shock!

"How could he do this to you Mom! How could he steal from his *own* mother!"

"Well Marty I've heard, with addicts there in no respecter of persons as far as money is concerned. When I gave him my code I never thought he'd steal from me. At *no* time did that enter my mind. I thank God, no more than that was taken." Marty returned downstairs and left for work.

Early afternoon, La Raine came over and took me to the market. I'd explained to her earlier about Bryan taking my money. She suggested I needed a change in environment. After an hour we returned home. She helped me hop up the steps with my crutches, to the porch. Before I opened the door, Bryan's yells on the phone caught me by surprise. When he saw me, he told the person he'd call back. He entered the dining room from the kitchen. I stared in shock! His blazing bloodshot eyes, wiry hair and disheveled dirty clothes baffled me. He acted like a mad man! His frantic outcry to me pleading for help was beyond belief!

"Ms. La Raine I have to talk to my mother, would you *pleaaase* leave! I have to talk to her *alone*!"

I hopped to the door with La Raine. She understood. She too had a relative who'd been strung out on drugs. She hugged me tight.

"Dawn, don't worry. Everything will work out. Give him time. Call me if you need me for *anything*."

My dear friend understood—or did she? Separated from a recovering alcoholic husband, recuperating from a six-week old surgery, just lost $540 in theft and now I must confront my enraged addicted son—and I'm not to *worry*? Bewildered, perplexed and confused. I'd never seen anyone in that condition before. What was I, supposed to do? How was *I* to handle Bryan having stolen my money? I stood balanced on both crutches, and listened to Bryan's attempt to explain why he'd stolen the money. He paced frantically back and forth between the living room and dining room.

I was scared! Unsure of his next moves, I watched and listened. He snatched my pocketbook from the table, flung it in the living room where it crashed against the wall!

"Why did you do that Bryan?" One mad person was enough. I kept my voice level low, still dazed by his actions. He trudged back and forth between the two rooms flaying his arms as he yelled and pleaded.

"I just want you to understand why I took the money!" He fell down on his knees in front of me on the hardwood floor and grabbed my legs.

"Mommy *please, please* don't press charges against me! I'll pay you back! I'll pay all the money back!"

I watched my son, my helpless twenty-seven year old son, strung out on drugs, down on his knees pleading desperately not to be sent to jail. How could I send my son to jail? I could *not!*

With compassion, I reassured him I had no intentions of filing charges. He needed help now, otherwise one day he'd steal from the wrong person and *would* be jailed. He soon calmed down enough to sit at the dining room table for us to talk.

"What made you stop taking the money, Bryan?" I asked.

"When I tried to get money and the machine *ate* the card, I knew you had found out. No money, no crack." My voice remained low.

"You look terrible Bryan. You're trying to kill yourself aren't you? If you are you're doing a great job!"

"Mommy you *just* don't understand how that high makes you feel! The first high is the best! The other highs never reach the height of the first one."

"So when do you stop getting high?" I said.

"When the money runs out."

How grateful I was he hadn't cleaned out my checking account. I renewed my credit union loan to replace the money he'd taken. Stolen was a better word since he'd stolen my sanity, my trust in him and my true sense of punishment for such a selfish offense toward me, his mother.

"Let me get you some dinner. When did you eat last?"

"I haven't eaten or slept in *three days!* The only thing I wanted was to stay high. Addicts only live for that next high."

His keyed up body, rapid speech and waving hands helped him explain the life of addicts and why it's so hard to stop using crack cocaine. My heart pounded. My soul ached for my desperate son. I listened to him because he begged me to. He wanted me to understand his miserable life. He wanted me to know, to understand.

"Bryan how do you feel after the high has worn off?"

"Terrible! I think of all the money I'd wasted. I'm always broke afterwards and sit around feeling sorry for myself, for being *so stupid.*"

"I'll never understand how you can work all week then use *all* of your money on drugs." I said.

My voice yet calm—grieved for my weak ailing son, while my heart cried for a cure. I felt powerless; unable to find a solution. *I* couldn't stop him from using drugs. Only *he* could do that. *Only he* could solve his problem, not I. I'd learn *that* in Al-Anon.

"It's easy Mommy, addicts don't think about tomorrow, they only think about that *moment*, that high and the next high and the next one!"

He talked more than he ate. His intense emotional chatter continued. His anxious body shifted from side to side in the high back opened weave dining room chair. I stared at him then at the chair weave and thought *soon his brain will look like the holes in that chair, a sieve a strainer, destroyed from crack cocaine!*

I prayed as his babbling and gesturing arms explained the addict's suffering life. At last the human motor wound down. Again he begged my forgiveness then dragged his mentally mangled body upstairs to untangle the threads he'd woven. He slept until noon the following day. Had I pressed charges, he'd been jailed and the bank would have reimbursed my money. My heart ruled; my mind vacationed.

I rented a room to Terry, one of Bryan's coworkers about his age for $75 a week including board. Bryan gave him, his room and he slept on the pullout sofa in the upstairs den, next to my bedroom. Terry was ambitious and well mannered. He didn't own a car so he rode with Bryan. His six-foot lanky frame reminded me of the young Abraham Lincoln. However Terry's handsome looks paralleled my sons'. Terry and Marty paid their rent every week. Bryan—wasn't as reliable.

Getting up and down the steps became easier for me as the pain lessened. I went downstairs to cook and use the washer and dryer off from the first floor den. The three young men were responsible for their clothes and to keep the kitchen clean. Eventually their negligence to clean the kitchen each night created a major problem. I'd find dirty dishes piled in the sink, left over food and other debris spread across the stove and kitchen counter. Finally I bought inexpensive paper and plastic products for their use since they refused to clean. I placed masking tape across every cabinet that read in bold letters, *"Do Not Open!"* The next day Bryan asked in a most unpleasant voice:

"What's this Mommy! We can't use your glasses and dishes any more! What's going on here!"

"Well my dear, I've asked you many times, to keep this kitchen clean, but you don't! When you eat, you clean. 'No clean, use paper.' 'Wash dishes, use dishes.' Savvy?" He understood. They used paper and plastic until they realized that glass, china and silver were better.

I'd even placed signs in the bathroom over the toilet, "If you sprinkle when you tinkle, *wipe* the seat to keep it neat" and over the sink "Clean this basin *after you* bathe."

The signs helped. Sometimes I wondered however, if they'd forgotten how to read. The problem of irresponsible male boarders, house maintenance and thoughts of Bryan's stealing, reinforced my decision to move. He'd stolen the VCR a second time! That time I put him out! The next day he returned with the ticket.

"And what am I supposed to do with that? Get it out again with my money? You never paid me the $65 from the first time, remember!"

"Mommy I promise to pay you back this time."

"Your promises mean *nothing* Bryan! I don't want you in this house anymore! I told you I'd press charges the next time you stole from me but instead you can *leave this house, permanently*!"

"But where am I going to live? I don't know anywhere I can stay."

"You should have thought of that when you stole and pawned my VCR again. *Stop* using drugs, then maybe you can rent a room or share an apartment with your brother."

"Mommy please, *please don't* put me out! I'll start looking for somewhere else to live tomorrow, but please don't put me out!"

Whenever I asked if he'd found a room his answer was, "No, not yet." He said he was looking. I didn't believe him. This time he did get the VCR out and had it installed when I got home from school. He knew what to do in order to remain in that house.

The apartment complex called to confirm my interest. I had one week to decide. Convinced, I had to move before I forgot I was Bryan's mother, I toyed with ideas of how I could move and still handle both the mortgage and the rent. Several days passed before my answer crystallized. It emerged in school as I sat checking test papers at my office desk. A sudden urge to call the manager flashed in my mind. With April 1st only five days away I picked up the receiver unsure of my conversation.

"Hi Sonja, this is Ms. Winters. I'm still interested in the apartment but my house still has not sold. Has anyone applied for the apartment yet?" Her hesitant response answered my question.

"We-ll I'm not su-re. Ms. Winters, a man *was* here earlier who fell in love with it instantly but he's returned home to get his wife to see it."

"Oh my! I don't want to lose it. It's so beautiful and just what I need." I said.

"I need a confirmation and deposit today otherwise that couple may just get it."

I sank back in my swivel office chair, dropped my head in despair and thought. I didn't want to lose that gorgeous apartment, my road to tranquility.

"Sonja, I really don't see how I can rent it now, since my house hasn't been sold. Let me think on it and I'll call back tomorrow."

I hung up the phone, sat up tall, looked straight ahead and prayed, "Dear God please help me. Tell me what to do. I want to leave that house. I need *peace* and *quiet* but I can't afford to pay a mortgage and rent too. Please help me."

Instantly that *still quiet voice* said, "Yes you *can* rent the apartment. Use the rent money from the house to pay the mortgage and your salary to pay the rent for the apartment. Lenard will help." I thanked God for an answer, picked up the phone and called Sonja!

"Hi Sonja, this is Ms. Winters again. I'll take the apartment!"

"You will! What made you change your mind so fast?"

"God! I prayed. He answered my prayer and told me what to do."

After school I rushed to the Brittany Apartments located in that gorgeous isolated community to sign the rental lease agreement and pay my deposit. Sonja, an attractive, pleasant middle aged lady with lovely soft, salt and pepper gray hair was completing the paperwork. I sat in the upholstered burgundy and gray paisley patterned armchair opposite her desk, and waited. The sweet azalea fragrance from outside seeped through the slightly raised window while Sonja gathered all the documents. Her fingers rushed through small stacks of papers while removing the sheets needed. Meanwhile the other rental representative, a tall distinguished female blonde walked through the double doors and over to Sonja's desk.

"Sonja, this couple has decided to rent the apartment, the three-bedroom apartment I showed the husband earlier." I stiffened. Had I gotten there too late? Would that couple get my apartment? I stared at the reproduction of Turner's peaceful English landscape painting on the wall and prayed. Sonja noticed my worried expression.

"I'm sorry Martha but Mrs. Winters has already paid her deposit. I'm finalizing the paper work now. She'll be moving in Friday."

"But Mr. Fellmore was here earlier and this lady just got here." Martha was shocked at the news she'd just heard.

"No, Mrs. Winters saw the apartment two weeks ago, before you started work here. She called today and came to finalize everything."

All three persons looked perplexed at the immediate situation. *Again* God saved me. He'd told me to call the Brittany and check on the apartment's vacancy that day! It had *not* been my decision. He'd explained everything. He was totally responsible for me getting the apartment of my dreams!

Marty, Bryan and Terry were sorry about my move but understood my motive. They realized their rent would help pay the mortgage until the house sold. Now three young men were responsible for the daily care and maintenance of the property. I cleaved to emotional stability but future obstacles created severe mental trauma for me!

Spring break started Friday. I had *one* week to move and get organized before school reopened. Purple Heart took unwanted furniture, clothes etc. The moving van was scheduled for Wednesday, April 3rd. I hauled pictures, lamps small boxes etc. everyday. Eleven years accumulation in art, music, dance, interior design, drapery fabrics, and teaching materials were packed and ready to go. Of course boxes of books increased with every move. The attic, basement, under porch storage and outside shed held its share of *treasures*, most of which were useless.

Essential items Marty, Bryan and Terry needed to survive: dishes, cookware, bed linen, towels etc. remained. The apartment had a washer and dryer so I left them mine. The utility bill was theirs to pay. Day after day I packed my Cadillac and drove to the apartment. The apartment entrance was *all* the way around the other side of the building. My tired body and paining foot that walked and hauled from dawn 'til dusk, shouted for rest! My foot had *swollen* so much I wore the open blue canvas shoe I'd worn after surgery. I carried boxes, pictures, anything I could, around to the front entrance; opened the heavy metal locked door, then battled *three* flights of steps to my apartment. After six days of repeated stress and strain, my foot *screamed!!!*

Bryan promised to help me the day I moved. He never showed. As usual

I did everything myself: explained what to take to storage and the apartment; made sure my furniture was protected. Lenard helped me twice that week. Since he worked for someone else, his leisure hours were limited. I'd rented a storage bin in the basement of my apartment building for $40 a month extra. We finished moving Good Friday evening.

47...TRANQUILITY OR WHAT?

I never knew any man in my life
who could not bear another's
misfortunes perfectly like a Christian.
Alexander Pope: Thoughts on Various Subjects

The weekend's rest, was well deserved before I reported to work Monday morning. My cat Solace and I adjusted to our new surroundings. Did I rest? No. As I unpacked boxes, I played with Solace, listened to classical and contemporary music, watched a little TV and thanked God I didn't have to *climb* those three flights of stairs anymore until Monday afternoon!

Solace stayed Tuesday and Wednesday in the vet's while I moved. When I brought my white and black gorgeous companion home Thursday, he ran from room to room sniffing corners and carpet, checking out his strange new residence. He looked like a Calico breed minus the tan or orange mix—only black and white. Once again it was just the two of us: one human female and one feline male, a jealous male at that. Oh yes at times Solace was a terror!

He disliked being alone during the day and wanted to sleep in my bed at night. When I refused his company he'd go in the hall bathroom, open the lower cabinet door with his paw and let it bang shut countless times! He'd release his anger until I got up and swatted him with newspaper, after chasing him around the apartment. He was one *smart*, determined *male* cat.

I remember when I bought the new brand of cat litter from Amway. It was made of tiny balls of ground newspaper, the size of a BB bullet. I bought one bag to see if Solace approved. He *hated* it! After he'd use his cat box he'd unroll the toilet paper that was above his box and pile it high in his box. I *didn't* change the litter. Another time he pulled down my brand new peach towel with satin trim at the bottom that hung above his box and defecated on it. I *still* didn't change the litter. Finally one day when I came home, Solace had *dragged* the box from its usual spot. It straddled the marble threshold; half of the box was in the hall and other half remained in the bathroom on the carpet. He'd *won*! His persistence prevailed. I threw out the large bag of hated litter, cleaned his box and returned to his former cat litter.

Solace my unusual cat was sweet and kind one minute and devilish the next. I obtained him by calling around to various vets for a kitten when I lived in the large house. At one office the secretary said a kitten had been left on their steps in a box the day before. She described his coloring: black and white similar to a Calico I'd had prior. The next day I bought a litter box, litter and cat food. When I held the dear kitty in my arms we bonded instantly!

At home he stayed close to me. He'd jump on the bed then walk all over my body, his tiny claws alerting me of his presence. My neck and shoulders held his small bundle of soft cuddly fur. He'd fall asleep; his curled up body in the crook of my neck. Solace became my sole companion. Soon Lenard's absence was replaced with Solace (solace meant a source of relief). Yes he brought me peace, love and filled my lonely hours with love. He needed me and I needed him more. We fed off each other's love.

With all his peculiar habits, I loved him still. When I'd lie down on the sofa in the Den, he'd crawl up on my chest and sleep. When he grew older, he'd bring me a small empty raisin box I'd thrown on the floor. Each time I threw the box, he'd retrieve it bring it back to be tossed out again, just like a dog. I'd never seen a cat do anything like that before. We'd play until he got tired and retreated to his corner to rest. My sweet kitten loved me unconditionally. He'd hide behind furniture and play tag or patted my leg with his paw, when I walked by. Many stockings were damaged by his innocent pats.

Every week Lenard came by with money to defray my expenses. His kindness prevailed. In late May I removed the sale of the house from the market. I decided to return when my apartment lease expired. The upstairs would be rented again. Later I'd add a larger bedroom and extend the narrow kitchen. Two days after the removal I received an excited call from Darcy, my real estate agent.

"Dawn I have a couple very interested in *buying* your house. They know you removed it from the market two days ago but wondered if you'd reconsider? They've seen the outside and love it. They're anxious to see the inside. They love older homes and this one has plenty of land for their four children."

I should have been elated but I wasn't. I should have released sighs of relief but I didn't. I should have said "Oh yes how soon do they want to move in!" but I couldn't. Instead I paused and thought *as soon as I decided to return and convert the upstairs to an apartment again, somebody wants to buy it.*

Return of the I-Roc meant my monthly expenses were reduced by $400. With that reduction I would return to the home I'd spent eleven years renovating. To inhale the lilac's, apple blossoms fragrances; the forsythia's early bloom, white and pink hyacinths and assorted colors of tulips, what the rabbits didn't eat. Also yellow jonquils, sturdy red salvia, luscious grapes and pears in early fall. Oh yes I must not forget the luscious pink and white peonies in the back I'd planted over the filled in cesspool. Most of all, the entrance sidewalk had variegated hosta my favorite broad leafed green and white striped hearty perennial, on either side. A sprout of violet blooms appeared toward summer's end.

Every year I'd divided the larger plants to transplant in new areas. The yard was *spectacular*! Now for the major decision: should I or shouldn't I sell? If I kept the house, it would require constant repair, if I sold it, I'd be free from worry and hassle.

"Darcy, let me think about it. I'd already decided to move back after my lease runs out next year." I heard her deep sighs. I knew she wanted me to sell for two reasons, first my income barely maintained it; second because she'd lose a sale.

It was she who sat on the kitchen stoop steps with me before Theon and I bought it and estimated its worth. It was she who watched the old neglected unpainted eighty-year old house and abandoned yard blossom into a home of charm and beauty.

"Give me some time Darcy, call back in an hour." She agreed.

I examined the pros and cons as to why I should or shouldn't keep it. I knew that to keep it would weigh heavily on my pocketbook. I realized no matter how much I loved it; it had to go. I didn't have the resources to maintain it without neglecting myself. Reluctantly I picked up the receiver.

"Darcy, this is Dawn, I'll sell... I'll sell the house."

I met the interested buyers the following day and gave them a tour. Darcy had told them about the hardwood floors, two kitchens, pocket doors and the large unfinished attic and basement. They *loved* the house, as so many other people had in the eleven years I lived there. The wife's *ecstatic* interest was revealed in her eyes and mannerisms. Her quiet exhilarating presence enveloped the home's persona. She rubbed the balustrade and newel post with such caress and love as we strolled up the steps to the second floor. Each room's enchantment put sparkle in her eyes. Often her husband glanced down at her radiant face and absorbed her feelings; their shared feelings. As we sauntered through, I described all the hard work I'd completed in transforming the rundown property.

In the raw stone walled basement with new casement windows and new $2500 concrete floor Mr. Talbot asked.

"Does this basement leak? I notice you have a Sunk pump, over in that corner?"

"Yes it does leak sometimes when we have those heavy rain storms. I had two sunk-pumps installed to handle that problem. There's another pump in that small room where the oil drum is stored." Mrs. Talbot paid me a compliment.

"Mrs. Winters, you're the first person I've met that admitted water does come in the house when they have it on the market for sale."

"I'm honest Mrs. Talbot. I try to treat people the way I want to be treated."

Mr. Talbot was a Baltimore City Policeman. He was in control and *definitely* the head of *his* family. His curt sarcastic boorish questions turned me off. His wife was the opposite: sweet, gentle and had the most gorgeous sleepy brown eyes I'd ever seen. Had it not been for his wife's kindness I'd *never* have sold them my home!

In awe she said, "Our house would fit in your house three times!" She was in such wonder and made such complimentary remarks, she reminded me of myself whenever I first saw something I truly liked.

"Do you have to sell your house first before you buy this house?" I said.

Mr. Talbot spoke right up. "Oh no, we're going to rent it out. We own the house next door to us that we also rent out. We intend to keep them both."

I thought *what a smart man*. He has invested money for his family's future. Why couldn't I have had a husband who wanted property as an investment? I married men whose thoughts were elsewhere, all because I didn't *wait* on the Lord. I jumped into marriages because of loneliness and sexual desire.

"Where do you work Mrs. Talbot?" I asked.

"I don't work. I haven't worked since my first child was born." Mr. Talbot interrupted again. Only this time his voice softened as he placed his arm around his wife's shoulders.

"Yes, Marion doesn't have to work. She takes care of us, that's enough work for her." My previous thoughts of him altered—slightly.

"I agree. With four children, she does have her hands full."

Yes, they agreed to buy the house. The following two days were spent getting the contracts written. Darcy and I sat at the dining room table in my apartment and reviewed the sale price of $99,500. Minus all fees, I'd clear close to $15,000 which pleased me! As much as I loved the old house, it was *time* I let go and let God. It had become an over grown cancer! It required a man who desired an older home, a person with carpentry skills and heartfelt interest; of which I had neither.

I'm sure the original owners, Mr. Smith, his mother and the old house thanked me for what I'd done but it needed more help than I could give. How strange a third family would live in his home; only this time, devoted loving parents and four adoring children?

Mr. Smith and his mother were ostracized by family and friends since he'd been born out of wedlock. My chaotic eleven-year stay caused by frustrated humans, house repairs and extreme weather conditions would soon end.

Early Saturday morning three days following the contract signing I met with Mr. Talbot who'd paid an appraiser $250 to check the property. I walked with them as the appraiser jotted down notes. He said little but wrote much. Each note meant a dollar sign to me! One page, two pages three pages after the third page I went downstairs to breathe. I thought, *when he finishes I won't have any money left.* I returned to the attic where they discussed removing the antiquated overflowing water tank. I thanked God I'd had the attic windows replaced which ended in a financial fiasco.

When Theon and I signed to get the attic and kitchen windows replaced our Income Tax Refund check would cover that debt. Instead of a check for over $3000, we got a check for *$296!* Theon's back child support was deducted from our refund. I was furious! It was then I found out he'd *stopped* paying child support the day we married.

"How dare you stop taking care of your children, just because we got married!"

I *cried* and *cried* but the tears didn't return my $2800. Theon tried to console me but there was nothing he could say. Now we had *another* bill. An unnecessary bill he'd made because of his selfishness. I was *sooo mad* with that man! After we separated the bill was left on me. I had to refinance the house to pay him $5000, his share in the property when he hadn't invested one dollar. At first he told his lawyer *$25,000*. After both our lawyers conferred it was reduced to the $5000. He tried to take everything he could from me. As fast I saved my money, *something or somebody snatched it away!*

Bryan's young daughters, Briana and Nadia spent several weeks with me that summer in the apartment. His days off, Bryan took his children on city tours or visited friends with kids.

The girls improvised tunes on the piano with their small but long graceful fingers. Lengthy white sheer curtains swept the floor in a semicircular puddle manner at the French doors. The elegant living room embraced the century old cream sofa, large Italian contemporary breakfront and high-gloss ebony baby grand piano. My grandchildren's laughter added cheerfulness to the lonely room.

Weeks earlier my friend Tanya, who knew I had a piano, asked me to assist her in buying one.

"Dawn, do you have time this week to help me look for a piano?"

"Of course; can you play Tanya?"

"No, but I intend to take lessons after I get it."

As we walked through the front door of the music store we were greeted with an array of magnificent grand pianos: ebony, white, mahogany etc. That instant I imagined an ebony grand, in my new apartment. The salesman pulled out the soundboard then explained the purpose of the interior parts. A cast iron frame vs. the earlier wooden frames, felt covered hammers vs. leather hammers, the three pedals, strings stretched over the bridge to be struck by the hammers and of course the sparkling black and white keys on the outside. After his thorough explanation we *both* bought a new baby grand: her first piano, my third.

The outstanding, out-of-my-reach Steinways I admired, but eased by. I started lessons with the salesman the following week in the home that he and his mother shared. I sold the console piano I'd bought for Bryan and months later regretted that I had.

Early Saturday mornings I rose at 6:30, put on my jogging clothes and ran around the quiet, enclosed lovely complex four to five times. The manicured landscape, fluffy clouds and chirping birds, so early in the morning, lifted my spirits as I ran. Running helped strengthen my legs and physical endurance for karate classes which I resumed four months after my foot surgery.

Mr. Bun, my former Korean instructor and his American wife opened their own karate studio during my absence. Now I had a new teacher, Mr. Randall, superior in his techniques. Although he'd been there a few months, he'd not met me. I'd called earlier introducing myself on the phone and explained the former surgery. He suggested I return Monday since my next belt was scheduled the *following* week. He insisted I take the test. I insisted I wasn't ready. I had one *week* to review all the previous belt formations and kicks. I remembered the new form but after four months and no strenuous practicing I knew I wasn't ready. Mr. Randall *disagreed*! We met before the four o'clock class on Monday to review my *forms*.

Two weeks prior to calling him, I started exercising. I practiced in the house and in the yard: jumps, turns, kicks and the forms for each belt I'd earned. After I moved, only forms that required no jumping or kicking were practiced in the apartment. Karate released the day's pressures. Each punch was for someone who annoyed me that day. Each *yell* set free anguish and stress. I preferred 5:00 p.m. classes to 8:00 because my body had time to quiet down before I retired.

The young energetic Mr. Randall, an Afro-American dedicated to his job, watched the execution of my forms, a few kicks and jumps. They were *shaky* as I'd told him, but he convinced me that coming daily plus Saturday I'd be ready for the Red Belt test the following Tuesday. I practiced every morning before I went to school, in school on my lunch hour, and in karate class *everyday*.

I practiced behind the students unless it was my own class, where I stood on the first or second row due to my 5'2" height. Fifty-three years old, I kept up with the best although—I disliked sparring! But I knew Karate meant sparring; the forms were only a means to an end.

For every belt promotion test, two rows of folding chairs were lined up across the back of the studio for parents and guests. The back was actually the front entrance of the building. People walking by, were able to see inside the studio, while classes were in session, through the wall to wall glass window. What better way to attract a new student, than by watching the actual practice lessons, of Tae Kwon Do? I had one week to work hard improving my kicks, jumps, turns and previous forms: Dae Ryun Hyung, Kicho Hyung, Tae Kyuk Sa Jang, Tae Kyuk Oh Jang, Palgae Youk Jang, and my new form Palgae Chil Jang for red belt. During class I always did well. When test time arrived I was a bundle of ragged nerves!

Candidates for various levels of belts practiced and stretched on the main floor of the Dojang or in the back locker room. I usually stretched in the locker room unless it was too crowded. Usually three master instructors from other schools, sat at a table covered with a royal blue velvet cloth with the Karate Emblem attached in front. Their backs were to the mirrored wall as they examined each student's moves closely. Our regular instructors stood on the side encouraging those who might forget.

All candidates sat on the floor directly in front of the parents and guests, with crossed legs facing the testing instructors. Every nervous student including myself, avoided eye contact with the audience. Testing started with two or three students on the floor: lower belt levels first then higher-ranking belts. The order was No Belt to White Belt, Yellow Belt, Green Belt and Purple Belt. My heart pounded louder and louder! Finally it was my turn. Mike, an adult student in his early forties, tested with me for our Red Belt. He and his eight-year old son Winston usually performed together but Winston had a cold that night. We positioned ourselves on the floor facing the audience with our backs to the instructors.

My peripheral vision sighted Mike's moves and sidetracked mine. Our kicks and turns were not simultaneous. Cloudy concentration engendered error and caused me to stop and stand still until Mike completed his form. When he finished, I was allowed to start over. Performing alone I made no mistakes.

At last, the *breaking board* session arrived. I'd never worried about breaking boards before. But now I had to run across the room on a *healing* foot, jump high while making, a 360 degree turn in mid air, thrusting my right foot forward to break the board. My foot pained! I was crazy to have allowed my instructor to persuade me to test in the first place. The strenuous week's workouts and that night's testing had caused *intense* physical trauma to my foot. I responded robotically when my name was called.

"Next... Dawn!"

"Yes, Sir!" I jumped up. A usual response when a student's name was called.

The testing students lined up against the wall on the right. Across the room two *strong* older students held up the board or boards we'd break with our instep, heel or side of the foot. I knew exactly what to do. Every step of the breaking process was etched in my mind but my left foot *refused* to be abused anymore. On my first attempt, my right foot hit the board but slid off, scraping flesh from my ankle and leg, which almost kicked the student in the face that held the board! We were allowed three tries. I had two left. I returned across the room for the next attempt. I ran, jumped, turned swiftly then thrust my right foot forward knocking the board from their hands and into the wall as I landed on the floor! Embarrassed! Humiliated! This had never happened before. I'd always broken all my boards on the first or second try. A hand reached down and helped me up off the floor. Disgraced, I moved slowly toward Mr. Randall's office, trying not to limp. After I flopped down in his chair I covered my bruised bloody ankle and leg with my pants to keep Mr. Randall from seeing it. He was headed toward the office.

"Dawn why can't you concentrate? I've watched you do everything right until you thrust your foot toward the board. What's wrong?" He was compassionate in his concern for his senior citizen student who thought she was sixteen.

"It's my *foot* Mr. Randall, it hurts terribly. I told you it was too early for me to take this test."

"Stay in here and rest. I'll tell the testers what's happening. You can make your last try when everyone else has finished."

Seconds later Mr. Marshall, who'd tested me several times before, appeared in the door. Mr. Randall returned out front.

"Dawn you're doing fine. All you have to do is concentrate. Keep your eye on the *center* of the board then drive your foot all the way through the board with your *eyes* and mind. Remember you must *see* your foot go *through* the board!

"It's not the board Sir, it's my foot. The pain from my last jump diverted my attention from the board."

Mr. Marshall talked several minutes convincing me I *could* break that board and pass my test otherwise I'd have to wait *four* more months to try again. I sat, rested my foot and asked God to direct my foot correctly.

Once again I stood opposite the board held firmly by the same two men on the other side of the room. I prayed, started my paced run, jumped high before I reached the board, made a 360 degree turn then plowed my foot so fast into the board that it zoomed past the men's heads and into the wall! The split board *flew*; the audience *yelled!* Exhausted but relieved, I limped off the floor, past parents and guests gracious with compliments. I heard, "Look, she's limping; there's blood on her leg." I limped to my car, drove to my new home, an apartment, elated! Now I was a Red Belt!

The appraiser finished; we left. Mr. and Mrs. Talbot walked around the yard, checking trees, shrubs and flowers. I leaned out the window and yelled. "Stay as long as you like. It'll all be yours very soon!"

48...THE HOUSE, THE HOME

A creditor is worse than a master;
for a master owns only your person,
a creditor owns your dignity, and can
belabour that.
Victor Hugo: Les Miserables.
Ibid. Chap. 2

Negotiations began for the property's sale. My sons knew they'd have to vacate by the end of July. Packed boxes in the attic and scattered throughout the house had to be moved. Purple Heart had arrived for bags piled high on the front porch. Lenard brought a truck and loaded it with Marty and Bryan belongings to store in his mother's attic. I gave Aunt Betty's davenport (very old heavy sleep sofa) to Lenard's mother to place in her living room.

Two weeks before settlement I reviewed the sale contract. I detected an error in my profit amount. Rather than receiving $12,000 I'd only receive $8,000! I called my agent and revealed her error.

"Darcy in reviewing the contract I noticed you made a gross mistake in adding the columns and subtracting the repairs."

"What error, what column? What section are you talking about Dawn?" Anxiety reflected in her nervous twitchy voice.

"On the right hand side of my paper you've added up a group of numbers incorrectly. Your answer was $15,000 and it should have been $11,000. When I subtract the $3,000 for the repairs that leaves me with only $8,000! Darcy, I'd *never* have sold my house for a profit of $8,000!" I said in a firm voice.

She was speechless. "Dawn I'll be right over."

Fifteen minutes later, Darcy's perplexed face appeared at my door. She carried an attaché case filled with papers in her defense. Again we sat at the dining room table. She examined her numbers written quickly on the margin.

"Darcy here is where you made your mistake; you added this section rather than subtracting them."

She stared at the numbers and rewrote them repeatedly; nothing changed her error. The only thing that changed was my reduction in money. Nothing she did corrected the numbers written on the right hand margin of that paper. She checked over and over again, not believing her mistake. Her figures clearly stated I would profit $15,000 minus the $3,000 for repairs. Therefore I'd receive $12,000. *Wrong!* The amount as I had discovered days earlier was $8,000. In her defense Darcy derived her own conclusion.

"Dawn those figures were only an estimate. Nothing's final until the day of settlement." We talked at length about the grave error. She denied any error. And that the total was only an estimate.

"I disagree. On the day of settlement the seller and buyer know exactly what they are to pay and what they're to receive. Sometimes there are minor differences, but not *$4000 Darcy!* I've sold two houses. I'm familiar with property closings and I've never had an amount different the day of settlement than what the agent had written."

"But Dawn as I said those figures were not the actual amounts."

"I'm sorry Darcy, but that's what you *told* me, plus it's on the contract, I would receive $12,000 and that's what *I want* on the day of settlement." I was angry. I was mad! Darcy gathered up her papers nervously; placed them in the attaché case and left. The next day I contacted a lawyer by phone. I explained my problem.

"I'm sorry Mrs. Winters but I'm not experienced enough in that area to help you. However, I can recommend an excellent lawyer who only handles real estate law, but he is *very expensive.*"

"What do you call expensive?"

"About $1000," he said.

"*$1000!!* That's *way* out of my league! Could you recommend another one?"

"No, he's the best in the area. If I were you I'd use his service; he *is* the best."

I obtained his name and phone number then called his office. Whatever extra money I'd receive would pay his legal fees.

"Hello, my name is Mrs. Winters may I speak to Mr. Cabots please?"

"Are you a present client or new client?" The secretary asked.

"Hopefully, a new one."

"One moment please." Seconds later he answered.

"Mrs. Winters, how may I help you?"

I explained my problem; he stated his fee. I made an appointment for the following day. His office was located in an old house in a historic section about thirty minutes from my home in Towson.

I sat in the outer office and allowed my eyes to roam freely, around the most interesting office I'd ever seen. This old Victorian home, now converted into several law offices was far above charming. The woodwork and doors remained the original dark stain. Airy ethereal wallpaper lifted the room's subtle atmosphere. Mr. Cabot's secretary sat busy at her English mahogany pedestal desk while other staff moved back and forth over the Persian rug as though it weren't there. An *array* of eclecticism appeared throughout each office.

An Italian chair, an Oriental lamp, English desk, and a gilded framed wall grouping were impressive. A tapestry hung on the wall above the Regency styled three-seat canapé flanked by a love seat with caned back and seat and two Hepplewhite shield-back armchairs. My heart melted as I recalled studying those antique furnishings in my interior design classes. I thought, *now I see where my $1000 is being spent; although thousands before mine had paid for this office's exquisite décor?*

"Mrs. Winters, Mr. Cabot will see you now."

I returned to the present and stepped into an office walled with books, a huge mahogany desk and two chairs placed in front for his clients. Mr. Cabot, a fast talking Jewish middle aged man, around 5'9," extended his arm out toward the chair.

"Have a seat Mrs. Winters. How are you dealing with this hot weather?"

"It's not the hot weather that's annoying me, but this heated raw deal concerning my property."

"Yes I can understand how you feel. $4000.00 is a lot of money to lose especially when you'd been told another amount. I see you brought the documents."

I handed him the folder of papers; then sat patiently as he perused each sheet never raising his head. The cool office helped me maintain a sense of calm as I thought only of my *$4000.* He finally looked up.

"Can you help me Mr. Cabot?"

"Yes I can, but I'm not sure how much."

We discussed the papers and Darcy's error. After tossing up various questions and possible solutions we ended the consultation. I paid the *$300* retainer fee and left. Two days later he called regarding the phone call he'd had with Darcy's office manager, Mrs. Steele. He soon realized he knew the agent from a business luncheon and confessed if he'd known that, he'd not have taken my case.

The following day Mrs. Steele, the real estate manager, called and voiced her concern as to why I hadn't contacted her rather than seek legal counsel. The idea never occurred to me since they worked in the same office. I didn't expect any sympathy or financial relief from the company, so I called a lawyer. Not just any lawyer but one of the highest paid in the area; the best in his field, the one I *couldn't* afford.

A week prior to settlement, I obtained a book on real estate law from the library. After in-depth research I located the section on *verbal agreed contracts* and its validity. The section *upheld* my verbal and written agreement with Darcy.

The day before the settlement I finished moving boxes and other items from the attic downstairs to the living room. Lenard borrowed a truck from a friend, loaded and carried the remaining items to my storage locker not too far from his job. Everything had to be ready to load. He had an AA Meeting he couldn't miss since he'd already skipped the last one helping me.

Exhaustion won! All day I'd cleaned, packed and hauled. The last day in my house and everything had to be removed *that* day. I dragged boxes down from the attic one step at a time. When I'd reach the second floor, I almost passed out! I heard Bryan's drained voice from the den where he slept on a fold up cot as he recovered to the real world from a night of crack cocaine.

"Mom-my, lea—ve those bo—xes 'til tomorr—ow?"

The cot would be placed on the truck the next day leaving Bryan to find residence elsewhere. How pitiful was my situation; I moved from my lovely home, because I gave in to my sons when they needed a place to live. I refused to say *No*!

"Bryan, settlement is tomorrow. Everything has to go today, even *you*."

He never heard a word I said but returned to his dream world. He was supposed to help me move all those boxes but instead he got high and slept all day. I dragged a large box until I got to the head of the staircase and collapsed on the floor as my head fell on both arms.

"Oh God, Dear God *please, please help me!* I'm *sooo tired. Please* give me the energy to finish moving everything today."

Suddenly my fatigued body was *revived*! I felt as though I'd rested all night. The foot still pained, but God *answered* my prayer! *He'd supplied the energy I needed to complete the job.*

Later when Lenard arrived, everything was ready. He and his friend loaded the truck then pulled off for the storage bin. I followed behind in my car. Marty and Bryan moved the next morning, the day of settlement.

I arrived at my lawyer's office the following morning but I'd left the book on real estate law I borrowed from the library at home. Instead I told Mr. Cabots about the information I'd gathered. He was quite impressed with my curiosity to delve deeper on my own.

"I'm sorry you didn't bring the book Mrs. Winters. Where did you say you got it?

"From the library; I searched until I got the right one. If I had time I'd go back home for the book, but we don't have enough time."

"It sounds like you'd be good in this field."

"What do you mean—a lawyer?"

"Yes, I mean you'd make a *good* lawyer."

"*Me*, a lawyer? There have been times I've thought about it, but there're so many things going on in my life I wouldn't have time to study."

What a *great* compliment! Especially, since it came from one of the best attorneys in the area. On occasions other people had assumed I was an attorney. Even my students said, "You should be a lawyer. You shouldn't be teaching. You're wasting your time here. Lawyers make a lot more money."

I'd never have survived the pressures as a lawyer. They surmounted the tensions in education, besides lawyers had to *lie* and *connive*. I was too honest to deal with the deceit involved even though attorney salaries were greater.

We left in our separate cars and met at the settlement office in Baltimore.

It wasn't held downtown in a swanky office but rather in an older house similar to Mr. Cabots' only minus the magnificent décor. We arrived and joined Mrs. Talbot already seated in the office along with my agent Darcy, her supervisor Mrs. Steele and the title company's agent seated behind her desk. Mr. Talbot arrived later. Introductions were made and the settlement proceeded.

My lawyer started his case. He presented the documents I'd signed to the title agent. Mr. Talbot, a policeman arrived just in time wearing a yellow and white *tank top!* I was appalled and offended by his appearance as were the others seated in the office and dressed professionally! To think he'd come to our settlement half dressed. I noticed their frowned expressions when he walked in the room and sat next to his wife on the two-seater sofa. He wanted to expose his muscular physique, but that was a business appointment not a cookout! We continued the transactions.

I argued I wanted the $12,000 due me rather than the $8000. Mrs. Steele, the real estate supervisor argued in Darcy's defense, that those figures were only estimated. I refuted her statement repeatedly. Tears swelled in my eyes; furious, my voice escalated! Finally my lawyer and Mrs. Steele excused themselves for a private conference in the adjacent room. Returning they agreed on the sum of $700. The exact balance I owed my lawyer. I screamed and cried!

"$700! You must be crazy! I've invested $35,000 and eleven years of my *life* in that house! That $35,000 in repairs and improvements increased the value of the property. No one wanted that thing but me. And *No One* can pay for the eleven years of my own hard, *hard labor!"*

"My digging, planting shrubs, cutting grass, replacing the basement floor, replacing the cesspool and having county sewage installed. I cleaned the adjacent lot we bought then removed the overgrown climbing vines and trash that had accumulated over the years. I did *all* that work almost single-handed! Darcy remembers how that property looked before I bought it! She knows better than anybody else! Now Mr. Talbot wants $3000 for other repairs. *It's not fair!* I've spent thousand and thousands in repairs already. *It's just not fair!* You started off with me getting $15,000. I anticipated minor repairs but not *$3000!* Now you're taking, another *$4000!* You've taken half of my money. Had I known I'd only be getting $8000 I'd *never* signed those papers." Mr. and Mrs. Talbot sat opposite me with lowered heads.

"We're not arguing that you've spent a great deal of money improving the property but you've forgotten that you've refinanced twice, otherwise you'd be getting far more money than you are. The money you received from refinancing is actually part of your profit that you've already enjoyed, Mrs. Winters."

"I know what the refinancing money was used for and it wasn't for enjoyment! I'm the one who borrowed it, so I'm the one who knows the truth. It paid off my former husband in our divorce suit, when he never put a penny in the house in the first place. He hated the house. Next, it paid for the new basement floor, new gutters, security system, flood lights and county sewage. And finally to repair a car I'd purchased for my son and he couldn't maintain after my car burned. During that time I was nine months without a car."

Blood rushed to my overtaxed brain as I stared into strange faces. Their raised brows and eyes questioned my words while other heads bowed in shame.

"Yes I understand everything you've said but you still enjoyed the money," she said.

"I *never enjoyed* anything lady! Haven't you been listening to what I told you! I paid *out* everything. Enjoyed meant that I traveled or bought diamonds. My last refinanced mortgage jumped from $630 to $940 because I believed a cheat and a liar! The loan officer promised I'd be able to refinance in a couple weeks. I believed him. Yes, I believed and was denied another mortgage. I've received nothing but pain from people and they've benefited from my stupidity!"

As Mrs. Steele continued her appeal, I buried my head in my hands and *cried!*

"You ju-st don't un-derst-and. You ju-st don't und-erst-and!" I jumped up, ran out the room to the front porch and cried non-stop! I was drained! I was enraged and furious with everyone involved. People who walked by the house, stared, as I yelled and screamed. *I did not care!!* I'd been taken advantage of; another disaster to grapple with; another hurt to experience; another grief to suffer. I didn't deserve this! I cried and cried 'til my body throbbed in pain! The meeting inside, resumed on the outside; the front porch. My lawyer, the title agent and Mrs. Steele's attempts to console me were useless. I refused to listen.

Later…much later after my frayed exasperated body realized my loss and that *I had* lost, I returned to the room and accepted their final offer of $1000. The exact fee owed to the lawyer minus $300, which I'd already paid. I'd wasted my time, my tears and gained *nothing!!!* Everybody involved profited sizably except me.

Drained, debased and downtrodden I returned home. *Three* days passed, before I talked on the phone or left my apartment. I ate only to stay alive. My close friend Valarie called every day! Each time she called, I cried unable to talk—then hung up. Finally I removed the receiver. My pity party ended when I picked up my Bible and asked God to help me through the agony and pain. He would have helped earlier but I never asked. Instead I wallowed in hurt, humiliation, degradation and misery—an inner emptiness that felt like a ladle had scooped out my insides leaving a vast cavity where I could crawl inside, curl up and die!! That too did pass.

49...ANOTHER RAMBLING ROAD

...It is for the artist to do something beyond this:
in portrait painting to put on canvas something
more than the face the model wears for that one
day; to paint the man, in short, as well as his
features.
James McNeill Whistler: The Gentle Art of
Making Enemies. Propositions, 2 Ibid.

With school opening soon little time remained to brood over lost money from the house. Paintings and drawings amassed during my teaching career spoke softly, "It's time Dawn. It's time to have your *own* art exhibit."

Shows cost money. Something I didn't have, at least not for what I wanted to have. Business cards, invitations, a photographer, a caterer and mild wines were essential. The $300 plus the $8000 helped to pay my summer expenses and bills.

Marty visited me alternate Friday evenings. He'd moved in with his girl friend temporarily, only because she'd offered to share her home with him until he found a place of his own.

During one of his visits, as we sat at the small kitchen table talking and sipping wine, I mentioned having a One-Woman Art Exhibit. As we talked, I read my mail, mostly from loan companies begging me to borrow money. One was from the company which had financed my piano. I read the letter, tore the $2500 check in half then tossed it in the trash can with other useless mail.

"Mom was that a check you tore in half?" Marty asked.

"Yes it was; a check for $2500. But it's not real. Besides I don't need another bill, I'm trying hard to get out of debt."

"But Mom, that's the money for your exhibit!" Marty's eyes widened; his surprised look caught me off guard.

"Ah, no Marty that's just a come-on letter to make the reader call."

"That's right; let me read that letter."

I reached in the trash; retrieved the letter and torn check. Marty read and reread the letter as I watched his eyes brightened even more. He was right, all I had to do was deposit the check in the bank and the funds were available as soon as the check cleared.

"But Marty I've torn the check in half. The bank may not accept it or maybe the finance company won't allow me to deposit the torn check."

"Mom I'm telling you, the check is alright!" Marty, a bright young man was usually correct in business matters.

"Okay, I'll call on Monday and find out." I called.

Marty was right. Now I had enough money to finance the exhibit. I contacted several art galleries but they were booked for months or a year in advance. Others said I needed to have another artist exhibit his work with mine. Each gallery had its own standards which I didn't fit. The Lyric Theatre was booked, along with other theatres. There was one I hadn't called, The Arena Playhouse, an Afro-American theatre that also exhibited art works in their lobby. I called. They had a vacancy the first two weeks in November *free* of charge. I was overwhelmed! At last I'd reveal my God given talents, other than teaching.

The next day I met with the director, Mr. Chantel. He showed me the long oyster white exhibition wall opposite the large brown ornately designed theatre entrance doors. Five large woven blue/turquoise ottomans occupied the lobby's center used by guests for relaxing during intermission. Before the exhibit in November, I had to present the list of works by title, size, and value for insurance purposes. The total had to be under $10,000. It was August two months before the exhibit; plenty of time, I thought, unaware of the mammoth undertaking that lay ahead. But God, who'd blessed me with these talents, provided my strength. How great to know God was on call twenty-four hours a day. There were times when I needed Him twenty-eight!

The postman had just left my apartment building. I sauntered along the sidewalk around to the front admiring the large oak tree centered in the courtyard. What a gorgeous sight! Dogwoods of varied sizes were set at intervals to complement the massive oak. I opened the main door, unlocked my mailbox and retrieved the mail. I fumbled through the mail then opened one.

August's *Welcome Back to School* letter had arrived. I scanned the usual contents until I reached a part that caused my body to fall *limp* against the wall. Rereading the sentences but slower this time, I knew there must be a mistake. This letter's from an *elementary* school! My hands trembled, as they held the unwanted *bad news*. Baffled, again I felt betrayed by the school system! I expected a transfer, because my high school was adding a vocational education department thereby eliminating music, art and several foreign language teachers, but not to elementary.

All my teaching experience had been in junior and senior high schools except for two summers when I'd taught an elementary accelerated art program. In addition I taught a summer K-12 program with student teachers under my supervision at a local college. I'd never taught elementary all year. I balled up the letter; stuffed it in my pants pocket and rushed upstairs to call my art supervisor.

"Tess why didn't you call me earlier?"

"Dawn I'm sorry. I didn't have anything available in secondary, so I gave your name

to Mrs. Butts, the elementary supervisor. The other alternative was *no job*. I'm positive you didn't want *that* to happen. Besides I think you'll enjoy elementary."

Yes I needed a job. I had to survive. To survive I had to earn money. No I wasn't angry. I was *MAD!* Perturbed because no one called to prepare me for the *profound* changes I'd face in September. Elementary teachers were known as art resource teachers. I'd disliked the title. A resource teacher traveled from school to school, like my friend Lily did everyday. She kept art visuals, materials etc. inside her car and in the trunk. She serviced two or three schools each week, sometimes two in one day. No, I didn't want to teach elementary art!

"Tess I've already moved twice in four months, first from my house to this apartment. Plus everything left in the house had to be removed since I sold the house last week. Now a week later I'm notified I've been transferred and must move all of my visuals and materials from one school to another school. How much can one person endure Tess! How much!"

"I didn't know you'd moved to an apartment! You sold that *gorgeous* Victorian house. You'd invested so much time and money in that house Dawn. I thought you'd be there forever."

"So did I Tess, so did I."

"What caused you to sell it?"

"My sons. I couldn't put them out, so I moved. I was tired of being used by them. It was time to go. Besides the house was more than I could maintain financially and physically." I avoided telling her the entire truth, the main reason, Bryan's addiction and stealing.

"Dawn I promise, after you stay in elementary a while, you'll never want to return to secondary." Was she in her right mind?

"Everyone who left secondary for elementary, has *loved* it!"

I listened as she tried to soothe my hurt with comforting words. Her words were barely heard; my mind was still in shock. I grieved! The previous house move's wounds had not yet healed and now I had to *move again!*

The new principals understood my plight. Yes, I was assigned *two* schools! On Mondays I taught in a very, *very* old building, one of the oldest schools in the city, in a regular classroom on the third floor with no elevators. Antiquated thirty-year old tables, chairs and desks, no sink or water or cabinet space comprised my art room. The first time I visited the school, the principal a sweet middle aged attractive lady, walked up the steps with me. I thought we'd never get there! My sighs said *you mean I have to climb these steps every week?* The idea of regular teachers, who'd been there for years, having to climb Mt. Everest everyday, was astounding! Their excellent health thanked the steps, not to mention muscular legs!

My main building, where I taught four days, also ancient, but had a new art room a few years old, on the first floor at the end of the hall from the main office. So there I was, once again ready to tackle *dirt* left by a former teacher. Only this time I had *two* art rooms to clean, in *two* different schools, *twice* as many bulletin boards and three flights of steps to climb several times a day, every Monday, all in the name of *survival*. As I cleaned and reorganized each room, once again tears stained my face. Again Christian and classical music eased the stress I endured those next few weeks. I felt as though I was witnessing someone else's dilemma; not mine.

I removed my teaching materials from Southwestern High School before starting the massive cleaning job of the two new art rooms. Third floor again but this time I used the elevator to help move that enormous load. It took *three* full days to move. The materials were split between the two schools. Before returning my keys to the main office, I strolled through the six-room art suite, reminiscing about the happy and sad moments from the past two years. The purple and yellow *fadeless paper* I'd used to decorate the stage for senior graduations zoomed before my eyes! I loved my students. Why did I have to leave? We needed each other. Every time I settled into a situation I relished, I was transferred. When the school system had cutbacks, the last teacher on board, was the first one to go in art, music, and foreign language, *never physical education*; how sad.

Mournful regrets of leaving Northern Senior High School surfaced each time I moved on to another assignment, another staff, another art room, another pupil personal adjustment and another principal. Nat my second husband's constant nagging and alcoholic tantrums ignited my decision to retire in the first place. That decision rested on my shoulder, a reminder of why I was moved to a different school, every other year. A decision—I *always* regretted! Had I not retired when I did, my position at Northern Senior High was secure until I retired at thirty years.

The secretary's greeting was warm, yet not happy. She shook her head and pointed to Mr. Amos' office to the rear of her desk.

"Hi Mrs. Winters, I'm *sooo* sorry you're leaving. This school will definitely miss your beautiful artwork. Now who's goin' to do my office bulletin boards? I never had an art teacher to volunteer to do them before you came. Mr. Amos wants to see you before you leave."

I had *nothing* to say to that man! I walked around the counter, passed through the lower swinging door and stepped over the threshold into the tyrant's office responsible for my three days of *misery*!

"Hello Mr. Amos, I understand you wanted to see me before I left."

"Yes I did. How are you Mrs. Winters?"

"I'm drained; disappointed. I feel deceived."

"That's the reason I wanted to see you before you left. I didn't want you to think I transferred you because you refused to do that *banner*. I had to cut back in many areas. Our only music teacher has also been transferred." He cited other departments that had lost teachers.

"I understand all of that Mr. Amos but the art, music, home economics and foreign language departments *always* lose teachers first. They're the subjects that liven up the schools. Students need those subjects *just* as much as they do the academics; I notice physical education *never* loses a teacher." He lowered his head and spoke sympathetically. Nothing he said softened my grief.

"Again, Mrs. Winters I am very sorry."

"That's alright, God's in control. Everything will work out. I'm carrying materials to two schools, so I better leave before it gets too late. It's really been a strain on me these past three days, physically, emotionally and mentally. You have a good year Mr. Amos." My firm handshake received his limp hand. I said farewell to the office staff; gave and received hugs, then left, never to return!

September arrived. I'd survived the leg aching, back breaking move to the schools. I lugged boxes, visuals and books up three flights of stairs in one. Three weeks passed before I taught. Moving, meetings and workshops *absorbed* the first week. Putting up bulletin boards, organizing each room squeezed in between the maze moving.

I needed double of everything to assure a smooth opening. "Everything in its place and a place for everything was my motto." It was the *only* way to work. I taught my students organizational skills as well as art. After four weeks of hard work and writing lesson plans, I was ready for my babies. I stole a few minutes on several days, strolled around each school and observed my new soon-to-be-students.

One day as I stood next to a kindergarten classroom door fascinated by the *little ones* my principal, Mr. Peterson of my four-day school walked toward me. (He'd suggested I tour the school and its two usable floors to observe the students). I taught *every* child in the building.

"Oh Mr. Peterson, they're *so* cute. I've never taught kindergarten students, all I want to do is hug them, they're *so* precious!"

They sat on the floor dressed in school uniforms with crossed legs in a circle listening to a story their teacher read from a large picturesque book. As she read, she pointed to the large colorful pictures and asked questions. Their little eager hands shot in the air. The classroom walls had colorful learning visuals of all kinds. Multiple teaching stations appeared at various intervals to assist students on different levels.

The principal said, "Yes most of them are. A few months from now some *won't* be so precious."

"You mean those sweet little children will cause problems?" He nodded.

"Wait and see. Let's proceed with your tour of the building. The cafeteria is at the end of this hall and to the right." His comments resumed as we strolled down a hall that sparked my curiosity. I continued my tour of this grand old architectural building. The first, second and third graders were a pleasure to watch.

Finally the big day arrived. I stood at the window staring out at the vacant lot next to my room. The view from the span of three huge connected windows was unbelievable! I visualized numerous colorful cityscapes to be drawn and painted. A soft pleasant voice from the hall interrupted my images.

I turned. A teacher peeked inside my door.

"We're here, Mrs. Winters."

I'd not heard anyone in the hall. I rushed toward the door and saw my *babies* standing in line two by two, my *first* kindergarten class!

"Thank you Mrs. Bryston. Are they always this quiet?"

"We're working on that aren't we class?"

They answered in unison. "Yesss, Mr-s. Bry—ston."

I stared down and thought *God how am I supposed to teach these little ones? I just left senior high school. Please help me!* His still quiet voice responded, "Teach them like you always teach; just break it down."

The class entered, sat wherever they wanted to until I switched seats, separated friends, and made a seating chart. Every class had its own seating chart. Every chart helped me to learn their names, their places, plus each class's trouble makers—instantly!

50...NEW TERRITORIES, NEW ADVENTURES

The perfection of moral character consists
in this, in passing every day as the last,
and in being neither violently excited nor
torpid nor playing the hypocrite.
Marcus Aurelius: Meditations, Book VIII
Ibid. 69

Multiple adventures faced me in September, three not yet healed (sale of my home and two arduous moves) and new ones to handle! I stepped from the looking glass into reality and felt more thorns on my roses than I'd expected.

Dividing flowers from weeds became a burden; a burden too heavy to bear. Daily problems flattened my spirits! Handling them became unbearable mentally and emotionally. The still small voice, whispered softly, "Dawn leave those problems at school. Don't carry them home; they *don't* belong to you. You have enough of your own." The change from senior high to elementary was a drawn—*out* disaster; every morning I'd dread the drive.

Years of attending evening school during harsh winters resurfaced. Some evenings I was *sooo* tired I dragged my body up that massive marble curved staircase leading to my second floor classrooms. I attended evening and summer classes at three colleges to become the best teacher possible and was thanked with a slap in the face! Fifty-four credits beyond a Master's Degree, paid on a Ph.D. salary scale, I felt *cheated*! I'd prepared myself for senior high, *not* elementary! My conscience's advice was difficult to heed since my spirit chose to soar freely as a lovely butterfly. But life's blockade intervened in every journey.

Problems in the Monday school increased. A cramped classroom filled with antiquated wooden tables provided me little space to walk between back to back chairs to help students. As warm days changed to cool weeks then to cold months my students learned, as I earned respect from staff and administration. They discovered I was not the normal resource teacher but a dedicated artist. Since I was there, only one day a week, I survived. Why? I *loved* my students.

The sale of my home, the school moves and preparing for my first One Woman Art Exhibit in November soon took its toll. Each day the weight intensified. Each day's struggle seemed endless. Each day I prayed for strength! Strength *was* given. Often I used my lunch hour to drive uptown while eating lunch to discuss my folded-business cards with the printers. Since I'd hand lettered and drawn my own design, an approval on each step was required before mailing the final copy to their printer in Arizona.

My close friend Valarie recommended an artist who framed artworks. We made an appointment by phone. Twenty-seven pieces were spread out on the floor and tables at his request. Used frames sprayed to complement the paintings and drawings reduced the cost to $800. His art studio, located in a downtown art section of the city, was awesome! From my downtown school I visited his studio twice a week. As I checked on the framing downtown, my business cards uptown, while teaching downtown, I was soon *drained*!

The mixed-media artwork unveiling of Thomas Jefferson and Sally Hemings, his mistress of thirty-seven years was the main reason for the exhibit. The unacknowledged love affair deserved to be revealed artistically as well as it had been in literary form.

Often, my *car* automatically went to one school when I was scheduled at the other one. Every Monday morning was disastrous and depressing. I felt like nothing! I'd ask myself, why am I here? Why am I hauling all of this stuff up and down three flights of steps every week? Is this why I worked so hard to send myself to college?

Winter Monday mornings were miserable! All school furnaces were off on weekends. Turned on at seven a.m. Monday morning, classrooms were not warm until late afternoon or the following day. Often I taught downstairs in the library. My students' complaints were useless.

"Mrs. Winters we don't like being down here. We miss our art room. It's nothing down here but dreary looking bookshelves and old worn out books and tables. Why don't they fix that old heating system or get another one?

We'll never finish our projects. We only *have* art twice a month. It's just not fair!"

Other students chimed in with their complaints. After listening to their repeated criticisms I quieted their discontent and started our lesson.

"Listen, we must make the best of what we have. Button your coats. Put on your hats and gloves then we'll watch slides of Michelangelo Buonarroti, the world's most famous artist, sculptor."

I taught. They listened and asked numerous questions, about his partially nude figures; why he didn't clothe them. By Christmas I'd adjusted to my elementary students. We related well, especially the Monday classes. I covered the dark *old* wooden tables with white oilcloth, decorated the bulletin boards with bright picturesque projects completed by previous students which inspired them.

Every Monday morning two students carried two to four buckets of water from the custodial closet at the end of the hall to our art room. The buckets of water were placed on a separate table. Water was needed to remove any adhesive or paint remaining on their hands. In addition it was used to dilute paints and clean their brushes. The students at that school were smart and well behaved. They deserved better than that old building in an uptown neighborhood of homeowners who'd worked hard with their children.

The downtown school was situated in the middle of poverty, drugs and crime. Many past students from that school however climbed above their sordid environment and soared to achieve greatness. I took pride in my classroom. It reflected me, my love of art as well as for my students. I was strict, but fair. Most students understood my goal but others rebelled. *Ohhh* how they rebelled and opposed strong discipline!

Each classroom teacher was responsible for escorting his class to my art room. The students stood quietly by the wall outside my room until I'd ask them to come in and take their assigned seats. The teacher left and returned at the end of their class. This procedure existed in both schools.

Every teacher responded well in both schools except *one* who taught at the downtown school. Mr. Ramone taught fourth grade and refused to bring his students to art. After reminding him several times that his students had missed their art class, I took my problem to Mrs. Clemons the assistant principal.

"Mrs. Clemons, Mr. Ramone refuses to bring his class for Art. I can't grade them if they've not completed any assignments. He brought them one time in September. He says he forgets, but his students have told me otherwise."

"Mrs. Winters, Mr. Ramone said we didn't need to come down here for art. He said he'd give us our art grades. He said we needed to stay upstairs and finish our work."

"I'll speak to Ramone Mrs. Winters. His students *won't* miss anymore classes."

They came on time twice. Subsequent days were ten, fifteen or twenty minutes late. Sometimes even *thirty minutes* into the period. During our next faculty meeting I mentioned the importance of my teaching time; that forty-five to fifty minutes for my students was required to teach my lesson. I pleaded with them to be on time. They were forewarned.

After that announcement I refused any class fifteen minutes late upon suggestion from the assistant principal. Very few teachers were late after that. Ramone, about thirty-five, 5'9," 160 lbs. was soft spoken, floated along as he walked and exhibited an air of aloofness. His persistent refusal to conform to my repeated requests required a formal meeting with him and Mrs. Clemons. We met in her comfortably decorated office one Wednesday after school. Now Ramone had plenty of time to give his excuses for denying his students the art period that belonged to them twice a month. He insisted he forgot or they were so involved in a project *they* chose not to come downstairs to their art class. We listened as his sorry excuses poured from a mouth full of evasiveness. Mrs. Clemons informed him that his students *didn't* have the right to make that type of decision.

He *hated* me! He denied me the privilege to teach his students. His dislike of art influenced his students' consequently his class was my *worst* class. Seven students refused to obey. I called their parents, had after school detention and parent conferences. Some did improve while others remained in the classroom with Mr. Ramone. At that point I decided if they wanted to fail my class then that was their choice. Of course, Mr. Ramone changed their failing grades to passing. This time I showed my grades to Mrs. Clemons who compared them with his homeroom grades. He'd changed several grades; said he couldn't understand the letters, however Mrs. Clemons had no difficulty, neither did the other teachers.

Tuesday, November 5th, the date of my One Woman Art Show was drawing closer. Initially the date was Thursday, November 7th but was changed because the minister I'd asked to pray, Sister Gibson, taught a Bible class at our church that night. Every phase of the exhibit was on schedule except exposure in the local newspapers and television. I was denied that service each time I spoke to anyone about coverage. My friends informed me why other local artists were given coverage before and after their exhibits.

"Dawn you're not in their cliques. You're not a native of Baltimore. Besides they won't allow you to compete with their artists friends."

They were right. I'd contacted three newspapers, submitted black and white photographs of two of the twenty-seven artworks, written the articles they'd requested and was still denied coverage. I called an art teacher, one I *thought* was my friend, a native of Baltimore, who socialized with the elite in getting my exhibit, advertised. She appeared in the newspaper frequently for her art shows and sorority events. I *knew* she'd help. *Wrong!*

"Dawn what happened to your drapery business? Aren't you still making draperies for people?" I detected something strange.

"Yes I do occasionally, but I'm an artist Lyris. I just happen to be an artist who also makes draperies. God's blessed me with many talents so I use them?"

"I understand all that Dawn, but why have you waited all this time to have a One-Woman Art Exhibit?"

"Why shouldn't I have an exhibit, Lyris? For years I've wanted this show but something always happened. The reason for my delay has been money. You have a fine husband who supports everything you do. I haven't had that luxury in any of my marriages. Making draperies wasn't for pleasure but for *survival*. Remember I've raised two sons and cared for my ailing mother for many years almost single-handedly. Now, is the time for my exhibit! Will you help me get coverage?" I heard deep irritable sighs.

"Dawn I wish I could help you but I really do-n't have the ti—me... I'll give you the name of someone who mi—ght be able to help you."

I listened to her enumerate various functions and minutiae that would consume her time in future months. I thanked her; then contacted the person she suggested. The lady embraced the artworks I'd carried to her home to judge.

"Dawn I'm not an art critic. I know very little about art. I don't know why Lyris asked me to critique your work? I like everything. Some I don't quite understand though."

"Which ones are they?"

"Those bright colored tissue collages; that large painting of four eyes overlapping each other. What does it mean?" I explained the content of the

The Eye an abstract painting, and the function and use of value changes in color. She held on to every word as I pointed out special lines and curves, size variation and color intensity and contrast. She understood better.

"Dawn I'm still curious why Lyris gave you my name." My heart and soul refused to be sidetracked. It was only another barrier, another hurdle to surmount and overcome by November. I denied the rejection and moved forward alone as usual.

After Lyris' refusal and her friend's lack of knowledge, I sat quietly at home and prayed, "Dear God please help me, show me what else I have to do. *Nobody* will help me." Ideas emerged as leaves flutter from a tree. Slowly I understood the short messages and wrote them down.

An agenda listed items to purchase. My entire life had been budgeting: the market, the bills, Christmas cards mailed and received etc. The $2500 was my entire budget.

Between school and preparing for the exhibit I had other commitments: Church, two Bible classes on Wednesday night, karate twice a week, piano lessons once a week. Also the director of the theatre asked me to paint a mural on one of the small lobby walls. *Exhausted,* my heavy eyes drooped, reddened knees resulted from crawling on the floor as I completed the mural while my stomach pleaded for nutritional meals. Karate classes helped to release my daily built-up stress.

Time to work on the Thomas Jefferson and Sally Hemings artwork seemed almost impossible! The work wedged deep in my mind needed completion, but when? Each day Solace greeted me at the door. I'd spend a few minutes with him, grab something to eat; then flop down on the den's sofa totally drained! At times I slept there all night still dressed only to rise early, shower, dress, and start the senseless cycle all over again. Three months of slavery were devoted to a *thing,* an exhibit. The overwhelming *desire* to culminate everything for the exhibit single-handedly would soon end! My sons weren't able to help me. Bryan had moved to Virginia and Marty still chauffeured for a limousine company long hours into the night.

Agnes, my close artist friend asked her husband's secretary to type my three-page price list; an enormous job! I assumed the strength of many and proceeded with the mission. My dear friend Lauren would handle the coatroom. Lenard's friend a local TV Videographer would tape the exhibit.

The agenda for the exhibit was complete: the caterer, taped music, coat checker, business cards, invitations all mailed, artworks framed, all twenty-seven works titled, sized, and priced. Batiks, collages, pencil drawings, pastels, watercolors, tempera, macramé, needlecraft, mixed media and weavings were ready. The artist, Romano, had bagged the framed artworks in large extra heavy-duty plastic bags to ensure their protection from scratches. Everything was completed except the main attraction, the Jefferson/Hemings work! When would I ever find time to *finish* it before the show?

Three days before the exhibit, I *started!* The art, sewing and catchall room, my third bedroom, housed the artwork placed on the tall brown easel. Half was completed, the other half developed as I worked. The evening before the exhibit, my friend, Aria who lived in Florida, called. She and her husband were in Baltimore and wanted to stop by and discuss my joining their family business.

"Aria, I'd love to see you and your husband but I'm getting ready for my first One Woman Art Show and I still have *soo* much to do. Can we discuss it another time?"

"Dawn it won't take that long, we're leaving early Wednesday morning and I don't know when we'll be up this way again."

"I'm sorry Aria I just can't, not this time." She refused to take *no* for an answer.

"Dawn Tuesday is Election Day and schools are closed. Won't you have time then?" Weariness stole my dismay but our friendship made me relent. It was I who'd taught this determined young woman how to sell when I recruited her into an art business years earlier. I felt obligated!

"Alright, but it can't be long because I have *so* much to finish."

"I promise you Dawn it won't take that long."

On that cold Monday, November 4th, around 6:00 p.m. when Aria and her husband rang the doorbell, I'd fallen asleep on the sofa in the den. I jumped up and dragged my slumberous body to the foyer and pushed the buzzer.

"Who's there please?"

"It's Ai—ria and Looo-gan." I pushed the button that unlocked the main door to admit the female with that charming southern accent. Their strained footsteps trudged up the three flights of steps as though they were ascending the fifty flights of 897 steps of the Washington Monument in our Nation's Capitol. With no elevator they had to bear it as I did twice a day seven days a week.

"Gi-rl, how *do* you han-dle these steps? I'm just woo—rn out!"

"Ah, you get used to it after a while. Besides they're terrific for building my stamina and endurance for karate."

"Well I'm not ta-king kar-ate and they're *toooo* much for us." Her husband nodded. We greeted each other with hugs. Once inside, she wanted to see every room. They were highly impressed with its spacious 1400 sq. ft. the same as a house.

Aria, a strong Taurus, was my best friend for several years, before she returned home to Florida. After a light dinner, I listened to Logan explain the Amway business.

As he explained, retaining my composure was *arduous*! My eyeballs felt like lead, ready to drop out. I reminded them often of the exhibit the following night and even showed them several framed works. Neither one was interested. I understood. After I signed the contract, they left.

"I knew I could count on you Dawn because you recruited *me* into TransDesign."

They left at nine. I dined with Jefferson and Hemings along with Solace until three the next morning. Four hours later, I got up, finalized the work then rushed out at 10 a.m. to purchase forgotten items for the artwork.

Bitter cold breezes grazed my face as I dashed from store to store procuring the necessities required to put the last touches on my *masterpiece* including a sterling silver locket. The historical thirty-eight year forbidden love affair was etched in my heart, just as the heart shaped silver locket had hung around Sally's neck on a black velvet ribbon which held the likeness of Thomas Jefferson. Their love affair was carpeted by society. The love between an American President and a black slave, who looked white, plus being the half sister of Jefferson's wife Martha, was unacknowledged for 211 years.

In 1989 I read *Sally Hemings* written in 1979 by Barbara Chase-Riboud. Mesmerized by its contents, I decided to depict this tragic segment in American History in an artwork. Two years later my composition, titled, *Love in Bondage* was finished the day of the exhibit. The covered canvas was placed on an easel and unveiled that evening.

I forgot the exhibit date was on Election Day! When I remembered, the 150 invitations were already mailed, many to out-of-town friends. Attendance was fair if you take into account the *freezing* temperatures. I applauded the ones who braved that frigid weather and attended anyway! The attendees at the Arena Playhouse performance held in the auditorium that shivering night joined my guests.

Every weekend of November, I was available in the lobby to answer any questions concerning the exhibit. Many strolled from painting to drawing to collage to weaving to watercolor etc. *Love in Bondage* was displayed after being framed in a shadow box because of its 3-Dimensional mixed media qualities.

In December the new director called and asked if I'd return in January since that month's artist was unable to exhibit. I said *Yes!* Once again every weekend I stood in the lobby and answered questions. The main attraction was *Love in Bondage* and its *unknown* history. By that time it was copyrighted in the Library of Congress. The 24"x36" original was reproduced for sale but a little smaller. I felt terrific! Now I was a *real* artist with an artwork reproduced! Now I was respected as an artist and not just as an art teacher or *the lady who made draperies.* The guests listened attentively to the sad historical love story and asked multiple questions.

After my repeated requests, media coverage was still *zero.* Not *one* person from either school came to the exhibit the entire split two-month period, not *even,* my principals or assistant principals! Reminders were made every Friday on the school intercom to staff. Administrators and staff, however, never stopped asking me to put up bulletin boards and showcases, hand letter large banners for assembly programs, plus decorating for other school functions. Since I'd only been there five months, I thought, maybe that's the reason. They appeared to accept me, but not enough to see the exhibit. No excuse was acceptable unless they were *sick, dead or dying* as my college band instructor said if we missed a band practice!

Many reproductions of *Love in Bondage* were sold during those January weekends. Besides I met marvelous people! Also interaction with the actors and actresses comforted my spirit. I watched many rehearsals and helped out wherever I could.

One actor overheard I needed a house in order to get my belongings out of storage.

"Dawn I know of a gorgeous housing development that rents, but it's in Essex. They're having a special on right now."

"I don't mind, Essex isn't that far from where I teach, thirty to forty minutes at the most. Besides one of our office secretaries lives out there. When can you show me where it is?"

I leased the lovely two story row house with finished basement including a half bath and a *large* storage area. The partially paved back yard provided parking for one car with soil space left on both sides for flowers or plants. Once I saw the beautiful section I knew I'd move in April when my lease expired. A hundred dollars *less,* it would accommodate everything in my apartment basement *shoe box* storage and the outside paid storage. I'd save $165 a month.

Before I moved to Essex, my Cadillac Seville had problems. One sunny Saturday afternoon as I returned from a friend's house, steam spurted from under the hood! I pulled over on the shoulder of the highway. As tears rolled down my quivering cheeks I prayed for help. I got out of the car and propped up the hood. A trucker noticed my car and the little helpless lady who stood looking bewildered at her unsolvable problem! He stopped and repaired the problem, refusing any payment except thank you. Truckers have *always* been helpful to me during a highway emergency! The second and same problem occurred as I drove down Liberty Road. Fortunately, I was close to a service station as steam escaped from under the hood like a volcanic eruption! I'd been embarrassed twice; I'd bought a lemon! Never had I seen a Cadillac's hood up on a highway. I'd wasted my money! More problems required more money. I had the problems but not the money. The third problem occurred one night on my way home. It was *cold* and raining. Oh how it *rained*! Putt, putt, putt the car's too familiar unhealthy sound said, "Pull over! Can't you see I'm choking! What's the matter with you!"

Cars passed by, not one stopped. I reached over the back seat for the umbrella. The rain fell slower now but remained constant. I left the parked car and started the half mile walk home. The rainy peaceful stroll provided time to evaluate my life and its multiple problems, most of which would not have occurred if I'd not had:

Boyfriends—hurts and disappointments
Marriages—adulteries, physical and mental abuse
Children—worrying, talking back, headaches,
Cars—payments, insurance, problems, maintenance
Houses—payments, lawns, roofs, furnace, repairs,
Pets—cleaning up, vet appointments, feeding
Jobs—harassment, mental and physical abuse, prejudice
Bills—impulsive buying for the house, clothes, family and others

But then I thought *all of this is part of life. Its how I handled each one that caused my crises! Yes, yes,* I'd drawn the conclusion that living *alone in the woods* brought happiness! The Indians survived without tall buildings and cars that polluted the air. They lived off the land and survived without these types of headaches. Why couldn't I? Residing in a mountainous section would be divine, peaceful, harmonious and bonding with God—only if *I* didn't interfere.

At least nature didn't talk back or hurt if I minded my own business. I'd read about people who lived off the land and were *extremely* happy. Yes, but could *I* live like that? Caught up in mad cycles of *buy, buy, buy and have, have, have,* just because I had the money*!* I *must* change! But *could* I! The fourth car problem occurred after I'd moved to Essex that April.

At the rear of our houses a huge farm hid behind a dense row of trees. Outstanding! In the front my house resembled city life, while the back was country. The birds, squirrels, rabbits and other qualities were characteristics of rustic scenic serenity.

The move was hectic as usual, by this time I'd moved over *twenty-two* times since attending college thirty-six years ago. In fact, I could have bought my own moving van with the money I'd spent moving. Strange as it seems, moving never bothered me, especially when it always improved my living conditions. Space, that's what I needed, plenty, plenty of space! My friends called me a gypsy. My aunt said I was crazy. My mother just shook her head. And my children, my dear children were never surprised every time I'd say, "We're moving next month." With all the moves and all the husbands my job remained constant. Well, something had to pay for all the transitions. Besides, I needed stability and money to qualify for each new location! It never occurred to me I was running—in search of something—but what?

After I settled in, I let Solace go outside to live like a cat. *Big* mistake! Early Saturday morning, I opened the back kitchen door, then storm door. He looked up at me, stared at the opened doors then tiptoed outside cautiously one paw at a time, on the doorstep landing. His slow careful motions continued as he proceeded down the wooden steps even more deliberately one paw, one step at a time. He'd never been outside, except on both third floor balconies at my former apartment. After five minutes of sniffing the outside world, I brought him in, although he resisted. Each day I'd let him out for a few minutes when I came home from work until he refused to come in and would scamper off into the wooded area to meet his friend, another male cat.

Eventually he stayed out, all night, and returned in the morning when I called. At first he'd ignored my calls but soon learned; he'd be outside all day if he didn't come home. Most mornings he'd be under the back porch wooden steps asleep or somewhere near the house. The car's absence notified him I'd left.

The last day of school in June, one of my co-workers Terlise, a marvelous teacher, stopped by my room to bid her farewells until we met again in September.

"Hi there, Dawn I see you're still here. Do you hate to go home?"

"No indeed! I've *been* ready!" I said.

"And what are your plans for the summer; are you going away?" She said

"No I'm not going anywhere this summer. My four granddaughters are supposed to come for three weeks so that's enough vacation for me."

"Four! All at one time! You're a brave soul after teaching all year."

"Well their parents are young and don't see the necessity for the girls to visit each other. Since I do, it's left up to me to bring them all together. I don't want them to become adults not knowing each other. Neither mother wants the responsibility of four girls for two or three weeks."

"And what are your plans for this summer, Terlise?" I said.

"Nothing, I plan to do *nothing* but rest. My daughter and I may take a few short trips but other than that I'll stay in the city."

"Terlise, do you know of a house I might rent. Right now I'm living in Essex but the drive is rather far from all the things I have to do in the city."

"I think I do."

"You *do*, where!"

"Where I live; it's not far from here; almost walking distance. They're called co-op homes. I think you'd really like them."

Instantly I thought *she lives in this neighborhood? But these houses are very old. Why would she want to live down here?*

"If you're not in any hurry Dawn, you may follow me in your car to our main office and we'll talk to Mr. Skinner the Manager," she said.

"Sounds great, to me! When you're ready to leave come by and I'll be *glad* to follow you to the office." I said.

I couldn't believe what I said. I'd just moved two months ago and was ready to move again. *Wow*, did I really tell her I'd follow her to the main office? Is something wrong with my reasoning? I followed Terlise several blocks until we reached the charming housing development I'd *forgotten*. Yes, now I remembered that interesting gated community all to itself. It was a diamond in the midst of the rough.

The main office was across the street from my favorite school where I'd taught for five years. A nearby hospital had bought the property and was renovating it for a Children's Rehabilitation Center. I paused; the fun-loving times I'd shared with staff and students surfaced. I reminisced about the assembly programs, dance recitals, field trips, semester break trips our principal Mrs. Perkins sponsored for her teachers. Yes, my *best* teaching years were in that huge old dark building, Rollin Mazell Junior-Senior High School, la crème de la crème!

"Hello Mrs. Mason is Mr. Skinner in today? I have a friend who's interested in a house."

Mrs. Mason extended her hand to me and released that gorgeous smile as her blond hair hung loosely around her face. Those brilliant blue eyes reminded me of Paul Newman's, only she didn't have his sensual mouth.

"No, Mr. Skinner isn't in at the moment. But I think I can help you. We will have one available, but not until next year." My heart skipped a beat as my eyes met Terlise's eyes, also beaming!

"Oh that would be perfect! My lease is only for a year anyway."

Mrs. Mason continued, "Mrs. Hearson has been a resident in that house since these houses were first turned into co-operative homes ten years ago. She's one of our oldest residents and has the *only* detached house in the entire development. Terlise has a house but it's a row home."

"What are co-operative homes?" I asked.

Mrs. Mason moved from behind her desk toward the front where we stood.

"As I explain, we'll visit a few apartments, some two bedrooms and some three bedrooms so in case Mrs. Hearson doesn't move you'll be able to select something else."

We walked up the block then turned on Baltimore Street. I'd never known those row houses were part of the co-ops.

"In co-ops you never own the land, only the unit. There are 216 units in this group. When you purchase a unit you buy into all 216 units. No one makes a profit. The profit goes into a fund, for repairs or replaces anything needed in the units. The best part is that you are not responsible for any maintenance inside or outside. The lawns are cut, the snow is shoveled and the leaves are raked."

"You mean I wouldn't have to cut any more grass, rake any more leaves or shovel any more snow? *Oh yes*, that's exactly what I'm looking for! How soon can I move?" They both laughed at my exaltation in less manual labor and agreed with my eagerness to move.

The following week I met Mrs. Hearson. A plump pleasant lady opened the door. She gave us a grand tour of the entire three floors and basement. We stepped through the kitchen door outside onto the small patio that would hold my custom made round wooden table with four seats, yellow vinyl tablecloth and matching umbrella. My heart swelled with anticipation, a dream come true. A few yards of gorgeous green lawn and shrubs from the patio was a *monkey bar and sliding board set* for small children. All this beauty was enclosed by six-foot chain link fencing. Residents had a key to the gate nearest to their building. The house was mine from the moment I stepped in the front door. It would be completely renovated after I selected the options in new kitchen and bath cabinetry. All new appliances and new carpeting throughout the house included the steps and halls. Mrs. Hearson was tired of climbing steps. Besides, since her two sons had moved, she required less space. My children were grown and gone too but I *still* needed more living and storage area than she—for my unforgettable years of accumulated *junk!*

51...AN EMBRACEABLE SUMMER

Children have neither past nor future;
They enjoy the present,
which very few of us do.
La Bruyere: Les Caracteres

Two weeks after school closed my *paid-for* Cadillac Seville barely made it home. It crawled down the street, and finally rolled into the backyard. After one year and $4500 cash, AAA arrived and towed it where Lenard worked. The mechanics agreed with Lenard, it was useless to waste money on repairs but better to buy another car, a newer model.

I realized all the money I spent could have been the down payment on a better car; I just didn't want another bill! In Sunday's paper I spotted a three year old Cadillac reduced from $17,000 to $15,000 and called the dealer the next day. The formerly $35,000 car was white with blue interior and in excellent condition from my view. The salesman allowed me to drive the car to my mechanic (Lenard) to be checked out. When everyone saw me drive up in that gorgeous car they stepped *waaay* back in disbelief!

"Well Dawn you sure got a *fine looking* car there!"

"It's not mine yet. I brought it over to be checked out before I sign the papers." I felt at ease sitting in that seat knowing this car would last longer than the other one.

"How much did they allow you on the Seville?"

"Not that much, only $1000 trade in. I expected more but since it needed work I guess that sounds fair."

After the car passed their inspection I returned to the dealer and signed the contract. Before I drove off the lot I noticed a red light on the dashboard. The salesman said it would go out. As I drove to Essex the light remained on. I stopped at a phone booth and called the salesman. I was distraught with the entire situation! He said they'd pick it up the following day if the light stayed on. Their tow truck arrived the next morning and towed my car away. Now I had no way to get to work. I was *sooo* angry! One day I bought the car and the next day it was towed!

It cost $1000 to repair, at their expense! My anger changed to *gratitude*. Once again, God *was* definitely in control.

On July 13th two of my four beautiful granddaughters arrived by plane from Elkart, Ind., Rolanda eight and Marvis five and a half. I financed their trip. They were tagged and supervised by an airline stewardess. The other two sweethearts from Fayetteville, N.C. Briana seven and Nadia four arrived three days later. These were two of the four summers all four of them visited me at the same time. It was *significant* they knew each other. Since their parents refused to have all four together, I took them for three weeks. They were growing up so fast! Soon they'd be grown, gone stumbling and fumbling into a vast world of the known and unknown.

Before the girls arrived I had an agenda of places and things we'd do. Of course they'd add their own wishes and needs.

"Grandmommy may I read your list! I know you have one because you wrote a list for us last year."

"Of course you may read it Briana, here it is." She took the list and crossed her legs as she sat on the beige carpeted floor in the upstairs den. Her eyes scanned down the list until she stopped and turned her head toward me.

"Grandmommy you forgot to include your karate classes. Aren't you going to take *us* with you when you go to your classes?"

"Of course I am, just add it to the list."

Briana and Nadia's mother was from Thailand. She came to America at age 12, not knowing one word of English; now she knew thousands. She still had more to learn since there are over 750,000 words in the English language. My son Bryan's resemblance was slight in the faces of his two small China dolls with long black hair. They were as one; I'd never seen such love and closeness between two sisters. They *never* argued, complained or made any needless noise in the house. They played so quietly sometimes I'd check to see if something was wrong.

The previous year they had visited me at the Brittany Apartments. Twice that summer we used my key that unlocked the gate to the subway station's parking lot adjacent to my complex and rode downtown and back. We shopped, ate lunch, toured the local historic sites and returned home exhausted. I rode the New York Subway for many years, however I wanted them to experience the ride since Fayetteville didn't have one. Later they saw Baltimore's greatest attractions the Aquarium, the Planetarium and the Zoo, their favorite.

Whenever Nadia was tired of playing, she'd tell her sister.

"Bria I'm tired. I don't want to play this game anymore. Let's play something else. We've been playing this game all day." She didn't talk much, but when she did, her words were absolute. Briana on the other hand was a chatterbox unless someone made her angry, then she sat quietly in a corner.

My other two granddaughters were just the opposite. Marvis, the younger one usually picked on her sister or cousins. She and her sister argued most of the time about anything. Yet, Marvis was our family *sweetheart*. Her Mom called her *love bug* because she was such a lovable child! Hug, hug, kiss, kiss, nosy, nosy, tattler and picky were Marvis's nicknames. She refused to mind her own business or keep her hands to herself. I tired quickly of hearing her call my name.

"Grand—mo—mmy, Brr—iaaa, wo—n't gi-ve me so—me of that pieeee." Or Gran—mom—my theyyy— wo—n't sh—-are with meeee." I heard whining, continuous complaining *all day long!*

"Gran—mo—mmy, th-ey wo-n't let me playyyy with th—-emmmm." She sang every word when she spoke. I corrected her the entire summer, to no avail.

"Marvis stop *singing* when you talk. You're too big for that and besides it gets on *my* nerves!"

I had three weeks to listen to her whine and complain so I learned to pay attention and to respond accordingly. Poor child the other three children evicted her from all their games and hid in the house so she couldn't find them. Of course Marvis turned to me.

"Grann—mom-myyy will you pl-ayy with meee. Rolannnn—da and th-em, they don't waaa-nt to pl-ayyy with meee." Her sadness touched my heart.

She and her sister had the most beautiful smooth tan complexion. Their skin was as satin and their smiles as radiant as their mother's. I'd gather art supplies and spread a sheet over the dining room table. With scissors, crayons, Elmer's glue, assorted colors of paper and our *imaginations*, we drew, cut, glued and marveled over our pretty pictures. We cut out shapes, made designs using color schemes and remembered to vary the sizes. After she tired, I taught her new stitches for her pillow, which each girl was making. She'd run back and forth upstairs showing the girls her project but their unpleasantness toward her caused more tears to spill from her pretty brown eyes.

"Grannn—ma—meee, th-ey wo—n't lo-ok at myyy art pic—turrrres."

As she related her sadness, I stared at the numerous plaits her mother had taken time to braid and then added numerous crystal clear and multicolored beads on each plait that touched their shoulders. Their mother, Renata was a *wizard* with hair!

We visited the library, museum, went to the beach, movies, thrift shops and karate classes on Tuesdays and Thursdays at 5:00 p.m. Karate was their *highlight*. They sat eagerly in the chairs reserved for family and friends and watched their grandmother perform her kicks, jumps, turns and sparring techniques.

Of course their best outing was visiting my friend Agnes's home where we all swam in her huge 30'x 40' *fantastic* swimming pool. Agnes loved children, *anybody's* children! Her five were grown, and on their own, yet every summer she kept her grandchildren: two grandsons from Kentucky and her daughter's son and daughter. I thought teaching art nine months was enough children for Agnes but she surrounded herself with precious children seven days a week! She was a flawless gem!

As Rolanda requested, she celebrated her *ninth birthday* bowling with her sister and cousins. Nadia only four could barely hold the ball; we helped her. Usually she rolled gutter balls, but occasionally a few pins fell over. We had pizzas, sodas and took pictures dressed in party hats with noisemakers. Birthday cake and ice cream topped off her day. Making others happy made me happy! On Sundays we attended Church.

Their vacation ended and drained my wallet!

Bryan and his girlfriend Stella arrived by car to carry his children back to Fayetteville while Rolanda and Marvis were again tagged and returned to Elkart by plane. Relieved I thought, "Thank God, finally *peace!*"

On July 11th, two days before the girls' arrival, I attended my friend Valarie's family reunion. Each year, I went and was accepted as part of their family. I almost didn't go.

"Valarie, I don't think I'll come this year." I told her.

"Why not, Dawn? You've been coming every year so why not this year?"

"I just get tired of going places by myself."

My close friend had many male admirers even after her stroke six years prior. A cane enabled her to stay on the go! A busy, busy lady! It was while she recuperated at her sister and cousin's home that she met Lenard months before we married. Valarie insisted I be at her family reunion.

"Well, sit at my table there'll be men there you already know," she said.

"Yes and all of those men are in love with *you!*"

"Ah, come on Dawn you know better than that. I want you there, you *hear?*"

"Yes mom I'll be there, but I *won't* sit at your table." We understood each other; two Aquarians born one day apart, February 1st and 2nd but years apart.

When I arrived, guests waited in the lobby and downstairs. The assigned banquet room was not ready. An employee had scheduled their affair an hour too early, a costly mistake on their part. Had I not needed to hang the large banner I made I'd have left.

At the last minute I showered, slipped on a black sheath dress with white batiste sleeves that resembled leaves. Each petal overlapped the next creating an exotic look. As the attendants decorated the tables I managed to slip in, hang the banner, and then return to the hall. Valarie had been my close friend since the first day I stood in line to register at Morgan State University.

My dear friend *lived* to work! Excessive *work* is what initiated her stroke. She was involved in too many clubs and organizations. Her high ranking position, in Washington, D.C. was taxing enough without other dedicated missions. We were so much alike. By this time Valarie had bought a lovely home. Another sister Dawn moved in because no one wanted her living alone.

The banquet room was ready at last! We filed in and sat at various tables. I sat with people I didn't know. After fifteen minutes, Valarie walked to my table, which was across from hers.

"Dawn why are you sitting over here, do you know any of these people?" She said.

"No. In fact I was going to leave because I don't know anyone sitting here."

"*Don't* leave, come on over to my table."

"Your table? There are only men at your table and one lady. I'll stay here for a while then I'll come over."

Since nothing else was on my agenda that Saturday evening, I decided to stay. I excused myself and strolled over to the table of men and one lady, now three including Valarie. But since she didn't stay still long enough, she wasn't counted. The hidden leg brace under her long azure gown and cane didn't stop her mobility. It only slowed her pace.

I sat in the vacant chair, next to her boyfriend, Gregory Kingsley. He said nothing. After a few seconds I introduced myself.

"Hello Gregory do you remember me?" I said.

"Yes I remember you; you're Dawn, Valarie's friend."

"I thought you'd forgotten. The last time I saw you, I married Lenard and you read that beautiful poem at our Wedding."

"Yes, I remember." He answered.

"I didn't think you remembered me because you didn't say anything when I sat down." He dropped his head as if in deep thought as I stared into space. Minutes later the man seated opposite me spoke.

"Why are you sitting over there by yourself?"

I realized it was Gregory's brother Rory, even though we'd never met. They looked just alike, except that Gregory was a little shorter. I thought *he's the one I saw earlier downstairs walking swiftly back and forth with a program in his hand.*

"Well there's a vacant chair right here if you don't want me to be alone." I said.

He got up, walked around the circular table then sat next to me. With him on one side and his brother on the other I had brotherly love. We said little, until he reached up with his slender tan fingers and touched the white batiste petals on the left sleeve of my black dress.

"What's all this?" He flicked the white oval petals with his fingers and threw me his fantastic seductive smile, the Kingsley trademark. As lonely as I'd been the last few months I didn't need to see any man, especially a seductive one.

I turned my head and said sarcastically, "You see something you like in that sleeve, or do you just like playing with a lady's dress?"

His radiant smile remained focused on me.

"Yes I do see *something* I like."

Yes, he was interested, very interested, but I knew better. My mind said hands off, but my heart knew better. We chatted, danced, laughed, and joked as though we were old friends. That much fun had not crossed my path in years. Soon Gregory strolled over.

"Hi Rory, how are you and Dawn enjoying yourself?" We nodded that we were.

"Gregory, I enjoy your brother's company but he's married. I don't want my heart broken. It's been cracked too many times already."

"Ah that's not important! They go their separate ways; have been for many years. There's nothing there anymore. They just live in the same house.

Ask Rory, he'll tell you."

I recalled the first time I met Gregory five years earlier seated at Valarie's dining room table in front of his birthday cake. I thought *that is the handsomest man I'd ever seen in my life!* Indeed he was a strikingly good-looking example of the male sex. I rushed to the kitchen where Valarie had gone.

"Valarie, *where did* you find that man! He's *the best looking man* I've ever seen!!" She smiled. "What can I say?"

Now five years later, I had his duplicate seated next to me!

The family reunion ended; but not our friendship. Rory asked me to call him Roy. He didn't like his name, never had. He wanted to know where I lived. Rather than tell him, I drove him all the way to Essex, right to my front door, turned around and headed back to Valarie's where Roy was to meet Gregory. During our drive Roy revealed incidents about his childhood, his life, and children from his first marriage.

We sat in my car and waited in front of Valarie's house for Gregory. What a *long* wait. Long enough to know I wanted to see this man again. I felt sorry for him. He'd married a young woman twenty-five years his junior and spoiled her with love and materiality. His studies were sidetracked and forgotten after they met.

After two years of marriage he soon tired of the weekly dances and music she loved and stopped frequenting the weekend affairs. She refused to stop. He became more involved in his church while she pursued the party lifestyle. She refused to attend his church. As years passed the gap widened. Nothing was left except his obligation to care for her needs. I had heard this same scenario five years earlier from Valarie and Gregory. She never worked. Roy gave her everything.

In addition to his disability check from the Federal Government he worked two jobs. Soon his wife discovered she had cancer. Smoking attacked her lungs but the strong determined woman got her way! $300-600 dresses with shoes and handbags to match adorned her body at every affair. I listened as he poured out his soul. We had so much in common: we liked the same music, including opera, we loved to read, write poetry, travel but most of all we loved the Lord! I surmised that people usually end up marrying the wrong individuals. I'd heard that opposites attract. No, it's because the devil is *on* his job! He puts stumbling blocks in the Christian's path; desires that will divert his attention from God! That's Satan's ultimate goal!"

"Dawn I'm looking for a wife." Roy said without an introduction of conversation.

"Why would you say that; you're already married Roy."

"Not really, it's only a piece of paper. She doesn't care for me anymore. We just share the same house. I'm someone who supports her financially. I take her to visit her family and her daughter to school everyday. All I do is work and take care of everyone else. No one in our house truly cares for me."

"How do you know that?"

"It's obvious; that all."

By this time my head rested on Roy's shoulder. It shouldn't have been there, but it was, I shouldn't have been there either but I knew that too. He placed his gentle hand under my chin, tilted my head back, then put his soft sensual mouth on my lips and gave me a kiss that *lit* up the sky! We kissed. *Ohhhh* how we *kissed*! The chemistry was there! He knew it. I knew it. That kiss lasted several minutes and preserved my heart over *two* weeks! My kiss communicated, I care I'll take care of you.

He didn't call me after my grandchildren left. So after a few days passed, I called his brother. I wanted to hear his voice.

"Hi Gregory, Roy was to call me after my grandchildren left. I haven't heard anything from him. Is he sick? Is something wrong?"

"No, not that I know of. Stay right there. I'll call him on his night job. He'll call you right back." Within minutes Roy called.

"Why didn't you call me Roy?"

"I thought the kids were still there," he said.

"Are you sure that's the only reason?"

"Well...I thought...maybe there was too much chemistry there. I was afraid."

"Afraid of me? Why are you afraid of little ole meee?

"You're a *lot* of woman, Dawn. I don't know if I can handle that much chemistry at

this time in my life."

"Well, why did you start the fire, if you couldn't put it out?"

"I'll see you tomorrow evening after 5:00. Will you be home?" He said.

"Yes of course I'll be home." I beamed!

He arrived the following evening. Since I had waited two weeks, a few hours meant nothing! Soon I'd see that gorgeous smile, a smile that lifted my soul to heaven, a smile that spoke and eyes that penetrated my being. With him, I'd *live* again!

324

The doorbell rang. I'd watched him drive up and park in front of the house as I sat on the white antique sofa wearing white shorts and a loose white blouse staring out the half closed blinds. Hot temperatures required cool clothing even though the air conditioner was on. I wondered why I'd worn shorts that day. It was our first date. I should have worn pants rather than shorts, but I guess I wanted to get his attention. I did! We embraced and kissed, exhilarated to see each other.

"Did you get lost trying to find your way Roy?"

"You know I did. You gave me perfect directions but I always have a tendency to explore another route."

"Where did you stray?" He explained where he'd made his blunder. I listened patiently while we laughed at his silly mistakes. We ate the light dinner I'd prepared. In those few minutes his high intellect was obvious, so was his need for constant conversation. After dinner I cleared the table and put the dishes in the dishwasher. Roy joined me in the kitchen.

"That certainly was a great dinner Dawn. Are all your meals that good or did you prepare something special for me?"

"The answer to both questions is yes I am a good cook and yes I did cook something special for you. Are you ready for your dessert?"

He'd walked over to the kitchen door and looked out the window.

"That's an interesting view you have. Is that farmland being used or lying dormant this year. I know you enjoy the view since you're an artist."

"Enjoy it, I *love* it! Every pine tree, bird, climbing vine, squirrel reminds me of the south. I've driven down that old dirt road several times when I've wanted to get away. I'd sit in my car and look over the still serene calm water. What peace I've experienced back there! There are old farmhouses at the edge of the backwoods plus another spread of land and a lake."

"Tell me, did they own this land also?" He said.

"Oh yes! But the complex bought it. They wanted all of it but the owners refused to sell the part that's left."

We moved slowly upstairs to the den. Roy wanted to see something special on TV so I sat close to him and watched. My attention wasn't on television. It was about getting to *know* this man. But would I *ever* know him? I never knew the other ones. The men I knew had a way of revealing a sliver of their true selves while I was more truthful in my romantic attachments. To know is to believe. If I dug too deep I might find something distasteful and discredit the man. To know is to grow. But the direction of growth is uncertain, as is romance.

Roy had been openly honest about his past, the first night we met. He'd explained his relationship with his first wife; his regrets about not knowing his children because of his working many jobs. I should have known Roy had an emotional problem similar to mine but the heart ignores the visible.

We continued our romantic interlude as he watched television and I watched him. We laughed and talked and fooled around. Soon he left for that long drive back and his family. From that day on he drove to Essex every Saturday to teach me Spanish. We rarely covered any Spanish. The third Saturday he arrived, I had a picnic basket, chairs, blankets and beach umbrella ready to go.

"We're going where?"

"To the beach! You do remember the beach don't you; the sand at the water's edge, where people swim, lounged on blankets, and had fun. The place where sand gets in between your toes as you watch sea gulls zip back and forth while super high waves rush toward the beaches edge." I explained poetically.

He stared down at me with his sensual smile and those doting penetrating eyes.

"Yes Dawn, I remember. It's been *many* years though since I've been to a beach. My family goes every year but I work. Somebody has to pay, for all her *wishes*.

A head taller than I and twice as heavy, he was a woman's man. He clearly possessed those three "T's," Tall, Tan and Terrific! Our relationship blossomed as weeks burst into months! Love was easy so was the intimacy between us.

After Labor Day, schools opened. My last year's kindergarten students were now first graders. In both schools I was amazed at the growth spurt and maturity incurred over the summer. I knew my influence would help improve their behavior and morals if I taught them every year until they left the sixth grade. Along with the younger student's growth, the older student's misbehavior had exacerbated! Ramone had his same students from the year before. His negative *attitude* about art remained the same, as did his class. I foresaw a rough year ahead with his class and the two Special Education Classes.

Each Special Education Class had two boys who *didn't* belong in the school! They were *terrible, terrible!* By December my nerves had *exploded!*

I volunteered to sponsor an assembly Christmas program at the school where I taught four days. I'd use excerpts from The Nutcracker Suite in dialogue, song and dance. I wrote all the speaking parts and attempted to teach the dances on my planning and lunch periods. No staff member replied to my urgent petition for help. Teacher Aides brought their participating students to the auditorium and left. Struggles to instruct twenty-five wiggling boys and girls were in vain! Some listened while others ran behind the curtains, picked at the girls or did anything mischievous to upset our rehearsal. The dances progressed although they still needed lots of practice. Some lunch periods were allocated to Sarah, the Sugarplum Fairy and to other students who were struggling to remember their parts. I——-was——- *sooo——-ti—red!*

Saturdays I washed clothes, cleaned the house, cooked dinner, might cut the grass and prepared for Roy's weekly visit. Sundays I drove to church in downtown Baltimore, where I took piano lessons once a week with Mr. Zanick, a music teacher and a former colleague at Rollin Mazell.

Karate classes were twice a week. I saw Amy Smothers my therapist twice a month. Some obligations were scheduled on the same day. When I had one or two afternoons free, I went straight home. Traffic to Essex was bumper to bumper for miles! That was a main factor that influenced my return to the city. I cherished the wide open countryside each time I traveled those spacious highways. There no problems existed. Heaven and I were one! Those were daydreams. Soon I returned to reality; the hard knocks of life.

On Sunday morning, December 13, 1992 my life made a drastic change! Roy called me early Sunday morning as usual.

"Buenos Dias, Mi Chiquita. Are you ready for church?" His sensual voice caused my face to brighten and heart to flutter.

"Buenos Dias, Mi Amor. No. I feel very light-headed. I'm too dizzy to drive."

"Well my love, I think you should go. This is the time you need to go, when you don't feel like going..."

"I guess you're right. I really don't feel like driving but since you're not here to drive me, I'll have to drive myself, won't I?"

Sunday morning's traffic was sparse. The dizziness remained. Any idea of sickness was rejected. I drove and listened to inspiring Christian hymns that eased my pressure inside the car. At church I sat down front as usual; I thought I'd feel better. I didn't. Instead my body swayed each time I stood with the congregation to sing. I needed to hear my pastor preach. But I felt faint, too weak to stand. I picked up my Bible and purse excused myself in front of the gentleman on my right and walked slowly up the isle toward the rear of the church. Some people might have seen me wobble rather than walk. In the lobby of this huge two-year old church, one of the largest in the city, I stumbled toward one of the ushers.

"Please help me. I feel as though I'm going to faint."

Immediately the male usher took my arm and assisted me to the nurse's suite about ten feet away. I was asked to have a seat. The nurse took my blood pressure and said:

"How *did* you make it to this office! Your pressure is *sooo low*! I suggest you go to the hospital when you leave here and see a doctor as soon as possible." After ten minutes I went to the lobby and attempted to call my doctor's office but it was closed. I got the answering service.

"I'll see him tomorrow after school. I knew something was wrong. That's why I started not to come, but my boyfriend encouraged me to drive anyway."

"Drive! I *know* you didn't drive! You're in *no* condition to be driving!"

"Yes I did and have to drive back home."

"*Men!* They don't understand a thing. They think we're made of steel! I don't know what they'd do without us. I think we need to sit down and let *them* wait on *us!*"

The two middle-aged full-figured nurses dressed in white uniforms and white starched caps were overly concerned about me driving back home. They mumbled and laughed about males and their insensitivity toward women. I agreed completely but saved my vocal energy for driving home.

"Here drink these small cups of orange juice. If you don't have any at home stop and buy some."

"How do you feel now, Ms. Winters?" One of the nurses asked.

"I feel a lot better since you gave me that orange juice." I answered.

"Well orange juice is good for just about anything. That's why we should have it everyday. If not the juice then have an orange." She was right.

"Orange juice used to make me scratch, but I treated it the same as I did tomatoes. A friend once told me to keep eating them until my system got adjusted and that's exactly what happened."

"Are you sure you can drive all that distance to Essex?"

"Quite sure. I'll be all right. God will take care of me. He has all this time."

I knew God expected us to use wisdom but since no one could drive me home I was forced to act foolishly and drive myself. I waited thirty minutes then left not forgetting to buy the orange juice.

I drove to work the following morning. Less than an hour I was light-headed again. During lunch, I called my family physician and made an appointment to see him *that* day. I notified the office and canceled the Christmas pageant. I was sick and had to take care of myself. During the day students kept popping in my door asking such questions as:

"Mrs. Winters did you stop the Christmas play?"

"Mrs. Winters, why did you cancel the Christmas Program?"

"You mean I can't be in that play now?"

These questions persisted all day. I apologized, explained I was sick and had to cancel the program. After school I drove directly to the doctor's office. Again I nearly fainted as I walked through the Mall, avoiding eye contact with anyone. My swaying could have meant I was high on something. I floated in the office then up to the registration window. When the nurse took my blood pressure, she too was shocked!

"Mrs. Winters did you drive to this office!"

"Yes I did."

"I don't see how! I don't know how you managed to walk from your car, through the mall and to our office. Your blood is *wayyy* down! Here, drink this orange juice right now, before you pass out!"

"The nurse at church yesterday gave me orange juice. She *also* said my blood pressure was very low."

My limp body lost *all* its energy as it waited for the tall, bald but handsome, ultra conservative tan man in his late thirties. A man of few words, but his eyes, yes those heavy eyes said it all. A few minutes gave me enough time to reflect on how I'd met his parents.

I'd been hired as an interior designer for their new huge impressive two-story brick home, four years prior by his parents Major and Mrs. Sierra. The married doctor was their only child and how *proud* they were of him!

Both families lived across the street from each other in the city but were having the new house built in the county so they could live as one family. His mother and father were the principal owners and lived downstairs. Their son, wife and two young sons occupied upstairs with four bedrooms and two baths. They were a loving family; the living room, dining room, den, kitchen etc. were shared by all. His parents planned the house so, after their passing their huge bedroom and sitting room plus bath downstairs could be converted into their son's medical office, if he chose. Doctor Sierra entered the office in his slow casual manner.

"Good afternoon Mrs. Winters, I haven't seen you in a while. I see you're having some dizziness. Tell me about it."

I re-explained the dizziness I'd been experiencing since that previous day. I don't recall his exact medical terms but I was not to work, get plenty of rest plus add more sugar and salt to my diet. The medication would help control the dizziness in my stress-related problem.

"How are your parents and family doing?" I asked.

"They're doing just fine. The boys have grown so much since you last saw them."

"Your mother, has she finished designing her flower beds?" I said.

"No, mother never finishes. I hope you've finished your holiday shopping because you'll be confined to the house for quite some time."

"You mean I can't drive? I live alone and there's no one to help me."

We discussed my problem then I left. At his advice I stacked up on sweets, orange juice and anything else I needed. Christmas was ten days away. I hadn't completed addressing, my Christmas cards or mailing my family's presents. The next couple of days I finished the cards, wrapped my few packages then mailed them. The line wasn't too long in the post office but my dizziness remained constant. I sat on the floor against a wall on a pillow from my car until it was my turn in line. No one offered to let me go first. They saw how bad I felt, but God protected me. It was my pleasure, my joy to mail Christmas cards to my friends every year. That's the one time I communicated to all of my friends. I thanked God I'd finished almost everything before I got sick.

I traveled back and forth to Dr. Sierra's office without help. Of the many tests he'd taken, all were negative. Finally I started making trips to an Essex hospital which was closer. They found nothing. Relieved that nothing was fatally wrong; I still needed to know why I was sick; why was I so dizzy?

Roy visited Christmas Eve. My next door neighbor had sent dinner over by her son much earlier; a pleasant and welcomed surprise. Roy gave me a lovely soft pastel blue bathrobe and other small tokens for Christmas. I'd gotten him a shirt and tie. As usual I received *nothing* from my children. My *only* gift was from Roy, my sweetheart.

During my time home, friends called daily. Valarie contacted a relative named Adell Chapman who didn't work and lived close to me. Adell volunteered to take me to the hospital any time I called! What a blessed message those words were to my ears! Mr. and Mrs. Wilson who were like my adopted parents also offered to drive from Baltimore and take me to the hospital but they had *too* many years to be driving all that distance.

I recall his exact words. "Dawn, so you think we're too old to drive that distance, huh? I've driven farther than that."

"No, but it's just too far for you and Skipper to come."

After three months of attending various hospitals, subjected to multiple tests, an MRI, mental and physical tests, still nothing was detected; yet the dizziness remained. There were times I barely made it from the bathroom to the den. Holding on and leaning against the wall was the only way I got from one room to the next. Feelings of nausea and dizziness occupied my life seven days a week. Still nothing was found. On two occasions I asked my neighbor next door to carry me to the hospital. Another time I called my son early one morning.

"Marty I'm *so* sick would you please come and take me to the hospital?"

"Mom you live so far from me and I'd be late getting to work. Do you know somebody closer you could call?"

"No Marty I don't." I hung up the phone and drove to the hospital myself, very carefully. The two-hour emergency room stay confirmed my blood sugar was low. They fed me intravenously then sent me home, again.

On Roy's Saturday visits he did the marketing with my grocery list. I ate only one main meal a day. Getting up and down those steps to the kitchen was a major job. Orange juice, fruit, crackers, sweets etc. remained in the den. I'm sure my recovery would have been shorter if I'd had more nutritional meals.

Roy's visit was robbed by illness. His wife's cancer returned. She refused to accept the doctor's diagnosis; ignored his advice, and continued her life style of dances and parties. Week after week her weight dropped. She ignored her serious medical problem while his girlfriend sought anxiously for identification of hers.

At the advice of my senior friend Simone, I drove to the Greater Baltimore Medical Center in Baltimore one early Saturday morning. This had been her hospital for years. She praised it daily. After a thorough physical examination, they detected the usual low blood pressure in addition to something I don't recall but they *admitted* me. I thought *finally someone will locate my problem*. Wrong! After four days of multiple test and young female interns probing daily and asking their rapid questions, the hospital sent the On Staff Psychiatrist for a final decision. He walked over to the left side of my bed and sat in the chair. His extended firm handshake confirmed his welcome.

"Hello Ms. Winters, I'm Dr. Bernard. How do you feel?"

"I feel the same way I did when I came in here four days ago. I'm not leaving here until someone finds out what's wrong with me."

"I've been told that's the way you feel but you don't have anything physically wrong so you'll be discharged tomorrow. Since all your tests results were negative the staff has concluded that your problem is psychological rather than physical." He read his agenda of questions. His third one ended our session.

"Ms. Winters, have you been under any pressures lately?"

To answer that third question accurately could have taken days!

"Oh yes! My life has been nothing but built up stress, a volcano ready to explode any moment!"

"That bad huh; tell me about these problems you've experienced."

"Let's see, where do I start? Well, I've been married five times. I've had two-alcoholic husbands one alcoholic boyfriend, one son on crack cocaine who's stolen money and other items from me, my second son gambles, daily stress from very bad students and little help from administrative staff. Also I've moved three times in two years..." Dr. Bernard's hands flew up!

"Don't, don't tell my anymore! I've heard enough." He shook his head in disbelief and stared at me in awe.

"I'm a *man* and I couldn't have gone through what you've just told me. I *don't* see how you've made it this long! I noticed on your chart, you've seen a psychiatrist. Are you still seeing her?"

"No, not—since I've been sick."

"Well I suggest you start back immediately! Your problem is mental, not physical. There's nothing else we can do for you here."

"You mean they can't find out what's wrong with me? This is one of the best hospitals in Baltimore. It's also the fourth hospital plus several doctors I've consulted. I told the nurse yesterday that I wasn't going to leave until someone tells me why I'm so dizzy. I need help Dr. Bernard!"

"I'm sorry Ms. Winters but we can not keep you if you don't have any physical problems."

"So you'll discharge me? Just like *that*. Suppose I have an accident on the way home?"

"I don't think that'll happen. As soon as you get home tomorrow make an appointment to see your doctor. Until you see your doctor, get as much rest as you can."

"Rest, that's all I get, is rest. I'm an active person. I'm not used to lying in bed all day and night too! It's depressing not knowing why I'm so dizzy and not getting any better."

He bid his farewells and left. So did I the following day. The weary drive home, the dizziness and jump from bed rest to driving on a hectic highway was overwhelming! I whizzed past God's magnificent miles of peaceful landscapes; I soared with the trees as they opened their arms in gratitude for His abundant guardianship. Solace my dear feline, awaited my arrival. He'd disrupted several things in the house. Marty came by once and checked on Solace.

My comfort and recovery would be my responsibility. The need to control stress was ultimate. The necessity of saying *NO* was paramount to my recuperation and survival! Dedication in job duties, home and other multiple activities must be curtailed if I planned to reach the grand age of 100 plus!

The highlighted April moving date on my calendar, to the three-story co-op in Baltimore, became my priority. For years my calendar, my daily diary, recorded a confused woman's transient entangled life. A life so embroiled and knotted with threads of silk, wool, jute and cotton, all in search of that idyllic unrealistic happiness owned only by a few human souls.

52...SLOW, SLOW RECOVERY

The cure for the greatest part
of human miseries is not radical,
but palliative.
Samuel Johnson: The Rambler No. 32

Weeks of medication and rest produced a prolonged—drawn out gradual recovery. In time I ventured outside in my light blue and white jogging suit, braving cool February temperatures—attempting a first walk. Each hesitant wobbly step looked like a child's first endeavor to walk. The uneasy steps conquered the challenge to walk past two houses. Dizziness was ever present. I needed fresh air. I needed exercise and got neither lying on the Danish sofa in the den all day. Roy was worried I'd fall but I assured him whenever I felt unsure in my steps I'd return home. On his next visit I persuaded him to let me go to the market with him. He did, reluctantly. The joy of shopping in the supermarket again jogged my memory; I strolled slowly through the aisles while leaning on the basket for support. Each time I staggered, Roy reminded me of his presence.

"Oops, I almost fell." Laughing like a child who's just taking his first steps, I'd turn around for Roy's approval.

"Don't worry, I'm here. I would *never* let you fall, darling." I loved him sooo much.

We supported each other. Finally I felt loved and needed by someone. Roy had *not* allowed me to spend Christmas or New Years Eve alone. Our love was rich, sincere and simple. Neither of us required an abundance of materialism.

Each day I'd walk the same distance from the house. When I couldn't pass another house, I'd return home. This challenge of walking past another house continued until I'd walked the entire block. It took almost two weeks before

I walked around the entire housing development where only months prior I had *run* up and down those same streets and alleys with the ease and speed of a fawn.

Now my steps were slightly faster than a baby's. This slow pace allowed me to examine the tiny blossoms on various weeds I'd run past previously. The uniquely cracked sidewalks under foot and leafless trees on my left brightened the morning's stroll as I inhaled breakfast aromas from house to house: freshly perked coffee, sometimes bacon and sausage, eggs, home fries and occasionally pancakes or stewed apples, my favorite. These were meals I no longer prepared since I lived alone. Besides they were *too* fattening!

The *glorious* day arrived! I returned to work, Wednesday March 3, 1993. Yes it was time to return to my profession of releasing bottled up hidden artistic talents in children's minds. After months of monotonous repose, it was time I rejoined the human race. Yes, the race with drivers as they wove in and out of highway traffic in their man made mobile machines! I was ready, willing but not that able. The children I loved inspired my early return. They needed their art teacher, not a substitute. The first days were rough but as usual I survived and thrived on happy smiling faces with beaming eyes when they crossed the threshold and saw me!

Many small students hugged me around my legs while others tugged on my sweater or simply held my hand or laid their small heads on my arm, dress or just stared up into my surprised face! The smaller precious children clapped when I expressed my happiness in being back. They were as happy as I was joyful. Of course the main office staff and administrative staff exhibited their mirth in, "We're *so* glad you're back! Thank *God* you're back! *Finally* you're back! Those kids have *really* missed you! *Please* don't stay out that long again!"

Since I taught each class only twice a month, if a class missed their art period because of testing, assembly programs or another mishap, some classroom teachers weren't aware I was out or even sick! The main office deemed it unnecessary to post notice of my illness. Many teachers *never* knew I was home sick—for months!

I received a Get Well card from the Hospitality Committee at each school. Since I wasn't an official faculty member of either school or a part of their school functions no one thought it necessary to send flowers or a fruit basket. However, my many decorated bulletin boards, huge stage banners and numerous school activities were forgotten—as usual. I was considered a part of their staff *only* when it came to creativity, a position I never understood.

On April 5, 1993, I appeared in the judge's office for my divorce hearing from Lenard. Since this was my fifth divorce, I was well apprised of the procedures. Never proud of having been married so often, I still defended the termination of each marriage. The wedding vows never said I had to be a *doormat* for any man. I knew with all the men on this earth there had to be at least *one* for me! Nevertheless I'd made bad choices in my selection of husbands. Why? I had not waited on the Lord. Mama used to say:

"Dawn, a man hasn't been born *yet* to satisfy you!"

Mama failed to remember that I didn't want to be satisfied, but to be justified in deserved respect from a husband. She didn't understand wives were a husband's pacifier, sympathizer, supporter, sustainer, a shoulder to cry on, a consoler and a friend. She couldn't be any of those comforts to her husband if he *cursed* her, *beat* her, *screamed* at her, *committed adultery, insulted* her in public, threatened to *kill* her or *demeaned* her in front of family. For better or worse did *not* include being mistreated and humiliated by her husband who stood before God and promised as the minister read him one of these vows:

Version I

"You now take this woman, whose hand you hold, to be your lawful wedded wife. Do you solemnly promise, before God and these witnesses, that you will love, honor, and cherish her; and that, forsaking all others for her alone, you will faithfully perform to her all the duties which a husband owes to a wife, so long as you both shall live?"

Version II

"Do you,_____take,_____,whom you now hold by the hand, as your true and lawful Wife; and, God helping you, will you love, cherish, honor, and protect her, cleaving only and ever unto her, until God by death shall separate you?"

Version III

"Do you take the lady whom you now hold by the hand, to be your lawful and wedded wife?

Do you promise to love and cherish her, in sickness and in health, for richer for poorer, for better for worse, and forsaking all others keep thee only unto her, so long as you both shall live?"

A Mutual Promise

"You mutually promise in the presence of God, and of these witnesses, that you will at all times and in all circumstances, conduct yourselves toward one another as becometh Husband and Wife?"

The Promise didn't say *sometimes* or *when you felt like it* but at *all* times and under *all* circumstances; not only in public but at home as well, behind those *locked* doors. *God sees* everything! *God knows* everything!

I wondered why married couples didn't renew their vows annually; renewing the radiant love that flowered initially? If so then pledged promises at the altar would be awakened and not forsaken so easily. I'd noticed married couples attending wedding ceremonies often smiled at each other, while the minister repeated the marriage vows. Of course I've seen others whose solemn sad expressions evidenced unhappiness. In several of my marriages the vows were *forgotten* that *week* or that *month!*

Yes, I too was guilty. Guilty of dating men who were unyoked, not Christians; who didn't attend church as they said; guilty of needing a man to shower me with lots of love and sex, which I confused as love. I was guilty as charged! Guilty of not marrying a devout Christian, someone with moral values; someone to build me up and not *drag* me through the horrors of hell!

My son Bryan floated from town to town. Drugs had him hooked! He had no problem getting a job, but *keeping* it was his major problem. At each job interview his vast business knowledge always impressed the employers. After a month or so the cycle of taking off those three crucial weekend days resurfaced time after time. Stella, his new girlfriend, also an addict, helped to exacerbate his usage. She, a beautiful young woman with a teenage daughter, also allowed drugs to control and ruin her life.

I first met Stella the previous summer when all four granddaughters had visited me in Essex. She and Bryan had come to get his daughters Briana and Nadia, to carry them back for a two-week visit with him before their school opened. Knowledge of her addiction was unknown to me then.

Eventually Bryan *moved* to Fayetteville and to another pizza company. His intention to flee from Stella whom he still loved, and get a fresh start, failed. He wanted to live alone. I persuaded Ms. Redmond to let Bryan rent her furnished vacant home, the home which she'd raised her five children. Since her husband's death, she'd remarried and moved to her new husband's gorgeous custom built spacious home.

Stella's life threatening crisis persuaded Bryan to send for her. A *big* mistake! Soon violent bouts erupted between them. Terry, Ms. Redmond's older son, called me regarding their neighbor's complaints. Stella had been seen outside, running around the house in her slip. On another occasion she'd gone next door to call the police because they didn't have a phone. They were asked to move! He moved to Virginia. Two weeks later Ms. Redmond called.

"Dawn, this is Aunt Miriam. I guess you're surprised to hear from me. I called because I have two bills that Bryan has not paid. When he left he owed me close to $200 between rent and utilities. He promised he'd mail the money but I haven't heard from him." I listened as she explained her financial situation. Her problem was the same one I'd dealt with for

The obligation was mine since I was the one who'd asked. I mailed the $200. She'd helped Bryan and allowed him to live in her lovely home. Once again I got stuck paying *his* bills. My heart directed my thoughts while my brain vacationed tired of making unnecessary decisions for Bryan! That mother/son bond dug deep into my wallet because of his twisted reasoning. He knew the right buttons to push that made me jump!

My newly renovated detached co-op was scheduled for completion the latter part of May. All week I packed boxes between appointments to see Dr. Romley or Amy Smothers my therapist. Both music and karate classes were held on Wednesday. Friday was the second day for karate. The co-op office changed the settlement date *twice*. Saturday, May 22nd I made the official move to the lovely house on Manor Street. Going to work every morning with a car packed with clothes, lamps, pictures etc., lowered the moving cost. After I moved I returned to Essex three more times and crammed the car to its capacity *without* any help—as usual. The Banner Homes issued parking permits to each homeowner. This allowed its residents to have a space near their homes plus it kept outsiders from parking in the neighborhood. Permits were placed inside, on the dashboards.

Our homes were located downtown near the Fells Point area, a well-known historic section of Baltimore. Tourists, city employees and neighbors benefited from parking on our charming treed streets. Why? They were just blocks away; walking distance from the waterfront, nightclubs, pubs, outdoor restaurants, art galleries, markets, marina and theatres: where plays, musicals and workshops were held. The open-air market was my favorite spot in addition to a well-known fabric and knick-knack store where I'd spent thousands of dollars in drapery fabrics for my customers in years past.

Banks, senior citizen organizations and several thrift shops that sold everything from plastic forks to furniture lined the streets. Apartments were located over many stores. So finding a parking space was a *premium*, especially on weekends. My search resembled trying to squeeze a *big* foot into a size five shoe. Often I walked the several scenic blocks rather than waste gas circling and waiting for someone to back out.

Tuesday night was *exhausting*! Three weeks of packing; moving on Saturday had depleted my energy! My eyeballs throbbed; my overworked body endured the pain determined to fight its rebellious nature to retreat. After midnight my car, packed in every possible corner, backed out of the driveway and headed toward home, my new home. I prayed for strength and for a parking space close to the house. It was past one a.m. By that time all resident cars were already parked. As I drove down Manor Street and approached the house I spied a parking space across the street in *front* of my home! I beamed! God had answered another prayer. He'd *provided* a parking space. He also gave me strength to unpack. I spread everything around in the living and dining rooms and kitchen. I'd been forewarned *not* to leave anything valuable in my car. Items left overnight *would* be stolen.

Thursday afternoon I returned to Essex and retrieved the last carload of leftovers and finished cleaning. Every house or apartment I rented was *always* left clean. Once again I arrived at my new home after *one a.m.* I crept down Manor Street and prayed for another parking space in front of my house.

Jesus says, *"You have not because you ask not. Anything you ask in my name will be given."* Yes He *heard* me! *Right in front* of my *door* under the huge oak tree was *another* parking space! I parked the car then sat a few minutes and thanked God over and over again! He knew what I needed and *He provided* my need! In my weariness He lifted my spirits and guided me home to park in front of my *own* door. Once again I unpacked *everything*. Too tired to climb those peach carpeted steps to my third floor bedroom, my haggard worn out body reached the second floor den; flopped down on top of blankets and clothes spread across the blue Danish sofa and slept all night in my clothes. I'll *never* forget those three draining days!

Friday's school dismissal inched closer and closer. I missed karate class and drove right home from school. Five to seven minutes away from school was *great* compared to that forty-five minutes to an hour drive twice daily!

I recall that wonderful day of settlement! The moment Mr. Skinner handed me the key; the excitement I experienced receiving the key to my newly renovated detached home!

"I'm finally here Mr. Skinner. No more running back and forth to Essex." I said.

"I hope you find everything in order Ms. Winters. If not, just call us and we'll send someone down there to correct the problem immediately." He meant every word.

Mr. Skinner, a very proud young man in his thirties, about 5'9" of average build, dressed impeccably. He appeared afraid to let down his guard unless he might collapse. He stayed to himself. He constantly pushed his eyeglasses up on his nose but they insisted on sliding down. His secretary, Mrs. Mason was just the opposite: sweet, caring, humorous and relaxed. What a combination they were. Her warmth soothed his cool persona.

With key in hand and feet in motion I walked the short distance down the hill to the house rather than drive, so eager to see the final results. The unique quaint neighborhood resembled Georgetown in Washington D.C.

I'd check the workmen's progress on my lunch hours. Each visit increased my excitement. The transformation of the house was like *This Old House* on TV. In two months the interior was almost new. It served my purpose *well*. Now I had sufficient room for all of my junk!

I put the key in the door and opened it slowly. The Bible held in my hands was extended before me as I stepped on the small linoleum foyer. This was truly God's house. I was only a resident passing through. The long awaited peach carpet covered all the rooms except the kitchen and bath areas. Off white painted walls welcomed me as I closed the door and knelt down on the floor with my Bible. I kissed the carpet and thanked God for my newly renovated home. My feet moved slowly to the kitchen with its new cabinets, stove, refrigerator and linoleum. I ascended the peach carpeted staircase to the second floor with two bedrooms and bathroom just waiting on a new sink. Soft blue tiles over the bathtub matched the blue commode with a window above.

As my heart raced so did I, up the steps to my bedroom on the third floor. The huge bedroom had enough space at one end next to the closets to put the drafting table and any art supplies—my art corner. Three wide windows spanned the front of the house; a perfect spot for the brass bed. The old house was my new home!

June 15th was our last day of school, while my piano recital was that Saturday, June 19th. Mr. and Mrs. Wilson and Roy attended the recital, held in the huge choir room where I also had my weekly lessons with Mr. Zanick. Risers extended high to the back windows. The baby grand and the console were placed next to each other. Each student had to play a duet with our teacher or with another student. When I approached the piano I refused to look at the audience until I'd completed my two selections. I thanked God I'd played well without any noticeable mistakes.

My four granddaughters returned in July, just in time for another birthday party for Briana on July 21st. The yellow umbrella hovered over the round wooden picnic table covered with its yellow vinyl tablecloth to match. The girls played games and various relay races on the grass. Bright colored birthday party hats, gifts, plenty of junk food plus ice cream and birthday cake covered the picnic table. Pictures taken that day captured their falls on the grass and rotating movements, laughter and winning moments. What a marvelous day it was; so *much fun* and excitement. Later Bryan took a picture of us posed in the living room. Sheer white tablecloths covered each person's attire of shorts and shirts. The five of us stood in front of a large green plant flanked by the piano and dining room table on either side.

Also that summer my older son Marty and his girlfriend, Michele rented a house and moved in together, she carried his child. The day after they moved in, the girls and I bought food for the family and visited them. It was in the same development where a friend of mine lived years earlier. *Neither* room had furniture. In one room I saw a mattress on the floor with a sheet and blanket for the children; all *five* slept together. Michele and Marty slept on a blanket spread over *stacked* pillows. I was *appalled!!!*

Since I'd eliminated most of my debt, I had excellent credit. So *free hearted me* opened an account in my name at a furniture store and bought them a bedroom suite, bunk beds and mattresses for her five children, including linens for all the beds plus towels and wash cloths. I refused to allow anyone to sleep on the floor and not help. I thought *Marty works too hard to be sleeping on the floor.* I approached them with a suggestion.

"Marty if I open an account in my name and buy everyone beds would you be able to pay the bill every month?"

He said, "What do you think the monthly payments might be?"

"Anywhere between, forty and fifty dollars."

"Okay, that sounds fine to me, what do you think Michele?"

"Yes we can make that payment. That's *noo* problem."

The furniture was delivered days later. They promised to make the $46 monthly payment. The next week I also bought a new $800 washer and dryer on my Sears account, my gift. In her condition, I didn't want Michele lugging clothes back and forth to the Laundromat. The following week I took her to Sears and bought them a kitchen set. I didn't have one myself. We both liked the new styled white and tan wooden kitchen table with inlaid white tiles on the tabletop. I put it on my American Express account, $700. With nothing in the living room to sit on but the kitchen chairs I asked Marty the following month about a soft cushioned turquoise sectional sofa and recliner set I'd seen advertised in the newspaper for $999. I didn't buy anything that I couldn't handle in case Marty became incapacitated in any way and couldn't work.

"Oh Mom, we can't afford that! Besides you've already done enough for us!"

"Marty didn't you tell me you were expecting a large sum of money in October or November?"

"Yes. But won't your American Express bill be due before that time? How will you pay it?"

We discussed the bill and due date in depth. After calculating, he realized the money *would* arrive in time to pay the bill. I ordered the furniture. Now I'd furnished their *entire* house, something *I did* all by my little self and *insisted on doing* and eventually *regretted!!!*

During that summer my granddaughters and I went to the beach several times. I'd stop at Marty's and pick up three of Michele's older children. What a glorious time we had, all eight of us! We swam and played in the sand together. I even made sand castles with the smaller ones while the others tired themselves out as the waves knocked them back to shore. What happiness I breathed to see my grandchildren all together learning and loving each other at that young impressionable age. What fun and festive unforgettable memories they'd shared! What a splendid summer! With childhood years so short, their reminiscences should be gratifying.

One day as I sat in the sand, building castles with Nadia, inhaling the morning's fresh air while cool breezes from dashing waves brushed my body, two of my sweet little girls in third grade spied me and ran over.

"Hi, Mrs. Winters, what are *you* doing out here!"

"The same reason you're out here, to swim and have fun with my family."

"Are these your grandchildren?" They asked.

"Yes they certainly are."

"But you're wearing a bathing suit. And I see your legs."

"Yes I am wearing a bathing suit. Do you like it?"

"Yes Ma'am I... like... it but you're a teacher. I didn't kn—ow teachers wore ba—thing suits at the beach."

"Everybody else is wearing a bathing suit, why can't I wear one?"

"I know all that but you're a teacher." That child was sincere. I was amazed at her reaction to me wearing a bathing suit at the beach.

"You mean teachers aren't human? Can't we have fun like everyone else?"

"No ma'am I didn't mean it like that." She did.

"Well why don't you and Cathy sit down and help me build this sand castle?"

"We were hoping you'd ask us. Do you have any food?" As usual, Tamika was outspoken.

"Yes I did but my grandchildren have eaten everything. I think I might have some extra cookies. Would you like a few cookies?"

"Oh! Yes ma'am we sure would. We ate up all our food long time ago and now we're hungry agin."

Hungry, they ate ravenously! The fresh air and water had done its job. Children from a rough neighborhood, they were my well-mannered courteous sweethearts. They reminded me of the few times Mama and Daddy had taken Sister and me to Coney Island during my young years.

Tamika and Montrey were always obedient students. They belonged to a summer camp that provided bag lunches for the children. Many children brought extra food but Montrey and Tamika had none. I took pictures of them swimming and playing in the sand by themselves and with my grandchildren. At my request and using my camera, a lady took pictures of our entire group including the two campers. What a splashing exhilarating day!

Before my grandchildren returned at the end of the summer to their separate homes I bought everyone including Michele's children a gift from Sears on my account. I allowed each child to select something he or she desired. Out of nine children there was only *one* boy, Theo! He was the *little prince*. The bill was high, but who cared? I'd made children's faces beam! There was nothing like the smiling face of a precious child, especially one in need; and all of those were quite needy!

School started. My happiness ended. I'd gone in two weeks early as usual to prepare the art rooms and hall bulletin boards in both schools. I made my own class schedules. Art resource teachers taught on an A-Day, B-Day schedule. Each class came twice a month every other week. I taught *every* child in the building.

When my 2nd graders entered the classroom, most of them took the same seats they'd had the previous two years. I didn't mind. Two years prior they were my kindergarten babies. But, *now* they'd grown so tall, a few, I didn't recognize. Rarely did I encounter any major problems from my K-3 graders because I'd been their *only* art teacher. Not so with many other students since they had difficulty adjusting to my classroom rules and civilized standards. I demanded their respect and undivided attention. Every time I transferred to a new school I inherited another teacher's problems, substandard qualities and expectations.

As I watched the eager faces seated before me I recalled the two years prior when I first arrived at the elementary school and met my principal.

"Mrs. Winters we're really happy to have you here. I know this is your first time teaching elementary but I feel you'll make the adjustment as I did and learn to love this level. I've been here five years and never want to return to secondary. Your secondary supervisor recommended you highly. Have you had a chance to meet your new elementary supervisor?"

"No, I haven't. I'll meet with her later on today in her office."

He knew my displeasure of change and sympathized. Disgust etched in my face, I tried hard to absorb what he said. Lack of interest drizzled through our conversation. As he talked, I stared. I gazed into his gorgeous eyes that picked up the tan in his white and pinstriped shirt. The necktie complemented his smooth tan complexion. He was kind and handsome; an easy paced, understanding human being I could work with in peace. On the wall was a picture of his wife and family and a larger one of his daughter seated on a horse.

"I see your daughter likes horses."

"Like, she *loves* horses! She'd rather *ride* than eat!"

"How long has she been riding Mr. Peterson?"

"Since she was ten. She's won several ribbons in competitions in the last six years." I watched his face brighten as he discussed his daughter's first love and how expensive it had been those past years.

He continued, "I understand you're a firm disciplinarian Ms. Winters; that's *exactly* what these students need. In the last six years they've had *six* different art teachers."

"*Six*! You mean they've had a new art teacher every year for the past six years?"

"Yes that's right, six. I hope you'll stay here because they need stability in that art room."

"Why so many teachers?"

"Various reasons. One teacher became pregnant, another one decided teaching wasn't for him, three were transferred to other schools and one moved to another state."

"Well Mr. Peterson I hope this is my last move. I'm tired of hauling my visuals from school to school every two years. You're familiar with the city's policy: the last teacher on board is the first one to be transferred when they make teacher cuts. And of course the teachers of art, music, foreign language, home economics go first. I'm so disgusted with this school system. They have no feelings for their teachers. They treat us like we're robots!"

"What happened that you got on this circuit, Mrs. Winters?" I explained my dilemma as briefly as I could.

"When I taught at Lakeview High School, my husband decided he wanted me home. Since I made draperies part time I decided to leave the system and open a shop in my garage. Two weeks after school ended and I'd already submitted my resignation, my husband started to complain. So—I rescinded my resignation and hand carried it to the personnel office. It was never received. After school opened, I had no teaching position. Two days later I stood in that long line of teachers at 25th Street and was assigned to a junior high school. I stayed there five years and then left on disability. After two years I returned and was placed at a middle school. Ever since then I've been bounced from school to school whenever there were teacher cuts."

"Well, I hope you like it here because we need someone as badly as you need a permanent school."

Most of the students were courteous and did marvelous work. Creativity burst from their small hands and their energized minds. But working two years with some rude malicious special educational children and Ramone's former students had taken its toll on me. I needed another rest!!

I thought, "This will be a great year. I've taught three of the classes starting this year from kindergarten. They understand me, and know my expectations. Besides this is the last year for Ramone's *former students*. They will be promoted to middle school in June! *Wrong again.*

When I first arrived at the school, Ramone's students were fourth graders. That year they'd be sixth graders. Not young sixth graders but *overgrown* sixth graders. Some had failed twice and were trying for their third. When they strolled into my classroom, that first day, some boys bopped in, others dragged along, while others brushed by me as though I weren't there. Two-thirds of the class was okay. One rebellious child could ruin a class but this class had many. The class's negative events required only a leader.

My Monday students were respectful and smarter. Apart from climbing three flights of steps, some cold mornings, no sink and water in the classroom, the school wasn't so bad. The students' kindness and excellent work overcame the building's physical defects.

With Ramone's bad students and the problem children in special education, I felt like screaming! Toward the end of September, I resented going to work!

I felt humiliated when students said, "Don't touch me!"

"Why are you looking at me like you're crazy!"

"I ain't goin' no where and *you can't make me!*"

"Shut up you white b—— or half-breed b——!"

"I'll *punch* you in your face!"

"I'll get my Mama down here and beat your a—!"

"She called me black!"

"Ms. Winters Randy's shaking his thing at me!" (Randy was an exhibitionist in a special education class.)

"I ain't leaving this room and whatcha gonna do about it anyway!"

I'd heard this type of language and worse over twenty-eight years; my breaking point had arrived. My nerves erupted one afternoon when a male student stood at my door.

He yelled, "Ernest, come on to practice! We started already!"

I moved toward the door, "Dupont stop yelling in my classroom. If you want to see Ernest you must get my permission. Do you have a pass from your teacher?"

"I wasn't *talkin'* to you. *I was talkin' to Ernest!*"

"Do you have a pass?" I said.

"*No!* I ain't got *no* note! Ernest, come on. *Why* you still *sittin'* there man!"

I stood in my doorway as Dupont yelled past me into the classroom. Appalled, I couldn't believe that boy had the nerve to yell at me! I was one minute from grabbing him. I knew what his problem was and so did he.

"Dupont, Ernest isn't going anywhere unless he has a note from a teacher.

Go back and get a written pass."

"You *betta'* let Ernest go right now or I'll come in there and *punch* you in your face! *You always in somebody's business you b——!*"

That sixth grade class was Ramone's *former* students. Had he not instilled such hatred for me and my subject they'd never acted that way. No other class did.

I rushed out of my classroom, past Dupont who stood in the hall still yelling foul language at me! At the end of our short corridor, I turned and headed for the main office where I saw our principal standing in the hall. He stopped his conversation with the student when he saw me in a state of turmoil. I explained what happened as I trembled in anger. Other adults standing in the hall had witnessed Dupont's bad behavior and confirmed my statements.

I was *furious* with that boy! In all my years of teaching I'd *never* had a student threaten me to that extent! Mr. Peterson said he'd heard Dupont's outburst as he talked to the student in the hall. He said he'd handle it. He took Dupont to his office and I returned to my classroom.

Minutes later I escorted the same class to the auditorium to see the Student Counsel's office elections for that school year. After my class settled and all of their books, were on the floor under their seats, I sat in a seat at the end of the center aisle. When I looked toward the stage, I couldn't *believe* what I saw. My head strained forward to confirm what I *thought*—I saw.

Yes! My vision wasn't impaired. Seated on the stage and running for an office in the Student Counsel was *Dupont*. Yes, the same Dupont that had just cursed me and threatened me at my door. *Shocked, disgusted and overwhelmed with disbelief,* I rose from my seat and walked up the aisle toward the back of the auditorium where Mr. Peterson stood by the opened door.

"Excuse me Mr. Peterson, I like to know why Dupont is seated on that stage?"

"Oh, he's running for the vice president of the Student Counsel." He spoke in an unassuming manner as though nothing had occurred just minutes prior.

"Yes, one of his classmates told me but I didn't believe it. I couldn't believe you still allowed him to run for an office after the way he yelled and cursed me just minutes ago? I thought those offices were for students with *good* behavior. Dupont's behavior is *awful!*"

"I've taken care of that problem already," he said.

Obviously my principal accepted Dupont's bad behavior as appropriate to run for that Student Counsel's office.

"But Mr. Peterson you mean after his horrendous behavior he's still allowed to run for an office of honor and respect?"

"Well, Mrs. Winters this program was already planned before any of those problems happened a few minutes ago."

Was he deaf; had his brain collapsed? Had I misunderstood what he'd just said to me?

"Mr. Peterson, his classmates heard everything he said to me. Now that they see him seated on the stage, they'll think it's alright to curse and threaten a teacher and still run for a school office."

"All of these activities were planned before today Mrs. Winters."

He had no intention of punishing that obnoxious boy. I thanked him, returned to my seat, humiliated, demeaned and dishonored! Tears filled my eyes. They struggled to pour out. I yearned to cry out *what is wrong with this school system!!*

Offended with the situation, helpless, powerless and unprotected, I rose again and *walked out* that distorted sick environment. As I moved down the hall slowly toward the teacher's lavatory, hot tears rolled down my face. The hall was empty. So was I!! After crying in the lady's room I regained my composure and started down the hall again. This time I met Ms. Kenny the master teacher. She stood in the hall next to her office door.

"What's the matter Mrs. Winters?"

Before I answered her question, tears burst out as I rushed into her office! I explained what had happened. She understood; but she and the principal were *tight*! It was her job to relate *everything* to him. She acted as supervisor to all the teachers in the building. As I proceeded toward my classroom I met Mrs. Clemons the assistant principal. I asked to talk to her privately. We went inside her office.

"Mrs. Clemons will you get someone to watch my last period class? I can't teach anymore today." I explained my problems.

She witnessed my perturbed emotions but her *lack* of concern was obvious. My infamous day ended! The shameful vile conduct displayed by disrespectful students and the unconcerned administrators overpowered my thoughts as I drove home. Tears streamed down my face. Minutes from the old dismal building, I parked under the aged oak in front of my red historic front door, went inside and continued my *pity party.*

Monday after school I called several offices in the school system concerning what happened. They *agreed* with me but again there was nothing they could do.

Finally I called the school's superintendent, explained my concerns and then asked the big question.

"Dr. Dramer, do you have any other positions available I might switch to? I simply can't teach anymore." Desperation drowned my words. Even I had difficulty understanding myself. My soul screamed, for mental relief, from daily strenuous encounters of verbal humiliating attacks.

"Mrs. Winters, a thousand teachers ask me the same question everyday," he said.

"It's not that I don't want to teach. The fact is I *do* want to teach but can't teach because of bad students."

"Now Mrs. Winters, you know how I feel about our students. We don't have *bad* students. We have students who *do* bad things."

My mouth opened to scream! But instead, I covered it with my left hand! Was this man crazy? Did he realize what he'd just said?

"Thank you, Dr. Dramer for listening to my problems. You have a good remainder of the day. Good-bye."

That instant I made up my mind. To save my sanity, I had to *quit*, retire on disability. If I didn't leave I'd hit someone's insolent child. I'd been teaching twenty-eight years. It should have been thirty years but I was on disability two years prior for the same problem. My nerves were shot! I couldn't work any more, anywhere for any one! My working days were over if I planned to remain *alive.*

That Monday I informed my new principal Mrs. Ackerman, I was sick and would not be back. Her eyes bulged! She voiced low uncaring utterances that I shunned.

"Maybe if you took a few days off you'd feel better."

"No, I did that last year when I struggled with severe dizziness. Stress in teaching caused my illness. My mind can't handle any more stress. I'll start taking my visuals and supplies home today, and return after school during the week and get the rest."

She stood stunned while the sense of relief zoomed through my body! I'd taken the *first* step! Tuesday would start the second. I told no one at the other school my plans. At the end of every *hard* day, I carried home my visuals, pictures, books and other articles I'd used for my students to draw. I never allowed them to *copy* from books. They learned to draw from what *they* saw; not to copy what *someone else* had drawn.

The devil was busy. Everything happened that week that could happen. It was only October the second month of school, but I knew I couldn't last another week! I'd either have a stroke, heart attack or be committed to a mental institution!

In one obedient class as I stood next to a boy correcting his lettering, I patted his shoulder with my left hand encouraging him, while my right hand pointed to areas of his work that needed improvement.

"Charles don't worry, it takes time and lots of practice to learn how to use a lettering pen." He jerked his head around, as his satanic eyes rolled at me!

"*Take* your *hand* off my shoulder!"

His brutish face exposed his inner spirit! I removed my hand slowly as the class focused their attention on his wicked outburst and my reaction. Still in shock at his attack on my character, I helped the next student who *was* grateful to be corrected and smiled after he understood how to correct his mistakes.

Thanking God I only had a few days left, I entered the building the following day knowing, I'd *soon* be free. Free to live in peace at least for a while. When I corrected a girl that afternoon, she tossed her head high in the air.

She said, "I don't have to listen to you! I don't listen to my mother so why do I have to do what you tell me to do...!"

She strutted across the room, threw her art project in the trashcan then returned to her seat. Her disrespect only deepened my wounds enhancing the need to leave school before I *hit* somebody's rude child! My clenched hands held behind my back tightened as I gave her an assignment from our text book. No need to send her to the office, nothing would be accomplished except wasting my time by writing a useless note.

Students thought we were robots without any feelings. We were human beings. Blood ran through our veins. We had hearts, minds and feelings just as they did. As I thought, I realized, I'd forgotten about the neighborhood in which I was teaching. These poor children *had to fight* to survive. They were exposed to wickedness, depravity, poverty and every sinful deed and act of violence that mankind had initiated. I understood, but after twenty-eight years I *couldn't* take anymore!! I'd had enough of taking students out into the hall and discussing their problems while other students needed my help. In trying to save the world I was killing myself!

Thursday afternoon I carried home my last large bundle of materials. The few minor possessions that remained would be taken home the next day, *my last day!* Everyday that week I prayed, "Dear God, please forgive me for leaving. You blessed me with these artistic talents to help others but I simply *can't* work anymore! I can't take anymore verbal abuse and disrespect from children, parents and inconsiderate staff.

For years I'd taught my students how to enjoy the everyday beauty that God had given us. They understood everything man-made was an art form, not only drawing, painting, sculpture and ceramics. But also architecture, interior design in homes and buildings, furniture design, clothing, jewelry, shoes, automobiles, boats, toys, cooking and eating utensils, package design, book covers, greeting cards, school supplies! The list was endless. It hurt to know most students and parents cared very little about art.

Everyday that ended closed another day in my teaching career. As Friday grew closer I prayed for His guidance and support.

"God please help me get through this week! Please give me the strength to endure what's thrown my way. I know I can depend on you! Remove me from this *jungle* before I go absolutely insane!"

All day *Friday*, I worked and prayed for strength to get through *that* day. Ramone's former students arrived after lunch. I stood at the end of a table attempting to teach my lesson. As I talked, the students who sat at the same table refused to stop talking. They whispered across the table right in front of me. I shook my head and walked to another table. I refused to allow them to get the better of me! My nerves were shot! My rattled mind and body trembled as I watched them. My hands flew into the air and I screamed!

"Shut up! Shut up that noise! Don't you have any manners *at all!* You see I'm trying to get my class started and some of you will *not stop talking! What's the matter with you!"*

I turned, walked out my classroom diagonally across the hall and asked the school psychologist, Mrs. Fineman to watch my class until the bell rang. My nerves were shot! I'd *screamed* at those children, as I never had before in my teaching career! I knew that loudness had damaged my brain, at *least* the part that remained.

No one knew it was my last day, I did!

No one knew I'd spent my life being a firm disciplinarian, only to end up damaging myself internally and mentally, I did!

No one knew I'd *eat grass, concrete, tar, tree bark, or leaves* before I'd teach in another Baltimore City Public School to be *humiliated, demeaned* and taken for granted by some teachers and administrative staff. But *I did!!!*

The next class was my last for the day and *forever*! The middle of October and this was the *first* time they had reported to art. That fine intelligent group of students was the school's best! The system thought other activities were more important than art. How sad our school systems had such low regard for art since past artists had recorded our *world's history.* The system denied children the right to record contemporary events and express in creative ways their feelings and emotions.

Those well-behaved children were eager to learn. Since I taught each class only twice a month it was difficult for some students to retain what they'd learned weeks earlier. There was nothing I could do about class scheduling or our system's priorities.

I stood in front of the talkative students and managed to get most of them to pay attention while, Mrs. Fineman sat in the rear of the classroom at my request. She sat and listened. I sat in a chair at the front table and attempted to talk when suddenly my head dropped down on the table. At that precise moment Mr. Peterson walked into the classroom and placed his hand on my shoulder.

"What's wrong Mrs. Winters?"

"It's my head again. I am *sooo* dizzy."

"Have you taken your medicine?" He said.

"Yes. But it hasn't helped."

He assured me I'd improve later but I knew better. The students' silent sympathetic stares warmed my heart. Why couldn't my other classes have been as cooperative? The guilt of leaving my students pained deeply. However I knew my working days were over. The bulletin boards remain decorated and lesson plans stayed on my desk as I walked out that room forever!

During my short sorrowful drive home bitter thoughts of injustice flashed through my mind. My principal had offered me the opportunity to work there five days a week the following year since the two unused top floors would be used for the additional junior high students that would come from neighboring elementary and other junior high schools.

Had my principal not informed me, I'd *only be teaching junior high* I might have stayed. However, *never,* would I teach those *obnoxious students* from Mr. Ramone's, former class! They'd remain there throughout the seventh, eighth and ninth grades! I thought it's *not* fair to me or the good students that bad behavior must be tolerated. It's not *fair* that I must leave my job because bad students are allowed to remain in class and deny other students the right to obtain a well-rounded education! It's not right, it's *just not fair!!!*

53...SELF REVELATION, EXPOSÉ

'Tis the part of a wise man
to keep himself to-day for to-morrow,
and not venture all his eggs in one basket.
Miguel De Cervantes: Don Quixote

Confident I'd get retirement disability I made an appointment with our Baltimore Teacher's Union's president, Mrs. Fineman. Drenching rains only increased my misery as I drove uptown to the office. As I opened the building's main door I experienced a surge of calm. After Mrs. Fineman confirmed my appointment I was shown to her office. Seated behind the desk was an attractive lady. I introduced myself and had a seat. She'd taught school and was *well* acquainted with the mental pressures teachers endured. I'd explained my problem briefly on the telephone but she wanted more detail.

"I *know* you qualify for retirement disability Mrs. Winters but there's a *lot of paper work* involved and it may take several months. Are you financially able to wait that long?"

This former teacher understood my grief. Her large dark sympathetic eyes shared my sorrow. As warm tears flowed down my troubled face I answered slowly.

"Yes, I have enough sick days until the end of January."

"It might take longer than that Mrs. Winters but there is a sick bank that's available if you need it."

"That's good news Mrs. Fineman I might have to use it."

She explained the long drawn out process I'd have to follow. Positive thoughts lifted my spirits as I rushed toward my car that cold rainy wintry November morning. Meanwhile the same attorney handled my retirement disability who was filing for my social security disability.

Roy's wife's cancer had spread rapidly. She refused to take chemotherapy or radiation. By the time she relented it was too late. Weeks sped by without seeing Roy although he called daily. Working three jobs, recovering from recent surgery himself, taking his wife to various treatments had taken its physical and mental toll on him. It began to show.

"Oh Dawn, she's lost *so* much weight. I've walked in the bedroom and caught her examining her thin emaciated body in the full-length mirror. Her severe drop in weight from 150 lbs. to 95 lbs. has devastated her! Most of the time now, she spends in bed. No more card parties and dances. I have to give her daughter credit; she does a wonderful job of caring for her mother. Many nights I've come home from work and found her sitting in the lounge chair next to the bed, fully dressed and sound asleep waiting to administer the morphine as her mother's pain increases. I just *couldn't* do what she does. Watching someone die from cancer day after day is draining. I feel so helpless because there's nothing I can do to *stop* the pain and the problem."

"Don't feel guilty. You're blessed. Her daughter and mother care for her while you work and don't have to pay a nurse everyday."

"I realize that but the mental strain is still there. She stopped loving me *years* ago. I soon realized I was *only* her meal ticket to America, and her family. We have not had sex for over two years. Even though we'd gone our different ways, and slept in the same bed, I still feel sorry for her in all that pain. All that misery could have been avoided had she listened to her doctor and taken the treatments."

"Roy, remember determined stubborn people always reap what they sow."

Ironically Roy's wife and Lenard's mother, still my mother-in-law, died on the same day, January 1st. I attended Lenard's mother's funeral. The family and I were happy to see each other. Her death hit Lenard hard even though their personalities clashed when they drank.

The end of January Roy received the insurance check. He paid $10,000 for the funeral, doctors bills not covered by his medical insurance and gave his sister, his mother-in-law and daughter-in-law $10,000 each. He also sent several thousand to her other family members and paid off some of my bills including my car and piano. For my birthday he bought me an engagement ring. This *generous man* had given all of his money away. Months later I learned he only had $2500 left in his checking account.

One cool February afternoon Bryan called speaking in his usual sad solemn tone, when he'd done something stupid. I listened but wasn't surprised at what I heard.

"Mommy I need your help."

"What's wrong now Bryan?"

"Stella and I had a fight. A real bad brawl! She ended up hitting me in the head with a baseball bat."

"And what did you do to provoke her Bryan? Remember—I know you."

"I know you do Mommy. I was hitting her with my belt. We were all drinking and she started that stuff about me not having anywhere to live and not keeping a job, and I got mad, so we started fighting. You know how Stella is," he said.

"Yes, I also know how you are. I've told you to keep your hands off your girlfriends."

"I know that but she made me mad and now I'm in jail because of her."

"No. You're in jail because of your drinking, drugs and associating with the wrong people. But those have always been the kind of people you like."

"Not really. I really need your help Mommy."

"How much this time?"

"$250. A friend of mine will stand the bond but he doesn't have the bail bond money."

"*$250!* What do you think I am—your bank!"

"No. But you're the only one left that can help me."

I listened as my son explained his dilemma; words from an ongoing record that played on and on and on refusing to stop! I wondered how long I'd continue to say yes, until I learned to say *NO!*

"Give me the guy's name and address Bryan. I'll wire the money tomorrow."

"Thank you Mommy, *thank you!* I knew I could depend on you."

"Well my dear this is the *last* time I'm sending you any money to get out of jail. From now on you're on your own! The next time you get *in* jail you get *yourself out*! I'm not working now and I just received my last payroll check. I know it's foolish to ask you when I will get my money since I've never gotten any of the prior *$100,000* you owe me."

"Well just add it to my bill and when I get rich you'll get it all plus more," he said.

"Yes dear. I've heard those same words for years."

The following day I wired the money to his friend in Waynesboro. Bryan had been living with Stella in her sister's house but now he rented a room with

356

a lady who worked at the pizza business, where he was employed. At the end of the month I received another call from my son.

"Hi Mommy, it's your son. I need to get out of Waynesboro. That's the only way I'm going to kick these drugs. I love Stella but we're not good for each other. She uses drugs as much as I do. Please say you'll let me stay with you for a while until I'm able to get a place of my own?"

Well, another bombshell! Stampede I should say. I sold my house to keep my sons from living with me. Now one of them wanted to return since I had *another* house. What was I to say, "No way, stay out there on your own or yes you may stay for a while?"

"Bryan I don't have any money for your bus ticket however if you get here you may stay with me for a *short while.*"

I *was* his *mother*. How could I say no? He was a sick, suffering, confused soul, hanging on to life by a string, a string that could snap—any moment. I refused to see my son fall and get lost between Satan's cracks. Only an inch away, he could drop deep down any day.

"I don't need any money. I'll borrow enough for a one way ticket to Baltimore. I'll arrive tomorrow afternoon at 3:20 at the bus station."

My wait in the bus station supplied sufficient time to meditate on various travelers in search of their diverse destinations. I recalled lyrics from a children's Christian song:

"Red and yellow, black and white
They are precious in his sight,
All the little children of the world."

I saw Native Americans, Asian Americans, Afro-Americans and White Americans seated or standing around in the bus station's waiting room. The passengers talk among themselves, played with their children, read magazines or newspapers, while they waited. To help pass time, some travelers slept until their bus arrived, to be carried to their destinations not by horse, bicycle, rickshaw, car or limousine but by a Greyhound Bus that seated forty or more passengers.

Those passengers of mixed races sat anywhere they pleased on that bus. And why, because they were God's children made in His likeness and image! Too bad mankind could not delight in the variety of skin tones given us to enjoy just like the animals, birds, fish, flowers, trees etc. I thought we have such a short time to share love and kindness on this earth why is it so difficult?

I remembered reading that in 1830 the English had their *first* steam driven bus. In 1895 the Germans welcomed a powered gasoline engine bus that carried *eight* people. In 1922 America's first bus was released. Double-decked buses also existed in New York City and European Countries.

Bryan's bus arrived on time. I saw him stroll inside the opened doors, carrying a small white plastic bag. I thought *that must be his lunch.* We embraced. He kissed me on the cheek.

"Where's your luggage Bryan? Do we have to wait until it's removed from the bus?"

"No. Here it is right here?"

"Right where?"

"Right here in this white plastic bag." He held up the small white bag that held a few pieces of fruit, his toothbrush and a change of underwear.

"While I was in jail the landlord put all my stuff outside because he needed the room for someone else."

"Didn't he know where you were?"

"No. I didn't tell him. He'd been *so* good to me Mommy I was ashamed to tell him I was in jail for something dumb and stupid! I was only in there a week. I realize I should have told him though."

"Well come on. We'll stop by the thrift Shop. It's just a few blocks from my house."

"No, no Mommy! You've done enough for me by sending the money to get me out of jail and now letting me stay with you. I feel terrible about crawling back home to you again. My *life* is a *wreck*! I just can't seem to get it together."

"I've told you repeatedly what to do but you refuse to heed and follow what you know is true."

"Yes I know you have but I'm just not the Christian you are Mommy."

"Bryan I'm far from being perfect. But the thing I do that you don't, is turn to God when I'm in trouble and not to drugs or alcohol. If you continue this style of living you'll *die* real soon. No drug is more important than your *life* and your *two lovely daughters!*"

"I know; I know; that's why I came here to try and get myself together."

As usual Bryan got a job *right* away at another pizza business. This time it was in the heart of downtown Baltimore. This was his first time working downtown; just a few miles from where we lived. At first he rode the bus to work; then he bought a used bicycle. The bike was great until it rained! He'd get home late at night drenched! Finally he asked the *long*—anticipated question.

"Mommy would you co-sign for me to get a truck?" I knew I didn't hear what I thought I heard.

"I've been working for a month now and the weather is starting to change. That bicycle won't make it when the weather gets real cold not to mention the ice and snow."

"Do you *really* think I'll co-sign for another car for you and end up paying for it like I did the I-Roc?"

"Mommy, just go with me tomorrow and we'll talk to the sales lady. I'm sure she'll work something out."

After his constant nagging and begging I relented and took him against my will. I should have been *whipped!* Again my mother's heart overruled my intellect and any common sense I had left. Looking back I realize my brains took a sabbatical leave *every time* Bryan asked me to help him get a car. A smooth talker, Bryan seized my emotional side; my rational side slept though the entire conversation. I thanked God we weren't able to get it; my salary wasn't large enough for *two* car payments. My undefeated son searched the used car ads until he found a Toyota that suited his needs and definitely *his wallet.* He greeted me at the front door before I even stepped inside.

"Hi Mommy, would you have time to take me to see a used car? I called the dealership and they described the car in detail. It sounds like a great deal for the amount of money."

"You don't give up do you Bryan?"

"Nope! I guess I got that from you."

"I guess you did since I don't give up either."

We examined the $2700 Toyota. I signed the contract. Once again I was responsible for two cars. Every month Bryan handed me the monthly payment of $275 in cash. There were times he was reluctant in paying because his room and board was also due. The car payment/room and board left his hand hesitant while my extended hand accepted his cash eagerly. Since he worked, he paid room and board, a modest affordable amount, far less than he'd paid renting rooms when he'd lived in Richmond, Waynesboro, Fayetteville and Columbia.

A previous pizza employer needed a manager in another city two hours away. He called Bryan and asked him to consider the position. Bryan discussed his options with me. He wanted the position since the job paid more money however he'd travel two hours home on his days off to see Stella who'd moved to Baltimore fleeing her drug friends.

Stella lived with me a few days before she was hired as a waitress and rented a room at their motel. Employees paid a moderate fee. Bryan moved to his new job and shared his employer's apartment. My son could talk his way into *any* pizza business. With his skill, determination, gift for business gab, he *always, always* got a job!

His weekly trips back and forth to Baltimore soon took its toll on the aged Toyota. The exhausted car screamed for relief! It choked and coughed, and spilled oil. It pouted and rattled and refused to move. Bryan soon decreased his weekly visits to every other week. After one and a half months the foreseen happened sooner than I'd expected.

At two a.m. as Bryan was unlocking his car door a man rushed from the rear of the building, grabbed him around his neck from behind with one arm while a gun pushed into his back with the other hand. They stole the $4000 he had to be deposited and fled the scene! Bryan lay on the ground knocked out with a battered head and a bruised body. After he regained consciousness he managed to stumble back to the store, open the door and called the police!

He'd advised his manager several times to put the money in the safe. The manager still insisted that Bryan deposit it in the bank on his way home every night. Bryan surmised it was an inside job. Every night the cash never matched the receipts. Of course missing money taken by the inside and outside employees was deducted from *Bryan's* salary.

Disgusted with nightly stealing, the robbery, his injury plus the long distance from Baltimore he eventually returned home and got a job at *another* pizza business. Freezing temperatures, ice and snow had damaged the Toyota's body and Bryan's spirits even more. One night he borrowed my white Cadillac Deville to deliver pizzas. His car cried, *no more, no more!!*

The night it collapsed was one of the coldest nights that winter! The following day we managed to get it towed to a nearby repair shop. After three days of waiting, because many cars had been towed due to frigid temperatures, he was told it would cost $1000 to repair. I said okay and put it on my American Express Card, knowing I'd *never* get it back. Two days later they'd found all the parts they needed. Once inside the car, more trouble surfaced another $1000! Roy agreed. Again I put it on my American Express Card. $2000 in four days! Roy, Bryan and I went to pick up the car. We were greeted with additional surprising news.

"I'm afraid you'll still need that transmission. We've done everything we could to keep from replacing it, but it's just in bad condition."

"And how much would that be?"

"$1000."

"$1000! No way! I'm not spending another dollar on that car! I've already spent $2000 now you're asking for another $1000."

Roy and I left in my car while Bryan drove his half functioning Toyota. We fought snow, slush and ice piled high on side streets where city ploughs weren't able to reach. White fluffy flakes fell gently resting on homes, cars and streets. The accumulated gentle beauty always caused harsh traveling conditions. The admired whiteness eventually became dirty brown slush and mounds of packed muddy ice.

Rather than investing more money into the Toyota, Bryan suggested we check with Roy's nephew, an assistant manager in a Nissan dealership about getting a new car. We did. The Toyota barely made it to Jonathan's business. After discovering I had impeccable credit, Jonathan started the search for the *right car* and the right price. Only because of *Roy's* trust in Bryan did I agree to sign for another car. Of course Bryan would make the monthly payments. With a new car he could resume his job of delivering pizzas.

I preferred a small sedan rather than a sports car. Of course Bryan disagreed.

"Mommy why can't I have what I want since I'm the one that's has to pay for it?"

"Why? Your personality changes when you have a new sports car Bryan. You need a sensible car especially since you're delivering pizzas."

"I know how to deal with this situation. I've been in the pizza business a *long* time. I don't like those other cars. I think I should have what I want since I'm paying for it."

Roy and I excused ourselves went outside the building and discussed the feasibility of his reasoning. It appeared Bryan wasn't using drugs anymore. Since he was working, making his present car payments and rent on time we agreed to the sports car rather than the sedan. The new black Nissan 240 SX/SE left the parking lot driven by my son with his girl friend Stella seated by his side. Days later his attitude changed. Once again he washed his car but not mine. His excuse, "I didn't have time" was always his answer. He missed days of work, came home unbelievable hours and disrespected my home. He denied using drugs. I knew better.

His first car payment was due the end of the month. He stayed at Stella's most of the time where they both used drugs. The ultimate was unavoidable;

he lost another job. Jonathan offered him a position as a car salesman. Bryan attended one training session but never returned. Drugs had devoured his brain. The downward plunge into hell's inferno of addiction and self-annihilation consumed my son. I prayed *unceasingly*!

"Oh God *please* help Bryan. *Open* his eyes; *clear* his mind; *touch* his heart to feel the agony he's causing himself, his mother and his daughters! Make him understand the hideous state these drugs are claiming on the most precious sacred life you've given him!"

Angry, disgusted and bewildered I called Jonathan, explaining my situation.

"Jonathan, would you please help me, by picking up the car and driving it back to the dealership. Let it stay there until it's sold."

He guaranteed nothing but retrieving and returning it to the dealership. I had an extra key. Late that night I drove to the motel, anxious, frightened and cold. Now I had two car payments if it didn't sell. *Dumb, Dumb, Stupid, Me!*

Jonathan parked his car near Stella's room then walked to my car for the extra key, which he really didn't need. Why, Bryan had left the car door unlocked with his *keys* in the ignition! The fuel indicator pointed to, *empty!* I followed Jonathan to the closest gas station; then we drove to the dealership where he parked the Nissan close to the side of the building. As I drove back to his car we discussed my *serious* financial problem. I could *not* return the car. My only recourse was to sell it. We'd traded the Toyota with a balance due. I felt like *screaming*! Within *one* month before the first car payment was due I'd retrieved the car and returned it to the dealership, temporarily.

Memories of the multiple problems I'd had with the I-ROC resurfaced: wasted money, agonizing pain, friends who'd help me rise up to conquer each harsh hurdle. Was I to experience those same problems again? Less than a month, I was stuck with a new car and another car payment. Only this time, the payment was more, $405, since the Toyota's balance was added to the Nissan. Was I feeble-minded or just plain crazy? Was I stupid, thick headed or needed a new brain? I needed lots of help to have signed for another car for my drug addicted son! An hour after I returned home the phone rang. I knew who it was.

"Mommy, do you have my car?"

"No I don't have your car."

"Well do you know what *happened* to *my* car!"

"Yes I do. I had it picked up and returned to the dealership."

"You b——! *You took my car!*"

His screamed obscenities forced me to hang up. I sat staring at the television, dazed, stunned, emotionally wounded at the words my son had yelled at me, his mother, the mother who'd *done too much* as always for her second born who'd nearly died at birth. Minutes later the phone rang. I ignored its rings. Bryan called back repeatedly until I answered and listened to his apology of callous words he'd hurled at me.

"Mommy I'm *sorry. I'm sorry* for the way I talked to you. I'm *really sorry.* You've been so *good* to me. I just got *so* mad." He expressed his feelings at length.

"Bryan I told you if you started using drugs again, I'd take the car. I *meant* that. The fuel gage indicator pointed to empty. You don't have a job so you can't make the payment due next week."

"How do you *know* what I'll have *next* week!"

"I don't. But I do know you've never stopped using drugs; that's enough for me. I won't have that car impounded and sold if drugs are found inside."

As far as I was concerned the Nissan/Bryan issue was closed! The car *would* be sold! After negative responses from newspaper ads, I thought of Marty's former wife, mother of my two granddaughters and called Elkhart, Indiana. We chatted briefly then I popped the *big* question.

"Renata how would you like to have Bryan's car. He's still on drugs and I've taken it back?"

"A *car*, Bryan*'s* car, how can I get it. I'm all the way up here?"

"The monthly payments are $405. If you pay $250-300 with insurance included, it's yours." She was speechless. The soft whispery voice wasn't hers.

"Yees I can han-dle $250 a mon-th. I can't bel—ieve you're do-ing this for me."

"Well Renata we're helping each other. You need a car and I need help with the payments."

The following week Roy and I met Renata and a girlfriend at the airport. They'd share the long drive back to Indiana. Roy drove us to the dealership while I discussed my business arrangements with Renata. Upon our arrival at the company, Roy's handsome nephew greeted us in his usual charming manner. We then walked outside where the new month old shiny black sport's car was parked. When Renata opened the Nissan's door and slid inside on the soft black leather seats behind the steering wheel; her glowing smile lit up like fireworks on the Fourth of July!

With three children, Renata needed a sedan but the sports car would have to do. Once I arrived home I called my insurance company and removed Bryan's name as a driver and replaced it with hers. She gave them her driver's license number plus other information. She also gave me her first month's payment, $250. The following day they departed from Baltimore, MD for their nine hour, 600 mile, north/west drive for Highway 1-70 to Elkhart, Ind., *beaming*! I thanked God I had help and also helped! Even though I still paid the insurance, some money was better than nothing at all. However, gloom and grief waited around the corner patiently—for that special moment of attack.

54...LEAVING SILVER SPRING

Be not disgusted, nor discouraged,
nor dissatisfied, if thou dost not
succeed in doing everything according to right
principles...
Marcus Aurelius: Meditations Book V
Ibid. 9

I stared at my last paycheck and wondered when my retirement disability would be determined. My last month's prescription bill had been *$168!* I'd never paid that much for medicine in my life because of my Blue Cross/Blue Shield Insurance discount. But now it no longer existed. The disability insurance was my only source of income and would last two years. Still it wasn't enough to cover monthly expenses and medication. With some assistance from Roy I managed but still—he had his own debts.

Roy had rented a two-bedroom apartment in downtown Silver Spring across the street from the school where he taught English to foreign students. Living there was ideal since he saved on gas. A realtor handled the sale or rental of his house. His in-laws moved in with a relative, until the mother returned to her native country. My arduous trip of transporting heavy awkward items from Baltimore to decorate his apartment soon lost its initial appeal. Why? Locating a parking space in the poorly designed underground parking garage was a disaster!

Finally Roy paid the attendant a fee for his *own* space rather than wait months for an available one. His cramped corner parking space next to a large old burgundy van was difficult to maneuver. Backing up/pulling out where two cars parked in front of each other, not side by side was *unbelievable*! *Every inch of space* was used in that garage!

After I parked the car, I stared at the elevator on the other side of the parking lot—dreading the long awkward walk. Carrying artworks, weaving between parked cars and dodging moving vehicles was a challenge. The slow, tired elevator hoisted its passengers up sluggishly as conveyor cleats squeaked noisily to the third floor. After it stopped, I'd lift the heavy load and start my second walk down a long hall, on plush carpet to Roy's apartment, *exhausted!*

As I stood in the elevator each day, monopolizing most of the small enclosure, I thought *there must be another way to transport these items.* Yes, a happy thought glowed. I'd resolved my problem! I bought a *grocery cart* the vertical one, consumers used to pull their groceries home from the market. It was a blessing!

Paintings adorned the apartment's walls; royal blue towels and rugs enhanced the two white bathrooms. A paisley designed bedspread with values of blue, green and tan brightened the dark bedroom furniture. The once plain rooms now breathed in subtle refined colors and design.

One day as Roy and I sat in the huge living room off from the dining/kitchen area listening to easy music flow from his stereo he said.

"I can't handle both of these payments. I was sure the house would have rented by now. The rent is comparable to the other houses renting in this area. I don't understand what the problem could be?"

"What happened to the family who was moving from Arizona?" I said.

"The agent said they saw another house they liked better."

I'd never been inside Roy's house. He'd driven me by it once to see the outside. It was now time to see the inside. The next day I met Roy at the house. The problem was obvious. His house was an absolute wreck!!

Broken cinder block on peeled brick front porch
Broken metal folding closet door in foyer
Filthy kitchen wall oven, base boards, cabinets and refrigerator
Broken garbage disposal, hall linen closet door off track
Dirty red torn shag carpet revealed hardwood floor
Dingy blue walls and carpet in master bedroom
Torn dirty window shades; cracked shower door
Rusty medicine and base cabinets in both bathrooms
Greasy return vents; huge grimy basement and half bath
Dirty glass sliding patio door and windows

The 20' back yard and remaining sloped area behind the gigantic elm was

366

unbelievably trashy: branches, dumped grass, linoleum pieces, boxes, cans, jars, etc. lay at the bottom of the hill at the chain-linked fence.

Several non-repairable window screens lay on the ground behind the house. The property was a *disgrace*! I stood dazed! How could an intelligent man allow his property to fall into such disrepair?

"Roy I *see* why your house has not rented. It's *filthy*!"

"Well, my mother and daughter-in-law said they cleaned, up everything. I guess they didn't finish."

"Finish! They never started!"

Roy looked perplexed. He didn't have the slightest idea what I meant. Why, because he never *saw* the broken hanging closet doors, torn shag carpet, filthy stove, twisted window screens strewn and scattered across the yard behind the house. Was he blind? No. He *really* had not seen them. The only thing he saw was green—*money*! He didn't *live* in the house. He was a boarder; renting a room. He worked all the time. When he was home, his short visits were to eat and sleep.

"With Savina dying, everybody cared for her. No one had time to clean the house and the yard. I know I didn't! I was working trying to pay doctor's bills and my bills."

"I understand Roy but these problems didn't happen over night. This is many *years* of neglect." It was useless. He refused to understand.

"I thought the renters could clean this yard. Why should *I clean it,* when they would be renting the house?"

"Why Roy? This is your house, your junk and your dirt. It's *your* responsibility to clean it, if you want to rent it, otherwise it'll just remain dirty and vacant. I'll get it ready. I guarantee it'll be rented by the end of the week."

He agreed to help me as best he could. I found out he was absolutely *no help whatsoever!* He knew zero about maintaining a house. He bought what I needed and gave me moral support.

Off white paint in the master bedroom and smaller room with the red torn shag carpet, which we pulled up and threw out, brightened the rooms. I painted the bathroom cabinets white, repaired and painted the closet doors, cleaned the wall oven, etc. The young man who cut Roy's yard studied the backyard for a few seconds and said, *No!*

It took me *three* whole days to clean that *filthy* yard! It was mind-boggling the debris I carried and dragged up that steep hill. Gradually the house and yard took shape. It evidently looked so good that Roy's decision to keep his apartment changed. He said:

"Dawn, you've got this house *looking so good* I think I'll move back instead of renting it."

"What was that again?" I couldn't believe his words.

"I don't want to rent the house now. I've thought about how hard you've worked so I decided it should be *your* house."

As I cleaned and painted I'd also grown attached to the house, an unexplained closeness.

"Do you think that's wise? Savina's just died months ago. You bought this house for her, *not* for me. I'd never feel right living here. I only cleaned and painted it to rent."

He insisted he would terminate his lease at the end of the month and return to his newly decorated home.

No rental interest was shown during my preparation days. I spent Saturday night in Silver Spring to complete the painting and the yard. Roy and I stood in the empty clean house Sunday morning, happy he'd made the decision to return. Not to my surprise the expected happened.

"Dawn I called the realtor early this morning and told her to remove the house from the market. I also notified my apartment office, I'll be moving back to my house the end of the month."

"What did she say?"

"Everything's okay. I was renting month to month anyway because I was waiting for a three bedroom."

As we stood in the kitchen talking and making plans for the house we saw a small blue car stop in front of the house. I froze. Intuition apprised me what to expect. Roy answered the door. I rushed into the living room where I needed to touch up a few spots of paint to avoid the expected conversation. Roy stepped outside. It was the real estate agent. Roy returned.

"Dawn this family wants to see the house. They're interested in renting it."

I grabbed the broom from the kitchen broom closet and rushed out the front door. At first I stood stunned on the sidewalk under the tree with my hand and head on top of the broom handle. I thought, *suppose they decide to rent this house after all the hard work I've done. What would I do?* I swept the sidewalk, avoiding the pain of such a decision. Again I thought *isn't that why you decorated it in the first place, to rent?*

Peripherally I saw Roy crossing the lawn, toward me. His head was lowered as he walked slower. The scene reminded me of a military officer standing at a front door, to notify a family of their deceased loved one. Before he completed his sentence I became enraged.

"*NO, NO, NO!* I've worked too hard in this yard and that house. You made the decision a few days ago to keep the house. I'm *not* a yo-yo! You can't raise my feelings and then let them drop! Had you not come to the conclusion yourself it wouldn't be so bad but *you're* the one who said you wanted to keep the house, *remember!*"

He stared as I waved my hands frantically, glaring at him enraged! This was my other side, the side he'd not encountered. He'd *never* seen me that angry.

"Dawn if I rent the house it would eliminate the hassle of maintaining it and you wouldn't have so much to do after we get married. Besides the rent would pay the mortgage and I'd only have to pay the apartment's rent. It would save money."

"*No!* If you rent the house when I return to Baltimore today I *won't* come back! You can find yourself *another* girlfriend because I won't see you any more!"

He strolled over to me, rested his hand on my shoulder and expressed his feelings in his normal low toned voice.

"Dawn I didn't realize you felt so strongly about the house."

"It's not the house Roy. It's the switching back and forth you do that I can't handle. I'd geared myself to planting flowers in the yard, and even a small garden. Then you change your mind. After you said we'd live here I did *more* than I'd planned to make the house more comfortable for us, *not for someone to rent!* I did *too* much anyway." He understood my anger, returned inside. He told the realtor No!

Days later we started his move back to the house. I carried nothing as heavy as I did before. I wrapped all my paintings in sheets and towels placed them in large plastic bags allowing the *movers* to put them on the truck. The double driveway was a plus. *We'd never miss that poorly planned underground, garage!*

We married the end of May, two months earlier than planned because my B/C B/S insurance plan had expired. My low income wasn't enough to pay for my *necessary* medicine. Roy's insurance plan covered everything. I called Renata, prior to the marriage and offered her various pieces of furniture, the washer/dryer unit, Roy's bedroom and dining room sets along with other odds and ends she could use for her three children and herself. She flew down from Indiana with her same girlfriend. We rented her a U-Haul truck. Bryan and his friends helped load the truck in Baltimore then drove to Silver Spring and packed the furniture Roy had offered. I recalled Bryan moving that tall *heavy piggy back* washer/dryer by himself. Not a year old, I gave it to my former daughter-in-law, the mother of my two precious granddaughters. They returned to Elkhart with a house full of furniture: living and dining room, bedroom, trundle bed, two Danish sofas, odd chairs etc. and glowing faces once again!

I'd informed my friends I was getting married and moving to Silver Spring the end of May and needed to rent my co-op. The first family a young married couple Mr. & Mrs. Arnold Talbot with one small daughter saw the house and loved it instantly!

On Friday, May 27, 1994 at 4:40 p.m. we were married in Baltimore, by and in the home of my dear friend Rev. Cecil Monroe, the wife of the late Rev. Ernest Monroe who'd officiated my mother's funeral nine years earlier.

Roy's sister Malina and her boyfriend Ian, Bryan and Mr. and Mrs. Wilson, both in their eighties, my beloved adopted parents, stood as Best Man and Maid of Honor. We stood in the living room in front of Cecil's elegant white marble fireplace decorated with antiques chosen by her late husband Ernest, a collector.

After the intimate wedding ceremony ended, Malina the family's personal photographer took pictures. Malina, Ian, Roy and I returned to Silver Spring. Roy had a six p.m. class. He *ignored* my pleas *not* to work on our wedding day, but to notify the school of our marriage so we'd have dinner together. A stubborn man, set in his ways, was adamant about *not* missing his class, went anyway! He *knew* I was hurt. That was one of many instances where Roy exerted his stubbornness, a negative trait he revealed too often. However he had more pleasing traits.

Roy ascended the steps to the evening job he could not miss. I pulled away from the curb and headed toward the mall where Malina deposited the film, in a 1-Hour Photo shop. She purchased a wedding album and strolled through the mall, as people eyed our wedding apparel.

At 8:00 p.m. we returned for Roy. He climbed into the car and was greeted with our stunning white embossed wedding album filled with memories of our small intimate ceremony just four hours earlier. His sister agreed with Roy to marry me then; not to wait until July. The album held treasured moments of our wedding and dinner party shared by his sister and her male friend. Toasts, jokes, and amusing anecdotes from blissful restaurant guests at nearby tables heightened our romantic evening.

Round trip drives from Baltimore to Silver Spring were three-four times a week, moving light items in the car to my new residence. Bryan remained in my house and cared for its needs while I packed my possessions, getting ready for the *major* move the end of June. The Talbots were to move in on July 1ˢᵗ.

I wondered, "Will this be my final husband? Will this be my last move? I certainly hope so. I've spent my life marrying, divorcing and moving! This must be the final marriage and final move because I'm getting too old and too weary.

To my friends I was still a *gypsy*! But I knew it was my Indian ancestry that urged my moving without a second thought. Wide opened spaces and a region to roam was my home. Nature was my habitat; rural out-door settings were my choice dwellings. Trees, water, birds, squirrels and a soft cuddly kitten to rub sufficed my needs. Being boxed in, unable to move at will was not for me. In the past four years I'd moved *five* times in addition to helping Roy move twice and didn't fret. In fact I looked forward to a new home; new rooms to decorate.

I recall the morning of the wedding. Roy's telephone rang. I answered wondering who was calling today.

"Hello, this is Elroy may I speak to Dad."

"Hi Elroy this is Ms. Dawn how are you?"

"I'm great, what about yourself?"

"Well I'm ecstatic! Roy and I are getting married today! I'm nervous and happy at the same time: another bride to be; no longer loose and free; but safe, in the sanctity of marriage."

"Married! Why didn't you guys tell somebody?"

"Well we just decided last week. We'd planned to do so in July but Roy decided *now* was the time."

"I called because Simone and I'd planned to stop by today and pay Dad a visit."

"Where are you now?"

"We're at my sister's home just outside D.C."

"Tomorrow would be fine if you want to."

"*No* that's too soon we'll give you guys a day. We'll come over Sunday and treat you to a fine wedding dinner."

"Sounds great to me!"

I set the time and relayed the message to Roy. Sunday's dinner was splendid. We returned home, sat around the dining room table and discussed memories of Elroy's childhood with his dad. Those recollections induced energetic laughter and exuberance. Simone's pronounced British accent still remained after living in America over twenty years. I could have listened to her talk for hours. Elroy said she'd often tease him about his American accent. She believed Americans *didn't* speak correct English. Contrary to her opinion, Elroy like his father spoke perfect American English!

Our bedroom was surrendered to Elroy and Simone since there wasn't a second bed. We slept downstairs in the basement on a sofa, two sofa chairs pushed together. The make shift bed backed with several heavy pieces of furniture anchored it close to the wall. "Twas a restless uncomfortable second honeymoon night."

They left the following morning while we burst with laughter for days, regarding *our shifting chairs* during that awkward but *loving* night.

Bryan moved out of my house, the Talbots moved in, and I'd moved to Silver Spring to start a new life with my first Christian husband.

My retirement disability was denied. I reapplied. I also applied for regular retirement, one third of the disability retirement. Years earlier I'd withdrawn the $10,000 paid into the city's system and reinvested two-thirds into an annuity with better interest. That withdrawal automatically placed me with The State Teacher's Retirement System. A few years later, while on disability for two years, I terminated my disability insurance sure I'd have a position that September. *I didn't!*

Without disability insurance and no job, I withdrew the entire balance from my annuity account in order to pay the $6600 credit union loan. That way my co-signers were not responsible for my debt. It was *my* obligation; not theirs. My close friends thought what I did, was admiral; I didn't think so. What I did was the right and *only* thing to do. Why, because the same dilemma had happened to me.

An amount of $79 per pay was taken from my salary bi-monthly over a year for a part time employee Nat had vouched for on his job. Months later he quit. Two of his relatives and I paid his loan. Months after the loan was paid he was rehired in Baltimore City. When he applied for another credit union loan they had him borrow enough to repay his co-signers! Most co-signers weren't as fortunate as we had been. Usually the borrower obtained another job or moved to another state.

But, "The Lord is good to those who love Him and follow His Word." I tried not to worry because I knew my Father would take care of everything. *He did!*

Seated at a birthday party the first of May, in the midst of many friends, Roy's niece, Malina's daughter offered him a free trip to Las Vegas if he'd go on the trip. She was expecting a large settlement check from her job.

"Uncle Roy if you agree to go on the trip, I'll pay the $500 for your ticket then Dawn would only have to pay for hers."

He answered her slowly, "I'd have to think about that Arlene. Dawn and I'd planned to drive to Atlantic City for our honeymoon. Going to Las Vegas is *expensive*! Besides we don't have that kind of money right now. That's why we chose Atlantic City. We'll let you know."

It was May; the church's trip was in July. We both agreed to go. Disappointment surfaced when Arlene *didn't* receive the amount of money she expected. We couldn't cancel our tickets! We couldn't retrieve our $500 deposit. We were stuck! $500 for Roy's ticket plus $1000 borrowed from his sister Malina who *insisted* we go.

We didn't like Vegas outside our magnificent hotel, *The Excalibur*. The hotels were electrified with majestic contemporary architecture. Each one contained its own ambience, its own impressive interior décor welcoming visitors, their money which enhanced their entertainment. Since unwavering heat refused to lower its intensity we spent most of our time inside our luxurious hotel. Exciting activities, festive restaurants, floor and dinner shows encouraged most guests to stay put until darkness cooled the day with breezes from several exotic outside fountains. Crowds lined the streets with sightseers and thrill seekers anxious to *waste* their money at hotel gambling tables and slot machines.

Our only tour of the city was a day to remember! An antiquated air conditioning unit on the bus refused to cooperate. We heard sounds from the unit but nothing cooled our bodies. Soon, perspiration covered passengers' faces including ours. The bus stopped numerous times at various sites. The cooled interior of the buildings soothed our wet and clammy bodies. We saw homes of movie stars as the bus cruised by vast wastelands sparsely covered with greenery and other growth. Trees were few, but I viewed the open spaces with objectivity. The bus driver revealed that jobs were plentiful in Las Vegas. I understood why; a 126 degree temperature was enough to discourage any tourist from living there.

The Excalibur, one of the finest and most exquisite hotels in Las Vegas housed our group. The hotel, packed with people of all ages monopolized floor space not in jeopardy, leaving only enough room for guests to squeeze through while passing from one area to the next.

After the plane landed loud music, slot machines with flashing lights and ringing bells greeted us as we opened the doors to the airport. Slot machines of every kind lined the walls of the ladies and men's restrooms. Slot machines, gambling tables, roulette wheels etc. bombarded our space as we strolled through the maze of iniquity toward the elevators located on the *opposite* side of the casino area. The sight was frightening yet awesome, while unbelievably inviting to others. A quick stride propelled me through the network of sin as fast as I could. The rat race of gullible tourists and gamblers longing to lose their hard-earned money was distressful.

I thought *what a pathetic sight!* Illnesses, divorces, suicides, lost businesses and drained bank accounts resulted from gambling. Human pride had been stomped on, pounded deep into the ground and sealed! The casinos grew wealthier, more affluent and in demand! They stole money needed for rent, food, clothes, medical and other family expenses. Gambling was an addiction; as bad as drugs, alcohol, food, nicotine or shopping. Each one posed a threat to sick people that refused help and allowed their families to suffer. Vast sums of savings had been squandered; tender lives were headed for decay, crumpled and dispersed in graves with thousands of other ill, weak, sick souls. For what, *nothing*! *Greed*!

Neither Roy nor I gambled therefore we preferred to rest in our room and view the sites from our window. His sister Malina and her church friends frequented the casino. I recall early one morning our telephone rang. It was Malina's roommate.

"Hello Rory, this is Nettie. I'm sorry to call you so early but Malina's bed hasn't been slept in all night. Do you have any idea where she might be? I'm worried about her."

"Don't worry Nettie, I'll find her."

Roy dressed quickly and rushed out the door on a major search for his sister. He didn't say where he was going. I didn't ask. Forty minutes later he returned with Malina, exhausted mentally and physically from her long wasted night. She'd spent all night at a poker table trying to recover her $800 loss. After ten hours of a win/loss situation she recovered most of her money. I knew she'd been a gambler years earlier, but thought she'd stopped. Roy said there'd been times she'd gambled for days at a time, winning and losing, losing and winning.

"Dawn she isn't as bad as she used to be. I've seen times when she'd be on a roll for weeks taking just a few hours out for sleep and food and then return to another game at someone else's home."

"Well, believe me I do understand, there are many kinds of addictions. Mine is searching for love in the wrong places." Roy placed his arm around my shoulder.

"Darling you won't have to worry about that anymore. I intend to give you all the love and support you'll need."

Those were kind insuring words but I needed more than words to express love. I needed *action!* Positive action!

I recall the morning as we ate a hearty breakfast of fluffy pancakes, scrambled eggs, sausage, home fries, bacon, juice and coffee. We sat at the table with Malina and her roommate. That lady asked Roy an appalling question.

"Rory, which one of your wives was prettier, Dawn or Savina?"

I continued eating as though her dumb, insensitive, immature question had not *shocked* me into a state of oblivion! How dare this *so-called Christian* have the nerve to sit in front of me and ask such a question in my presence! Anger elevated my heartbeats that jumped into my throat inhibiting my ability to swallow. I chewed my food slowly by habit, waiting for Roy's answer to her stupid, half-witted question. Savina was fifteen years my junior, a party, party person, a far more fashionable dresser and *not* a Christian. After I'd seen many pictures of her, my friend Valarie and I knew it was her heavy makeup that enhanced her looks. Even Roy admitted it was the makeup. She was not a beauty, by far.

His statement had been, "When I first met Savina she was an ordinary looking young woman until our first date. She looked completely different with all that makeup. After that she never left the house without her makeup."

He kept his eyes glued to his plate and spoke not a word. I knew his answer. His sister Malina spoke up.

"Of course Dawn is."

She continued describing my positive attributes while my husband of one-and a half months continued eating his breakfast without one word. Needless to say I felt absent. After our morning stroll inside the hotel we returned to our room to change clothes. It was then I released my pent-up angry emotions.

"You made me feel just like a fool at breakfast. You said nothing. How do you think that non-response appeared? You could have said something. You may think Savina was beautiful, but others and I don't agree."

"She *was* beautiful! She *was* beautiful!" He answered.

He explained his reasons and rationalized his beliefs that I shouldn't let that problem ruin our trip.

"She may have been beautiful to you. With all that make-up she used, anyone would be beautiful. She stopped loving you two years after your marriage; she spent your money recklessly causing you to work three jobs in addition to receiving your Government Retirement. She disrespected you as a minister, she cursed you, she never worked the fifteen years you were married and she took advantage of your natural kindness. And you call that *beautiful!*"

Roy tried to soothe my hurt. I cried several minutes before I stopped.

"I may not be beautiful but I'm *here!* Where is Savina? I'm your wife *man* and you have the *audacity* to tell me how beautiful your deceased wife was! I don't wear make up. You said that was one of the reasons you were attracted to me in the first place. I'm your wife! I helped you get your filthy house together. I'm the one who cuts your grass, washes our cars, does the marketing, washes and irons our clothes, hangs wall paper in the bathroom, paints the inside and outside of the house. I may not be beautiful to you, but I've always been told I was pretty, smart, intelligent, a hard worker and ambitious. Besides I always worked until now. No I'm not beautiful but I am *not lazy,* I'm a Christian and I'm the one here!"

After his insensitive remarks our honeymoon was *over!* I wore the happy face of the new bride but I was *far, far* from happy. I always felt Savina's presence. I learned something about that man that day I hadn't seen during our dating. He was insensitive to others' feelings. Weeks and months ahead unveiled other inconsistencies. Determined not to allow a deceased person's memories cloud our *costly unwanted* trip, I adjusted and *tried* to enjoy myself.

Our return to Silver Spring, MD entailed a two-hour layover in Columbus, Ohio. A layover was understood but lasted longer than anticipated. We sprawled around on wooden benches, curled up in chairs, slept on opened garment bags or walked around touring the nearly deserted airport. Only a few shops were accessible to the public the wee hours of our stranded morning. Restaurants and snack shops to supply our brewed aromatic coffee and buns were closed.

Exhausted and hungry, we finally dragged our weary bodies and luggage aboard the long awaited plane and headed home. The honeymoon had ended. Had our marriage too? We should have gone to Atlantic City *alone* as planned, not to Las Vegas, with inconsiderate people who'd known his young pretty late wife.

I shook the dust off my shoes, stepped into our house and stumbled into a new marriage. My shoes grasped the new milieu and endured its discomfort. I realized I could not compare myself to a woman fifteen years my junior!

At first waiting on my kind, handsome articulate husband was pleasant until he made an astonishing request! One Tuesday evening after work Roy entered the kitchen, kissed me hello then went downstairs to watch television in his new lounge chair I'd gotten him for Father's Day. Seconds later he yelled upstairs lovingly.

"Darling, would you bring me a glass of water please?"

I stopped washing dishes, stared out the window puzzled by what I *thought* I'd heard? "Did he just ask me to bring him a glass of water? No, he couldn't have, he was just in this kitchen, and now he wants *me* to take *him* a glass of water!"

Yes I carried the glass of water down the steps to my husband. His hand, as smooth as satin, never used to hard work as mine, reached up for the chilled glass. Before I surrendered its release, I revealed my painful thoughts.

"Roy this is the *last* time I'll bring you a glass of water downstairs unless you're sick. You walked in the kitchen; came down these steps then yelled upstairs for *me* to bring you a glass of water. Don't you think that was a little selfish?"

"I didn't want any water when I was upstairs."

I soon realized Roy always had a sorry excuse for something he'd said or had done while never admitting his wrong about *anything.*

"You didn't answer my question dear. Don't you think that was selfish?" He faced me with that gorgeous smile.

"I didn't think you'd mind my dear." Still laughing as he spoke.

"Well I *did* mind. Just remember next time to get your own water when you come home. I was born in America, not in Santo Domingo where women wait on the men like they were kings! I tried to come close to their culture but I'm sorry, I can't. Besides I don't see anybody waiting on me, do you?"

He laughed heartily having found my words amusing. I *didn't!* It's wasn't amusing, for an overgrown man to take his wife for granted. One day as we strolled through the supermarket aisles I commented why some men expected their wives to wait on them. He replied.

"Well Dawn, aren't *you* my maid? Am I not your king?" He was proud of himself to have a wife that did *everything*.

"*No*! Indeed I'm *not* your maid or your slave! I'm your wife not your servant!"

Roy's sister mentioned to me before we were married that he did nothing in the house. However she hadn't said he wouldn't do *a-n-y-t-h-i-n-g!* Our first month of marriage proved he was the *laziest human being I'd ever met!* He did *absolutely, nothing,* unless I asked. If I didn't ask he'd walk through the house as though nothing was out of place or needed cleaning. His mother, sisters, late wife and relatives had spoiled him. I had to get him *unspoiled!* Unaware of the severity of his problem, it would take *years and years* to crack the surface of his laziness!

He once said, "Before I got the word water from my lips someone was handing me a cold glass of water, removing my shoes, bringing me the newspaper or setting a tray of dinner on my lap."

"Well Darling, those days are over! I don't mind doing some things for you but many things you're capable of doing yourself. You've met your Waterloo now. Today is your first day of *I Will Do It Myself Day.* "

I knew I couldn't expect that man to change over night. His family, girlfriends and wives had waited on him *allll* of his life. It would take years to alter that pattern; it did!

When he was young the women did everything, the men worked outside the home. Roy had that special something that towered over his shortcomings: gentleness, intellect, patience of my artistic temperament, kindness and love for our Lord. He never argued, raised his voice or criticized anything I did. So I rationalized. Since he doesn't hit me, curse me, belittle me or spit in my face as another husband had, I tried to adjust to his laziness because I *thought* he'd eventually change. One of his former doctors told me, "Rory is a highly intelligent man but he's also a *very stubborn* man."

Indeed he was *exceptionally stubborn!*

Before we married we'd planned a budget. He refused to allow any IRS deductions from our salaries; he wanted *all* of his money. He'd been used to paying the Internal Revenue Service monthly payments for *years*. I'd never paid but *always* received a refund. Why, because I had money deducted up front. Not Roy, he insisted his way was the better way. I insisted I was right; he said no. Since I no longer worked and only received a disability check of

$1500 monthly, I relented. I said nothing else about his monthly deductions to the IRS. I *thought* he knew what he was doing.

I visited Roy's former psychiatrist just before moving to Silver Spring because I wasn't satisfied with mine. He increased my Zoloft immediately from 50 mg to 100 mg. My depression and nervousness appeared to be under control. The additional medication always made me extremely sleepy afterwards. Every morning I stared out the basement window until I drifted off to sleep.

His house's gutter spouting needed cleaning, also the clapboards under the eaves around the house. Roy was afraid of heights so I climbed the tall ladder that leaned against the front of the house, next to the huge oak tree whose branches needed pruning! Roy held the ladder firm in its place. We had so much fun! He sang while I cleaned the gutters and sawed off oak branches that dumped their dead leaves and debris on the roof. To *save* money as usual, I climbed the ladder once again and painted the white exterior wood above the brick while Roy held the ladder. It looked *great* compared to the original dull, dreary green color. The brick home's front door needed a face lift. Days later I painted two feet of brick all the way around the door. When Roy arrived home he was startled!

"Well I guess I'll get used to your new paint job. It is different though." He adjusted sooner than I had anticipated.

A few days later he said, "Dawn I really like that white paint you put around the door. It makes the door look so much larger." His nods reaffirmed his approval.

"Yes. That's the whole idea. Extending the door color onto the brick gives the illusion the door is twice as wide. I'm glad you like it Roy. I thought you would. The dark red brick next to the bright white paint gives a strong degree of contrast. Thank you darling for liking what I've done." I hugged him.

One night when Roy held the tall extension metal ladder while I painted beneath the clapboard section under the soffit board, I decided to stay a little longer after he left to see his favorite game show, *Jeopardy*. I painted 'til dark. After I descended the tall heavy ladder that leaned against the roof, I attempted to lower it to the ground by myself. In doing so, its weight and my awkward handling made it *slip* from my grip, slide down the side of the house *so fast*, that it struck the top of my head, knocked me to the ground up against the chain linked fence, into shrubs and flowers, before I realized what had happened!

Thinking I was dead, I lay there. Seconds later I lifted my head slowly, looked around to see if anyone had seen my dumb deed then touched my head with a trembling hand. I saw no blood. I was alive! Once again I'd done something stupid and God saved me. I told Roy a few evenings later; too embarrassed to tell the truth that night and how I almost lost my life.

Later I painted the small concrete front porch rust, a strong reddish brown color, planted tall red Salvia flowers with Silver Dust in front as a low border on three sides of the house, seeded bare lawn spots then planted assorted colors of Impatience in back of the house. The former dismal looking brick home looked *magnificent*! Neighbors complimented me often on our new façade and the work they'd seen me do.

"Dawn you've done *wonders* with that house! I can't believe it's the same house! When you finish you're welcome to come over and decorate ours." We laughed at all the work I'd done and still needed to do in time.

Roy's French speaking African student Armal edged the front sidewalks. He removed *deep-rooted* grass, which had grown far across the concrete's edge, with a sharp knife. He worked all day in scorching temperatures against my advice to wait and finish another day. Armal did a *marvelous* job! I watched him from the kitchen window on the front of the house. Such care he took in each area he dug out. He performed his task like a watch repairman or an artist working in a tight area on a painting.

I felt complete, just as I had when I'd transformed my former old Victorian home. My life had been spent, decorating houses and apartments. Cleaning and beautifying my surroundings was my life, whether helping a friend, redecorating my home or my work environment. I relished every moment!

Roy proposed we visit different churches and find one we'd both want to join. During our search his friend Pastor Ledon, of Orlando, FL suggested Roy contact his aging father, Pastor of his family church in Washington, D.C. He did. We attended one Sunday morning and were greeted warmly by the congregation in the small store front building while my eyes perused its interior.

To Be Continued...

Printed in the United States
55084LVS00003B/61-90

9 781413 756364